Spiritual Alchemy

OXFORD STUDIES IN WESTERN ESOTERICISM

Series Editor
Henrik Bogdan, University of Gothenburg

Editorial Board
Jean-Pierre Brach, École Pratique des Hautes Études
Carole Cusack, University of Sydney
Christine Ferguson, University of Stirling
Olav Hammer, University of Southern Denmark
Wouter Hanegraaff, University of Amsterdam
Ronald Hutton, University of Bristol
Jeffrey Kripal, Rice University
James R. Lewis, University of Tromsø
Michael Stausberg, University of Bergen
Egil Asprem, University of Stockholm
Dylan Burns, Freie Universität Berlin
Gordan Djurdjevic, Simon Fraser University
Peter Forshaw, University of Amsterdam
Jesper Aa. Petersen, Norwegian University of Science and Technology

RECYCLED LIVES
A History of Reincarnation in Blavatsky's Theosophy
Julie Chajes

THE ELOQUENT BLOOD
*The Goddess Babalon and the Construction of
Femininities in Western Esotericism*
Manon Hedenborg White

IMAGINING THE EAST
The Early Philosophical Society
Tim Rudbøg and Erik Sand

INITIATING THE MILLENNIUM
The Avignon Society and Illuminism in Europe
Robert Collis and Natalie Bayer

GURDJIEFF
Mysticism, Contemplation, and Exercises
Joseph Azize

SPIRITUAL ALCHEMY
From Jacob Boehme to Mary Anne Atwood
Mike A. Zuber

Spiritual Alchemy

From Jacob Boehme to Mary Anne Atwood

MIKE A. ZUBER

Oxford University Press is a department of the University of Oxford. It furthers
the University's objective of excellence in research, scholarship, and education
by publishing worldwide. Oxford is a registered trade mark of Oxford University
Press in the UK and certain other countries.

Published in the United States of America by Oxford University Press
198 Madison Avenue, New York, NY 10016, United States of America.

© Oxford University Press 2021

All rights reserved. No part of this publication may be reproduced, stored in
a retrieval system, or transmitted, in any form or by any means, without the
prior permission in writing of Oxford University Press, or as expressly permitted
by law, by license, or under terms agreed with the appropriate reproduction
rights organization. Inquiries concerning reproduction outside the scope of the
above should be sent to the Rights Department, Oxford University Press, at the
address above.

You must not circulate this work in any other form
and you must impose this same condition on any acquirer.

CIP data is on file at the Library of Congress
ISBN 978-0-19-007304-6

DOI: 10.1093/oso/9780190073046.001.0001

1 3 5 7 9 8 6 4 2

Printed by Integrated Books International, United States of America

For Lana

Contents

List of Illustrations — ix
Acknowledgements — xi
Conventions — xiii

Introduction — 1

1. The Radical Reformation, Paracelsian Networks, and Pseudo-Weigelian Alchemy — 14
2. A Nuremberg Chymist and a Torgau Astrologer Read Pseudo-Weigel — 30
3. Jacob Boehme's Spiritual Alchemy of Rebirth — 48
4. Abraham von Franckenberg and the Ancient Wisdom of Rebirth — 69
5. Georg Lorenz Seidenbecher, Franckenberg's Spiritual and Philosophical Son — 87
6. Friedrich Breckling, the 1682 Boehme Edition, and Spiritual Alchemy — 106
7. Collaboration, Counterfeit, and Calumny in Amsterdam — 125
8. Dionysius Andreas Freher, Boehme's Apostle to the English — 142
9. Mesmerists and Alchemists in Victorian London — 160
10. Mary Anne Atwood and Her First Readers — 175

Epilogue — 197

Notes — 203
Works Cited — 271
Index — 305

Illustrations

1.1. Pseudo-Weigel, *Azoth et Ignis*, as copied by Paul Nagel. Karlsruhe, Badische Landesbibliothek: Ms. Allerheiligen 3, p. 397. © BLB Karlsruhe, Digitale Sammlungen.   22

2.1. Johann Siebmacher, *Introduction hominis*. The Hague, Koninklijke Bibliotheek—National Library of the Netherlands: PH404 M315 (Ritman Kerncollectie), title page. © KB Beeldstudio.   33

5.1. Abraham von Franckenberg, *Sæphiriel*. Zurich, Zentralbibliothek: Bibliothek Oskar R. Schlag, SCH R 809, f. 12r. © ZB Zurich, Digitalisierungszentrum.   102

6.1. Friedrich Breckling, undated autograph letter. The Hague, Koninklijke Bibliotheek—National Library of the Netherlands: 72 E 14, unpaginated. © KB Beeldstudio.   117

7.1. Bartholomaeus Sclei, *Theosophische-Schrifften*, frontispiece designed by Michael Andreae. The Hague, Koninklijke Bibliotheek—National Library of the Netherlands: PH2762 (Ritman Kerncollectie). © KB Beeldstudio.   129

10.1. Mary Anne South, autograph letter pasted into *A Suggestive Inquiry into the Hermetic Mystery*. London, Wellcome Collection Library: EPB/B/49072, back flyleaf. © Author.   176

10.2. Dionysius Andreas Freher, *Jesus Immanuel* [*Fundamenta Mystica*, vol. A], formerly owned by Alban Thomas and Mary Anne Atwood, vol. 2, title page. Private collection of S. Brown. © Owner.   190

Acknowledgements

A scholar inevitably incurs many debts while writing a book. I am very grateful to the assistance of all those mentioned here and also to those I may have inadvertently neglected to include. Special thanks to my supervisors and colleagues at the University of Amsterdam, the University of Oxford, and the University of Queensland, particularly Peter J. Forshaw, Wouter J. Hanegraaff, Howard Hotson, Rob Iliffe, Peter Harrison, and—last but by no means least—Leigh Penman. My revisions greatly benefitted from the rigorous and collegial feedback practices at the University of Queensland's Institute for Advanced Studies in the Humanities. Many read the book or parts of it at various stages of completion, including Jacqueline Borsje, Christine Ferguson, Olav Hammer, Ian Hesketh, Eric Jorink, Lucinda Martin, Cecilia Muratori, Guido Naschert, Lawrence Principe, Aren Roukema, and Vincent Roy-Di Piazza. I received important, indeed crucial, pointers from Scott Brown, Carlos Gilly, and Frank van Lamoen. Others engaged with my ideas, responded to queries, supported my research, or taught me much: Bo Andersson, Rosalie Basten, Günther Bonheim, José Bouman, Hartmut Broszinski, Paul Dijstelberge, Marcel Elias, J. Christian Greer, Yaniv Hagbi, Cis van Heertum, Ariel Hessayon, Tünde Beatrix Karnitscher, Andreas B. Kilcher, Martin Mulsow, Sonja Noll, Tara Nummedal, Julian Paulus, Horst Pfefferl, Rafał Prinke, Joost R. Ritman, Esther Ritman, J. Jürgen Seidel, the late Joachim Telle, Andrew Weeks, and Matthias Wenzel. Among my former students, I would like to thank Samuel Dooley, José Vieira Leitão, David Sterkenburg, and Kateryna Zorya. Thanks also to many librarians and archivists across the world who competently and patiently facilitated my quest for primary and secondary sources, foremost among them the late Monique Fasel of the University of Amsterdam's Special Collections. I gratefully acknowledge the funding I received from the Society for the History of Alchemy and Chemistry (New Scholars Award 2015) and the Fritz Thyssen Foundation, in collaboration with the Research Centre Gotha (Herzog Ernst Scholarship 2015 and 2019). Despite all the help and feedback I received, I take sole blame for any remaining imperfections.

Conventions

Most quotes are translated from the German. Only key expressions appear in the original language, italicised and within parentheses, as opposed to other interpolations placed within square brackets. Since unconventional spellings are to be expected, I have kept the use of [sic] to the absolute minimum. Most quotations from the Bible are mediated by historical sources, which I have translated accordingly with reference to various English translations. When quoting the Bible directly, I use the English Standard Version unless otherwise indicated. Libraries and archives holding manuscript sources or specific exemplars of printed books are given in full only upon first citation; afterwards they appear in abbreviated form.

A special note concerns Jacob Boehme and his writings. Rather than quoting from the (reprinted) 1730 edition of Boehme's works, which has been uncritically accepted for too long, I quote the best text available. In practice, for texts preserved in autographs, I rely on Werner Buddecke's *Jacob Böhme: Die Urschriften* (2 vols., 1963–66), whose *Aurora* was recently reprinted alongside Andrew Weeks's 2013 translation. Otherwise, I use the earliest manuscript version or print edition to which I have had access. When there is reason to believe that historical actors themselves used a specific edition, I follow their lead. As a concession to the status of the 1730 edition as *textus receptus*, I include the coordinates for the corresponding passage according to it, giving an abbreviation for the work, followed by chapter and paragraph or alternative indicators as appropriate. The following abbreviations are used to refer to Boehme's writings:

A	*Aurora*	IV	*De incarnatione verbi*
AS1–2	*Anti-Stiefelius I–II*	MM	*Mysterium magnum*
AT1	*Apologia I. contra Balth. Tilken*	PV	*Psychologia vera*
		SR	*Signatura rerum*
C	*Clavis*	TaP	*Tabula principiorum*
CS	*Christosophia*	TP	*De tribus principiis*
ET	*Epistolae theosophicae*	TV	*De triplici vita*

Introduction

What was alchemy? Or what *is* alchemy? Whatever it might be, it is clearly not a thing of the past alone or the exclusive preserve of historians. Instead, alchemy is something that continues to fascinate not only self-professed contemporary alchemists but also scientists, artists, psychologists, and a variety of spiritual seekers. It also appeals to readers of popular fiction such as Paulo Coelho's 1988 novel *The Alchemist* or J. K. Rowling's series that began with *Harry Potter and the Philosopher's Stone* in 1997.[1] Some might say, and with good reason, that these are questions that cannot be answered, presuming as they do that it would be possible to provide a single definition that captures the meaning of 'alchemy' over the course of almost two millennia. Yet throughout the past three centuries there have been three dominant attempts at answering these questions. In a nutshell, alchemy has been viewed as superstition and fraud, as religion and psychology, as science and natural philosophy. These answers closely reflect an underlying triad of highly problematic reifications that have underpinned grand narratives of humanity's history since the nineteenth century: magic, religion, and science.[2] Despite the many problems of these categories to which scholars have been drawing attention for years, they continue to powerfully inform the way we think about history, its long-term trajectories, and our place within them as modern, rational, and secular individuals in an age dominated by science.

The very fact that such divergent answers to what alchemy was and is could be taken to suggest that its complex history and that history's reception defy these fundamental categories. By resisting a straightforward definition, alchemy unsettles the all-too-neat triad of science, religion, and magic. Indeed, the very term that appears in the title of this book, 'spiritual alchemy,' seems to undermine any attempt at classification: it hints at something that is neither fish nor fowl, neither science nor religion as they are commonly understood. In this introduction, I first explore three widespread views of alchemy and outline a new stance regarding the two more important ones, a strictly historicist perspective that affords us the privilege of not having to commit to either. Second, I define the subject of this book and clarify why 'spiritual alchemy' is the most appropriate term for it. The introduction concludes with a brief outline of the book's chapters.

Competing Views of Alchemy

The three main views of alchemy just described continue to be defining for both public perceptions of and scholarly debates on the art of the adepts. Starting in the 1720s, Enlightenment polemicists such as Bernard le Bovier de Fontenelle, spokesman of the Parisian Académie des sciences, denounced the art of the philosophers' stone—the fabled transmuting agent that would turn base metals into gold. He painted alchemy as utterly misguided and fraudulent, associated it with superstition and dishonesty, and contrasted it with chemistry.[3] Later proponents of this view classed alchemy as a 'pseudo-science,' and until 2002 that was the category where the annual bibliography of *Isis*, the leading journal for the history of science, placed research on the subject.[4] This view would lead us to neglect alchemy as the worthless intellectual 'rubbish' produced by a superstitious past.[5] In fact, engaging with it might even harm our sanity: in an oft-quoted statement, Cambridge historian Herbert Butterfield famously pronounced that historians of alchemy seem to incur 'the wrath of God' and 'to become tinctured with the kind of lunacy they set out to describe.'[6] While this attitude still occasionally surfaces, historians no longer take it seriously.

From the middle of the nineteenth century, a considerably more flattering understanding of alchemy developed, one that viewed adepts as engaging not primarily with material substances. Instead, the alchemists of old were allegedly concerned with the transmutation of their inner selves, a process that might be construed in a religious, spiritual, psychological, or moral manner. In 1850 Mary Anne South, who became better known as Mrs Atwood, anonymously published a sprawling work titled *A Suggestive Inquiry into the Hermetic Mystery*. Engaging with the unconventional interests of her father, Thomas South, she presented alchemy as similar but superior to Mesmerism as a means for attaining the ancient aims of mysticism. Independently and almost simultaneously, the American major general Ethan Allen Hitchcock presented a moral interpretation. As he explained in 1855 and 1857, the philosophers' stone stood for 'truth, goodness, moral perfection, the Divine blessing': these were the goals that medieval alchemists, who were really '*Reformers*' and '*Protestants*' *avant la lettre*, pursued and discussed throughout their treatises.⁷ Hitchcock's work became an important point of reference for the Viennese psychoanalyst Herbert Silberer, a longtime member of Sigmund Freud's circle. He influentially linked alchemy to both mysticism and psychology in his 1914 book *Probleme der Mystik und ihrer Symbolik* (Problems of Mysticism and Its Symbolism).⁸

In the twentieth century, this second understanding shaped scholarship on alchemy to a significant extent, in part because the first view discouraged active engagement with the mysterious art. Romanian-born historian of religion Mircea Eliade viewed alchemy as a 'spiritual' quest 'pursuing a goal similar or comparable to that of the major esoteric and "mystical" traditions.' He clearly stated that 'alchemists were not interested—or only subsidiarily—in the scientific study of nature.'⁹ The Swiss psychiatrist C. G. Jung is probably the most prominent exponent of a psychological conception of the royal art, and his work on alchemy informed scholarship for a considerable part of the twentieth century. In fact, it provided the dominant paradigm for research on the subject from the 1940s to the 1990s.¹⁰ In contrast to Eliade, Jung viewed the experimental study of nature as defining: he described an ideal or classical alchemy, 'in which the spirit of the alchemist really still wrestled with the problems of matter, in which the inquisitive consciousness faced the dark space of the unknown and believed that they recognised shapes and laws therein, though these did not originate in the matter but in the soul.' In contrast to simplified accounts, Jung clearly held that actual laboratory work provided the basis for this to occur and lamented its neglect in the wake of Jacob Boehme, who died in 1624.¹¹ It is thus no coincidence that Boehme, the theosopher of Görlitz, plays a pivotal role in the story told in these pages.

Even as he acknowledged the experimental side of alchemy and considered it foundational, Jung—the inventor of analytical psychology—was chiefly interested in alchemical imagery. He interpreted it as the projections of the unconscious. His 1946 contribution to *Ambix*, the leading journal for the history of alchemy and chemistry, described the art of the philosophers' stone as 'a real museum of projections.' Jung provocatively claimed that 'its history should never have been treated by chemists, for it offers an ideal hunting-ground for the psychologists.'¹² According to him, the approach to alchemy taken by chemists obscured much of its richness, which he as a psychologist was better able to appreciate and communicate. Jung's interpretation of alchemy was an attempt to understand its nigh-impenetrable language and fascinating symbolism that was fresh and stimulating at its time. It played the important role of establishing that alchemy was worthy of serious inquiry rather than dismissal. Even pioneering historians such as Betty Jo Teeter Dobbs, who worked extensively on Isaac Newton's alchemy, initially approached the art through Jungian lenses.[13] To this day, Jung's views inform popular portrayals and perceptions of alchemy and still continue to stimulate interest in the subject.

While mild criticism of Jung's ahistorical approach accompanied his reception in the historiography of alchemy from the start, only in 1982 did Swiss art historian Barbara Obrist call for its abolition and present a convincing critique.[14] According to her trenchant analysis, the very popularity of Jung's work had led to 'general confusion' due to an inflationary use of the term 'alchemy' that saw it applied to all sorts of evocative art, including mythological depictions and the work of the famous Dutch artist Hieronymus Bosch.[15] If all intriguing imagery could be studied as alchemy, the term risked losing any analytical value it possessed. Two historians of science, William R. Newman and Lawrence M. Principe, have since expanded on Obrist's criticism of Jung. Through a series of studies, they successfully replaced Jung's approach with a new paradigm, known as the New Historiography of Alchemy, and firmly integrated alchemy into the history of science.[16] In particular, Newman and Principe reproduce alchemical processes experimentally by decoding arcane language and imagery, thus demonstrating an alternative, historical interpretation for what Jung viewed as timeless 'psychic processes expressed in pseudochemical language.'[17] Among specialists working in an Anglophone context, the 'old historiography' is now definitely a thing of the past. Scholarly debates in other linguistic contexts have been struggling to keep up with the rapid developments brought about through the New Historiography.[18]

In a classic article, 'Alchemy vs. Chemistry: The Etymological Origins of a Historiographic Mistake,' published in 1998, Newman and Principe challenge a widespread dichotomy as based on faulty etymology. Chemistry traditionally represents 'the modern, scientific, and rational,' while alchemy is alternately viewed negatively as 'the archaic, irrational, and even consciously fraudulent' or idealised and romanticised as having a defining 'spiritual or psychic dimension.'[19] Newman and Principe argue that both terms were employed synonymously prior to the late seventeenth century. Early-modern authors routinely used the term 'alchemy' to refer to what we would recognise as chemistry and 'chemistry' for what we deem quintessentially alchemical, for example the transmutation of metals. Establishing this discrepancy is a key insight that cannot be passed over and that highlights the complexities of the historical record. To name but one famous example, Andreas Libavius' voluminous *Alchemia* of 1597 'is usually and fairly described as the first textbook of chemistry' or 'a landmark in chemical literature. '[20] To avoid the problem of a false dichotomy, Newman and Principe recommend that scholars use the archaic 'chymistry' as well as other, more specialised terms encountered in historical sources.[21]

Principe and Newman further explore this issue in a crucial study titled 'Some Problems with the Historiography of Alchemy.' This landmark publication criticises 'a "spiritual" interpretation of alchemy,' which views 'alchemical adepts as possessors of vast esoteric knowledge and spiritual enlightenment.' Principe and Newman locate the historical origins of this view in 'nineteenth-century occultism,' among writers such as Atwood and Hitchcock. Projected back onto earlier alchemy, their interpretations amount to anachronistic misrepresentations: Principe and Newman 'find no indication that the vast majority of alchemists were working on anything other than material substances toward material goals.'[22] Instead of portraying alchemists as otherworldly initiates, the New Historiography thus places them in the company of miners, metallurgists, assayers, distillers, pharmacists, and even balneologists, all of whom drew on chymical techniques to work with material substances toward many different practical, entrepreneurial, and medical ends. Taken together, the importance of these two essays cannot be overstated, as Principe and Newman made a cogent case for a fresh start that has come to define the field for the past two decades. Whereas it seemed clear to earlier generations of researchers that alchemy was either an outright pseudoscience or primarily spiritual, religious, moral, or psychological, the New Historiography has led historians to see alchemy as predominantly scientific and experimental or, to use a more historic term, related to natural philosophy.

Nevertheless, there are also scholars who criticise the New Historiography from various perspectives.[23] Though they all have different aims and angles, all of these critics agree that the New Historiography implies an overly restrictive view of its subject and downplays important aspects in favour of chemical content and experimental technique. This tendency can lead to an implicit portrayal of alchemy as a kind of proto-chemistry obscured by strange imagery and secrecy. Due to the very success of the New Historiography and its approach, there is the danger of a latent essentialism that could lead, and in some cases already has led, to an implicit view of alchemy as '"really" science (and not religion).' This is simply the antithesis of earlier views holding that 'alchemy may sometimes look like science, but it is really psychology or religion,' as Wouter J. Hanegraaff summarises them.[24]

My aim in this book is not to continue a long-standing tug of war regarding the essence of alchemy, which in effect, as Hanegraaff points out, goes back to the 'conflict thesis' of science and religion, formulated in the nineteenth century.[25] In view of the changing faces of the philosophical art through history, it seems unlikely that either the 'alchemy is scientific' or the 'alchemy is religious' team will ever succeed in pulling its opponents across the line. To transcend this futile contest, we need to adopt the perspective of an impartial observer and identify alchemy itself as part of the game: it is the rope. Even as the teams pull it toward the 'science' or 'religion' side, they both hold on to integral, if different, parts of the same rope, which reaches across the entire playing field. By its refusal to neatly fit either label, alchemy can actually call into question science and religion as categories of analysis too often taken for granted. This tendency is heightened further by narrowing down the subject to 'spiritual alchemy,' a contested term sometimes used to highlight the religious elements encountered within alchemical literature.

Spiritual Alchemy

Based on the advances of the New Historiography, the aim of this book is to study the religious aspects of alchemy seriously and rigorously.[26] This entails a different approach than viewing alchemy as primarily religious, spiritual, moral, or psychological: one would simply take religious elements for granted. Yet it is a rather curious fact that, from the very oldest surviving sources, we do encounter religious dimensions in alchemical sources. The alchemist Zosimos of Panopolis in Hellenised Egypt, for instance, was familiar with gnostic teachings that emphasised humans' need for salvific knowledge to escape the prison of the mortal body and return to the divine. He interspersed his alchemical treatises with various dreams or visions. Based on the apocryphal Book of Enoch, Zosimos even held that fallen angels had taught humankind the art of alchemy.[27] From the beginning, according to Pamela H. Smith, the literature of alchemy 'included a remarkable accretion of religious and gnostic concerns with the relationship of matter and spirit.'[28] Even in much later sources, this situation persists. In the fourteenth century, the Italian author Petrus Bonus wrote a treatise on alchemy titled *Pretiosa margarita novella* (Precious New

Pearl), which contains a chapter arguing 'that this art is both natural *and* divine.'[29] The earliest known German work of alchemy, the *Liber Trinitatis* (The Book of the Trinity), composed in the 1410s, details extended analogies between Jesus Christ and the philosophers' stone.[30] Though the text of the work remains largely inaccessible, its cycle of images became part and parcel of later alchemical literature. The *Rosarium philosophorum* (Rosary of the Philosophers), first published in 1550, was an early and widely disseminated example of this reception. The alchemical process described in the *Rosarium* culminates with the philosophers' stone that is visually portrayed as the risen Christ.[31]

Scholars have used a variety of terms, including 'spiritual alchemy', to draw attention to these conspicuous elements of alchemical literature. Unfortunately, the usefulness of these terms is at times exhausted in doing just that. The late literary scholar Joachim Telle, during his lifetime the outstanding expert on the manuscript record of German alchemy, frequently employed the deliberately vague term 'theoalchemy' (*Theoalchemie*) to describe the mingling of alchemy with theology that could take place in any number of ways.[32] Apart from its evocative, signalling power, this coinage is of very limited analytical value. More problematic still are terms that suggest easy binaries, such as 'exoteric alchemy' and 'esoteric alchemy' or 'material alchemy' and 'spiritual alchemy'.[33] Principe rightly notes that such distinctions go all the way back to the nineteenth century and basically amount to the old dichotomy of chemistry and alchemy.[34]

The term I have chosen for the phenomenon scrutinised throughout this book is not unproblematic. It has frequently been used to advance claims regarding the allegedly religious essence of alchemy. Moreover, a certain confusion surrounds 'spiritual alchemy': it is used to refer both to scholarly (and not-so-scholarly) approaches to alchemy and to actual content in historical sources.[35] The problem here is not that either of these meanings—interpretive approach versus historic ideas or practices—attached to the term 'spiritual alchemy' are wrong: actually, the interpretive approach to alchemy as something religious or spiritual has a very rich history of its own. It is, however, imperative to keep these two significations of spiritual alchemy apart. Only if we reserve the term 'spiritual alchemy' for precisely circumscribed historical and textual phenomena can it serve as a useful category of analysis. Despite the problems of 'spiritual alchemy' and the various alternatives scholars have proposed, I argue that there is no term better suited to the phenomenon investigated in this book.

Unlike some of its alternatives, spiritual alchemy has a number of historic approximations. Here are examples that appear in sources dating from around 1600 to the mid-eighteenth century: 'divine alchemy' (*gottliche Alchimiam*), 'spiritual alchemy' (*alchymia spiritualis*), 'spiritual *chrysopoeia*' (*geistliche Goldmachung*), and 'mystical alchemy' (*Alchymia Mystica*); even English 'Spiritual Chymistry' and German 'spiritual *chymia*' (*geistliche Chymie*) or 'true spiritual *chymia*' appear.[36] While the occurrence of 'mystical' and 'divine' signals an intriguing overlap with the religious domain, 'spiritual alchemy' as studied in this book has little to do with contemporary notions of spirituality. Boaz Huss notes that spirituality is now frequently defined 'in opposition to religion,' which contrasts with 'the early modern and modern perceptions of spirituality as a subcategory, or the essence of religion.'[37]

While some of the protagonists we shall encounter indeed viewed spiritual alchemy as defining for true Christianity, that is not the main point. Instead, the term 'spiritual alchemy' highlights early-modern understandings of *spiritus*. This term carried a bewildering array of meanings in vastly different contexts, particularly medicine and theology, but also anthropology, cosmology, and, last but not least, alchemy.[38] Intellectual historian D. P. Walker has perceptively noted that, against this background, the word *spiritus* could give rise to 'dangerous contaminations or confusions' that might 'lead towards religious unorthodoxies.'[39] *Spiritus* vacillated between the divine and the physical, between medical and theological anthropology, between the matter of heaven and the products of the alchemist's distillery. The interplay, interference, or even conflation of these various notions of spirit is crucial but often remains implicit.

To gain an understanding of what this looked like in practice, we might begin with the general medical understanding of *spiritus*. It was, writes Katharine Park, 'a subtle vapour or exhalation produced from blood and disseminated throughout the body,' serving as the soul's instrument to control 'all activity in the living body.'[40] In a clear hierarchy, spirit thus mediated between the more noble soul and the inferior body. Credited with the recovery of Platonic philosophy for the early-modern world, the Florentine physician, philosopher, and translator Marsilio Ficino extended this scheme to the macrocosm and posited the spirit of the world (*spiritus mundi*) as a subtle matter that mediated between the soul of the world (*anima mundi*) and its body, the material world.[41] Moreover, he identified the *spiritus mundi* as the quintessence and transmuting agent of alchemy. In so doing, Ficino inspired many alchemists to pursue the *spiritus mundi* for centuries to come.[42] Partly due to the Florentine philosopher, partly independently of him, the situation gets exceptionally tangled in alchemy. In a widely used collection of alchemical texts, for instance, the roles of spirit and soul are swapped, and we read that 'spirit and body are one, through mediation of the soul'.[43] Medical historian Marielene Putscher notes that this is not an isolated occurrence and that it is frequently difficult to assess 'whether soul or spirit is the medium that establishes the connection to the body'.[44]

Furthermore, in a theory popularised by medical iconoclast Theophrastus Paracelsus Bombastus von Hohenheim and his followers, the three principles mercury, sulphur, and salt corresponded to spirit, soul, and body.[45] In this manner, alchemical Paracelsianism contributed to the spread of a trichotomous anthropology among religious dissenters in the late sixteenth and throughout the seventeenth century, particularly in German-speaking Lutheran contexts: it was in this intellectual, religious, and cultural environment that spiritual alchemy developed. On the trichotomous view, spirit could refer to the divine spark, either preexistent within a human being and awaiting activation or implanted through rebirth.[46] Rather than mediating between soul and body, the spirit could thus become the noblest component of the human being. This represented a notable departure from the dichotomous anthropology espoused by Aristotelian philosophy and orthodox Lutheran theology. From the perspective of the latter, the crux was that this third part of humans was not only immortal but divine: it was, quite literally, a part of God and would return to God after death.[47] This view had far-reaching heterodox implications: sometimes the third component was effectively tied to an internalised *Christus in nobis* or participation in Christ's heavenly, ubiquitous body, doing away with the need for the outward rituals of baptism and the Eucharist.[48] Indeed, in the late seventeenth century, Lutheran heresy hunter Ehregott Daniel Colberg described 'the delusion of the three substantial parts of man' as the foundational error of 'Platonic-Hermetic Christianity' from which all other heresies flowed.[49]

Bearing in mind the layers of meaning accruing around 'spirit' in the early-modern world, I define the spiritual alchemy investigated here as *the practical pursuit of inward but real bodily transmutation*. This transmutation amounted to the reversal of the Fall and its consequences; furthermore, it prepared the faithful for the resurrection of the dead at the Last Judgement. This spiritual alchemy is thus closely connected to the idea of spiritual rebirth, which it helped shape and by which it was shaped in turn.[50] Apart from the fact that, from Jacob Boehme onward, all the figures studied here drew on his theosophy, there are three key elements of this alchemy. First, there is a three-way *lapis-Christus in nobis* analogy between the philosophers' stone, Christ incarnate, and the believer who mystically identifies with Christ. This element harks back to the more traditional *lapis-Christus* analogy but significantly expands it by including the individual disciple. The mystical identification of Christ and the believer could be summed up in a single phrase: *Christus in nobis*, the notion that Christ dwells within his faithful who mystically relive his life on a daily basis. In the seventeenth century, this phrase became popular in heterodox circles on the fringes of Lutheranism. Through the immediate access to the divine guaranteed by the divine *logos* within the individual believer, the implications of *Christus in nobis* effectively made the clergy, the church, and at times even the Bible unnecessary.[51]

Second, there is a physical process toward restoring the prelapsarian body, characterised as subtle or spiritual, in preparation for life in Heaven. With regard to the resurrection of the dead, the second element is fairly amenable to Lutheran orthodoxy. The reformer Martin Luther himself had praised alchemy as a visible demonstration of this article of faith, and a court alchemist's obituary explicitly called it 'spiritual alchemy' (*geistliche Alchymia*) around 1660.[52] Yet there are two important differences that concern timing and agency. In contrast to the delayed bodily transmutation at the end of time, Boehme and his followers held that it began in the here and now, albeit imperceptibly and in ways that cannot be measured with the tools of science. Furthermore, the orthodox understanding reserves agency solely for God, in keeping with Luther's principle of *sola gratia* (by grace alone): on this view, believers are passive matter in God's hands rather than spiritual adepts who participate actively in the cultivation of their resurrection bodies.

The issue of agency leads on directly to the third aspect, which is the practical pursuit of that process of spiritual rebirth and its bodiliness through devotional acts or mystical paths. By practising spiritual alchemy, the individual believer actively nourishes the new birth within by means of prayer, penitence, ascetic deeds, or other rituals, which may also be purely internal or contemplative.[53] By pursuing these practices over a prolonged period of time, spiritual alchemists attain higher stages in their quest for ever closer union with the divine. Sometimes the language of mysticism, particularly that of the three stages of *purificatio*, *illuminatio*, and *unio*, appears in these contexts. These devotional acts or mystical paths are explicitly described in terms of manual operations, alchemical techniques, or stages of the great work. In a way, then, spiritual alchemy is a peculiar form of Protestant mysticism. Contrary to a widespread perception, there is nothing that should cause us to view this term as self-contradictory; in fact, mysticism had a rich and largely positive reception within early Protestantism.[54] Yet the core three elements of spiritual alchemy do subtly depart from Lutheran orthodoxy by internalising Christ, emphasising rebirth, and requiring individual agency, respectively.

I cannot possibly stress enough that, in the interaction of these aspects, spiritual alchemy ceases to be merely metaphorical. If I had to reduce this entire book to a single point it would be this: Boehme and his later disciples believed that actual bodily changes—albeit not subject to the ordinary laws of physics or conventionally measurable—were taking place within them as they pursued the spiritual alchemy of rebirth and its processes.[55] This is the defining feature of spiritual alchemy proper, as opposed to any number of religious tropes, conceits, or metaphors one might uncover in alchemical literature. It is the reason that this book focuses on Boehme and ends with Atwood rather than Hitchcock, whose moral interpretation of alchemy remained entirely allegorical. While we would tend to understand rebirth, deification, or mystical union as non-physical processes of religious transformation, that is not how Boehme and his followers viewed them. In other words, even though spiritual alchemy did originate as a metaphor or conceit, it did not remain so. Instead, spiritual alchemy came to be viewed as *literally* describing the *physical transfiguration of the human body* through rebirth in this life, culminating in resurrection at the Last Judgement.

Even as it is challenging to transcend the hard-and-fast distinctions between mind and matter, soul and body, that is precisely what we need to wrap our minds around. Otherwise, it remains impossible to understand spiritual alchemy, predicated on the early-modern notion of *spiritus*. In important ways, therefore, the spiritual alchemy of rebirth is the alchemy of *spiritus* as the subtle matter of the new birth, the kingdom of heaven, and Christ's human body turned heavenly. Through the spiritual alchemy of rebirth, believers could *literally* become members of Christ's body, as the Pauline metaphor put it.[56] Irrespective of what we might think of this nowadays, the most methodologically sound way of approaching spiritual alchemy is the suspension of disbelief. For the historical actors studied in this book, it was real. Consequently, we have to also view it as real in precisely the same sense as the sun used to revolve around the earth, astrological influence determined the fate of people and nations, and (perhaps most appropriately) many alchemists successfully transmuted lesser metals into gold and had witnesses to tell the tale.

From a historical perspective, it is a moot point to note that these views no longer have a place in our current understanding of the world: borrowing a phrase coined by E. P. Thompson, historian of astrology Patrick Curry has described this as 'the enormous condescension of posterity' that privileges winners over losers among both historical actors and ideas.[57] In her study *Alchemy and Authority in the Holy Roman Empire*, Tara Nummedal makes this point with particular clarity: 'whatever we think of alchemy today, it is essential to remember that many people accepted the basic principles of alchemy in early modern Europe, even the transmutation of metals, and could point to religious and natural philosophical justification for their belief.' For all intents and purposes of historical inquiry, 'we must accept that, in the eyes of early modern Europeans,' alchemists 'did indeed transmute metals.'[58] While there may have been comparatively few who gave credence to the bodily reality of spiritual alchemy, this circumstance does not diminish the argument.

Based on the features just described, I establish that spiritual alchemy was shared, transmitted, or semi-independently rediscovered from Boehme to Atwood. This book traces the continued existence of the spiritual alchemy of rebirth in heterodox and specifically Boehmist circles from around 1600 to the early twentieth century. The basic claim of continuity from Boehme to Atwood argued here is not new. A particularly apt expression may be found in F. Sherwood Taylor's 1949 book *The Alchemists*, in which the founding editor of *Ambix* notes 'the existence of a school of mystical alchemists whose purpose was self-regeneration.' With Boehme as an important early exponent, this 'tendency culminated in 1850' with Atwood's *Suggestive Inquiry into the Hermetic Mystery*.[59] Taylor's statement, it turns out, could hardly have been more accurate yet has so far lacked the support of a comprehensive presentation. This led Principe and Newman to describe such claims of continuity regarding spiritual alchemy as mere 'conjecture' without 'clear historical evidence.'[60] This book marshals that hitherto elusive evidence, much of it found in obscure manuscript sources, and thus documents the continuity of spiritual alchemy that links the early-modern to the modern era.

With broad brushstrokes, the story begins with an attempt to sketch the Reformation-era developments that provided the necessary preconditions for the spiritual alchemy of rebirth to take shape. Going beyond the usual suspects such as Paracelsus, I argue that pseudo-Weigelian texts that have previously gone largely unnoticed played an important role in this (chapter 1). Early readers of these cryptic works included the chymist Johann Siebmacher and the astrologer Paul Nagel. It remains difficult to assess whether Boehme also encountered them directly, yet thanks to Nagel we can be sure that pseudo-Weigelian alchemy circulated in the theosopher's network (chapter 2). In Boehme's mature writings, the spiritual alchemy of rebirth comes into its own (chapter 3). Among his first generation of disciples, it was particularly the Silesian mystic Abraham von Franckenberg who absorbed and articulated the lessons of spiritual alchemy, presenting them as part and parcel of ancient wisdom shared by pious pagans, gnostics, and early Christians (chapter 4). He then actively communicated these insights to his spiritual and philosophical son, Georg Lorenz Seidenbecher (chapter 5).

Later to become notorious as a millenarian, Seidenbecher befriended Friedrich Breckling, who eventually rediscovered Boehme's spiritual alchemy and added his own accents in the 1680s (chapter 6). He did so partly in unmarked additions to the writings of an obscure sixteenth-century author, Bartholomaeus Sclei (chapter 7). Subsequently, Dionysius Andreas Freher took the spiritual alchemy of rebirth to England after spending a formative decade in Holland. In London, he introduced it to an English audience through his manuscript works (chapter 8). Freher received a delayed reception in the nineteenth century. Christopher Walton, a collector of Freher manuscripts, and Thomas South, the father of Mary Anne Atwood, discussed their shared enthusiasm for Boehme's expatriate expositor in letters written around the same time South's daughter composed her *Suggestive Inquiry* (chapter 9). Early readers correctly perceived the mystical thrust of this sprawling treatise, and Atwood herself expressed her understanding of alchemy more succinctly in later years (chapter 10).

1
The Radical Reformation, Paracelsian Networks, and Pseudo-Weigelian Alchemy

Whereas most proponents of spiritual alchemy have tended towards viewing it as timeless, it actually originated in a very specific historical context. In an important sense, the alchemy of spiritual rebirth at the origins of born-again Christianity was a quintessentially German affair. When talking about rebirth, most other European languages use the technical Latin term *regeneratio* or its vernacular derivates such as the French *régénération*. In stark contrast, German features the graphic *Wiedergeburt*, which Christ discussed in the Gospel of John.[1] References to rebirth occur in the writings of late medieval German mystics, yet they only play a marginal role.[2] Only during the late sixteenth century did *Wiedergeburt* really come into its own and emerge as something distinct from baptism. Around that time, the German-speaking world witnessed the confluence of two important currents, the older one of German mysticism from Meister Eckhart onwards and the more recent development of alchemical Paracelsianism.[3] These currents found their melting pot in underground networks, in which Paracelsian and potentially heterodox works circulated. The activities of such networks intensified towards 1600. It was in this context that the abstract language of rebirth that had already baffled the Pharisee Nicodemus became more tangible through recourse to the concrete phenomena of alchemy. Previously neglected pseudepigrapha attributed to the unconventional Lutheran theologian Valentin Weigel appear to be among the oldest sources in which this took place.

Reformation-Era Developments

The preconditions for spiritual rebirth emancipating itself from baptism arose during the age of the Reformation, due to Paracelsus, Caspar Schwenckfeld von Ossig, and Valentin Weigel, among others. Charles Webster has placed Paracelsus, chiefly famous for his medical innovations, in the context of the radical Reformation despite the fact that he remained nominally Catholic.[4] According to Paracelsus' baptismal theology, a simple ritual involving water and accompanied by prayer imparted to those baptised a new, immortal body. This spiritual body of rebirth then had to be nourished through Christ's body and blood in the Eucharist.[5] Boehme was to take up these core ideas, yet several important differences separated him from Paracelsus. Generally, there was a change in the state of alchemical theorising about the mineral world. In the early sixteenth century, Paracelsus stood at the very beginning of a time during which there was a 'porous boundary between alchemy and the world of mining,' exemplified by Petrus Kerzenmacher's *Alchimi und Bergwerck* (Alchemy and Mining) of 1534. It is in this context of alchemists' engagement with vernacular mining lore that a new understanding of the underground mineral realm began to take shape, one that was marked by 'death, decay, and rebirth just like the earthly surface.'[6] Such an animate conception of the mineral world led alchemists and others who engaged with miners to increasingly speak of the birth, death, and, occasionally, rebirth of metals towards the late sixteenth century. In view of this trend, it becomes less of a coincidence that the spiritual alchemy of rebirth began to take shape in the 1590s.

For that to happen, two further important shifts had to occur, and these also separate Paracelsus from later developments and Boehme in particular. First and foremost, Paracelsus himself hardly ever used the vocabulary of alchemy to describe his theology of the immortal body that was acquired through baptism. In fact, Urs Leo Gantenbein notes that 'the consistent use of alchemical terminology' is 'untypical for authentic Paracelsian theology,' although on rare occasions Paracelsus did establish parallels between theology and transmutational alchemy.[7] To put it another way, while many components of the spiritual alchemy of rebirth were already in place in the writings of Paracelsus, he did for the most part not yet construe them as *alchemy*. This is the reason why my account does not begin with the Swiss medical reformer. The second major discrepancy between Paracelsus and Boehme is theological and concerns the changing relationship between baptism and rebirth. Originally and even in later orthodox Lutheran practice, the terms were largely synonymous: sermons and obituaries habitually spoke of 'holy baptism and the bath of rebirth' (*Widergeburt*), effectively conflating the two.[8] By 1600, however, Anabaptism and spiritualism had brought about 'a dissociation of baptism and rebirth,' something I have described in more detail elsewhere. Anabaptists rejected infant baptism and 'highlighted an adult's conscious decision of faith as a crucial requirement for baptism and rebirth, even as the two remained closely linked.' Subsequently, spiritualist theologians such as Schwenckfeld and Weigel 'privileged the spirit over the letter, the invisible church over the visible, and consequently viewed external rituals as irrelevant.'[9]

Interiorised and spiritualised notions of baptism, the Eucharist, and the 'new birth' were central to Schwenckfeld's theology. It is possible that he borrowed these aspects of Paracelsus' theology, and Schwenckfeld may well have met the controversial physician in person on various occasions.[10] Particularly in his native land, the reformer of Silesia had many adherents into the seventeenth century and beyond, and it was in this vicinity that Boehme developed his theosophy.[11] Another minister among the second generation of Reformers also contributed to the devotional literature Boehme read: Valentin Weigel. After a quiet life as a pastor in the Saxon town of Zschopau, Weigel posthumously embarked on an impressive career as a heretic. Throughout the seventeenth century, his name became synonymous with what theologians and church historians now call spiritualism: orthodox clergy and authorities aggressively cracked down on Weigelians.[12] While most of them had been baptised as infants, their theological convictions led Schwenckfeldians, Weigelians, and Lutheran spiritualists to dismiss outward rites as ineffective.[13] They therefore turned rebirth into something that was distinct from baptism, purely interior, happening continually rather than just once. The baptism of infants or adults ritually imitates the death and resurrection of Christ once in their lives; rebirth does so daily through the mystical identification of Christ and the believer. Due to these shifts, spiritualists used rebirth to articulate an alternative Christianity, running counter to the church establishment they despised, claiming a truer faith of the few in contrast to the empty ceremonies of the masses. Whereas baptism had played a prominent role for Paracelsus as he wrote about the spiritual body, Boehme's mature works discussed spiritual rebirth as something unrelated to baptism.

Those who espoused the doctrine of spiritual rebirth departed from Lutheran orthodoxy, as codified in the confessional writings, particularly regarding the doctrine of justification. The position of Luther and Philipp Melanchthon, as well as the Lutheran church in general, is often described as forensic, although recent scholarship has complicated the picture somewhat.[14] On the forensic understanding, the righteousness of Christ is imputed to the believer in a legal manner, per decree, as it were, irrespective of that believer's past or future actions. One of the first to criticise this view was the theologian and mathematician Andreas Osiander, known to historians of science chiefly for the infamous anonymous preface he added to Nicolaus Copernicus' *De revolutionibus orbium coelestium* (On the Revolutions of the Heavenly Spheres) in 1543. In a fateful disputation held at the University of Königsberg on 9 November 1550, Osiander developed an alternative theology of justification centred on 'becoming united with Christ, born again (*renasci*) out of him, he being in us and we in him, living through him, and believing ourselves righteous through his righteousness dwelling in us.'[15] Almost immediately, Justus Menius, a minister in Gotha, attacked Osiander's interpretation as 'alchemical' (*Alcumistisch*), and soon enough a knowledgeable reader combined the theologies of Osiander and Paracelsus in pseudepigraphic writings attributed to the latter.[16]

Valentin Weigel also read and copied Paracelsus, and his writings featured an insistence on rebirth construed as a physico-spiritual but not yet alchemical process.[17] At the same time, the pastor of Zschopau followed Osiander in stressing the mystical incarnation of Christ within the believer: this was a vital, post-Paracelsian contribution that would eventually be absorbed into spiritual alchemy.[18] In a change of emphasis compared to Osiander, Weigel particularly positioned 'the new birth' (*die newe geburt*) as a replacement of the forensic understanding of justification.[19] In so doing, he preceded such towering figures as Johann Arndt and Jacob Boehme.[20] Arndt referred to the 'new birth' (*newe Geburt*) and 'rebirth' (*Wiedergeburt*) many times throughout his devotional bestseller, *Vier Bücher Vom wahren Christenthumb* (Four Books on True Christianity). Published from 1605, with a first complete edition in 1610, parts of the *Vier Bücher* had been lifted straight from Weigel's writings, which caused a controversy around Arndt and his work.[21]

Alongside Weigel, it was probably Arndt who shaped Boehme's views on the subject most, and Sibylle Rusterholz plausibly asserts that the theosopher was familiar with Arndt's voluminous work from early on.[22] In a rare instance of admitting to reading the works of others, Boehme expressed subdued praise for Weigel, who had written 'beautifully on the new birth (*neuen Gebuhrt*) and the unity of humanity through Christ among us.' Yet Boehme went on to claim: 'I described it [rebirth] more clearly in my writings.'[23] The eminent German church historian Martin Brecht lends support to the theosopher's self-flattering claim, as he notes that particularly Boehme had a lasting impact in spreading the notion of spiritual rebirth among radical

Pietists in the late seventeenth and early eighteenth centuries.[24] By way of Pietism and, particularly in England, Methodism, the idea of spiritual rebirth reached modern Evangelicalism, where it continues to thrive among born-again believers. The midwifing role of alchemy is now all but forgotten, yet this kind of Christianity continues to exist until today in congregations and communities that emphasise rebirth or in individuals who describe themselves as born again. Scholars of Evangelicalism and Pietism, such as W. R. Ward and Douglas H. Shantz, have perceptively noted that such debts to alchemy do exist in these movements.[25]

In parallel, a number of alchemical writers around 1600 showed an increasing awareness of their art's analogies with Christianity. The Paracelsian alchemists Gerard Dorn, Heinrich Khunrath, and Oswald Croll were remarkable for the extent to which religious concerns shaped their alchemical works.[26] In his famous *Amphitheatrum sapientiae aeternae* (Amphitheatre of Eternal Wisdom), first published in 1595 but vastly expanded in the 1609 edition, Khunrath wrote the following as a commentary on a verse of the apocryphal Wisdom of Solomon:

> Happy he to whom is shown, and having been shown rightly knows: the person, passion, and resurrection of JHSVH CHRIST; the matter, preparation, and more-than-perfection in the glorified body (*corpore glorificato*) of the PHILOSOPHERS' STONE; and your rebirth (*regeneratio*), formed in the image and likeness of GOD according to body, spirit, and soul.[27]

Thus, Khunrath was among the very first to explicitly posit a linkage between the Incarnation of Christ, the preparation of the philosophers' stone, and the rebirth of the individual believer.

Despite the clarity of this passage, there are reasons to look elsewhere for the beginning of the story to be told in these pages. Khunrath used the abstract Latin term *regeneratio* and did not dwell on this complex analogy to explain it further. Since he died in 1605, this commentary would have been composed several years prior to its appearance in print. If Johann Arndt's Christmas day 1599 letter to Khunrath's associate and later editor, Erasmus Wolfart, is any indication, the alchemist did indeed give rise to discussions of rebirth as analogous to alchemical transmutation much earlier than 1609.[28] Yet in this letter, the mystical identification of Christ and the believer is missing. Instead of originating with Khunrath, spiritual alchemy began to take shape in pseudepigraphic texts attributed to Valentin Weigel.

Pseudo-Weigelian Alchemy

Neither Schwenckfeld nor Weigel—who both contributed to shaping Boehme's theosophy—explicitly described the new birth and its bodiliness in alchemical terms. Indeed, according to Andrew Weeks, the genuine Weigel was 'without interest in medicine or alchemy.'[29] Yet pseudepigraphic additions to his oeuvre, were quick to make up for this perceived shortcoming. Previously largely ignored, two pseudo-Weigelian texts established a close connection between spiritual rebirth and alchemy. The first of these, *Azoth et Ignis* (Azoth and Fire), was composed between the mid-1580s and 1599 but first printed only in 1701. An exceedingly cryptic text, *Azoth and Fire* combined Weigelian spiritualism with alchemical terminology and apocalyptic speculation. The strange term in *Azoth and Fire* was a mystifying corruption of the Arabic word for mercury, *az-zā'ūq*, rendered as *azoc* in Morienus' *Testament*, the first alchemical work to circulate in Latin Europe from 1144.[30] The second and considerably more accessible text was written after the former and published in 1614. *Ad dialogum de morte* (Concerning the Dialogue on Death) presented an addition to Weigel's genuine *Dialogus de Christianismo* (Dialogue on Christianity), composed in 1584 and printed in 1614. Both works feature striking statements on spiritual rebirth and outline parallels between it and alchemical transmutation. Moreover, they strongly emphasise an alliance of rebirth and alchemy as an alternative to the doctrine of forensic justification. Instead of the law, with all the negative associations of the Old Covenant, superseded by the New Testament, alchemy provided another theological paradigm, based on the natural world as God's creation. The story of the spiritual alchemy of rebirth thus begins with two short and obscure works that were the first to systematically outline correlations between the great work of alchemy and the believer's mystical identification with Christ as spiritual rebirth. The remainder of this chapter discusses both texts of pseudo-Weigelian alchemy in turn.

Azoth and Fire

Most manuscripts of *Azoth and Fire* only run to a handful of leaves. Yet for all its brevity, the work establishes significant parallels between the heavenly cornerstone, Jesus Christ, and the terrestrial stone of the philosophers, as well as between spiritual rebirth and alchemical transmutation.[31] In the late sixteenth and all throughout the seventeenth century, *Azoth and Fire* circulated in manuscript and found readers as well as copyists among alchemists, religious dissenters, and some who qualified as both.[32] Its pseudepigraphic attribution to Weigel contributed to this relative popularity. Two older manuscripts of the text conclude with the following statement: 'These are the choicest secrets (*secreta secretorum*) out of Weigel's autograph, not to be revealed to any but the faithful sons of wisdom.'[33] This claim was part of the pseudepigraphic fiction but also hinted at a process of compilation.

While it remains difficult to identify many of the sources the anonymous compiler used, one of them was the *Theologia Weigelii* (Weigel's Theology), a work composed in 1584 and published in 1618. Horst Pfefferl has attributed it to Benedict Biedermann, Weigel's deacon, collaborator, and successor, who wrote many pseudo-Weigelian treatises.[34] Indeed, a number of elements and statements in *Azoth and Fire* already occur in this work. However, the *Theologia Weigelii* completely lacks the dominant emphasis on alchemy, which only appears as one branch of learning among others.[35] This distinctive aspect of *Azoth and Fire* points away from Biedermann and renders Weigel's cantor, the Paracelsian Christoph Weickhart, a more likely candidate for its authorship.[36] There is, however, not enough evidence to attribute the text to him. Furthermore, *Azoth and Fire* not only included Weigelian material. It begins with a stark revaluation of the number of the beast (666), which is held to contain all the secrets of God's two books, Scripture and Nature.[37] This positive reinterpretation of the number of the beast is an idiosyncrasy that goes back to Paul Lautensack, a Nuremberg artist and visionary of the Reformation era. For him, as Berthold Kress puts it, 'this number had ... divine connotations.'[38] Weigel and Lautensack represent important traditions of spiritualist devotion and apocalyptic speculation that found themselves combined with alchemy in *Azoth and Fire*.

In the contexts of the work's transmission, we encounter the same intriguing combination of normally distinct intellectual currents. A consideration of the textual neighbours of *Azoth and Fire*, the texts alongside which it was copied and read, bears this out. The oldest dated version was completed in 1599. In this witness, *Azoth and Fire* occurs as an appendix to a more substantial work inspired by Lautensack. Like most *Azoth and Fire* manuscripts, it concludes with a magic square whose lines add up to 666, clearly harking back to the Nuremberg artist.[39] Yet for some reason the copyist ascribed this volume filled with Lautensack material to Weigel.[40] Conversely, another copy of *Azoth and Fire*, attributed to 'Wigellus,' appears in a massive collection of Lautensack tracts in two volumes, compiled in 1611.[41] In a large book of alchemical excerpts acquired for the library of the Palatine Electors prior to the sack of Heidelberg in 1622, *Azoth and Fire* follows a brief passage derived from the pseudo-Paracelsian *Liber Azoth sive de ligno et linea vitae* (The Book *Azoth*, or: On the Tree and Line of Life).[42] Its first copyists and readers studied *Azoth and Fire* in the contexts of Weigelian spiritualism, Lautensackian apocalypticism, and Paracelsian alchemy.

The one copy of *Azoth and Fire* whose scribe can be identified further corroborates this assessment. The astrologer and millenarian Paul Nagel of Torgau included 'Weigel's *Azoth and Fire*' in his book of alchemical excerpts.[43] Despite being mainly known for his numerological speculations, Nagel devoted considerable efforts to the mysterious art, as this manuscript documents. He corresponded with the famous Polish alchemist Michael Sendivogius and accumulated the bulk of his alchemical excerpts around 1614.[44] As Nagel collected these texts, he copied pseudo-Weigel's *Azoth and Fire* between two prayers for alchemical success and a process of ten operations towards the philosophers' stone. The latter was attributed to Heinrich Khunrath, 'the highly renowned theosopher and physician.'[45] Along with the Paracelsian alchemists Gerard Dorn and Oswald Croll, who also figured in Nagel's excerpts, Khunrath was a key representative of a growing trend towards emphasising religious aspects within alchemical literature. Furthermore, Nagel added marginalia throughout his copy of *Azoth and Fire*, documenting his attempt to interpret this challenging text. Eventually, he also took up its ideas in his own scribal publications and became an important node in the network of Jacob Boehme. While noting relevant discrepancies in other witnesses, I chiefly rely on Nagel's version of *Azoth and Fire* throughout the following discussion (fig. 1.1).

Azoth and Fire integrated the Lautensackian number 666 into an alchemical frame of reference. The text claimed that it corresponded to the one subject of the art: the eponymous '*azoth* and fire.' At this point, Nagel added a marginal note that glossed *azoth* as 'mineral gold and silver' and fire as mercury, that is, presumably *mercurius philosophorum*, not to be confused with common quicksilver.[46] While just about all alchemists would have agreed that the mercury of the philosophers was of crucial importance, it was also subject to wildly different interpretations. Nagel likely understood *mercurius philosophorum* to be a powerful solvent, able to dissolve gold into its *prima materia*, or undifferentiated metallic matter, as the Swiss alchemist Raphael Egli construed it in a manuscript discussed by Bruce T. Moran.[47]

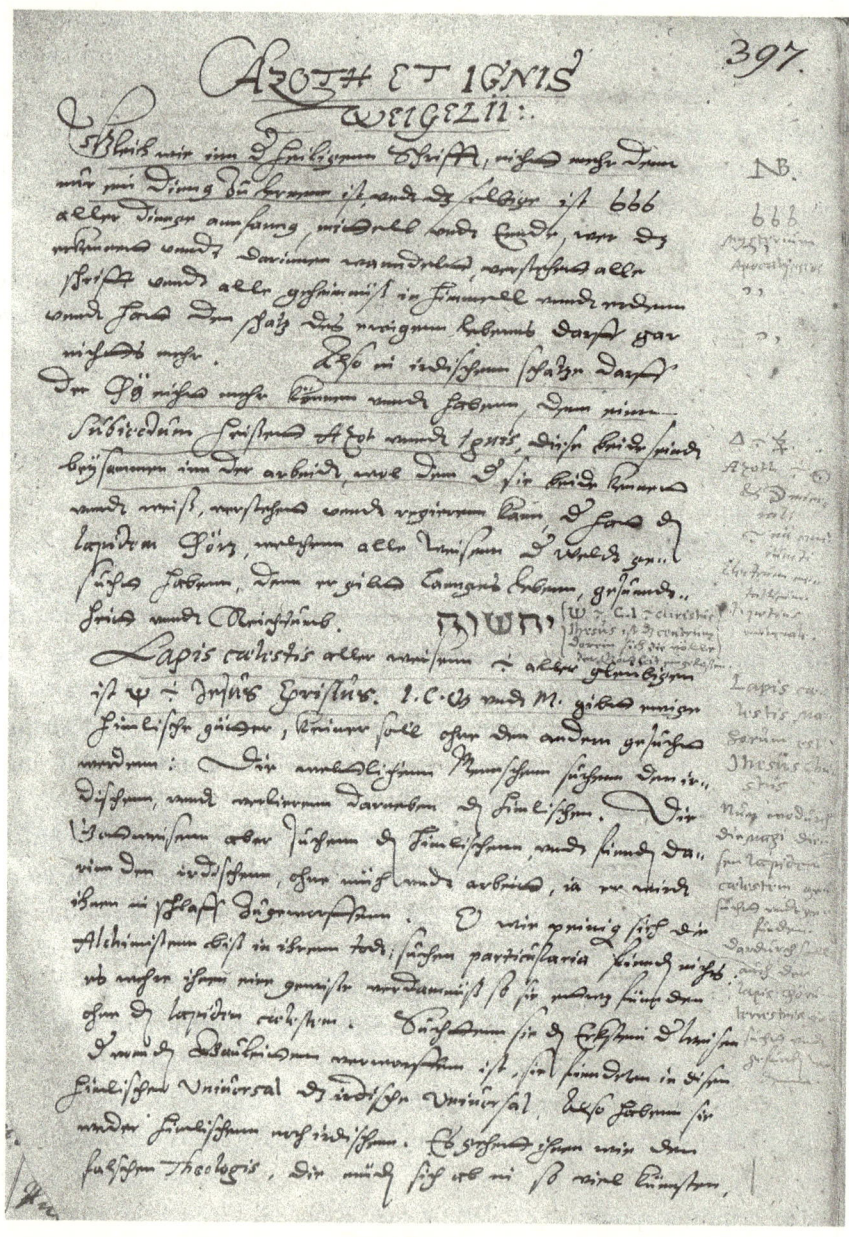

Fig. 1.1 Pseudo-Weigel, *Azoth et Ignis Weigelii*, as copied by Paul Nagel. The first page of *Azoth and Fire* in Nagel's hand documents how the millenarian grappled with the text, adding marginalia with his interpretations. Karlsruhe, Badische Landesbibliothek: Cod. Allerheiligen 3, p. 397. © BLB Karlsruhe, Digitale Sammlungen.

Pseudo-Weigel promised that 'whoever knows and can understand and rule both [*azoth* and fire] has the philosophers' stone.' From the terrestrial stone, pseudo-Weigel moved instantly to the 'heavenly stone (*lapis coelestis*) of all the wise—of all the faithful: Jesus Christ, God and man' (*J. C. G*[*ott*] *undt M*[*ensch*]).⁴⁸ The other manuscripts lack the phrase about the faithful, which could thus be a gloss added by Nagel. This simple addition effectively conflates true believers and alchemical adepts.

If the philosophers' stone and Christ as the 'celestial stone' are analogous, familiarity with the latter entails alchemical success. One only ought to seek Christ, 'so you will have proper alchemy and, in addition, true theology.' Consequently, pseudo-Weigel contrasted misguided alchemists and their toil with Christian adepts, noting that 'theosophers seek the heavenly [stone] and find the terrestrial one besides, without effort or trouble; indeed, . . . in their sleep.' In addition, the reader learns that 'you cannot be a proper alchemist unless you are also a true Christian.'⁴⁹ Disregarding Christ, impious alchemists toil in vain; they discard 'the cornerstone of the wise that the builders rejected,' according to a verse from the Psalms recalled repeatedly throughout the New Testament. This cornerstone is none other than 'Jesus Christ God [and] Man—666.'⁵⁰ For pseudo-Weigel and some of his readers, in the wake of Lautensack, the number of the beast was no longer associated with the Antichrist but with Christ himself. In a 1618 scribal publication, *Leo rugiens* (Roaring Lion), Nagel provided a possible rationale for this complete reversal. The Book of Revelation explicitly states that it is 'the number of a man,' and Christ is 'the Son of Man.'⁵¹ 'Therefore,' Nagel continued, 'this number also carries within itself the secrets of Jesus Christ and all his saints.'⁵²

In keeping with Weigel's *Gnothi seauton* (Know Thyself), composed in 1571 and first printed in 1615, *Azoth and Fire* extols self-knowledge in a succinct prayer. The stance it articulates corresponds to the scathing criticism of academic learning pervasive among religious non-conformists:⁵³

> I thank you God, father of our Lord Christ Jesus, that you hide theology and alchemy—that is, all celestial and terrestrial wisdom—from the wise and learned of the world and reveal it only to the simple (*einfeltigen*) who study the 'Know Thyself' (*Gnothi se auton*), that is, to recognise oneself in God.⁵⁴

Here as elsewhere, the intricate connection between knowing oneself and knowing God hints at the underlying concept of *Christus in nobis:* if Christ dwells within the believer, introspection is tantamount to contemplation of the divine. *Azoth and Fire* further specifies the analogy between alchemy and theology in the more specific domains of eschatology and soteriology, the doctrines of final things and salvation, respectively. Mirroring the alchemical process as well as Christ's redemptive work, both macrocosm and microcosm have to suffer death and destruction in order to be made new: 'Just as Christ does not bring anyone to life or salvation without cross and death, so gold cannot be, nor become, the tincture or [philosophers'] stone without death in the mercurial water.' Just as the destruction of the world by fire would have to precede the creation of a new heaven and a new earth, so the individual believer has to die with Christ in order to be saved and resurrected.

Based on this reasoning, pseudo-Weigel very explicitly criticised the Lutheran doctrine of justification that construed human salvation in forensic, legal terms as the imputation of righteousness. Instead, he presented an alternative:

> Christ's cross and death do not have to be imputed from the outside, as the pseudo-theologian pretends, but by a corporeal union and essential implantation. How should Christ's cross and death tinge [transmute] me into a new, heavenly man, unless I really died to sin and were killed in, with, and through him?[55]

Mystical identification with Christ lay at the core of this spiritual alchemy, which was to effect the transmutation of man into a heavenly state. An apodictic statement in Latin did not mince words: 'Therefore, imputative righteousness from outside is fictitious theology and of the devil.'[56] Heightening Osiander's critique to the extreme, pseudo-Weigel used alchemy to launch a frontal attack on a core doctrine of orthodox Lutheranism. While the polemical aspect may have been more important to pseudo-Weigel, mystical identification with Christ was central for spiritual alchemy.

The alternative paradigm espoused by pseudo-Weigel was that of rebirth. Pseudo-Weigel insisted that spiritual rebirth and the making of the *lapis philosophorum* were analogous: 'Rebirth (*renascentia*) is necessary, we have to be born again (*renasci*) out of spirit and water; the same goes for the stone.'[57] The use of this term established a conscious contrast against the more common *regeneratio*. Compared to other manuscripts, Nagel's version highlights this aspect most emphatically, while simultaneously stressing the identification of Christ and the born-again believer: 'Jesus Christ is the new Jerusalem, the city of God in which the deity lives incarnate. *Homo renatus,* the born-again human, is the new Jerusalem, the city of God in which the Trinity lives incarnate.'[58] Nagel underlined this passage in red. It combined the mystical identification of Christ and the believer with the much more contentious notion of *Christus in nobis*. Whereas leading theologians of the Reformation era had previously used that phrase, it came to acquire heterodox associations as spiritualists and other dissenters used it to claim independence from regular church instruction and asserted divine authority for their own prophetic revelations. Mostly ignored by previous scholarship and printed only after a century of scribal transmission, pseudo-Weigel's *Azoth and Fire* was likely the very first text to draw an analogy between laboratory alchemy and spiritual rebirth while emphasising the mystical identification of Christ and the believer.

Concerning the Dialogue on Death and *A Conversation on Death*

Many of the core ideas of *Azoth and Fire* reappear in *Concerning the Dialogue on Death*, the pseudepigraphic addition to Weigel's genuine *Dialogus de Christianismo*. Indeed, the later text derived some of its most poignant statements from the obviously spurious *Azoth and Fire*. Since *Concerning the Dialogue on Death* is not contained in the most reliable manuscript witnesses of the *Dialogus*, Weigel scholars have classified this piece as an inauthentic contribution and consistently excluded it from modern editions.[59] Yet as already noted by Will-Erich Peuckert, the additional dialogue emulates the real Weigel quite convincingly, certainly more so than *Azoth and Fire*.[60] Accordingly, *Concerning the Dialogue on Death* found inclusion in the first edition of Weigel's *Dialogus* in 1614, printed at Halle.[61] Within five years, in 1616 and 1618, the *Dialogus* was reprinted twice by Johann Knuber of Newenstatt (New City), a pseudonym and fake imprint that probably concealed the identity of Johann Francke of Magdeburg.[62] The pseudo-Weigelian addition was thus readily available in print. A single extant copy shows that *Concerning the Dialogue on Death* also circulated in manuscript, likely before it was printed, albeit under a slightly different German title: *Ein Gesprech vom Tode* (A Conversation on Death). Compared to this older manuscript version, the printed edition preserves the exact outline of the conversation between the three interlocutors Death, Preacher, and Listener. However, it is much shorter, omitting almost half of the text by drastically shortening some of the conversation's longer contributions. Nevertheless, the print edition should not be disregarded, as the manuscript contains various imperfections that can be corrected based on it. In what follows, I draw on both versions and highlight significant differences.

Proposing an alternative theology of rebirth based on alchemy, the main thrust of *A Conversation on Death* was directed against the Lutheran doctrine of justification, a concern Weigel shared with his imitators.[63] The pastor of Zschopau prefaced the authentic *Dialogus* with an explanation of the significance of each interlocutor, according to which Death represents Christ: '*Mors*, Death, entails Christ Jesus, ... everything that Christ discussed, suffered, did, and lived. He is one with Christ.'[64] As Christ's *alter ego*, Death also figures in *A Conversation on Death*. In one passage, Death specifically attacks the forensic understanding of justification proposed by the Preacher, the representative of the clergy and orthodox Lutheranism: 'If you want to attain true life, you have to die first, uniting with me bodily (*leibhafftig*), instead of letting something be imputed to yourself from the outside.'[65] This derives directly from *Azoth and Fire*. Whereas that text contains a frontal assault on orthodox Lutheran theology, *A Conversation on Death* tempers its radicalism somewhat, and the explicit final clause mentioning imputation from the outside is only found in the printed version. In contrast, the manuscript version is much clearer in its presentation of the alternative model of rebirth: 'True and permanent life comes from resurrection (*Resuscitation*), regeneration, and rebirth *(Wieder geburdt)*. [The Gospel of] John in the third chapter: "Unless someone is born anew, he cannot see the kingdom of God." '[66] Through the mystical identification of the believer with Christ in death and resurrection, the believer is born again.

Regenerated life thus depended on a prior death. Through processes such as putrefaction and fermentation, alchemy showed that the same held true for nature generally. While praising the art, pseudo-Weigel particularly emphasised the alchemy of rebirth, both spiritual and natural. In the shortened, printed version of *A Conversation on Death*, the Listener, representing lay Christianity, announces that he holds alchemy in high esteem, 'for it is a gift of the Most High and teaches the new birth (*newe Geburt*) so that one can see it with one's own eyes.'[67] Luther had said something similar in praise of alchemy, yet the contrast is illuminating: for the reformer, alchemy prefigured the physical resurrection of the dead at the Last Judgement.[68] With recourse to the Gospel of Matthew, 'palingenesis' (*Wiedergeburt*) could also refer to the restoration brought about at the Last Judgement, including the resurrection of the dead.⁶⁹ Luther thus assimilated alchemy to Christianity by embedding it into a providential and eschatological frame of reference. For pseudo-Weigel, however, alchemy became the model for spiritual rebirth and helped articulate Christian beliefs in alchemical terms.

This tendency is even more apparent in the manuscript version. The corresponding passage emphasises rebirth and describes alchemy as divine, conflating it with both the apocalyptic woman clad with the sun and the eternal virgin of wisdom. Pseudo-Weigel thus presented divine alchemy as the mother of born-again believers who subsequently dwelled with them, making them wise like King Solomon:

> But divine alchemy, which is a chaste and eternal virgin, I esteem highly, for she shall be my mother (Revelation 12). She is clad with the sun and steps on the moon, and on her head she carries a crown of twelve stars. To whomever she gives that same crown, he will be her son. She is a gift of the Most High; she is called Wisdom, for she has been with God from eternity; a virgin chaste and without blemish, she admits no bestial man with two horns, only the unicorn, the unsplit horn, the godly, who is born of God himself, by the Spirit of God. She teaches the new birth.⁷⁰

In this passage, pseudo-Weigel effectively used the term 'divine alchemy', centred on rebirth, to refer to what I call spiritual alchemy.

While the religious dimension dominates in *A Conversation on Death*, the text also contains some practical information for aspiring alchemists. There are several references to antimony and hints regarding the crucial role of this substance in transmutational alchemy. The fundamental importance attributed to antimony allows us to contextualise the pseudo-Weigel behind *A Conversation on Death* as one of the 'wretched antimonialists' denounced by Heinrich Khunrath.⁷¹ This school of transmutational alchemy found its most prominent representative in Basilius Valentinus, the fictitious Benedictine monk whose writings appeared from 1599.⁷² Yet prior to that, Khunrath specifically mentioned Alexander von Suchten—a former *protégé* of Copernicus—as a prime exponent.⁷³ Hence, it is no surprise that *A Conversation on Death* also contained a reference to Suchten's writings.

Alluding to the iconography of Christ as saviour of the world (*salvator mundi*), the Listener notes that since the world despised him, Christ 'also carries such a character ☿ in the left hand.'⁷⁴ Usually, the cross-bearing orb in Christ's hand is a symbol of his dominion and authority, yet here it is reinterpreted as antimony in an alchemical frame of reference. The disregard often accorded to this substance paralleled the rejection Christ experienced throughout his life on earth:

> He has created a thing which the magi paint in his left hand ☿ and not in his right hand. This is also disdainfully despised, no one knows it, only the wise; all people search only for gold and silver, leaving behind that through which they could attain gold and silver.[75]

In the jargon of Weigelians, or spiritualists more generally, true believers were sometimes called magi. The manuscript version emphasised the sinister associations of the left hand, highlighting the low esteem in which the world held what this symbol represented. Pseudo-Weigel thus presented antimony as the crucial substance that was 'above,' or better than, 'sun and moon,' gold and silver, yet 'mean and despised among all people.'[76] Suchten's antimonialist influence here caused a departure from *Azoth and Fire*, where antimony figured alongside lead as 'the core (*principal*) of alchemy' for transmuting other metals into gold and silver.[77]

Since antimony was often neglected by alchemists chasing after gold and silver, this reinforced the analogy between Jesus Christ and the philosophers' stone. Christ was 'the stone that the builders rejected,' and the notion that the philosophers' stone was hiding in plain sight was a common staple of alchemical literature.[78] The manuscript version of *A Conversation on Death* even quoted the *Practica* of the fifteenth-century German alchemist Bernardus Trevisanus to that effect: 'The whole world has it in front of its eyes and does not recognise it.'[79] Though the Preacher was dismissive and ill-informed regarding alchemy, he cannot but concede the force of the analogy between Christ and the transmuting agent: 'It is true, Christ is humble and mean for all people, and yet he is the saviour of the world; if such a thing ☿ should exist in nature, I had not heard of it before.'[80] Only by cultivating this awareness would potential adepts be able to recognise the value of such a despised substance. Fearing that the Listener was revealing too much, Death repeatedly tried to stop him: 'Beware that you do not reveal everything, lest people pursue this in heated desire! You have already done much in revealing the character.' Responding, the Listener emphasised that only those born again and 'taught by God . . . in Christ Jesus' would be able to make anything of his clues.[81] Since Jacob Boehme emphatically met both requirements, it may well be that he felt called to simultaneously expand on alchemy and spiritual rebirth, as adumbrated in *A Conversation on Death*. In Boehme's extensive discussion of alchemy in *Signatura rerum*, for instance, the symbol for antimony also figured prominently. As in the printed editions of *Concerning the Dialogue on Death* (where this appears to have happened unintentionally), Boehme too analysed that character in its constituent parts.[82] It is thus highly likely that the theosopher encountered *Concerning the Dialogue on Death* in one of the three editions printed between 1614 and 1618.

This chapter has sketched how spiritual rebirth gradually came into its own and found itself closely associated with alchemy in pseudepigraphic texts attributed to Valentin Weigel. Pseudo-Weigelian alchemy presented an embryonic stage of spiritual alchemy. For all the prominence accorded to him throughout this study, Boehme was not entirely innovative when writing about spiritual alchemy: he owed much to earlier writers such as Paracelsus, Schwenckfeld, and Weigel, as well as to inauthentic texts that circulated under their names. Yet due to his many later readers, the cobbler, trader, and heretic of Görlitz became a towering figure in intellectual history and did more than anyone else to propagate the spiritual alchemy of rebirth. Before we can turn to Boehme's writings to see what he made of this combination, we have to consider two early readers of pseudo-Weigelian alchemy as possible avenues by which it could have reached the theosopher.

2
A Nuremberg Chymist and a Torgau Astrologer Read Pseudo-Weigel

It is very likely that Boehme encountered aspects of pseudo-Weigelian alchemy in print, but that would only have been the proverbial tip of the iceberg. Excepting the shortened version of *A Dialogue on Death*, almost all pertinent passages remained unprinted during the theosopher's life. As *Azoth and Fire* circulated exclusively in manuscript throughout the entire seventeenth century, it quickly found readers such as the Nuremberg chymist Johann Siebmacher and Paul Nagel, the astrologer of Torgau. Existing scholarship on Boehme and alchemy frequently attaches great importance to Siebmacher's *Wasserstein der Weysen* (Water-Stone of the Wise), printed anonymously in 1619. After all, it is the only alchemical work to which the theosopher referred by its title. However, the assumption that the theosopher relied on the *Wasserstein* while composing the treatises of his late period hinges on a letter mistakenly dated 1622; actually, it dates to May 1624, a mere few months before Boehme's death, when all his major treatises had already been written.[1] Once this is taken into account, it becomes much more difficult to claim that the theosopher's work was shaped by the *Wasserstein*. Nonetheless, the *Wasserstein* still merits attention as a very early example of the reception of pseudo-Weigelian alchemy. It becomes recognisable as such once the question of its authorship is resolved and *Wasserstein* is read in conjunction with a related work, *Introductio hominis* (Introduction of Man), published in 1618. The second part of the chapter explores Nagel's reception of pseudo-Weigelian alchemy, documenting how a member of Boehme's network elaborated its ideas further in his own scribal publications.

Johann Siebmacher and His *Wasserstein*

Ever since the eighteenth century, the authorship of the *Wasserstein* has been shrouded in confusion. General agreement exists only regarding the author's surname: Siebmacher. His first name is given as Johann, Johann Ambrosius, Ambrosius, or even Wolfgang.[2] As a consequence, there has so far been no distinct authorial profile allowing for contextualisation of the *Wasserstein*. Although two scholars arrived at what I take to be the correct solution more than twenty years ago, earlier, mistaken identifications continue to be repeated in much more recent publications.[3] Based on a thorough survey of the evidence and various clues in scholarship, Johann Siebmacher emerges as the author of the *Wasserstein*. A contemporary, the well-connected Augsburg physician Carl Widemann, described him as a 'philosopher and chymist at Nuremberg,' not to be confused with his more famous namesake, the engraver-publisher of a heraldic work.[4]

Surprisingly, the most important clues regarding Siebmacher's authorship appear in a 1736 edition presenting the *Wasserstein* under a very different title as *Das Güldne Vließ* (The Golden Fleece).[5] Rather than deriving from the 1619 edition, this publication must have been based on independent manuscript transmission of Siebmacher's treatise. Despite appearing more than a century after the first edition and featuring modernised spelling, this alternative version of the *Wasserstein* ought to be taken very seriously. It contains numerous playful allusions to the author's identity throughout.[6] The first of these occurs already on the title page, where the author is described as 'an unnamed but well-known, etc. *I Say Nought*,' a play on the initials 'J. S. N.'[7] A poem titled 'Why I do not mention my name here' contains a highlighted anagram that can be reshuffled to render 'Johann Siebmacher of Nuremberg' (*Johannes Sibmacher von Nurnnberg*).[8] Since none of these riddles provide any reason to believe that the author was called Wolfgang or had the middle name Ambrosius, we can safely discard these alternatives.

Siebmacher deliberately used one of the more elaborate plays on his name to create the impression that a second person had been involved in the composition or compilation of his treatise: the pseudonym 'J. Bachsmeier von Regenbrun.'[9] 'J.' stands for Johann, 'Bachsmeier' is an anagram of Siebmacher, and 'Regenbrun' thinly disguises Nuremberg. Once resolved, this plays the important role of linking the *Wasserstein* to two other productions by Siebmacher, in which a very similar pseudonym appears that replaces the first-name initial 'J.' with 'Huldreich.' Translating to 'rich in mercy,' this is a semantic cognate of Johann derived from the Hebrew for 'God is merciful.'[10] The relevant works are *Introductio hominis*, published in 1618 as part of the *Philosophia mystica* (Mystical Philosophy), an important collection of writings attributed to Paracelsus and Weigel, and *Zwey schöne Büchlein* (Two

Beautiful Booklets), containing two Weigelian treatises edited by Siebmacher either in 1618 or 1621.[11] A lavish manuscript copy of the former text, under the ungrammatical title *Introduction hominis*, dates the composition of the treatise to 1607 and contains clues and riddles very similar to those encountered in *Das Güldne Vließ*, leaving few doubts about their shared author (Fig. 2.1).

In fact, careful reading of the *Introductio hominis* reveals that it was composed shortly after the work known as the *Wasserstein*. In the 'Appendix' signed with the Bachsmeier pseudonym, Siebmacher described how exactly the two treatises related to one another. Without acknowledging that he himself was the author, he showed several acquaintances a treatise he had written 'on the high secret of the philosophical stone,' that is, the *Wasserstein*.[12] Not satisfied by their incomprehension and greed for the *lapis philosophorum* but unwilling to reveal his authorship, he sought to elucidate some contentious points more clearly in his *Introductio hominis*. Siebmacher's wording indicates that the test audience was too caught up in the pursuit of gold to appreciate the mystical bent of his work. According to his description of these events, that treatise bore the following title: 'The Golden Fleece, or the highest, noblest and most artful jewel as well as most ancient and most hidden treasure of the wise.'[13] This was the very same title as that of the eighteenth-century *Wasserstein* edition, which thus presented the title Siebmacher originally chose for his work when he first composed it in 1607, immediately prior to the *Introductio hominis*.

Despite the sequence in which these two treatises were written, it makes sense to discuss the *Introductio hominis* first. Conceived as an addition and companion piece to the *Wasserstein*, this shorter treatise is more theological and has considerably less to say about alchemy. In a somewhat bewildering move, Siebmacher sought to defend his unconventional alchemy with recourse to heterodox theology. For him the two were intimately linked. This connection derived from the pseudo-Weigelian *Azoth and Fire*, and the Nuremberg chymist revealed his familiarity with this text in *Introductio hominis*. Significantly, the theological views he expressed in this treatise were also greatly indebted to Weigelian literature more generally, in which the emphasis on the 'Know thyself' imperative figured prominently. For instance, Siebmacher borrowed key ideas from the pseudepigraphic third part of *Gnothi seauton*, to which he must have had access prior to its print publication in 1618: it had been composed about thirty years earlier.[14] Beyond his

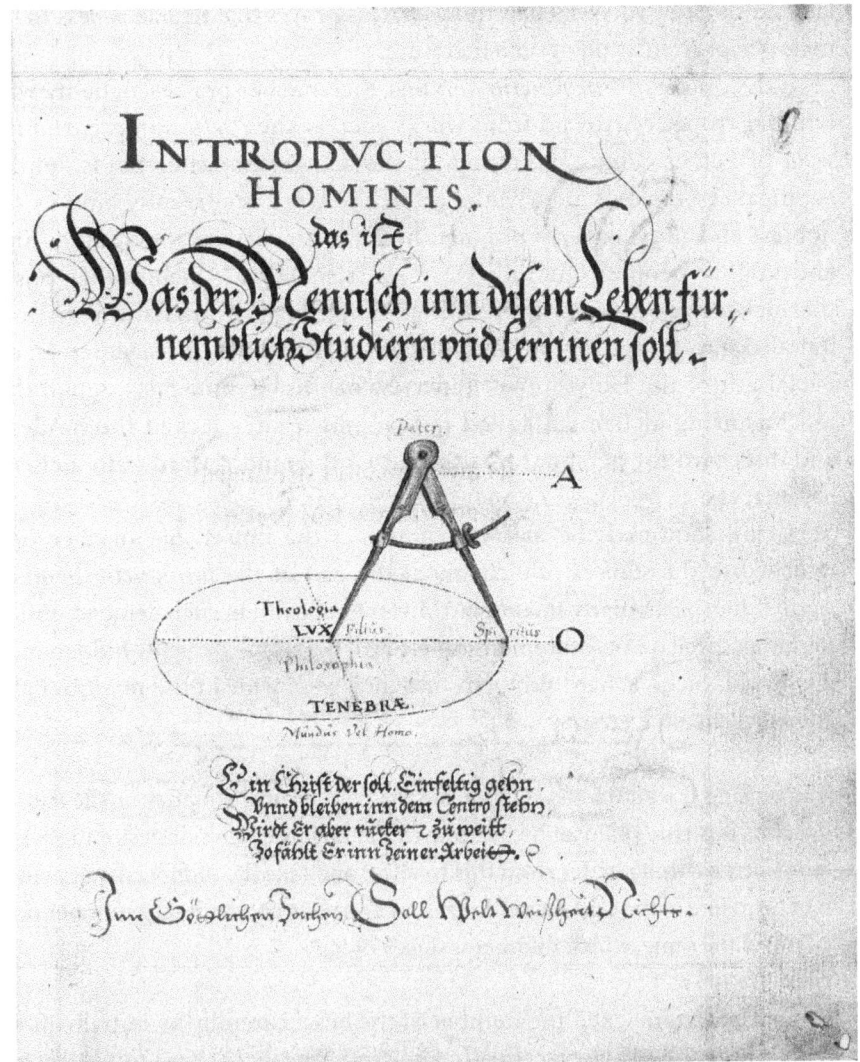

Fig. 2.1 Johann Siebmacher, *Introduction hominis* (1607). In this beautiful presentation copy, the line at the bottom hides Siebmacher's initials. This was lost on the printer of *Philosophia mystica*, who failed to highlight the larger letters J. S. N. The Hague, Koninklijke Bibliotheek—National Library of the Netherlands: PH404 M315 (Ritman Kerncollectie), title page. © KB Beeldstudio.

later edition of two Weigelian treatises, this proves that he had access to the manuscript circulation of such literature.

At the outset of *Introductio hominis*, Siebmacher praises alchemy with familiar tropes borrowed from works such as the *Pretiosa margarita novella* of Petrus Bonus.[15] Among all the arts, Siebmacher holds, 'philosophical *chymia* or, vulgarly, the art of the *lapis*' is currently among 'the noblest and most eagerly pursued by almost everyone,' including 'high and mighty people.' Quoting Hermes Trismegistus, Siebmacher posits that alchemy 'does not only provide complete insight into natural matters, but also into things divine, and it ought to and must be esteemed an especial gift of the Holy Spirit.'[16] In view of this, Siebmacher argued that most aspiring alchemists toiled in vain, since they lacked the modesty and disregard for personal wealth that God would reward with alchemical success.

Having showered the art with praise at the outset, Siebmacher only returned to the subject of alchemy at the end of the *Introductio hominis*. Addressing 'particularly those' who 'melancholically, in such deluded understanding, dwell on the aforementioned art of the stone so deeply hidden from this world,' Siebmacher told them that they were wide of the mark but also offered them advice:

> In closing, I want to clearly indicate the correct prime matter or the subject of this true philosophical stone to them (if they do not desire to seek or learn anything better from this treatise) and take the number-letters out of the name of the said matter known to everyone and name the number or sum of the same, which number is thus 999.[17]

Siebmacher approached the number of the beast carefully by initially introducing it as 999. However, treating this number 'according to philosophical custom,' it is at length 'opened and unlocked' and ultimately inverted to render 666, 'which is truly also the number of a man, of which mention is made in the Revelation of John, [chapter] 13.'[18]

Apart from linking it to the Antichrist, the relevant verse implied that this number contained great secrets. Since many early-modern alchemists suspected relevant mysteries in biblical texts, they would have expected to find important insights in Scripture. Siebmacher made this explicit and claimed that the number 666 contained the key to the philosophers' stone:

'Whoever learns to recognise the matter of the said art out of this, already certainly and truly has . . . the true beginning of the proper philosophical stone, for it (the said matter) is—and also will be for all eternity—the correct beginning and also the end, the *alpha* and the *omega* . . . of this whole art.'[19] As previously observed, Paul Lautensack's positive reinterpretation of the number of the beast was a striking idiosyncrasy that found inclusion in *Azoth and Fire*, where it was explicitly linked to alchemy. Consequently, if the *Wasserstein* only provided grounds for suspecting as much, the *Introductio hominis* leaves no doubt that Siebmacher must have known this pseudo-Weigelian text on alchemy. This familiarity also informed the Nuremberg chymist's earlier treatise.

Rebirth and the Alchemical Process of Christ's Passion

Siebmacher's *Wasserstein* restated the basic points of pseudo-Weigelian alchemy and expanded upon them while at the same time dampening its radicalism. As the idea that spiritual rebirth is a necessary precondition for alchemical success appears in both *Azoth and Fire* and *A Conversation on Death*, it is hardly surprising that the *Wasserstein* also contains similar statements. But rather than specifically discussing rebirth as a requirement for the successful completion of the philosophers' stone, Siebmacher held that one had to be born again in order to achieve an appropriate understanding of nature generally: 'If you want to understand [the quality and property of nature], you have to be like unto nature, that is, truly humble, patient, and constant, yes, God-fearing and harmless to your neighbour; in sum, be a born-again and new man.'[20] An unimpeded understanding of nature and, by implication only, success in laboratory alchemy therefore required the believer-practitioner to have been born again. In Siebmacher's take, the pseudo-Weigelian statements lost their narrow focus on transmutational alchemy.

When discussing laboratory alchemy, Siebmacher frequently employed phrases such as 'in the philosophical', 'terrestrial', or 'chymical work'.[21] These are to be expected in alchemical literature, yet he tellingly also used the analogous but considerably less common expression 'theological work' five times.[22] In so doing, he created correspondences between the alchemical work and what he described as the theological work. As his usage makes clear, his 'theological work' is tantamount to the spiritual alchemy of rebirth. One passage is particularly noteworthy for its clarity: 'Just like' the purification of gold through antimony while preparing the *lapis*, which, 'I say, happens and must happen in the chymical work, so it also has to be well-observed here in our theological work of the spiritual renewal and heavenly rebirth of man.'[23] In this way, Siebmacher instituted the analogy between alchemical transmutation and spiritual rebirth.

Yet, particularly when he first used it, the Nuremberg chymist employed the term 'theological work' to explicitly refer to the Incarnation of Christ as a historical event that also corresponded to the 'philosophical work.' Specifically, Siebmacher wrote that the *prima materia* required 'another metallic body' if it was to become 'a tincture to perfect the other base metals.' In the same way, 'in the theological work of the divine nature of God's Son,' Christ had to take on 'another likewise metallic and terrestrial body, that is, flesh and blood, humanity or human nature' in order to become an effective tincture of souls.[24] Just as the *rebis* (two-thing), or hermaphrodite, united sulphur and mercury, male and female in alchemy, Christ united the opposites of deity and humanity in himself through the Incarnation. In alchemical imagery, the formation of the hermaphrodite often precedes the destructive turmoil it has to suffer.[25] Siebmacher thus took for granted Christ's Incarnation and the redemption it brought about. But ultimately, he was more concerned with its internalisation as the birth of *Christus in nobis*, through which the believer was reborn. Through the phrase 'in the theological work,' Siebmacher established the three-way *lapis-Christus in nobis* analogy and summed up his spiritual alchemy.

Part of the significance of the *Wasserstein* lies in how it went beyond pseudo-Weigelian alchemy by extending the *lapis-Christus* analogy to apply to the entire biography of Christ. However, this extension could readily be found in earlier alchemical literature: what may well be the oldest extant German manuscript work on alchemy, known as *Liber Trinitatis*, posits extensive parallels between the alchemical work and the life of Christ.[26] The *Rosarium philosophorum* also portrays the philosophers' stone as the risen Christ.[27] Yet there is an important difference between these earlier contributions to alchemical literature and what we encounter from around 1600 onwards. In the early seventeenth century, there was a new insistence on the spiritual rebirth of the believer that cannot be expected in a late medieval work such as the *Liber Trinitatis*. This crucial element is needed to complete the three-way analogy between laboratory alchemy, the spiritual alchemy of rebirth, and the redemptive work accomplished through Christ's incarnation, death, and resurrection. This is one of the hallmarks of spiritual alchemy that also occurs in Siebmacher's *Wasserstein*.

The Nuremberg chymist also expanded more explicitly upon the analogy between Christ's Incarnation and the *opus magnum*. He held that alchemy mirrored the events described in the Gospels: 'The matter and preparation of [the terrestrial, philosophical stone of the wise], as stated, is a beautiful type and living imitation of the divine incarnation in Christ.'[28] Just as the substance of the work had to putrefy, Christ was 'placed in the furnace of tribulation and well-cooked therein' when, following his baptism, he spent forty days in the desert and was tempted by Satan.[29] Siebmacher also mentioned other events in Christ's life as described in the Gospels and related them to processes in the alchemical work. Christ's temptation and even more so his death on the cross were reflected in the black stage of death and decay (*nigredo*), both of which corresponded to the believer's ongoing process of rebirth.

Siebmacher compared the believer, who had to endure much in the hands of God, to alchemical substances manipulated by the adept: 'Like the compound in the terrestrial work, such a man will be placed in the furnace of tribulation by God and afflicted by all kinds of cross, suffering, and adversity, . . . until he is dead to the old Adam and the flesh.'[30] Apart from the blackness of *nigredo*, alchemists commonly also referred to other colour stages: the many-coloured *cauda pavonis* (peacock's tail), *albedo* (white), *citrinitas* (yellow), and *rubedo* (red).[31] Just as the various colours of the alchemical work were signs that the adept was on the right track, the manifold trials associated with them served to both identify and purify true believers.[32] Siebmacher described in colourful terms the manner in which the believer was boiled in God's furnace: in the 'digestion and cooking of the spiritual, dead body within man,' there would be 'manifold colours and signs (as can be seen in the terrestrial work).'[33] Siebmacher held that spiritual alchemy also involved a physical process, operating on an interior body with a subtle corporeality.

In describing the process of rebirth, Siebmacher attained greater specificity than pseudo-Weigelian alchemy. He declared that this rebirth was brought about through Christ, who related to humans as the philosophers' stone to the lesser metals:

> For if we, who are by nature impure, mortal, and imperfect, are to become pure, reborn, immortal, and perfect again, this must happen by no other means than only and uniquely through this one heavenly foundation and cornerstone, Christ Jesus.[34]

In contrast to alchemy but in keeping with salvation history, Siebmacher's wording suggested that the prelapsarian state of humankind was restored through rebirth: believers were made not perfect but 'perfect again,' restored to their prelapsarian state. This is a decisive aspect that will be encountered repeatedly throughout this book, particularly in Boehme.

Siebmacher further described this spiritual alchemy in technical language while alluding to mystical union as well. The augmentation and multiplication of the *lapis*, which served to enhance the potency of the philosophers' stone once it had been attained, corresponded to believers, who were 'like yet imperfect metals.' They were transmuted and became Christ-like themselves, 'purified and united with him, through his rosy-coloured and beatific tincture, and ... completed with a pure spiritual body.'[35] Christ propagated himself by transmuting sinners into little Christs. Siebmacher also made explicit that this process would undo the consequences of the Fall under which humanity laboured; only 'through a new [birth] and rebirth of the Holy Spirit' would believers be 'redeemed.' Literally rather than figuratively, Christ becomes one with born-again believers, 'just as the philosophical stone unites itself with the imperfect metals through its tincture and is made a perfect and indissoluble body with them.'[36] In this manner, Siebmacher transitioned from mystical identification with Christ to physical participation in his transmuted, spiritualised body.

Compared to pseudo-Weigel, Siebmacher adopted a less aggressive stance towards the doctrine of forensic justification: Christ's redemptive work is complete and believers 'are completely saved from all impurity,' yet they cannot enjoy the full benefits of 'his redeeming and wholly divine tincture' without also embracing God's 'holy word, which is pure and purified, like gold and silver tried seven times in the earthen crucible,' one's saving faith and love of one's neighbour.[37] The way Siebmacher construed rebirth was thus much more amenable to orthodox Lutheran theology, which viewed *regeneratio* as a natural consequence of the justification by faith that preceded it. Instead, pseudo-Weigel had posited rebirth as a stark alternative to the forensic imputation of righteousness, which would fail to save anyone. Even if Siebmacher agreed that the believer was saved on an imputative basis, he held that Christ could furthermore effect an alchemical projection. It was brought about by Christ's 'saving entrance,' that is, the mystical incarnation of Christ within the believer.[38] Once transmuted in this manner, the believer would experience salvation to a fuller extent than those who had merely been justified in a legal sense. This position, while integrating spiritualist notions, was much less radical than pseudo-Weigel's aggressive dismissal of forensic justification.

Although it was not as pronounced as in pseudo-Weigelian alchemy, the aspect of human agency also contrasted with the standard understanding of transmutational alchemy. Whereas the lesser metals were commonly portrayed as entirely passive and dependent on the application of the tincture, Siebmacher's spiritual alchemy implied that believers could become transmuting agents themselves. Initially, however, they simply needed to be transmuted, and Siebmacher drew on a familiar figure encountered in alchemical literature, that of the risen king.[39] Siebmacher's reference to the 'chymical king' alludes to an oft-depicted scene that particularly resembles the two last figures of the cycle preceding Bonus' *Margarita pretiosa novella* in its first edition.[40] Corresponding to the six lesser metals, the servants are shown as pleading with the resurrected king to receive the tincture. This chymical king corresponded to both Christ and the *lapis philosophorum*. Just like these, in a process compared to alchemical transmutation, the born-again Christian had to die and rise again, which was ritually symbolised through baptism 'by water and spirit.'[41] Yet, the initial transmutation would be followed by painful trials and tribulations, akin to those encountered in the preparation of the transmuting agent. Through *Christus in nobis*, the believer would then be able to tinge others in turn. Written in 1607, Siebmacher's *Wasserstein* is one of the earliest examples of the reception of pseudo-Weigelian alchemy. Even if the treatise did not influence Boehme as profoundly as previously believed, it shows how a chymist practically conversant with laboratory alchemy developed aspects of spiritual alchemy.

Paul Nagel on Divine Gold, *Azoth*, and Rebirth

Like Siebmacher, Paul Nagel was another early reader of pseudo-Weigelian alchemy. The astrologer and millenarian was keenly interested in alchemy, copied pseudo-Weigel's *Azoth and Fire*, and added comments that shed light on his interpretation of that cryptic treatise. Not only did the astrologer of

Torgau grapple with *Azoth and Fire* over the course of several years, he concurrently also became an important part of Boehme's intellectual networks. Nagel owed his introduction to his friend Balthasar Walther, the theosopher's widely travelled mentor, interlocutor, and student. Walther gave Nagel some of Boehme's writings in 1619. Nagel was absorbed in copying Boehme's *Aurora* as early as 1620; in fact, Leigh Penman has established that the Torgau astrologer was the first to see Boehme's words into print, in a 1620 publication by Nagel that included portions of the *Aurora*.[42] In 1621, about two years after its composition, Nagel copied Boehme's *Beschreibung der Drey Principien Göttliches Wesens* (Description of the Three Principles of Divine Being).[43] Eventually, Nagel also played a part in distributing the theosopher's writings. A letter Boehme composed on the Sunday after Easter 1623 mentioned Nagel affectionately: 'From Mr Nagel, MA, you will receive instruction where my works are known throughout Saxony; please greet him on my behalf.'[44]

While there is no conclusive evidence that Nagel himself had introduced Boehme to pseudo-Weigelian alchemy, I deem it highly likely that this happened directly or indirectly. At the very least, there can be no doubt that Nagel both appropriated and propagated pseudo-Weigelian alchemy in his network, which overlapped with Boehme's own to a very significant extent. Nagel's copy of *Azoth and Fire* shows that this work would have been available within Boehme's network by the second half of the 1610s. It was therefore potentially accessible to the theosopher of Görlitz himself. However, Nagel's engagement with pseudo-Weigelian alchemy did not exhaust itself in reproducing and annotating *Azoth and Fire*. In his scribal publications and correspondence, he repeatedly revisited key topics of pseudo-Weigelian alchemy. In *Aurum divinum 666. centenariorum* (Divine Gold of the 666 Hundredweights), Nagel meditated on the positively revalued number of the beast and described it as the divine gold of wisdom. *Leo rugiens*, a work Nagel composed two years later in 1620, contains a treatise titled 'Our *Azoth* Turned to Gold' (*Azoth nostrum solificatum*), which presents Nagel's spiritual alchemy at length. This material is complemented by his extant correspondence with the Leipzig physician Arnold Kerner.[45]

Nagel's *Aurum divinum* survives in Halle as a beautifully executed presentation copy. On 12 March 1618 he dedicated it to Duke August of Anhalt-Plötzkau, a Calvinist and eager supporter of the Rosicrucian cause. Nagel had first established contact with him years earlier in 1611.[46] In many ways, the manuscript is quite a typical example of the writings in which he advertised his millenarian views centred on the year 1624. The mathematician relied on numbers that occurred throughout Scripture and sought to explore their deeper significance. Even the number of years in the millennium was 'not a simple but a mystical number like the others.'[47] In *Aurum divinum*, Nagel was particularly concerned with the number 666, which appeared only twice in the Bible. According to the Old Testament, King Solomon annually received '666 talents of gold,' while in the New Testament 666 appeared as the apocalyptic number of the beast. The latter verse in Luther's Bible, which Nagel used, can be translated into English as follows: 'Here is wisdom. Whoever has understanding, let him consider the number of the beast, for it is a man's number, and his number is 666.'[48] In a way, Nagel's exegetical approach generalised this injunction to consider one specific numeral and applied it to all others that appeared in Scripture. Further examples he mentioned include the figures attached to other cases in which King Solomon obtained gold: 120 hundredweights from the Queen of Sheba and a shipment of 450 hundredweights from Ophir.[49] Ironically, it would seem that in the latter case Nagel did not have his numbers straight: the biblical figure is, in fact, 420.

Nonetheless, a lack of numerical accuracy did not get in the way of apocalyptic significance. Using the very same words as Luther's Bible, Nagel repeatedly insisted: 'Truly, here is wisdom. Whoever has understanding, let him consider the number of the [hundredweights of] gold.' Consequently, every numeral encountered in the Bible hid great wisdom, but only the one who first grasped the mystery of 666 would be able to unlock it. According to Nagel, who took his cue from a Lautensack-inspired pseudo-Weigel, this was a very special number indeed:

> It is a secret, mystical, divine, angelic, and prophetic number, with which the greatest secrets are sealed; therefore, whoever can properly consider and unlock it, to him the secrets will be open, and he will be counted among the prophets and have the spirit of prophecy; he knows what is past and what is yet to come.[50]

Through the association of 666 with gold based on Solomon's annual income, Nagel held that this numeral contained 'divine gold' (*aurum divinum*). Therefore, he viewed it as key to apocalyptic insights.

In a passage that closely resembles pseudo-Weigel's diatribe against worldly knowledge, Nagel chastised the learned for their disregard of this 'veritable number of marvels.'[51] In contrast, he praised 'one by the name of Valentin Weigel,' who had 'correctly understood the ground and the secret of this number, as can be seen from the book of his *Theologia*, but not everyone will be able to hear nor understand it; instead, many will be offended.'[52] Nagel was referring to the *Theologia Weigelii*, probably composed by Benedict Biedermann, Weigel's faithful deacon. The astrologer thus knew one of the sources for *Azoth and Fire*, which also relied on Lautensack's interpretation of 666 and emphasised John's Revelation as the most important book of the Bible.[53]

In order for their eyes to be opened, those who were learned according to the standards of the world had to endure the spiritual alchemy of rebirth. Only by undergoing that arduous process could the gold of wisdom be obtained: 'a spiritual dying and being buried, yes, an incineration and complete putrefaction is needed for this, namely, of the old Adam, so that the new one might live, who alone has the gold.'[54] According to Martin Ruland's *Lexicon alchemiae*, a famous dictionary of Paracelsian and alchemical terms, incineration was the technical term used for burning vegetable and animal substances to ashes, corresponding to the calcination of mineral substances.[55] Calcination was an ancient process to purify gold; incineration could be associated with palingenesis (literally, rebirth), which referred to the alchemical attempt to resurrect plants that had been burnt to ash.[56] After being likewise reduced to ash, the believer would rise with Christ and thus be born again. The use of alchemical language in this connection was no coincidence: writing to Kerner on 10 March 1622, Nagel quoted a phrase from Vergil's *Aeneid* popular among alchemists to refer to the death of the old Adam: 'This is the work, this is the labour.'[57] Dying to oneself and rising reborn in Christ was the true *opus* of spiritual alchemy.

Through this process, the believer obtained the 'divine gold,' which Nagel defined as 'the living, one and only, powerful, most dear, and holiest word of God within him'—*Christus in nobis*, to put it another way.[58] In his later work *Leo rugiens*, equally discussing 666, Nagel made this even more explicit and described it as the 'essential indwelling (*Wesentliche einwohnung*) of Christ.'[59] Another passage in the same treatise expanded upon rebirth: 'Furthermore, all of a reborn person's (*renati*) doing and living must also come out of God, . . . Christ must be born in every one, and nobody has any part in God . . . unless God the Lord through the Holy Ghost in Christ, his living word, has his throne and seat in him.'[60] Expanding *Christus in nobis* with the remaining persons of the Trinity, the Torgau astrologer must have had in mind pseudo-Weigel's *Azoth and Fire*. It expressly advanced the same idea, rendered in a particularly forceful manner in Nagel's own version.

The Supernatural *Azoth*

When Nagel wrote *Leo rugiens* in 1620, two years after *Aurum divinum*, he was probably also familiar with *A Conversation on Death*, the second text of pseudo-Weigelian alchemy that was by then readily available in print. Nagel could easily have obtained a copy of Weigel's *Dialogus de Christianismo*: Torgau was close to Leipzig, where important book fairs took place twice a year, as well as Halle and Magdeburg, where three editions of Weigel's work had been printed between 1614 and 1618. *Leo rugiens* is a rambling work filled with Nagel's usual numerological, astrological, and apocalyptic speculations. Its engagement with spiritual alchemy is largely concentrated in a passage titled 'Our *Azoth* Turned to Gold.' Near the outset, Nagel explained that the *azoth* of which he treated was 'twofold.' In the first instance, it was the *lapis philosophorum*, 'in which prime and ultimate matter are united, by which all metals can be transmuted into the purest and finest gold.' Yet in the second case, it was 'supernatural, heavenly, and divine; whoever has this one, he shall not lack the former one either.' Nagel referred to the first as 'their *azoth*,' that is, that of the alchemists, and to the second as 'our *azoth*.'[61]

Based on pseudo-Weigelian alchemy, we would expect this second kind of *azoth* to have something to do with rebirth. Indeed, Nagel had already given away as much before adding the distinction almost as an afterthought. Playing on the familiar expectations many associated with the philosophers' stone, Nagel claimed that 'our *azoth*' would deliver on these and even surpass them. It had the ability to turn sinful humans into 'children of God,' making 'them entirely spiritual.' Furthermore, it 'gives them clarified bodies like unto God's angels, able to survive in the heavenly essence (*Wesen*). In this our *azoth* lies hidden the treasure of reflorescence, regeneration, or rebirth (*thesaurus reflorescentiae, Regenerationis s[ive] renascentiae*), by which everything becomes green again, flourishes, and is rejuvenated or reborn.... Whoever attains this *azoth* has as much as Adam had in God's paradise prior to the Fall.'[62] According to Nagel's description, this *azoth* transmuted believers into deified creatures with angelic bodies fit for heaven, by the same token restoring them to the prelapsarian state.

Further comparing the two kinds of *azoth*, Nagel emphasises that the natural kind also has effects upon humans but that the supernatural one is far superior. Through the former, 'man is purified of all evil fruit and astral infections; he reaches the highest perfection of health and all of nature stands open before him.'[63] Quite apart from making one rich, the *lapis philosophorum* counteracts malign astrological influence, guarantees perfect health, and allows for a complete understanding of nature. The effects of the supernatural *azoth* are quite similar but operate at a deeper level:

> Through the other, heavenly, and eternal *azoth* and golden fleece, man is most highly purified of all his sins and misdeeds, attains the highest perfection and fulfilment, and man is thereby spiritualised, deified, or he becomes God's child, obtains a transfigured body, and becomes entirely spiritual, partakes of the eternal heavenly wisdom, sanctity, and justice as well as all heavenly goods, and also has eternal life through this. The tongues of men do not suffice to describe this surpassing, infinite, inexpressible treasure.[64]

If the natural *azoth* could cleanse human beings physically, undoing the effects of God's Curse upon creation imposed after Adam and Eve's transgression, the supernatural *azoth* could even undo the Fall, removing human sinfulness altogether.[65] Beyond enjoying perfect health in a mortal body, the physically transfigured and reborn believer could already participate in eternal life.

In a central passage redolent of pseudo-Weigelian alchemy, Nagel described the supernatural *azoth* not as a transmuting agent but as an instructive example. In effect, he recapitulated pseudo-Weigel's alchemical *imitatio Christi*:

> Our *azoth* teaches us . . . how one can attain this heavenly, surpassing, inexpressible treasure and how the new birth can be obtained; it must die and pass into incineration, if something new is to grow out of it: the grain, the seed must be thrown into the earth, putrefy, and decay, if it is to grow forth beautifully and gloriously. In sum, it has to become an *azoth*, that is, that God the Lord through Christ—the living word—in his Holy Ghost becomes all in all within us. Prime and ultimate matter have to come together and become one. The Lord must be *azoth*, that is, *alpha* and *omega*, beginning and end, the first and the last, God and man—that is, Christ: he must be revealed. Without and outside of him, man remains damned, and

imputative justice from the outside cannot save him. O ye humans, let us look for this surpassing treasure, our *azoth*, in which our blessed state consists, and it is the great mystery: Christ within us.⁶⁶

Through the mystical identification of Christ and the believer in death and resurrection, *Christus in nobis* became all in all within the born-again person. Christ within was the transmuting agent of Nagel's spiritual alchemy.

Nagel likened various stages of this process to alchemical activities throughout 'Our *Azoth* Turned to Gold.' He also did so in his correspondence, in which spiritual alchemy surfaced as well. In a 1620 letter to Kerner, the millenarian mentioned 'the angelic stone which rejuvenates through the new birth.' He further alluded to the spagyric art of separating the pure from the impure in connection with the spiritual alchemy of rebirth.⁶⁷ In a later letter, Nagel indicated to his correspondent that 'for my part, I still daily have to beg for the divine gold.'⁶⁸ This emphasised that constancy was a basic requisite in its pursuit. The *spagyria* Nagel described involved certain practices that would help believers attain union with Christ, comparable to the paths of mysticism.

In the first instance, the flame needed to be fed continually: Nagel construed 'our stone or *azoth* as a fire, first, ignited within us by the Holy Ghost; second, prepared by fire, consisting in fire and being fire. . . our *azoth* is nothing other than a fire of God's beloved children, naturally and supernaturally.'⁶⁹ This fire, which could be understood as the love of God, formed the basis for the work of spiritual alchemy. Its heat effected sublimation:

> So that the true union of the heavenly, the spiritual, and the corporeal mercury can take place and an *azoth* be formed out of it, the sublimation of the wise is required: that is, continual prayers, poured out incessantly in spirit and in truth. Thus the *azoth* develops, that is, CHRIST, who is the firstborn according to the *alpha;* he also becomes human in us according to the *omega*—hence AZOTH. Enough for the wise (*Sapienti satis*).⁷⁰

Through the practice of continual prayer, believers sublimated themselves, gradually giving birth to Christ within. If this sounded comparatively easy, other processes dissuaded many from pursuing spiritual alchemy: 'For faith is not everyone's work; if anyone wants to attain it, he has to enter into calcination, reverberation, putrefaction, and digestion—wholly becoming nought—by the annihilation, abnegation, renunciation, immolation, and mortification of oneself.' In this manner, Nagel established analogies between various alchemical techniques and mystical practices intended to subdue one's selfish will and to bring one to a state of 'serene equanimity' (*gelassene Gelassenheit*), as Nagel put it, using a key term of German mysticism and quoting Biedermann's *Theologia Weigelii*.[71]

With recourse to laboratory alchemy, Nagel further explained the significance of *azoth*. For him the core meaning of the term consisted in uniting two things, the first and the last, and one source for this assertion was once again the *Theologia Weigelii*. The *lapis philosophorum*, uniting prime and ultimate matter, met this requirement. But the term could also be applied to God himself:

> For it is at once certain and true: the one who let the Old Testament write about himself and himself confirmed in Revelation that he is the first and the last, beginning and end, *alpha* and *omega* among the Greeks. Among the Hebrews, he is also *aleph* and *tav*. And among the Romans and Germans A and Z—the first and the last.[72]

Nagel claimed that the term was formed based on God's very own statement, 'according to these four main languages': the first letters corresponding to A, 'together and taken as one; the other three letters form a syllable, *zoth*, and the whole word reads *Azoth*, that is, beginning and end' (*principium et finis*).[73] Christ not only united the opposites of deity and humanity; he also embodied the union of beginning and end, prelapsarian perfection and its ultimate restoration through rebirth. Christ could therefore aptly be described as the supernatural *azoth*.

Nagel did not stop there and tied this term and its meaning back to alchemical imagery, in which snakes figured prominently and concealed great mysteries. The first example he mentioned was the *ouroboros*, usually considered a symbol of eternity: 'The alchemists (*Philosophi*) have described their natural *azoth* with many marvels, speeches, or also figures and images, as when they posited a snake, with its tail in the mouth, consuming and devouring itself.' Even 'the two snakes on Mercury's staff,' the *caduceus*, and the two kinds of snakes with which Moses and the Pharaoh's magicians competed against one another ultimately drove at the union of opposites:

> Two snakes must become one. Behold, a splendid snake lies hidden within us, which is poison and death unto us, yes, it gives birth to damnation. But when this our snake is devoured and swallowed up by the heavenly and

Moses' snake, so that they become one and the heavenly alone exists, our *azoth* is at hand: in this God is beginning and end, prime and ultimate matter, God and man alone and at once. Thus Christ is revealed.[74]

Laboratory and spiritual alchemy mirrored one another: the alchemists' 'two snakes are a double mercury, a physical and a spiritual one, a poisonous mercury or snake, and a regulus or lion.'[75] This lion would vanquish and devour the snake, aiding the completion of the great work of alchemy.

As Nagel's chief obsession was the Book of Revelation, he was quick to identify this alchemical lion with Christ as the Lion of Judah.[76] Through his millenarian astrology and alchemy, Nagel had calculated that Christ's rule was only a few years away, scheduled to start in 1624 or 1625. The latter date corresponded to the numerical value of *azoth*, though Nagel had to resort to the trick of positing a dotted *tav*, which doubled it from 400 to 800. He concluded his lengthy chapter 'Our *Azoth* Turned to Gold' by exhorting readers to repent and persistently anticipate the roars of the Lion of Judah, who would vanquish the poisonous snakes within them and turn them into 'exceedingly strong lions.'[77] The Book of Revelation portrayed persisting and overcoming as crucial for believers. Those who overcame and emerged victoriously were to receive 'a white stone,' an object obviously amenable to alchemical interpretations.[78] In contrast to Nagel, who focused on the final book of the Bible, Boehme was less given to millenarian and apocalyptic speculation. Instead of Revelation, he emphasised Genesis and recognised that same snake in the *proto-evangelium*, the very first promise of the saviour who would remedy the Fall and Curse that Adam and Eve had brought on themselves and all of creation.[79] In so doing, Boehme firmly embedded the spiritual alchemy of rebirth into the whole arc of salvation history.

3
Jacob Boehme's Spiritual Alchemy of Rebirth

On the face of it, Jacob Boehme was an unlikely candidate to become the prolific author of speculative and devotional treatises. He was born to an affluent peasant family in Alt-Seidenberg during the year 1575. During his childhood, he evidently learned to read and write, but his schooling appears to have been limited to German.[1] From very early on, or so his biographer Abraham von Franckenberg claimed, Boehme had several visionary experiences, leading up to the most defining ones during his adult life in 1600 and 1610. The latter finally prompted him, a master craftsman and trader by that time, to take up the pen and write down the revelations he had received. In the first half of 1612, he produced a fair copy of his famous earliest work, the *Morgen Röte im auffgang* (Morning's Red Glow in the East), better known as *Aurora*, a work he never completed.[2] At this stage, the theosopher neither espoused a doctrine of rebirth that went beyond Luther's Bible translation, nor was he greatly familiar with alchemy. In fact, he emphatically distanced himself from being mistaken for an alchemist. He did, however, lay claims to alchemical knowledge based on his theosophical insights.

After briefly delineating the place of alchemy in *Aurora*, this chapter focuses on the spiritual alchemy of rebirth Boehme developed in works composed from 1619 to 1622. After 1612, he gradually became more familiar with alchemy, and his encounter with pseudo-Weigelian alchemy would have taken place soon after the beginning of his later writing period. In his mature works, he developed an increasingly distinctive understanding of rebirth, firmly embedded into salvation history and described in overtly alchemical language. He completed the fullest presentations of his spiritual alchemy of rebirth in the first half of the year 1622. Concluded in February, his famous *Signatura rerum* (The Signatures of Things) contained an extensive passage based on the three-way *lapis-Christus in nobis* analogy. Boehme described the central event of salvation history—Christ's Incarnation—as an alchemical process, corresponding both to the philosophical work of the laboratory and to the spiritual rebirth of the believer. Around the same time, Boehme engaged with another religious dissenter, Esaias Stiefel, who competed for disciples with him. In his *Apologia, Betreffend Die Vollkommenheit des Menschen* (Apology Concerning Human Perfection), the second treatise he addressed to Stiefel, the theosopher of Görlitz outlined the spiritual alchemy of rebirth and its intricate connections to salvation history from the very beginning until the end of time, from creation and the Fall to the Last Judgement.

Alchemy in Boehme's *Aurora*

Boehme's *Aurora* articulated a general stance regarding alchemy from which he did not depart even in his later writings. The most pertinent passage is found in chapter 22, in a section titled 'Concerning the metals in the earth.'[3] Here Boehme described the purification of gold in seven stages. Due to the great significance of the number seven, alchemists often structured their accounts of the *opus* in this manner.[4] While this already shows a measure of familiarity with alchemy (or metallurgy, at least), Boehme's term 'Salitter' can be situated more precisely. This idiosyncrasy, which occurs many times throughout *Aurora*, was Boehme's rendering of *sal niter*, which increasingly played a key role in alchemical theories around 1600. One of Paul Nagel's correspondents, the Polish alchemist Michael Sendivogius, contributed to this development through his *Novum lumen chymicum* (New Chymical Light) of 1604. Yet Boehme's appropriation had greater affinity to a work by the French Paracelsian Joseph du Chesne, also known as Quercetanus.[5] Already at the outset of his career as a writer, Boehme was at least vaguely familiar with transmutational alchemy and current trends in its literature.

Nevertheless, at the end of this *Aurora* passage, Boehme emphatically distanced himself from being mistaken for an alchemical practitioner: '*You should not take me for an alchemist.*' Professing ignorance and inexperience regarding laboratory alchemy, he indicated that he might still provide pointers for success in its great work. He argued that he could derive relevant insights based on his privileged access to the divine realm through Christ who lived in him. In addition, he claimed that he could offer astrological pointers for choosing the most appropriate time of day for certain operations.[6] He approached his subject—the mineral or metallic realm of nature—on the basis of analogy and correspondence with the divine world.

The metals, particularly gold and silver, were 'loved by human beings above all else in this world' as reflections, albeit dark ones, of the ongoing heavenly birth at its height: it was a distinctive element of Boehme's theosophy that he viewed the godhead not as static but dynamic.[7] He did not claim to have practised alchemy in the laboratory; rather, he asserted that he knew about the art based on his theosophical insights.

However, the theosopher did not yet make any connection between alchemy and rebirth in *Aurora*. In fact, at this stage he did not attach much importance to rebirth and used the term mostly in ways derived from Luther's translation of the Bible. In keeping with Paul's Epistle to Titus, rebirth appears in *Aurora* as the traditional synonym for baptism.[8] More frequently, in keeping with Christ's words in the Gospel of Matthew, rebirth in the *Aurora* refers to the restoration of creation and the resurrection of the dead at the Last Judgement.[9] It was precisely in this sense that Luther himself had viewed alchemy as confirming Christian revelation. 'Rebirth' thus referred to cosmic renewal, and the term also applied to restoration in the ongoing process of divine becoming, which involved God's seven source spirits. Derived from the Book of Revelation, they functioned as analogues of the seven planets and metals.[10] Only with the benefit of hindsight can we perceive the subtle germs of Boehme's later individualised and interiorised understanding of spiritual rebirth.[11]

The theosopher's life and works came to be indelibly marked by the controversy that erupted surrounding his first work. Independent confirmation remains elusive, but Boehme later claimed that a nobleman obtained a manuscript version, copied it, and disseminated it against the author's will. The person in question was probably Carl Ender von Sercha, Boehme's neighbour in Görlitz. The theosopher had had other plans: 'For I intended to keep it to myself, yet it was taken away without my consent and published' (*publiciret*).[12] The exact word Boehme used could also be translated differently: his manuscript was 'publicised' in the sense that it was copied and disseminated, and this in turn constitutes a case of involuntary, unauthorised scribal publication—perhaps one of the most famous in early-modern history.[13] Despite his protestations of innocence, Boehme was in trouble: in July 1613, Gregor Richter, the chief pastor of Görlitz and Boehme's nemesis for many years to come, denounced him from the pulpit. Boehme was briefly imprisoned, sternly admonished never to write again, and released only after his manuscript had been confiscated. Condemned to silence, he did not write any treatises for several years and meanwhile believed his *Aurora* lost: 'I also did not see that same first book anymore, I supposed that it was dead and gone, until copies were sent to me by learned people.'[14] Later on, Boehme reminisced that the whole affair had only served to make his work better known in the area and beyond.[15]

As a corollary, the notoriety Boehme and his *Aurora* gained allowed him access to increasingly larger networks, formed by Paracelsians, Schwenckfeldians, and Weigelians—religious dissenters and alchemists of various persuasions. Fascinated by the insights of the humble cobbler, many early readers across the region and its social classes began to send letters to Boehme.[16] His correspondence intensified accordingly, and so did the extent to which he was able to engage with the ideas and books circulating in his networks.[17] Perhaps for this reason, he evaluated his later writings very differently from his early ones: whereas to this day his fame chiefly rests upon *Aurora*, Boehme himself held a distinctly higher opinion of his mature works, 'which are much brighter, clearer, and more deeply grounded.'[18] These featured many learned terms he had picked up in the course of his reading, correspondence, and conversation, and those words took on new and at times surprising meanings as he integrated them into his works.

The Fall, Rebirth, and the Philosophers' Stone as the Holy Element and Christ's Body

Throughout the theosopher's mature works that reflect increased exposure to heterodox and alchemical literature, he engaged more deeply with both alchemy and rebirth. In the process, spiritual alchemy ceased to be merely a playful allegory and took on an independent reality within his theosophical understanding of the world. In so many words, Boehme even told his reader to take him literally when he spoke of the 'Process of Christ' and transmutation: 'we do not want to write anything parabolically but clear as day.'[19] In fact, spiritual alchemy even became dominant, more real than laboratory alchemy, which was but a physical shadow of the divine alchemy of becoming and the spiritual alchemy of rebirth:

> As the eternal birth [of the deity] is within itself, thus also is the process in the restoration after the Fall and thus also is the process of the wise with their philosophers' stone: there is not a dot of difference between them, for

everything originated in the eternal birth, and everything must have its restoration in the same manner.[20]

The model of divine becoming also explains why Boehme held that alchemists hoping for success in the laboratory needed to be reborn: they needed to live through the spiritual alchemy of rebirth to become proficient in its reflection, the alchemy of the laboratory.

The theosopher first penned a comprehensive account of rebirth in chapter 22 of *Description of the Three Principles of Divine Being*, his second major work completed in 1619. The views Boehme expressed here owed a lot to Valentin Weigel and Paracelsus.[21] Yet Boehme also added his own emphases, particularly in how firmly he embedded rebirth into the entire arc of salvation history. At the same time, he integrated rebirth into his theosophical cosmology: after all, he was both a profoundly speculative thinker and a writer of popular devotional literature, two aspects much too often considered in isolation.[22] Rebirth, particularly, provides a bridge between the speculative and the devotional Boehme, as it situates the individual's journey to salvation in the dynamic and layered cosmology of theosophy.

According to Boehme, the world consists of three principles, two of which are eternal: the first, the principle of fire and wrath; the second, the principle of light and love.[23] These eternal principles are opposites existing apart from one another, yet they mingle and struggle for dominance in the third, the temporal principle of the visible world. In its primordial state, the physical world was suffused with divine presence, and the second principle of light and love dominated. Similarly, Adam was originally created as God's image and likeness, with his will and imagination set on God and the second principle. Neither male nor female, Adam was originally intended to procreate asexually in this primordial state of perfection.

Yet soon the Fall changed this, taking place in two stages, as summarised in chapter 17 of the *Description of the Three Principles*.[24] First, Adam longed for a companion after the manner of beasts and fell asleep. Previously, he had had no need for sleep, but now it reflected his weakening and prefigured death.[25] As Adam slept for the first time, he was divided up into male and female, which Boehme, in his late *Mysterium magnum* (The Great Mystery), memorably described as his 'shattering' (*Zerbrechung*): God's mirror was broken.[26] The second stage of the Fall took place when the serpent seduced Eve to eat from the forbidden tree. Even as sexual beings, Adam and Eve had still retained some of their former glory, but they lost it as they ate of the forbidden fruit, found on the only tree consisting of the temporal, impure four elements, within a paradisiacal world.[27] By partaking of the terrestrial fruit, Adam and Eve unwittingly turned the subtle matter of their bodies into the gross matter of the four elements. They lost 'the body of the pure element,' which was eternal.[28] For Boehme, the Fall was not so much divine punishment for transgressing a commandment but rather a natural consequence of cosmological givens.

Rebirth literally undid the Fall on an individual basis: by being born again, believers could regain the subtle body Adam and Eve had lost. It consisted of the pure or holy element, which Boehme described as follows: 'It is the heavenly bodiliness, which is not only merely a spirit, in which the clear godhead dwells; it is not the pure godhead but born out of the essences of the holy Father.' The eternal Word was the divine *logos*, incarnate in Jesus Christ. Boehme sought to carefully articulate the status of the pure element in his emanative cosmogony: it was more than a spirit in which God could dwell but less than God. The theosopher also endeavoured to describe the pure element from another angle: 'If the Father always speaks the eternal Word, the Holy Spirit emanates from the speaking, and that which has been spoken is Holy Wisdom, and it is a virgin, and the pure element . . . is her body.' The pure element is thus the body of Sophia, the divine virgin of wisdom; conversely, she is 'the spirit of the pure element.'[29]

Boehme expanded on biblical and traditional personifications of Wisdom and described Sophia in a perplexing variety of ways.[30] She was 'God's companion' (*gespielin*) as well as 'God's likeness' and 'image' (like the prelapsarian human), but 'eternal, uncreated, and unborn'; she was the 'mirror of God' in which he 'saw all things from eternity.'[31] Yet Sophia was also closely associated with Christ: in a variation on traditional nuptial mysticism, she took on the role of Christ and became 'a bride to our soul,' female to male believers, male to female ones: like prelapsarian Adam and resurrected Christ, Sophia was androgynous.[32] Elsewhere, Boehme wrote that 'the beautiful and noble Sophia will be given to your soul as spouse,' and she 'now stands before your soul's door and calls out to you imploringly with her voice and knocks,' which alluded to a passage regarding Christ in Revelation.[33] Boehme then returned to Sophia as the heavenly bodiliness and identified her as 'Christ's body': 'Christ feeds the soul with the essence of Sophia, that is, with his body and blood.'³⁴ This statement firmly tied the heavenly bodiliness to the Eucharist.

In another context, Boehme summarised this series of identifications in so many words: the 'pure element' is 'the essence of heavenly bodiliness. The same essence or bodiliness... is Christ's heavenly flesh and blood.'³⁵ Without acknowledging it, the theosopher was much indebted to the Silesian reformer Caspar Schwenckfeld in this regard. As a spiritualist theologian, Schwenckfeld viewed rebirth as a continual partaking of the body and blood of Christ and thus construed it in terms of the Eucharist.³⁶ Schwenckfeld still had many followers among the local nobility, and some of them became Boehme's patrons and protectors.³⁷ Yet Boehme particularly emphasised that born-again believers regained the body, made of the holy element, that they had lost in the Fall: 'So, my dear soul, when you are born again in Christ, you put on the body of Christ out of the holy element, and the same [body of Christ] gives your new body food and drink.' Indeed, 'the holy element is Christ's heavenly body,' and Christ's disciples ate of it at the Last Supper in the very same way as the born-again faithful would many centuries later.³⁸ Here Boehme alluded to Luther's doctrine of the ubiquity of Christ's body, a position the theosopher defended at various points throughout his writings.³⁹ Through spiritual rebirth, believers literally and physically partook of the holy, pure element that was Christ's body and themselves received a new body consisting of the same subtle matter.

In many ways, the holy element resembled cosmological and alchemical conceptions of the quintessence, the fifth kind of matter that was radically different from the four elements of which the terrestrial world consisted. Indeed, Boehme viewed them as parallel, though with the important distinction that the holy element belonged to the second principle rather than the third: the 'pure element' is 'the movement of the inner spiritual world, and during the creation of the world it emanated (*Aus geflossen*) into being (*Wesen*), and it is comprehended in the quintessence' (*5ten Essentz*).⁴⁰ Yet, as so often with Boehme, these distinctions are so subtle that they sometimes give way to indistinction, if not identity. It is tempting to think that they were intended to ensure plausible deniability when the theosopher ventured into theologically dangerous territory. A similar shift towards the identity of two things elsewhere described as distinct also takes place in our case: the pure element *is* the quintessence. Through rebirth the believer was to return to that inner spiritual world and inherit the 'kingdom of God' by allowing the quintessence to dominate his four-elementary body: 'For whatever desires to inherit the inner spiritual world must be born out of the same.' Paraphrasing Paul's First Epistle to the Corinthians, Boehme emphatically noted that 'the terrestrial flesh out of the four elements cannot inherit God's realm... But the fifth essence, as the element out of which the four are born (that is, paradise), it must rule over the four elements in the same way as the light holds darkness within itself, as if devoured.'[41] The regenerate believer is born of the quintessence, which is the inner spiritual world and the body of Christ at once.

Particularly in *On the Threefold Life of Man*, Boehme went one step further and quite explicitly identified the holy element as the philosophers' stone. As I have shown, the holy element was also the body of Christ, and giving birth to *Christus in nobis* amounted to attaining the *lapis*. In a way, Boehme thus took very literally what had been a common religious metaphor in alchemical literature: now Christ was no longer analogous to the *lapis philosophorum*; he really *was* the 'noble and highly worthy cornerstone of the wise.'[42] Alchemists looked for this subtle, pure matter in vain until they participated in Christ's body through rebirth. If only Adam 'had remained in the will of God' instead of falling from grace, 'the noble stone *lapis philosophorum* would have been as easy to find for him as a stone for a wall.'[43] Through rebirth, the negative consequences of the Fall could be undone and the philosophers' stone attained:

> Whoever places his will out of himself into Christ ... he will be born again in Christ; his soul regains the eternal flesh in which God became man, an impalpable flesh of the eternal being. The old Adamic flesh of death does not become heavenly flesh: no, it belongs in the earth, unto death. Instead, the eternal flesh is hidden in the old, terrestrial man, and it shines in the old Adam like fire in a piece of iron or gold in a stone. This is the noble, precious stone *lapis philosophorum*, whom the magi find, which tinges nature and births a new son in the old: whoever finds it esteems it more highly than this world.[44]

To Boehme, the philosophers' stone *was* the ubiquitous body of Christ that believers put on as they were tinged towards the new birth. For him all of this was not to be understood in a purely religious or metaphorical way, disconnected from bodily realities. It was something that happened literally and physically.

The Incarnation of Christ as an Alchemical Process

The prominence many scholars attach to Boehme's dynamic, constantly shifting, and ongoing theogony obscures the fact that his view of salvation history is thoroughly traditional. Even as he criticised the institutional church for teaching a merely historical, literal faith, he took for granted the Incarnation of Christ as a historical event that made all the difference: only *after* God had truly become human could humans *truly* become god. To Boehme, the Incarnation was of profound mystical significance precisely because it had taken place in history, thus providing the precondition for the restoration of all that had been lost in the Fall. In *Von der Menschwerdung Jesu Christi* (On the Incarnation of Jesus Christ), composed in 1620, Boehme introduced the Incarnation as defying reason; it could only be grasped based on divine revelation. At the same time, it had a very clear purpose: 'It was all about the salvation of fallen man, that He [God] would bring him back into Paradise.'[45] As the second Adam, Christ had to undo the Fall caused by the first. Christ was only able to do so by fully becoming human, that is, by acquiring not only a human body but also a human soul from his mother, Mary: 'Christ received a soul out of Mary's essence, but without male seed.'[46] God thus became something he had not been before—human.

Only by fully becoming human was Christ able to undo the Fall and conquer its consequences. Boehme fully endorsed orthodox (Western) Christology as codified in the Athanasian Creed, composed in Latin during the fifth or sixth century and re-asserted in the Lutheran Formula of Concord.[47] The position outlined in this creed represents the straight and narrow path between two kinds of Christological heresies, which deny Christ's humanity or his divinity, respectively. Indeed, Boehme defended this delicate balance against other religious dissenters who strayed from it.[48] The theosopher particularly insisted on Christ having become fully human because 'Christ was the first from the dead,' preceding all believers who could subsequently participate in him, become born again, and be raised to life.[49] Conversely, if Christ had not become fully human, this participation would not be possible. Hence, Christ's death would have been in vain: 'If Christ is not in our flesh, he will not raise us up: what use are his wounds to me if they are in foreign flesh?'[50] Boehme's understanding of the Incarnation as a historical event with real, physical consequences led him to emphasise the mystical identification with Christ through rebirth. This placed him at odds with the forensic understanding of justification.

Explicitly mentioning the *lapis philosophorum*, Boehme alluded to the *proto-evangelium*, which promised that the woman's seed—interpreted as Christ, born of the Virgin Mary—would vanquish the devilish serpent. He construed the Incarnation as an alchemical process through which Christ became the true philosophers' stone, able to transmute human beings. Crucially, this understanding implied that Christ could not truly cause spiritual rebirth until he had wholly completed his life on earth. The Incarnation had to happen within the temporal, terrestrial world: 'Now in this lies the philosophers' stone, how the woman's seed tramples the head of the serpent; this happens in spirit and in being, temporally and eternally.'[51] Through Christ's victory over sin and death, he became the philosophers' stone; once it had been fixed within time during the Incarnation, it became available for eternity in the second principle of light as the ubiquitous body and blood of Christ. This was what made rebirth possible as the mystical incarnation of Christ within the believer, which entailed physical participation in the saviour's bodiliness.

Even as Boehme took the historical Incarnation for granted, this other kind of incarnation was of much greater concern to him.[52] The believer had to mystically enter into the incarnation herself, giving birth to Christ within. Boehme thus saw *Christus in nobis* as the only path to salvation, and he began a third of his extant letters with a phrase that summed this up succinctly: 'Our salvation in the life of Jesus Christ within us!'[53] Discussing Solomon, Boehme explicitly clarified that *Christus in nobis* was the philosophers' stone:

> Behold Solomon in his great, marvellous wisdom, who knew the properties of all creatures as well as herbs, which he had not learned at an academy; only through the noble stone, which he had in his heart, he recognised it.... This stone is Christ, the living Son of God; this is borne out in all who seek and find him.[54]

In an important way, then, the three-way *lapis-Christus in nobis* analogy became a three-way identity, in which the mystical incarnation of Christ in the believer *was* the philosophers' stone. This deceptively simple transition led to spiritual alchemy in its purest form.

Like the alchemical king, mentioned by Johann Siebmacher and illustrated in the first edition of Bonus' *Pretiosa margarita novella*, or the philosophers' stone, portrayed as the risen Christ in the widely disseminated *Rosarium philosophorum*, Christ had to undergo many trials and even death in order to acquire the power to tinge fallen humans.[55] Boehme described this process in great detail in *Signatura rerum*. According to him, any aspiring adept would therefore do well to study the Incarnation of Christ:

> Thus it behoves the wise one, who intends to seek, to contemplate the entire process of Christ's humanity, from its beginning in the body of his mother Mary, until his resurrection and Ascension; in this way, he will find Pentecost with the free spirit, whereby he may tinge, cure, and heal whatever is broken. We say this founded upon truth, as we have sublimely recognised.[56]

Through extended passages of *Signatura rerum*, Boehme repeated his variations on a single formula: 'Thus it also takes place in the philosophical work.'[57] This phrase served to both establish and assert the analogy of the great redemptive work of Christ's life and the noble alchemical work within the furnace. The theosopher encouraged 'the laboratory worker who is an earnest seeker' to contemplate his writings, 'so he will find the noble stone of the wise.'[58]

The Incarnation of Christ was central in this regard, and Boehme established many analogies between the 'process of Christ' and the 'philosophical work' throughout *Signatura rerum*.[59] Most of these parallels are difficult to translate into traditional schemes of transmutational alchemy, since Boehme extrapolated from the Gospels to the philosophical *opus*, rather than the other way around, as Siebmacher had done in the *Wasserstein*. Just as John had baptised Christ in the river Jordan, 'the artist' had to 'baptise the mercury... with the philosophical baptism.' Then, to make sure that this mercury had successfully been baptised, it had to be tried and tested for forty days, corresponding to Christ's temptation in the desert. If the mercury 'withstands throughout the temptation, the angels will appear to it after forty days,' which also means that 'the artist is able to do his work.' Yet if the angels fail to appear, 'he had better leave it be and deem himself yet unworthy of it.'[60] Laboratory alchemists also looked out for certain phenomena to confirm that they were on the right track; the *stella antimonii*, or star-shaped regulus of antimony, was a particularly impressive example that Lawrence M. Principe reproduced in recent years.[61]

Compared to the later events of Christ's life, however, the appearance of angels was but a preparatory phenomenon. Christ's death on the cross heralded the beginning of *nigredo*, the black stage of the work associated with decay and putrefaction: 'From this comes the great darkness in the philosophical work so that the matter becomes as black as a raven, ... as can also be seen in Christ, that the sun lost its splendour and a great darkness fell, against the ordinary course of nature.'[62] When Christ rose again after forty hours, this corresponded to both spiritual and laboratory alchemy as well, 'as this happens in the philosophical work, in which a new life rises up from death, just as God in Christ wakes us up within him, if we die to egoity and wholly enter into him.'[63] The philosophers' stone was formed but the work not yet completed.

If we were to put Boehme's alchemy of the Incarnation in more traditional alchemical terms, the resurrection of Christ would amount to the first *coagulatio* or *fixatio* of the tincture.[64] Yet to truly become the philosophers' stone, the potency of the tincture had to be increased repeatedly through *multiplicatio*, so that it would actually generate an increasing amount of gold. Boehme used this technical term of alchemy but did not exactly construe it in this specific sense.[65] Only afterwards would the alchemist enact *proiectio*, that is, apply the philosophers' stone to the baser substances that were to be transmuted. According to Boehme, Christ's process culminated in Pentecost. As the final stage of the redemptive process, the divine philosophers' stone was projected onto the disciples, who immediately became transmuting agents themselves:

> Until Pentecost he [Christ] goes around in a heavenly shape, sometimes also in his own, ... and then the Holy Spirit comes and goes out in his power out of the whole body consisting of body and soul. Then he tinges the dead and broken, as can be seen on the day of Pentecost, when Saint Peter with his heavenly mercury tinged 3000 souls at once and released them from death.[66]

By the time we get to the last sentence, it is no longer clear whether 'he' refers to Christ or the Holy Spirit or whether they are conveniently conflated. More importantly, Peter acted as a spiritual alchemist, whereas previously that role had implicitly been reserved for God and Christ. In this specific instance, the act of tingeing coincided with baptism: Boehme was, after all, paraphrasing the Acts of the Apostles, which states that 'those who received' Peter's sermon 'were baptised, and there were added that day about three thousand souls' to the community of believers. The passage thus carries an intertextual hint of baptism, previously synonymous with rebirth, even as Boehme and his contemporaries turned the latter into something distinct with recourse to alchemy. The theosopher's spiritual alchemy construed humans as base metals and the matter of the alchemical work that would become the transmuting agent, yet it also allowed for born-again believers to become spiritual adepts transmuting other, as yet unredeemed humans.

Playing on the double use of the philosophers' stone as a transmuting agent and medical cure for all ailments, Boehme continued: 'Dear seekers, in this lies the little pearl; if you had the universal, you would also be able to tinge like Saint Peter.'[67] By that term Boehme meant a general medicine applicable to sick humans and lesser metals, but he also used the word to refer to that cure's effect:

> The learned ... ought to study the entire process of how God restored the universal within man; this is entirely clear and revealed in the person of Christ, from his entry into humanity, until his Ascension and the sending of the Holy Spirit. This eternal process he ought to pursue, so he may find the universal, if he has been born again from God.[68]

Soon afterwards, Boehme provided a helpful gloss: in working his first miracle at the wedding of Cana, Christ advanced 'the process of the universal, towards the restoration of all that which Adam had lost.'[69] On the scale of the individual human, that medicine would therefore be the restoration of the prelapsarian state: in this sense, for Boehme the universal *was* spiritual rebirth. After attaining the medicine of *Christus in nobis* as the *lapis philosophorum*, the believer would be a spiritual adept with the ability to heal the sick and, perhaps more importantly, to tinge others who had not yet been reborn.

Esaias Stiefel's Challenge and the Fall as Reverse Transmutation

Around the same time that Boehme composed *Signatura rerum*, Esaias Stiefel criticised the theosopher's alchemical understanding of rebirth as inappropriate. Hailing from Langensalza in Thuringia, Stiefel was considerably more radical than the cobbler of Görlitz.[70] Initially, there had been a sense of potential alignment between them, since they both appealed to a very similar audience. Probably inspired by the hope of joining forces and relying on

Balthasar Walther as an intermediary, Stiefel's disciples in Erfurt submitted one of his treatises to Boehme, requesting his assessment. Honoured by such a request, the Teutonic philosopher showed himself charitably disposed towards Stiefel and acknowledged him to be 'pious, born-again, and holy in Christ through his new birth in the new man.'[71] Nevertheless, Boehme noted that he and Stiefel had markedly different conceptions of spiritual rebirth. He finished his *Bedencken über Esaiä Stiefels, von Langensaltza, Büchlein* (Assessment of the Booklet of Esaias Stiefel of Langensalza) on 8 April 1621.

Unfortunately, the relationship quickly soured and turned into vicious rivalry. Writing early in 1622, Stiefel responded to Boehme in his *Tractätlein von zweyen Sprüchen* (Treatise on Two Proverbs). He aggressively denigrated Boehme's concept of rebirth while placing him in dubious company:

> Not tinged according to the kabbalistic, Paracelsian, Rosicrucian Brethren manner and transmuted from the being of unbelief (*unglaubenß wehsen*) into the believing one; but according to the testimony of Scripture, a new birth, not out of the old, sinful being, but in the centre and the inward heart, in the love of the divine voice: a new beginning, a new heart, a new flesh and blood, new believing person in body and soul; a faith (*glaube*) not born out of unbelief (*unglauben*) but out of God.[72]

Since he could not harness an array of learned terms as impressive as Boehme's, Stiefel specifically reserved contempt for his adversary's alchemical language.[73] And with this attack on the theosopher's spiritual alchemy of rebirth, the antinomian of Langensalza inspired the most lucid treatment of spiritual alchemy that Boehme would ever pen.

Using the form of a point-by-point refutation that included the text of Stiefel's work, Boehme completed his *Tröstliche Erclärung Uber etliche . . . spruche der H. Göttlichen Schrifft* (Consolatory Explanation of Several . . . Verses of the Holy Divine Scriptures) on 6 April 1622. As was quite common in polemical writings, Boehme only acknowledged his opponent's identity in a pun on his name, the German word for 'boot': according to Boehme, Stiefel 'has to put on other boots (*stieffeln*) if he intends to ride across death and hell with Christ's spirit.'[74] According to Stiefel, the true, reborn believer was literally an entirely new creature in both body and flesh, having traded his or her human essence for Christ's. It was thus 'impossible that someone born again could sin,' and even their children will not be tainted by original sin but 'will be conceived entirely holily, without guilt,' as

Boehme paraphrased Stiefel's doctrine prior to dismissing it.[75] Stiefel's notion of *Christificatio* entailed that born-again believers literally became Christs, unable to sin. It was therefore no coincidence that Stiefel often signed his letter as 'Esaias Christ.'[76] Whether or not Stiefel was very familiar with alchemy, this doctrine made the transmutation of metals seem like a very inappropriate analogy for rebirth as *Christificatio*.

For his part, Boehme insisted that born-again believers were human and divine at once, just like Christ, with whom they mystically identified. For the theosopher as well as for Nagel, the proper understanding of transmutation entailed the unification of opposites, specifically of deity and humanity. With regard to substances or principles, alchemical literature often described the union of opposites as its goal, and Nagel in particular had construed spiritual alchemy as joining God and human together. Boehme very much thought along the same lines. For him the process of the new birth would only be complete at the final resurrection of the dead. In the meantime, the spiritual body of the new birth was merely internal, still covered by the outward, mortal body. Stiefel and his followers rejected this decisive distinction and denied the continued existence of the body of sin, skipping forward to the ultimate state and arriving at antinomian conclusions by the same token.[77] In claiming that they already were perfect, entirely new beings unaffected by sin, Stiefel skipped over important steps in a divinely ordained process of purification and transmutation, for which the life, death, and resurrection of Christ provided the blueprint.[78] Stiefel cancelled out the human element; consequently, his understanding of rebirth was far more radical: true believers were turned into Christ entirely and stripped of their former humanity completely. For Stiefel, the sinner came to be replaced by Christ in body and soul through rebirth.

According to Boehme, however, Christ did not turn us into a wholly new being with entirely different matter and form. As Christ had truly taken on a human soul so 'that Christ's soul is our brother,' Boehme insisted that 'no other soul is born in any man, but a new body is. The soul is only renewed through the pure godhead.'[79] In other words, 'Christ's body is our body in the new man.'[80] He deemed Stiefel's denial of the processes of spiritual alchemy all but incoherent:

> But what kind of fancies this author has when he refuses to concede the divine tincturation (*Göttliche Tingirung*) and transmutation through the new birth, despising and dismissing the same, cannot be sufficiently fathomed,

as in this manner he even claims blind and nonsensical (*ungereimtt*) things.[81]

Stiefel held that the incarnated Christ was fundamentally unlike other human beings. Boehme argued that Stiefel's heretical Christology and his antinomian doctrine of *Christificatio* contradicted basic tenets of the faith and undermined crucial events throughout salvation history, particularly the Incarnation. For Boehme, Christ's redeeming process was effective precisely because he had taken on human flesh and conquered death through resurrection. If his nature had been different, 'it would directly contradict the doctrine of the resurrection of the dead,' Boehme claimed in his *Apology Concerning Human Perfection*.

The theosopher further emphasised the transformation of a being existing continuously. He used the language of alchemy to make this point:

> I do not have to speak of another human being, of another creature, but of a transmutation; the rough stone into gold, the unholy into holiness. Now if this is to take place, the true alchemist (*Künstler*) has to enter me, that is, the Holy Spirit with the divine tincture, which is Christ's blood, by which he shattered the vanity of our humanity and guided our true life out through death. I have to be tinged, otherwise I cannot be transmuted. If Christ does not tinge me with his blood, my holy paradise life will remain faded in death; but if he tinges me, the Holy Spirit will move within me, who can transmute me into Christ's flesh and blood, according to the inner paradise man.[82]

Boehme argued that rebirth meant being tinged but that the actual transmutation would only take place later. In his terms, the tingeing of the soul—effected by Christ and wrought out by the Holy Spirit—was the precondition for the ultimate transmutation of the mortal body that was to occur only on the Last Day.

In keeping with the early-modern understanding of spirit as a very subtle matter, the spiritual rebirth and physical resurrection of the believer were closely connected in Boehme's spiritual alchemy. Reminiscent of the Pauline discussion of the resurrection body, the tincture planted the seed for the new, subtly material or rather spiritual body that was to flower only at the Last Day.[83] This corresponded to the manner in which Boehme described the effect of rebirth in *On the Threefold Life of Man*: 'This new body, which contains the reborn soul, is stuck in the old, corrupted flesh; it is impalpable and immortal. But the old Adam, conceived by the spirit of this world, must decay in the earth: he goes back to his mother, who will have to show and present him on the Last Day.'[84] Boehme playfully described Mother Earth's releasing of the risen dead as another new birth. For him, being spiritually born again was not a merely spiritual process: the reborn soul was tied to a new body that provided the basis for physical resurrection. Consequently, the tincture had different effects on the new birth and on the old body: 'My own essence of the inner man is tinged and transmuted in this temporality, and my outward, mortal man is tinged with Christ's death to die.' In contrast to this spiritual body, 'the outward man's mystery, that is, the quintessence (*fünffte essentz*) . . . will be tinged at the final deliverance and resurrection of the dead, which transmutation will take place on the Last Day.'[85] Whereas many alchemists prided themselves on the instant results their tinctures could furnish, Boehme's spiritual alchemy assumed a maximally delayed transmutation: it would only take place at the very end of time.

Equally with recourse to alchemical terminology, Boehme further explained this delay in *Signatura rerum*. To be fit for transmutation, the body had to die just like Christ's: 'But during this time, although the spirit is transmuted in divine power and baptised with the virginal baptism, putting on the image of Christ within, . . . the Adam of the same is not able to do so until he also enters into the transmutation of Christ, which happens in dying.'[86] Corresponding to the time during which Christ died and entered 'into putrefaction, . . . that is, in the tomb,' until his resurrection, the stage of putrefaction immediately preceded transmutation in the process of man's rebirth and resurrection:[87]

> Meanwhile, we poor children of Eve are not entirely transmuted instantly, according to the outer man, but we also have to enter death and putrefaction, so that the fierceness in the flesh would putrefy and the spirit rest in Christ's death, until the general resurrection and transmutation of the outward man, by which the earth of man is transmuted into heaven (*in Himmel*).[88]

In other words, humans had to be changed both inwardly and outwardly. Through rebirth, the inward human could be transmuted through mystical identification with Christ in death and resurrection, by which the soul was renewed (not replaced) and a new, inward, spiritual body received. In contrast, the outward human, the gross, carnal body, could only be affected through its actual physical death. Only with one's last breath did one physically relive Christ's death. And in death, the outward, physical body was forced to release the inward, spiritual body of the new birth.

In this regard, Boehme's spiritual alchemy of rebirth and resurrection corresponds to Christ's process but departs from traditional alchemy. Not only was the effect upon the body significantly delayed, Boehme also undermined the distinction between the transmuting agent and its subject: both the philosophers' stone (Christ) and the metals (fallen humans) had to undergo an arduous process. In transmutational alchemy, however, only the stone was held to go through this ordeal: once it had acquired the power of the tincture, that power was simply applied to other metallic substances in a process known as projection, upon which transmutation followed immediately. The most likely explanation for this departure from alchemical precedent is theological. Like Luther and a number of religious dissenters, Boehme endorsed the doctrine of soul sleep, albeit in a mild form.[89] In a valuable summary of Luther's views on soul sleep, historian Robin B. Barnes notes that the temporal lapse disappears from the perspective of eternity: 'From the point of view of the soul itself and of God, ... the final resurrection of the whole man, and the Last Judgment itself, follow instantaneously upon death.' Indeed, for Luther the Christian believer already 'lived outside of time through grace' but also still 'within time as a creature,' a dual existence that would conclude on the Last Day, 'the end of time in a fully literal sense.'[90] This description equally applies to Boehme's views: for all his arcane language and its potentially heterodox implications, he saw himself as a pious Lutheran and defended doctrines of his confession against religious dissenters such as Stiefel.

By April 1622, Boehme had come to think of rebirth in terms of spiritual alchemy to such an extent that even his understanding of the Fall had become alchemical. If rebirth amounted to transmutation and reversed the Fall, Boehme conversely came to view the Fall and its consequences for the human body as a transmutation in the wrong direction. Adam and Eve had originally had bodies like gold, yet they were corrupted and turned into lead.[91] Boehme began by describing an alchemical thought experiment:

> This is not to be understood in any other way than when I consider lead which had previously been gold and had then, through mercury (*Marcurium*), been turned into lead, in which the poisonous mercury

would be revealed, which had previously stood in great beauty and perfection in the gold. And there would still be the potential for gold within the lead, but it would not be revealed in the mercury. The mercury would not be able to turn itself into gold, unless the artist broke down the lead entirely and turned it into the first matter, from which it was created. Like this, the same matter could become beautiful gold again, as it had been originally.[92]

Boehme described a kind of transmutation not in the least desirable for any alchemist.[93] Yet he quickly proceeded to point out that the adept would be able to reverse it again by reducing lead to its prime matter. This was the undifferentiated metallic substance that could readily be transmuted.

The theosopher then explained that this reverse transmutation was analogous to the Fall. In *Signatura rerum*, Boehme described 'the paradise man' as 'bright, like a transparent glass ... in which the divine sun shines through and through, just like gold is pure through and through, without blemish.'[94] If the primordial, prelapsarian body could be compared to gold, the fallen human body was like lead:

> Similarly, spoken in a parable, the beautiful, golden body of Adam and Eve in divine power and being was turned into obscure, dark lead: the golden mercury woke up in the vanity of poison, thus the gold faded in disgust like the holy body. Then it became entirely terrestrial and had to return to earth. Yet the voice of God, which called them again, was conjoined with the prophecy of the snake-crusher in the womb of Venus.[95]

In a related passage in *Signatura rerum*, Boehme also alluded to the *protoevangelium* to express that *Christus in nobis* had to crush the poisonous mercury in order to effect the transmutation of rebirth.[96] Just like Nagel, who held that the lion of Judah needed to crush the serpent in each and every believer, Boehme also stressed this aspect but portrayed it in considerably more alchemical terms—and with emphatic reference to the saviour promised in Genesis.

Returning to the *Apology Concerning Human Perfection*, there is more to be said about the passage just quoted. Since the golden mercury became poisoned due to the transgression of Adam and Eve, their bodies deteriorated accordingly. The spark of the original golden or prelapsarian state still remained in the human body, though it was obscured in the resulting mixture of gold and lead. 'But (when the desire of the soul went out of it),' as Boehme went on to explain, it was

> faded in itself, so gold and lead were mixed in this marriage within the lead. Yet the gold was not revealed until God's mercury revealed itself in the word of the prophecy, in the lead, that is, in the flesh, so the lead was turned back into gold in Christ's humanity, and the process was conducted in the same manner as the transmutation of metals, which are turned into gold, takes place, as it is written very extensively and comprehensively in our book on the signature [*Signatura rerum*].[97]

As their desire turned outward, Adam and Eve's inward purity suffered contamination: the subtle, spiritual body became gross and carnal; gold turned to lead. This degradation could not be reversed until the divine mercury—Christ, God's Word, message and messenger at once—became incarnate in the lead of human flesh.

That was, of course, the very subject Boehme had expounded more fully in *Signatura rerum*, the more substantial treatise he had completed just two months earlier. Through the process of Christ's life, culminating in the Passion, an alchemical transmutation was enacted that provided the basis for the restoration of humanity's prelapsarian state. As the second Adam, Christ reversed the effects of the Fall, uniting deity and humanity, which the first Adam had sundered: 'Since we know that our life, which we are now leading, must go through a transmutation, if it wants to be called God's child; it has to put God on again, of whom it has stripped itself through Adam.'[98] According to Boehme, spiritual rebirth reversed the effects of the Fall: it reversed the reverse transmutation, as it were. Although this process would only be completed on the Last Day, it was held to begin here and now, during the believer's life on earth.

While it is a challenge to grasp Boehme's shifting theosophy, he did tend towards identifying the body of Christ with the holy element of Paradise and the second principle of love and light, as well as with the quintessence. All of these—Christ's body, holy element, and quintessence—Boehme designated *lapis philosophorum*. For the theosopher, the spiritual body of the new birth *was* Christ *and* the philosophers' stone at once—not figuratively and by way of analogy but literally and in reality. Going far beyond pseudo-Weigelian alchemy in its ambitious scope, Boehme's spiritual alchemy was intricately connected not only to the daily experience of the believer, but also to salvation history from the first week of creation to the resurrection of the dead at the Last Judgement. The Incarnation of Christ played a central role in this drama, and Boehme described Christ's entire life as an alchemical process that allowed the Messiah to truly become the tincture of souls in a very real, even physical sense. Only at Pentecost was that process truly completed: as the Holy Spirit entered the disciples, they themselves became spiritual alchemists able to work miracles and transmute the souls of unbelievers by virtue of *Christus in nobis*, the true philosophers' stone. The remainder of this book is devoted to how Boehme's readers—from Abraham von Franckenberg to Mary Anne Atwood two centuries later—rediscovered, adapted, and transmitted spiritual alchemy.

4
Abraham von Franckenberg and the Ancient Wisdom of Rebirth

One of Boehme's acquaintances and earliest readers was the Silesian nobleman Abraham von Franckenberg. Scholars have alternatively cast him as a mystical poet, Boehme imitator, Rosicrucian, or Christian kabbalist.[1] To the literary scholar, his chief claim to fame lies in his connections to various more famous poets, such as Georg Philipp Harsdörffer, Daniel Czepko, and Johann Scheffler, who is better known as Angelus Silesius.[2] To the historian of the book, the rarity of most of his works remains an enduring challenge.[3] Franckenberg reached his widest audience through his biography of Boehme, which painted a memorable, hagiographic picture of the theosopher's life.[4] Traditionally, he was included among Boehme's correspondents, yet Joachim Telle has thoroughly called into doubt the identification of Franckenberg as the addressee of Boehme's epistle dated 20 February 1623.[5] Franckenberg did, however, meet Boehme in person repeatedly in 1623 and 1624, the final years of the theosopher's life.

By 1625, as documented in his *Conclusiones de fundamento sapientiae* (Conclusions on the Foundation of Wisdom), the Silesian nobleman had studied no fewer than eight works by the theosopher, most of them in the intimate medium of manuscript. In 1627, he wrote his first extended epistolary treatise for the benefit of his Görlitz-based friend Ehrenfried Hegenicht: *Theophrastia Valentiniana*, ostensibly a discussion of the second-century gnostic Valentinus and his teachings.[6] This early work contains the most comprehensive treatment of Franckenberg's spiritual alchemy of rebirth. Although Franckenberg's later works do not dwell on spiritual alchemy, they continue to rely on it. This is especially true of what is arguably his most famous work, *Raphael* (The Healing Angel), composed in 1638 but not published until 1676.[7] In other writings, Franckenberg for the most part only alluded to his spiritual alchemy through isolated terms and references: after its early expression, it provided a significant but mostly implicit backdrop, appearing only in sublimated form, that is, as subtle references transparent only to those deeply familiar with his spiritual alchemy. In Franckenberg's hands, spiritual alchemy became inextricably tied to the wisdom of the ancients. By recasting spiritual alchemy in terms of *prisca sapientia*, ancient gnosticism, and kabbalah, Franckenberg considerably heightened its appeal among the learned of the early-modern age, sharing it with his correspondents as well as disciples in this new guise. In the broader story of spiritual alchemy, Franckenberg thus brought about an important shift.

Awakening

For much of what can be said about Franckenberg's early years, we are forced to rely on his own testimony. Two events are of paramount importance: the young Silesian nobleman's religious awakening and his encounter with Jacob Boehme. In 1617, having returned to Silesia from his academic tour, which had brought him as far as Strasbourg and Basel, Franckenberg found himself struggling with a crisis of faith. The deep doctrinal divisions among the rival confessions of Christianity troubled him.[8] While other Lutherans were celebrating the centennial of the Reformation, he despaired and 'fell into great disconsolation of the heart, could also hardly eat or sleep.' Soothed by his reading of the *Theologia Germanica* (German Theology) and other mystical and spiritualist texts, this crisis finally ended when he experienced a vision and was 'drawn into a calm sabbath' that ended his inner turmoil.[9]

Many years later, in 1649, Franckenberg described this as his illumination and tearfully related its details to Georg Lorenz Seidenbecher, his disciple. The vision, as Franckenberg related it, combined biblical imagery and kabbalistic speculation, emphasised love but also expressed longing for complete knowledge 'embroidered with gold,' such as the life to come would bestow upon the faithful.[10] The passage oscillates between an ecstatic vision of life in heaven on the one hand and bookishness on the other. In the same way, Franckenberg's illumination prompted him to become an avid consumer of the heterodox literature published from 1617 onwards. He documented his reading in his *Conclusiones*, composed in 1625 but not published until 1646: inspired by the genre of the academic disputation, he formulated twenty-five theses and supported them with references to the devotional literature he had perused. The *Conclusiones* thus contained Franckenberg's formative reading list, and he revisited these same works for the remainder of his life.

Thanks to this Silesian mystic's foible for bibliographical detail, the majority of the titles quoted can be identified with precision. Authors such as Valentin Weigel, Johann Arndt, and Johann Tauler were represented with more than three titles each. Albeit anonymously, Johann Siebmacher's *Introductio hominis* also appeared in Franckenberg's *Conclusiones*. It must have been a memorable reading experience: the Silesian nobleman still alluded to the alchemical, pseudo-Weigelian, and Lautensackian 999/666 passage as late as 1638.[11] However, it was Boehme, whom Franckenberg personally met in 1623, whose works were most frequently cited in the *Conclusiones*—no fewer than ten times. In addition to the three treatises of Boehme's *Weg zu Christo*, printed in 1624, these included references to manuscript versions of the theosopher's *Aurora*, *Signatura rerum*, and *Mysterium magnum*, among others. Franckenberg's reading and his close acquaintance with Boehme as documented here set the stage for the development of his own spiritual alchemy.

Though poorly supported by external evidence, it is well known that Boehme and Franckenberg met repeatedly in the last two years and even the last few weeks of the theosopher's life. In the 1630s, Franckenberg would refer to the 'illuminated Jacob Boehme of Alt-Seidenburg, our dear friend and brother in the Lord.'[12] Most of what we know about the relationship between the theosopher of Görlitz and the young Silesian nobleman can be gleaned from successive revisions of Franckenberg's biography of Boehme. In the final redaction, concluded on 13/23 September 1651, Franckenberg began by noting that he had recorded 'as much as my memory has retained until now from the personal conversations with the blessed late [Boehme] during 1623 and 1624.'[13] Sprinkling his biography with intimate anecdotes, Franckenberg described Boehme's ability to pick up foreign loanwords from his interlocutors and provided a personal example: the theosopher 'particularly delighted in the short Greek word *IDEA* [used] by myself.' Also in Franckenberg's presence, Boehme expressed regret at never having learned Latin, 'as I heard him say frequently.'[14] According to a much earlier, shorter version, Franckenberg related Boehme's visionary experience of 1600 'as I had heard [it] from his very own mouth.'[15] While scholars have often criticised Franckenberg for presenting the theosopher in the hagiographic manner he adopted, it is conceivable that this harked back to Boehme's conversational self-fashioning or, at the very least, his effect on an impressionable acolyte.

Even if we can no longer count Franckenberg among the recipients of Boehme's extant letters, he did belong to a group of admiring acquaintances and first readers. The theosopher even composed additional writings for the benefit of this inner circle. In the final version of the biography, Franckenberg's memory merged two separate visits Boehme made to Schweinhaus, the residential castle of the Schweinichen family. The first of these took place in the winter, the second in the autumn of 1624. During the first visit in February, Franckenberg and his friend Johann Siegmund von Schweinichen the younger successfully requested aids for understanding Boehme's writings. In response, the theosopher wrote a *Clavis* (Key) to his earlier treatises, as well as the *Tabula principiorum* (Table of the Principles), for their benefit.[16] Franckenberg noted that Boehme had personally 'commanded him to keep [the *Tabula*] secret.'[17] On this occasion, Franckenberg may actually have witnessed Boehme's writing process, which he later described as one of divine dictation: 'when writing he hardly changed or crossed out a word; instead, as the Spirit of God gave it into his mind, so he wrote it out cleanly and without copying.'[18] With the notable exception of a polemical treatise against the Görlitz minister Georg Richter, featuring copious corrections, Boehme's extant manuscripts largely succeed in not undermining this portrayal. If we take seriously Günther Bonheim's recent argument that there were two successive drafts of *Aurora*, perhaps the theosopher carefully sought to correspond to expectations surrounding divinely inspired writing.[19]

Boehme died on Sunday, 7/17 November, shortly after his second sojourn in Silesia that same year. Franckenberg's account emphasised how soon after their final encounter the theosopher succumbed to dropsy.[20] If we take into consideration another account, written on 21 November (New Style), shortly after Boehme's burial, it would seem that there was some intervening time: according to Tobias Kober, the Paracelsian physician who attended Boehme during his last illness, the theosopher had returned to Görlitz 'from Schweinhaus fourteen days ago, on Thursday, 7 November, very sick and weak, greatly swollen and exhausted.'[21] Allowing for a couple of days to travel from Schweinhaus to Görlitz and taking into account Franckenberg's even earlier departure, their last farewell would have taken place about three weeks earlier, towards the end of October or at the very beginning of November.

Subsequently, Franckenberg became more than Boehme's biographer. His exceptional knowledge of the theosopher's manuscript works allowed him to play a crucial role in promoting their wider dissemination and eventual publication: Franckenberg found himself at the centre of a circle of friends, mostly based in Silesia and Saxony, who treasured and copied Boehme's works in manuscript and then gradually passed them on to Abraham Willemsz van Beyerland.²² This Amsterdam merchant published a great portion of Boehme's works in German or in Dutch translation. With the generous assistance of Franckenberg and others, such as the Görlitz alchemist Johann Rothe and the Boehmiana collector Heinrich Prunius, Beyerland amassed the largest and most important library of Boehme manuscripts. In contrast to the Dutchman's tireless efforts as editor and translator, Franckenberg himself only saw a minute fraction of Boehme's oeuvre through to print: several chapters of the *Mysterium magnum* as *Josephus redivivus*, published in 1631, and a Latin translation of *Ein gründlicher Bericht* (A Fundamental Report), completed on 1 March 1639 and eventually included as part of *Trias mystica* (Mystical Triad) in 1651.²³

However, unlike Franckenberg, Beyerland lacked familiarity with Boehme's autographs and other copies. As a consequence, Beyerland repeatedly had to realise that he had based his editions on questionable manuscripts. The most egregious instances concerned Boehme's key works *Aurora* in 1634 and *Mysterium magnum* in 1640.²⁴ Franckenberg was particularly shocked by Beyerland's botched edition of the latter work. Franckenberg had access to several reliable witnesses and had already listed the *Mysterium magnum* as 'Commentary on Genesis' in his *Conclusiones*.²⁵ In an early version of his biography that emphasised the high opinion Boehme himself had of this late work, Franckenberg used the same formulation: it 'is a commentary on Genesis, which [Boehme] always held to be his final confession, and regarding the *Aurora*, it appeared to him that he had written the same only at first sight and thus imperfectly.'²⁶ Though this aspect is often eclipsed by his reputation as a hagiographer, Franckenberg was not only one of Boehme's earliest and most eager readers, as the *Conclusiones* document. By 1640 he had also become a leading expert on Boehme's literary remains in manuscript.²⁷

Spiritual Alchemy

In 1703 the controversial church historian Gottfried Arnold published an anonymous epistolary treatise. Titled *Theophrastia Valentiniana*, it has come to attract the attention of Franckenberg scholars: both Carlos Gilly and Sibylle Rusterholz have emphasised the significance of this work in various contexts.²⁸ Gilly has highlighted Franckenberg's sympathetic treatment of the gnostic heretic Valentinus, prompting Wouter J. Hanegraaff to hail the *Theophrastia Valentiniana* as 'the first known apology of Gnosticism.'[29] As the title suggests, Franckenberg sought to communicate the 'divine eloquence' of Valentinus and thus to compensate for the fact that none of his writings had been preserved: earlier church historians had reduced his entire literary remains to heretical snippets. In his disregard for such polemical labels, Franckenberg prefigured Arnold, whose sympathetic treatment of heretics in the monumental *Unparteyische Kirchen- und Ketzer-Historie* (Impartial History of the Church and Heretics) sparked outrage at the turn of the eighteenth century. Instead, Rusterholz notes that the treatise can be read as a subtle defence of the theosopher of Görlitz. She also draws attention to the way Franckenberg recast Boehme's theosophy in terms of ancient wisdom (*prisca sapientia*) and how he outlined his views on spiritual rebirth throughout the *Theophrastia Valentiniana*.[30] Indeed, to a significant extent, Franckenberg's *Theophrastia Valentiniana* reads like a study or paraphrase of Boehme's spiritual alchemy. The treatise is important for the manner in which its spiritual alchemy united ancient wisdom and Boehme's theosophy while linking individual rebirth to the restoration of all creation at the end of time.

In a radical departure from earlier accounts that inevitably described Valentinus as a heretic, Franckenberg styled him as the prototypical born-again believer. According to Franckenberg's treatment, rebirth was central to 'the philotheosophy of Valentinus' as well as to the story of his life. He construed the lack of understanding the gnostic Valentinus encountered in others, presumably especially those endowed with ecclesiastical authority, as the gnostic's main trial. In this he shared the fate of 'all born-again [believers] in this blind world,' Franckenberg noted. According to his account, Valentinus had initially been a 'Platonic philosopher, . . . like Zoroaster, Hermes, Pythagoras, Plato, etc.' who was then transmuted into a born-again Christian:

> In sum, what was previously dark, shattered, and unholy, that is now illuminated, healed, and sanctified within him to be a LIGHT, SALVATION, and SANCTUARY in the LORD. He retains his former body but [it is] clarified in the mystery, [retains] his former spirit but [it is] fixed and lit by a holy, pure flame of fire from the altar of the Lord. He is and remains a PHILOSOPHER, yet REBORN by THEOLOGY, that is, a Christian and scholar of the LORD, yes, under the lights of born-again nature and the rebirthing grace [he is] tinged, taught, and regenerated by the ray of glory.[31]

Inspired by Boehme, Franckenberg relied on alchemy to describe Valentinus' rebirth. The transformation was complete. Even the gnostic's body was affected by this process of rebirth: it mysteriously became subtler. And if Valentinus was a model for born-again believers and Franckenberg counted himself among them, it stands to reason that the foregoing description could equally apply to Franckenberg himself.

Adding alchemical symbols in the margin to accompany his text, Franckenberg described Valentinus' rebirth as a process of tincturation and fixation. The former implied that an impure metal was transmuted into gold. Alchemists often included the latter among the final stages of progess towards accomplishing the philosophers' stone.[32] Furthermore, Franckenberg insinuated that Valentinus was able to tinge others in turn: he had become a transmuting agent himself.[33] The remainder of Franckenberg's treatise—ostensibly devoted to the doctrine of Valentinus—described how the different stages of transmutation, augmentation, and projection in Valentinus' life prefigured the life of every true believer. Mystical identification with Christ inaugurated an individual process of rebirth, through which a restored, spiritualised or crystalline body would ultimately be attained.

For both Boehme and Franckenberg, the Incarnation of Christ represented the pivotal event in salvation history that made spiritual alchemy possible. Hence, it should come as no surprise that Franckenberg used alchemical terms to discuss the Incarnation. He likened the 'genealogy of CHRIST' to a straight line of deified patriarchs; in conjunction with the divine overshadowing leading the virgin to conceive, it had the effect of a 'flash,' descending 'to the depth of humanity, to the bright centre MarIAH, the favoured and blessed chosen birthing one.' Alluding to the ineffable Hebrew name of God, Franckenberg often highlighted the syllable 'IAH,' representing the first half of the divine tetragrammaton. The downward flash 'tinges as well as ignites the seed of light (as a ray of fire [kindles] saltpetre or grains of gun powder), from which the ray of triumph rises up to the sky, and exudes a bright, fiery glow, [and] also draws up all the other grains that are of its essence by touching them, according to the power of sameness.'[34] The triumphant ray alludes to Christ's Ascension; having previously tinged his followers and transmuted them into his likeness, he is able to lift them up and welcome them into his heavenly realm. The Incarnation of Christ thus had cosmic effects described in terms of Boehme's theosophy, complete with its recourse to alchemy.

Franckenberg's spiritual alchemy was based on a seed of light, which he elsewhere described as 'the spiritual essence' hidden 'in the terrestrial, corporeal matter of Adamic earth ... like light in darkness.' However, contrary to what might be expected in a gnostic framework, this did not refer to an immaterial component of humanity trapped within matter. It was material but more subtle, spiritual, and fit for heaven, harking back to the prelapsarian bodiliness of Adam and Eve: 'For the paradisiacal earth, out of which man was made prior to the Fall and Curse of the earth, lies in the centre and central point, that is, in the inmost, purest element of virginal earth in each and every creature.'[35] As such, this virginal earth provided the material basis for the heavenly body of the new birth. In a way, Franckenberg thus outlined an intriguingly physical variation on the notion of the divine spark that tied in with the topic of Valentinian gnosticism.[36]

Rather than from the tainted mixture of matter produced through intercourse, Christ was born from this primordial matter, or the virgin Mary's pure blood: 'CHRIST's body never saw decay, for he was [born] without male semen, out of the pure blood of the virgin, embalmed with the tincture of GOD's Holy Spirit.'[37] Since every creature carried some of its primordial, uncorrupted matter within itself, Mary was potentially anything but unique. 'HE was conceived from the Holy Spirit through overshadowing, ... out of the spiritual bodiliness, which is crystalline and the true humanity after our resurrection: the essential body and flesh of CHRIST out of the principle of light, and yet hidden in Adam.'[38] Yet it would seem that only those who experienced spiritual rebirth were actually able to benefit from this uncorrupted matter. In *Theophrastia Valentiniana*, Franckenberg spoke of the activation this spiritual essence required in terms of alchemical transmutation.

In his later *Raphael*, an extended, copiously annotated meditation on illness and health in spirit, body, and mind, Franckenberg gave the seed of light a more iatrochemical slant. He described this prelapsarian human matter as the 'holy, chaste, virginal, crystalline, translucent, blessed EARTH, or the true, rich, balm-like quintessential MUMIAH, paradisiacal ELeMent.'[39] Originally, the Paracelsian term *mumia* referred to the healing powers in the bodies of violently killed people; their lingering vital force could be harnessed in cures.[40] By linking the term to the prelapsarian human body, Franckenberg reinterpreted it positively, yet he did not stop there: this was also the matter of which Christ's flesh had consisted. Through his violent death on the cross, Christ literally became God's salvific *mumIAH*, which would bring eternal life to humankind. Drawing 'a sharp distinction between Christ's flesh and ordinary flesh,' Franckenberg's marginalia even enlisted none other than Martin Luther to support his own speculations and to defend Valentinus.[41]

Christ's biography, especially his passion, death, and resurrection, enacted a process that had to be repeated in believers' lives in order for them to be born again and ultimately attain Christ-like flesh. Whereas Boehme had seen the 'Process of Christ' as primarily transmutational, Franckenberg also viewed it as iatrochemical.

Despite the more medical perspective in later years, Franckenberg's most significant debt was to Boehme. Although the theosopher understood the new birth more as a newly implanted seed rather than a pre-existing component of man unaffected by the Fall, he and his acolyte both agreed that postlapsarian humanity had brought a deplorable state upon itself. In a later Latin work, Franckenberg described the consequences of the Fall in terms reminiscent of Boehme's reverse transmutation, due to which humans had been 'transmuted out of the image of God into the image of a beast.'[42] In his 1634 *Klage-Schreiben uber und wider den Greuwel der Verwüstung* (Epistolar Lament on and against the Abomination of Desolation), Franckenberg noted a change in Hebrew vocabulary to this effect. Initially, the Book of Genesis referred to man as *'adam*, yet subsequently as *'anush*. According to Franckenberg, this change was profoundly meaningful. The original word described the prelapsarian state: 'So that man would recognise why the Hebrews originally called him *'adam*, that is, a red, tinged earth from the orient, the power and vivid essence of which out of *'or*, αουρ, *AOUR*, light or fire; *dam*, blood or red wine; and *mayim*, the upper and lower waters.'[43] As a Christian kabbalist, Franckenberg interpreted each of the three letters that form the Hebrew word *'adam* as the initial of another word. The *'aleph* stood for 'light' (*'or*), the *daled* for 'blood' (*dam*), and the *mem* for 'water' (*mayim*). The prelapsarian human thus consisted of light, blood, and the etherial substance of the heavens. This would traditionally have been identified with the mysterious waters above the firmament mentioned in the biblical creation account, a passage that gave rise to profound speculations throughout the early-modern period.[44] By virtue of this, the prelapsarian human was tinged and able to tinge others, just like Christ's disciples after Pentecost, according to Boehme's description in *Signatura rerum*.

As an unredeemed, fallen creature, the human being had lost the benefits of that former state and the ability to tinge: 'yet later on (after the Fall) [he was called] *'enosh*, a sick, malevolent, despaired *mAn* . . . not without hidden meaning.' He did not similarly analyse this word, but the marginal annotation drew attention to a cognate: 'Νόσημος sick; *noshim* women.'[45] Due to the loss of prelapsarian androgyny, the Fall had left humans incomplete.

Franckenberg here alluded to several instances throughout Genesis in which protagonists received new names that reflected their providential destinies.[46] Conversely, in a negative sense, Franckenberg held that the change of terms used to refer to the human being hinted at the far-reaching consequences of the Fall. The Silesian mystic conveyed basically the same message as the theosopher of Görlitz, who had described this as a reverse transmutation from gold to lead. But Franckenberg further supported this argument with philological mystifications and kabbalistic interpretations. After discussing the terms used for humanity in Hebrew and other languages, Franckenberg concluded that they could serve as potent reminders of humankind's lost glory and spur a longing for seeing it restored. Considering these words carefully allowed believers to envision the prelapsarian state and to contemplate its recovery, and thus to actually repeat it, through mystical identification with Christ: 'Based on these diverse names,' the primordial, God-given 'virtue and nobility' of humanity could be 'remembered by recalling the First State and the Former Love,' and this act of contemplation could be 'complemented and restored by recapitulating' or repeating the restoration of that state 'in Christ.'[47]

Despite this broad agreement, there were important differences between Franckenberg's spiritual alchemy and that of Boehme. They differed on the preconditions of this restoration, for instance. Whereas the theosopher's lead of fallen humanity would appear wholly passive, Franckenberg argued that all human beings still carried within themselves some of the paradisiacal earth from which they were first created, prior to the Fall. The Silesian mystic described this seed of light as 'ash (*'epher*), the powder of lead, the ash of sixty colours according to the Arabs, the golden sand and purple grain of Ophir.'[48] This guaranteed the possibility of restoration; in alchemical terms, it was the material potential for gold within fallen humanity that made transmutation possible. Drawing on his knowledge of the sacred language, Franckenberg later developed his notion of an uncorrupted substance with recourse to the highly similar Hebrew words for dust and ash. In so doing, he followed in the footsteps of his namesake patriarch: Abraham had eloquently described himself as 'dust and ashes' (*'aphar va-'epher*), and the Silesian nobleman quoted this passage in his later work *Notae mysticae et mnemonicae* (Mystical and Mnemnonic Notes), composed in 1650. Due to the similarity of these two Hebrew roots, they were closely linked in Franckenberg's understanding and strongly associated with alchemy.

In the same *Notae mysticae* passage, the Silesian mystic explained 'to my dust' (*la-'aphroti*) as a return 'to the primordial chaos.'[49] This was a term used by alchemists to refer to undifferentiated metallic matter or mercury, attained by stripping a metal of its sulphur principle, thus preparing it for becoming, or at least receiving, the tincture. Elsewhere in *Notae mysticae*, Franckenberg also discussed 'within ash [of] Ophir' (*ba-'epher 'Ophir*). This phrase does not occur in the Bible, but it is derived from another one that does: 'from gold of Ophir' (*mi-zehav 'Ophir*). Franckenberg glossed this phrase with a reference to 'the Hermetics' tincture of gold,' thereby associating this substance with the transmuting agent of the alchemists.[50] In view of early-modern accounts that described the tincture as a red powder ultimately derived from gold through various processes, this association is apposite.

The interpretation Franckenberg outlined for the Hebrew word for dust interacted with its earliest occurrences in Genesis: God had initially created Adam with 'dust from the earth' and then cursed him to 'return to dust.'[51] In *Raphael*, Franckenberg paraphrased the passage on Adam's creation: 'Such dust,' out of which Adam was formed, 'is called '*aphar va-'epher*, dust and ash, . . . which also become gold.'[52] Franckenberg firmly integrated the death of the old body into the work of spiritual alchemy that would give rise to the new. In a marginal annotation, Franckenberg explained '*aphar* as 'dust of lead, ash of gold: the quintessence (*Q. E.*) of all bodies, the SMALLEST beginning of things.'[53] The Silesian nobleman interpreted the Curse that followed the Fall of Adam and Eve as a confirmation and a promise: humans' primordial matter was never lost, and eventually humanity would be restored to it, purified of dross. Through his spiritual alchemy, Franckenberg found a glimmer of hope even in the words of God's Curse.

Once tinged by the Holy Spirit or through identification with Christ, the new birth remained hidden within the old body but unaffected by it, 'pure and holy and without any stain of sin . . . like gold in dung or dross.' In a variation on the mystical identification with Mary, the believer was pregnant with *Christus in nobis* also in a very physical sense.[54] It is therefore no coincidence that Franckenberg spoke of himself in the same terms as of Mary, 'as a channel or tube, through which the water was led and flowed,' as he put it in a letter dated 18 September 1639.[55] This could be taken as a denial that Christ had become fully human through the Incarnation, and it was precisely one of the statements of Valentinus that his critics had deemed heretical. Yet it is more likely that Franckenberg, rather than denying Christ's humanity, wanted to emphasise the mystical identification of Mary and the believer, as well as the believer's passivity in the process of salvation, in keeping with the Lutheran insistence that it takes place 'by faith alone' (*sola fide*).

Reflecting the contrast between Adam's states before and after the Fall, the fundamental difference between Christ's flesh and human flesh posed a problem that had to be overcome. Unlike Boehme, who repeatedly spoke of the 'process of Christ,' especially in his *Signatura rerum*, Franckenberg did not emphasise as strongly that Christ's biography culminated in his transcending the mortal body. Consequently, Franckenberg portrayal could seem more static at times. Yet the basic contrast remained: if the human body could be described as reddish sand, dust, or ash, Christ's body resembled a precious gem. However, this gem-like body of Christ was hidden in terrestrial human matter. In order to fully assume the subtle body temporarily seen in his Transfiguration, Christ had to die and rise again, after which he was able to pass through closed doors.[56] Consequently, Franckenberg contrasted the baseness of the unrefined red earth with the purified substance of Christ's resurrection body: 'That man is terrestrial and made of earth is obvious... [in contrast,] Christ is of the heavenly loveliness [*recte*: bodiliness] of the ruby or carbuncle stone: which adumbrate noble, purified earth.'[57] By implication, the believer had to undergo a process of purification through which her body would be made crystalline like Christ's.[58]

Perhaps bearing in mind pseudo-Weigel's reborn human as the city of God, Franckenberg drew a connection to the 'heavenly Jerusalem made of transparent, bright jasper, transparent gold, pearls, emerald, and many other precious stones.' He argued that humans' 'celestial bodiliness' had to conform to this future habitat:

> We must admit that before the Fall Adam was very different from what he is now, and he also has to become very different, if he wants to enter the kingdom of heaven; 'flesh and blood cannot inherit the kingdom of God.' We shall be like angels, yes, like him and be where HE, CHRIST, is, and see him in us and us in him.[59]

Franckenberg here quoted Paul's First Epistle to the Corinthians to emphasise the need for bodily transmutation.[60] The human body had to be restored to its prelapsarian state; it had to become transparent gold in order to join Christ in the new Jerusalem.

This could only be accomplished through identification with Christ, which entailed participation in his death and resurrection. Franckenberg explicitly made his case by arguing from the analogy this process had in the natural world, as scrutinised by alchemy:

> We also see through chymical analysis (*Anatomia Chymica*) how the crystalline body lies hidden in the dark mass but becomes visible, comprehensible, and tangible when purified through the fire of calcination, separatory, or purgatory. Should there not also be found within man such a principle of heavenly relics—out of the uncorrupted body of the saints, out of the body and life of JESUS, the saviour of his own body—albeit hidden under the bark, ash, chaff, shell, cloud, etc. of the outward, dark body? Far be it! It would be something absurd in the light of grace and nature [if this were not the case].[61]

Franckenberg borrowed the term 'relics' in this connection from the *Libellus theosophiae* (Booklet of Theosophy), a short work he had already listed in his *Conclusiones*.[62] The potential for a crystalline body was a given, and it could only unfold if the depraved outer crust was removed. The analogy established with alchemical processes not merely served to aid the imagination; more importantly, it provided Franckenberg with physical proof, drawn from the Book of Nature, of what the Book of Scripture described in some of its more mysterious passages.

According to Franckenberg, the transition from a terrestrial to a crystalline body required a 'TheophiloSophical death, from which comes new life,' which was 'the goal of his—Valentinus'—doctrine,' as well as the aim to which all other true believers aspired. Just like pseudo-Weigel, Franckenberg stressed that new birth had to be preceded by death: 'That the new birth—through the holy death, . . . out of Christ, the new Adam, out of the Holy Spirit and the celestial upper waters—tinges man towards a new birth, towards a pure, untainted body, towards a heavenly, crystalline earth.'[63] Thus, spiritual rebirth ultimately had a physical goal. In fact, there is every reason to believe that Franckenberg held it to inaugurate a physical process, or at the very least one that called into question the modern distinction between body and spirit. It is worth recalling that spirit in the early-modern sense was not yet simply the antonym of body or matter.[64] In a letter dated 2 January 1640, Franckenberg spoke of the reborn believer as being '(according to the spirit and *the inner body of sanctification*) a new creature.'[65] Challenging the dichotomy between spirit/interiority and body/exteriority, the body of this new birth remained interior and invisible for the time being, yet it was a body nonetheless. Back in the *Theophrastia Valentiniana*, the death that had to precede the new birth pointed in the same direction: it 'is a melting away in the spirit, but concealed from the world.' The marginal remarks explicitly established a parallel with transmutational alchemy: 'Putrefaction is the key of the philosophers. While I putrefy, I am reinvigorated.'[66] *Nigredo*, the black stage of the philosophical work often associated with putrefaction, was a central accomplishment, after which the remainder of the path towards the philosophers' stone was held to be comparatively easy.[67] In this sense, putrefaction can indeed be seen as key to the *opus*, yet Franckenberg turned the believer into the alchemical matter.

Alluding to the persecution born-again believers would face just like Valentinus, Franckenberg gave a detailed description that featured alchemical terms. The challenges the faithful encountered served as repeated calcinations, through which God as the divine alchemist and *Christus in nobis* as the *archaeus* (a Paracelsian term that referred to humans' inner alchemist, responsible for digestion, among other things) were purifying them:[68]

> They [the born-again believers] are on trial, in purification, the closer and more they approach the centre of the *archaeus*, the internal smelter and rebirther in the spiritual, holy Vesta, GOD's holy fire, where they also will have to be attracted, protracted, extracted, and clarified, refined like glass and gold and seven times like silver; the more often the glass goes through the fire, the more beautiful, the subtler, purer, and brighter it becomes.[69]

As the mention of glass indicated, this process did not involve transmutation; in a sense, it had already taken place and thus given way to purification.

Correspondingly, Franckenberg also viewed the believer's mystical death and rebirth as a daily occurrence. In this regard, it would be misguided to posit too stark a contrast between the paradigms of transmutation and purification: rather than being mutually exclusive, Franckenberg saw them as complementary. The tribulations that believers had to overcome consequently corresponded to those encountered by Christ during his passion: 'For this reason, it is said that we have to enter in through much cross and tribulation, through many deaths in the Lord: Paul dies daily.'[70] The initial experience of rebirth can be seen as a transmutation; as Christ's biography is subsequently relived on a daily basis, this amounts to repeated cycles of purification. In a letter dated 1 August 1641, Franckenberg explained this distinction in the following terms: 'Though at first man has to be born out of Christ, yet afterwards Christ has to be born out of man—through true, indwelling faith (as can be seen in MarIAH)—and God revealed in man, just as man was revealed in Christ before God, according to rebirth.'[71] Once reborn of, or transmuted through, Christ, the believer gives birth to Christ daily, re-enacting his life repeatedly and becoming purer and purer in the process.

Like Boehme, Franckenberg viewed spiritual rebirth as an ongoing process that started inwardly in the here and now but also had eternal and physical implications. Rebirth was virtually a 'first resurrection' of the spirit that prefigured the final, bodily one:

> It happens here, according to time, as we fall and move in the flesh; yet according to the soul, it reaches into the principle of the spirit or the light of faith in CHRIST, from which originates—in the daily enactment of penitence—a foretaste and part of the tinctURe of the future, eternal life of joy, and it brings good fruit, both in this world and the next.[72]

For the time being, the effects of that divine transmuting agent could therefore only be felt to a limited extent. They did cause anticipatory 'delight in the resurrection of our bodies' among born-again believers and foreshadowed what was to take place at the final resurrection of the dead. The Silesian mystic described this in the following terms:

> As the mystery of the resurrection (of the paradisiacal life in the spirit, of the holy sabbath, of celestial bodiliness, of the spiritual ZION and holy Jerusalem, etc.) lights up beautifully every now and again in everyone, so born-again man is wonderfully refreshed and sees in this principle [the visible world], like in a mirror, the recapitulation and reminder of the effect—partly completed, partly yet to unfold . . .—of the divine will and Holy Spirit, feeling them with a foretaste.[73]

Franckenberg held that the lives of believers were punctuated by visionary experiences, during which they glimpsed what their lives and bodies would be like in the new Jerusalem, described towards the end of the Book of Revelation.

In passages already quoted here, Franckenberg repeatedly employed a key term of transmutational alchemy, for which he frequently used an idiosyncratic spelling: 'tinctURe' (*TinctUR*).[74] Simply put, a tincture was an extract from one substance that had the ability to communicate its essential attributes to another substance, thereby changing the nature of that substance to be like unto the first. Early in the seventeenth century, Martin Ruland's *Lexicon alchemiae* provided the following two definitions:

> A tincture is called that which penetrates and suffuses a body through its colour, just as saffron does to water; whatever penetrates and colours the bodies. A tincture is a specific secret which has, by means of the essence and the formal qualities, also the colour of a thing, so that it can tinge into a nature similar unto itself.[75]

On the same page of Ruland's dictionary, 'to tinge and to transmute' are listed as synonyms.[76] Transmutation of base metals into gold required a red tincture that was applied in a process known as projection. Usually, this was held to take effect in a very short time or even instantaneously, according to most accounts.[77]

Yet for Franckenberg and Boehme before him, the term 'tincture' acquired profound theosophical significance that cannot entirely be explained with recourse to alchemy. Boehme used it many times in his *Clavis*, a work he reportedly composed for the benefit of Franckenberg and Schweinichen, as well as the more private *Clavis specialis* (Special Key) composed for Schweinichen. There, Boehme defined it as follows: 'TINCTURE is the speaking of the word (the word in action).'[78] The term could thus refer to the very act of divine creation or its being sustained continually. In other cases, though, Boehme more obviously drew on the alchemical core meaning, describing the tincture 'as a penetrating being' that 'penetrates and sanctifies' others.[79] As it was closely associated with the deity, this divine tincture was a force that could render other things more like God. According to Boehme, it used to permeate all of creation: 'The tincture penetrated the earth and all the elements, tingeing everything; then paradise was on earth and within man.' Due to the Fall, 'the divine activity, [working] through the tincture, fled into its own principle, that is, into the inner ground of the light world': God's Curse, according to Boehme, was actually a withdrawal or flight, playing on the near-homophony of the German words for 'flight' (*Flucht*) and 'curse' (*Fluch*).[80] Conversely, the return of the divine tincture into the created world would bring about the restoration of its prelapsarian state.

Drawing on his familiarity with Hebrew, Franckenberg interpreted the very pronunciation and spelling of 'tinctURe' as indicating that it originated in the principle of light. He highlighted the letters *UR* because they transliterated the Hebrew word *'or* (light), with the *U* representing the letter *vav* and the *R* standing for *resh*. Yet the very same letters could also be used to transliterate *'ur* (fire): the spellings of both Hebrew terms are virtually identical and only differentiated by the position of the *vav*'s vowel dot.[81] The sacred language thus provided a striking confirmation of the intricate relationship Boehme had posited between the principles of fire/wrath and light/love, associated with God the Father and God the Son, respectively. In his later works, Franckenberg occasionally employed a more comprehensive transliteration of *'or* that included the silent letter *aleph* and the potential of *vav* to be vocalised as either *o* or *u*: 'AOUR'.[82] Only very rarely did Franckenberg draw attention to the distinction between *'or* and *'ur*, for example when noting that, on the Last Day, 'one part' of humanity 'would go towards OR,' the light or salvation, 'to the right, the other part towards UR,' the fire or damnation, 'to the left.'[83] In most cases, Franckenberg simply highlighted both OR and UR in words such as 'ʘRient' and 'natURe,' though these could potentially be ambiguous, as in Hebrew text without vowel marks.[84]

However, various occurrences of 'tinctURe' in Franckenberg's works create the impression that he quite consistently associated the term with light, paradise, and salvation, rather than fire, judgement, and damnation. In *Sephiriel* (The Counting Angel), an unprinted work Franckenberg completed in 1631, he explicitly mentioned the 'tinctURe of light' and linked it to the Transfiguration of Christ.[85] He used the German translation of the same phrase in *Raphael*, where he wrote of 'the bodily being of the tinctURe (*TinctURwesen*) of the spirit.'[86] For Franckenberg, then, the 'tinctURe' was quite literally reaching out of the divine world of love and light into the physical world, effecting a delayed transmutation in the believers it reached: like Christ on Mount Tabor, they experienced fleeting transfigurations and would at last permanently attain a body of transparent gold fit for heaven and corresponding to his resurrection body.

Such episodes would not have been wholly unlike Franckenberg's original illumination in 1617. After his religious awakening, he immersed himself in the heterodox literature of his day and eventually became acquainted with Boehme in person. The theosopher of Görlitz played a decisive role in shaping Franckenberg's views on spiritual alchemy. Beginning in 1623, Franckenberg very quickly became one of Boehme's most avid readers and, in important ways, not only Boehme's biographer but also the foremost scholarly expert on his works. Only a few years after Boehme's death, in 1627, Franckenberg penned a sympathetic treatment of Valentinus, the gnostic church father denounced as a heretic, for the benefit of another student of Boehme's works, Ehrenfried Hegenicht of Görlitz. In this context, Franckenberg presented his most elaborate treatment of spiritual alchemy. Later works, even *Raphael*, did not significantly add to this but referred back to notions already contained in the *Theophrastia Valentiniana*. In describing spiritual alchemy against the backdrop of the ancient world and its philosophy, Franckenberg considerably improved its credentials and appeal in ways that ultimately foreshadowed Mary Anne Atwood's much more comprehensive portrayal of spiritual alchemy as ancient theurgy. The mystical identification of Christ and the believer is crucial to the spiritual alchemy pioneered by Boehme and refined by Franckenberg.

5
Georg Lorenz Seidenbecher, Franckenberg's Spiritual and Philosophical Son

Although Franckenberg never penned a later treatise that could have superseded the spiritual alchemy outlined in the *Theophrastia Valentiniana*, frequent allusions in later works confirm that he did not abandon it. The Silesian nobleman increasingly engaged with the literature of laboratory alchemy in his later life. Early in the 1640s, the Thirty Years' War forced Franckenberg to flee his family's estate at Ludwigsdorf and eventually Silesia altogether. By 9 July 1642, he found himself in Danzig where he remained for more than seven years. During July and August 1649, just a few months before his return to Ludwigsdorf, Franckenberg met a young traveller by the name of Georg Lorenz Seidenbecher.[1] In him the Silesian mystic found a spiritual son and intellectual heir, who went on to become the author of an important treatise on millenarianism. In contrast to other discipleships Franckenberg cultivated throughout his life, his relation to Seidenbecher is particularly well-documented because this pupil was investigated on charges of heresy in 1661. Around Christmas of that year, Seidenbecher was removed from his office as pastor in the tiny hamlet of Unterneubrunn, then in the Duchy of Saxe-Gotha.

In the course of proceedings against him, the ecclesiastical authorities confiscated several manuscripts in Seidenbecher's possession. The original records of this investigation appear to be lost, but significant parts remain available in print. At the turn of the eighteenth century, Gottfried Arnold's *Impartial History* included a sympathetic portrayal of Seidenbecher's plight, documented by copious excerpts from archival sources.[2] Almost four decades later, the Danzig-based pastor and school teacher Albrecht Meno Verpoorten published his *De Georgii Laurentii Seidenbecheri vita* (On the Life of Georg Lorenz Seidenbecher). This hostile biography cast Seidenbecher as a heretical millenarian and Rosicrucian sympathiser. Franckenberg figured as the chief villain, sowing seeds of doubt concerning Lutheranism, as well as of heresy regarding millenarianism. He thus seduced a promising young man—the maternal grandson of the famous school teacher of Coburg, Andreas Libavius, author of the important 1595 textbook *Alchemia*.[3] To make matters worse, Libavius had even held a disputation against millenarianism and positioned himself as an intractable enemy of Rosicrucianism.[4] For his part, Franckenberg voiced the conspiratorial hypothesis that Libavius could have feigned his enmity towards the Rosicrucians.[5]

Though Verpoorten's account is obviously slanted, the significance it attributes to Franckenberg is surpassed in importance only by the primary sources through which his role is documented. Most but far from all of these also survive in a manuscript volume prepared with a view to the print publication of Verpoorten's *Seidenbecheri vita*.[6] These extant documents show that Franckenberg actively communicated his spiritual alchemy to Seidenbecher as his young disciple. After describing Franckenberg's increasing engagement with alchemical literature and his initial encounter with Seidenbecher in Danzig, the remainder of this chapter explores how the exiled Silesian nobleman initiated his pupil into the mysteries of spiritual alchemy. Seidenbecher's account and related sources highlight Franckenberg's strategies as a teacher of spiritual alchemy. In fact, manuscripts owned by Franckenberg that Seidenbecher copied and the correspondence between them contain many references to alchemical literature and terminology. These allow us to establish that even if Seidenbecher became known for his millenarianism, Franckenberg instructed him as a spiritual alchemist in a very real sense. This was in keeping with alchemical lore, which held that a laboratory practitioner communicated his secrets to a successor, who became his 'philosophical son.'[7]

Franckenberg's Increasing Engagement with Alchemical Literature

Franckenberg paid scant attention to alchemical literature prior to the late 1630s. In his *Conclusiones* of 1625, there is a reference to Oswald Croll's *Basilica chymica* (Royal Chymistry), a famous work first published around 1608, but that is the only relevant title among a host of devotional, mystical, and heterodox texts. While the *Theophrastia Valentiniana* documents some familiarity with alchemy, it is difficult to link its pertinent content to specific works or authors other than Boehme. This situation changed dramatically with *Raphael*, composed in 1638, which quoted Heinrich Khunrath without naming him, mentioned several alchemical authors, and drew on other relevant texts, some of them in manuscript.[8] In a letter dated 1 November 1639, there is also plenty of alchemical language and even a hint of familiarity with laboratory practice in 'the art of the philosophers'.[9] Closer reading suggests, however, that Franckenberg was merely showing off by liberally sprinkling a meditation on wine with alchemical terms and symbols. Marginalia that the Silesian nobleman added to his personal copy of Johannes Bureus' *FaMa è sCanzIa reDVX* (News Returning from Scandinavia) after 1639 also contain alchemical symbols and allusions.[10] Even if the precise contours of Franckenberg's alchemical reading remain unclear, there can be no doubt that he was considerably more familiar with relevant literature by the end of the 1630s.

Composed around the middle or towards the end of the 1640s, the *Speculum Apocalypticum* (Apocalyptic Mirror) echoed many positions already endorsed in the *Theophrastia Valentiniana*. Despite the preface bearing the date 13 May 1629, the work repeatedly referred to the *Oculus sidereus* (Starry Eye) and to *Von dem Ohrte der Seelen* (On the Place of the Soul), written in 1643 and 1644, respectively.[11] The *Speculum Apocalypticum* therefore dated to the mid-1640s and eventually found inclusion in *Trias mystica*, published in 1651. Among other things, it contained a variation on the alchemical initialism VITRIOL, that is, 'Visit the interiors of the earth; while rectifying you will find the hidden stone' (*Visita Interiora Terrae Rectificando Invenies Occultum Lapidem*). In Franckenberg's hands, this turned into 'Visit the interiors of the Adamic macro- and microcosmic earth' (*Visita Interiora Terrae Adamicae M^a_icrocosmicae*). In other words, one had to inspect not only the outside world but also the inner world of the microcosm. This injunction 'towards life' ([*ad*] *V.I.T.A.M.*) was followed by 'there a Christian ought to be reborn' (*IBI Christianum Oportet Renasci*), with the three capital letters forming the Latin word for 'heart'.[12] Put another way, it was within the heart of a body made of dust, ash, and earth that rebirth towards eternal life took place.

In correspondence throughout the early 1640s, Franckenberg emerged as a witness of alchemical experiments and asserted the superiority of older authorities over 'today's experience' on 5 January 1643.[13] He also exchanged letters with the mysterious Floretus à Bethabor, the likely author of an alchemical allegory. On 24 June 1644, Bethabor wrote that 'chymical matters

(*Chymische Sachen*) ... are very difficult, arduous, and more irksome than useful.'[14] That probably was not the kind of response Franckenberg would have hoped for, yet it did not deter him from further pursuing his alchemical interests. Towards the end of the decade, the Silesian nobleman corresponded with Tobias König, later ennobled as Von Königfels. In August 1649 Franckenberg wrote two letters to the 'distinguished artisan or mechanic' in Riga.[15] These missives only survived thanks to Georg Lorenz Seidenbecher, who copied them before they were expedited. As Seidenbecher's own letters to Franckenberg document, they exchanged information on alchemical books right until the end of his life: on 10/20 June 1652, Seidenbecher still promised his mentor a 'copy' of a text on the 'philosophers' stone' (*L. Φ.*).[16] Since this was a mere few days before Franckenberg passed away on 25 June, it is doubtful whether the letter reached him in time. But this only took place almost three years after the first encounter between the Silesian mystic and a young traveller from Thuringia.

Franckenberg and Seidenbecher in Danzig

Seidenbecher met the impoverished Silesian nobleman in his Danzig exile during the summer of 1649. The young traveller wrote a detailed account of these days and weeks, titled 'Conversation with Ancient Virtue and Faith' (*Conversatio cum Antiqua Virtute Fideque*), integrating one of the many playful devices through which Franckenberg concealed the initials of his name. Joachim Telle has prepared a modern edition of this text and emphasised what a vivid portrayal of Franckenberg's day-to-day life it contains.[17] Seidenbecher himself repeatedly referred back to the 'Conversation' in later years, as he continued to grapple with the topics Franckenberg had discussed with him. In some ways, his encounter with the Silesian nobleman parallels that of a younger Franckenberg and Boehme. The age gap was slightly bigger: Franckenberg was already a few years older than the theosopher had been at the time, and Seidenbecher met Franckenberg at a younger age. Seidenbecher's own letters from subsequent years leave no doubt that he viewed his contact with Franckenberg as defining for his life and faith.[18] Looking back, he wrote to Franckenberg that the Silesian mystic had 'sired' him 'just like Paul his Onesimus, so I duly accord you the title and name of a father.'[19] Onesimus was a runaway slave mentioned in Paul's Epistle to Philemon, and the apostle sought to appeal to Onesimus' former owner

Philemon for clemency. Not only did Seidenbecher become Franckenberg's spiritual son, there are indications that the younger man had to return to a harsh master, too: the relationship between Seidenbecher and his biological father was strained. On one occasion, Philipp Walther Seidenbecher, a high-ranking minister in Eisfeld, intercepted a letter sent by Franckenberg and confronted his son about it; another time, Georg Lorenz complained about the enmity of household members.[20] Against this backdrop, Franckenberg became an alternative father figure for Seidenbecher.

On the evening of Friday, 13/23 July 1649, Seidenbecher encountered Franckenberg for the first time. Suffering from poverty in his Danzig exile, Franckenberg talked about the devotional literature that had had such a formative impact on him: 'To begin with, Arndt's writings suffice; Thomas à Kempis, Tauler, and the *Theologia Germanica* rise higher.' After accusing the Jesuits of 'castrating writings of this kind,' he also criticised Lutheranism for paying so little heed to spiritual rebirth: 'On regeneration, but little is contained in the Augsburg Confession.'[21] This evaluation is defining for Franckenberg's stance towards the Lutheran church; to a significant extent, the spiritual alchemy he developed sought to address this perceived shortcoming. On Sunday afternoon, 15/25 July, Franckenberg derided the impiety of his age and extolled the virtue of pagan sages, such as Hermes Trismegistus. Seidenbecher noted that Franckenberg 'showed me a certain treatise written by himself, to be published in Holland at some point.'[22] Though the title is not mentioned in this context, the treatise in question was most likely Franckenberg's 1637 *Via veterum sapientum* (Path of the Ancient Sages) in manuscript—it was eventually published in 1675. He handed it to Seidenbecher to read a few days later, on 19/29 July, when there was no time for conversation. This work contains a whole section consisting of excerpts from the Hermetic writings.[23] Perceiving a kindred soul in Seidenbecher, Franckenberg warmed to him immediately, telling the young man about the devotional literature that had shaped him and letting him read a scribal publication that would only be printed a quarter of a century later.

On Monday, 16/26 July, Franckenberg confided his millenarianism to his disciple. Though this aspect is mostly ignored by scholarship, Franckenberg held millenarian views but articulated them only in the subtlest manner or in his least known works, such as the unprinted *Sephiriel*.[24] Specifically, Franckenberg and Seidenbecher discussed the impossibility of predicting the date at which the millennium was to begin. Referring to earlier writers, such as the Torgau astrologer Paul Nagel, Franckenberg cautioned against arriving at precise predictions based on rational procedures. As he pithily put it in a later conversation, 'reason is a strumpet.' However, it would seem that he did allow for the possibility of gaining further insights on God's timetable based on the interaction of textual exegesis and divine revelation. Avoiding the designations employed by the guardians of orthodoxy, Franckenberg used an exceedingly rare term in this context, 'sabbathism.' A decade later it would find its way onto the title page of Seidenbecher's *Chiliasmus sanctus* (Holy Millenarianism), composed in 1658 and published pseudonymously in 1660.[25] Based on the notion that world history mirrored the first week of creation, this term encapsulated the millenarian belief that, after six thousand years of turmoil, there would be a final era of peace, corresponding to the sabbath, the seventh day on which God rested from his creative work. On this fateful Monday in Danzig, Franckenberg planted the seeds of millenarian heresy that would prove to be Seidenbecher's undoing in the early 1660s.

On the very same day, Franckenberg gave Seidenbecher the rare opportunity to read some of Boehme's epistles, presumably in manuscript: 'He showed me the letters of Jacob Boehme I ought to read,' the young disciple recalled.[26] While individual letters or epistolary treatises had already been published in 1639, the first more comprehensive edition was only printed in 1658. Although published long after his death, Franckenberg was intimately involved with this project: he conceived it, provided the idea for the frontispiece, and contributed the preface to the *Theosophische Send-Schreiben* (Theosophical Epistles). Franckenberg may thus posthumously be counted among its editors, alongside Swedish diplomat Michel Le Blon, who also did not live to see the final product, and Amsterdam-based publisher Heinrich Betke.[27] In later years, Seidenbecher continued to engage with Boehme. On 9 June 1650, for instance, he reported on his encounter with Johann Angelius von Werdenhagen. Ennobled probably in 1637, this famous lawyer had translated Boehme's *Viertzig Fragen von der Seelen* (Forty Questions on the Soul) into Latin in 1632. Werdenhagen fondly showed to Seidenbecher the various Dutch editions of other works by Boehme which he had collected.[28] In a later letter, Seidenbecher remembered Franckenberg's critical remarks about some translations of the theosopher's works: 'Because Mr [Joachim] Betke,' a minister in Linum near Fehrbellin, 'recommended the writings of Jacob Boehme *Teutonicus*, I would like to know which are the choicest among them and which ought to be read before the others, also in which language, for I recall hearing you say in Danzig that they had been poorly translated.'[29] Once again, the repercussions of that summery Monday afternoon could be felt throughout Seidenbecher's *Chiliasmus sanctus:* in this controversial publication, he referred to Boehme repeatedly and even quoted an extended passage from the theosopher's treatise on the new birth.[30]

Over the coming weeks, Franckenberg and Seidenbecher usually met several times a week. Although they occasionally touched upon the shortcomings of the church, they spent most of their time discussing devotional literature and unpublished treatises. Authors that commanded their attention included the apocalyptic writer Julius Sperber, 'several of whose manuscripts' Franckenberg claimed to own, and Christoph Hirsch, 'an eighty-year-old celibate deacon in Eisleben, the author of the *Magical Jewel* (*Gemma magica*) not yet publicly seen in print.'[31] As Seidenbecher was planning to travel through Eisleben on his way home, Franckenberg wrote a letter of recommendation for his disciple, in which he also urged Hirsch to publish his treatise.[32] Despite this encouragement, it remained unprinted until 1688. As Franckenberg wished for Seidenbecher 'to make contact with the associates' of the Rosicrucians, he also tasked his pupil with tracking down a cell of them near his hometown, 'six miles from Eisfeld' and 'not far from Coburg at a monastery.'[33] Their conversations ranged from treatises to their authors and thence to the more mysterious societies that harboured secret wisdom.

One of Seidenbecher's later letters, dated 5 September 1650, indicates that he had indeed probed Hirsch for more precise directions regarding the Rosicrucians of Coburg. Unfortunately, the elderly deacon was not forthcoming. Although he did not deny that such a cell existed, he merely indicated 'by which guise those who are called chymists enter in.' Hirsch's suggestion that the Rosicrucians were chymical practitioners considerably dampened Seidenbecher's enthusiasm: 'Since I am currently a stranger to the chymical pursuit (*in studio Chymico*), although the case may be truthful regarding the aforementioned habitation, I have decided not to apply myself to it anymore or to investigate further: for I believe that I will not be able to learn more from others than I learned from you, by God's grace.'[34] Franckenberg's young disciple thus found himself disappointed in his quest for other guides on the path of spiritual alchemy; in comparison, laboratory alchemy was of less interest to him. As far as Seidenbecher was concerned, the Silesian nobleman had already assumed the role of a mentor who had revealed to him all the secrets of spiritual alchemy he needed to know.

In exchange for Franckenberg's guidance, Seidenbecher assisted him as an amanuensis, copying letters the Silesian mystic had written before they were expedited. In addition to the benefit of a further copy, the young disciple was also meant to derive spiritual edification from these assignments. A scrap of paper Franckenberg addressed to Seidenbecher made this explicit: 'Greetings. I kindly ask whether you may be able to make enough time, without too much trouble, to copy what is enclosed for me; you can also edify yourself somewhat through this.'[35] In this way, Franckenberg styled what was essentially a lengthy task to be completed on his behalf as a win-win situation: not only did Seidenbecher become privy to Franckenberg's communications with others, his spiritual progress would be furthered by the same token. The young disciple deemed the resulting manuscripts more precious than gold: one of his letters to Franckenberg recounted how a group of bandits robbed him of his financial provisions, yet upon his 'earnest entreaty' they restored his knapsack to him, which held the precious manuscripts.[36] Luckily, the robbers themselves were more interested in hard currency. If the very survival of these documents is anything to go by, Seidenbecher treasured these texts and perused them throughout his later life.

Franckenberg's Discipling through Reading Recommendations, Letters, and Manuscripts

Some of the material Seidenbecher copied during his sojourn in Danzig and fortunately received back from the robbers treated alchemical matters: Franckenberg's two letters to Tobias König and a sequence of shorter texts with arcane content. If the *Theophrastia Valentiniana* contains the most comprehensive statement of Franckenberg's spiritual alchemy, these texts and letters show how he tried to nudge his associates towards drawing similar conclusions. He did not present them with a complete outline; rather, he gave König and Seidenbecher various pointers, presumably hoping that they would elaborate on them individually. Another one of Franckenberg's disciples allows us to conclude that this procedure worked: Angelus Silesius, the physician Johann Scheffler who inherited part of Franckenberg's library and subsequently converted to Catholicism, integrated aspects of spiritual alchemy into the poetry of his celebrated *Cherubinischer Wandersmann* (Angelic Wayfarer), first published under a different title in 1657.[37] The material Seidenbecher received as part of this education provides the fullest documentation for Franckenberg's discipling activities.

Throughout the letters to König copied by Seidenbecher, Franckenberg drew on several familiar *clichés* derived from alchemical literature. In a variation on the Benedictine phrase 'Pray and work!' (*ora et labora*), which Heinrich Khunrath had taken up prominently in an alchemical context, Franckenberg exhorted his correspondent to 'continue on this path steadily, delicately with prayer and work, wakefully and without haste.'[38] Subsequently, he alluded to another borrowing from Khunrath that played an important role in his own *Raphael*: the grouping of 'the true kabbalah, magic, chemistry.' Discussing the Transfiguration of Christ, Franckenberg held that the disciples who witnessed it 'were so strongly tinged by this fiery aspect that they . . . wanted to call down fire from heaven.' However, as this was only a momentary prefiguration of the future 'glorified spirit and body of CHRIST,' Franckenberg explained that the time was not yet ripe for this.

Yet such anticipatory reflections of future glory did not only take place in biblical events. With the 'Know thyself' formula firmly in mind, Franckenberg held that the various stages of God's revelation throughout history were mirrored in the individual experience of the believer: 'which threefold secret of the heavenly Tinct☿Re can also simultaneously be found in every single born-again, believing human.'[39] Having concluded that 'the One Anointment can teach all of this,' Franckenberg contrasted the 'glorious, secret arts and sciences' of the 'old kabbalists, magi, and chymists' against the antics of 'the new artists.' Instead of looking to them, Franckenberg encouraged König to focus on 'the First FOundational F☉unt and AOURigin of all wisdom in God, the eternal, unique, and living WORD and his SPIRIT' (the Trinity), to avoid being seduced or deceived.[40] After a lengthy passage on the coming of Elias Artista, the biblical prophet to return as an alchemist towards the end of time, Franckenberg implicitly referred to his *Via veterum sapientum* and noted that the chief aim was to become 'fiery' like the transfigured Christ and 'finally to become conformable unto HIM in being and powers': deiform, as it were.

Franckenberg held that the potential for this transmutational deification was contained within the believer and that it had to be wrought out in a process of spiritual alchemy: 'for our heavenly spirit, our divine soul, and our paradisiacal body already has this within itself,' Franckenberg wrote, 'in and out of Jesus Christ, God with us (*ha-'Imanu'el*); through faith, love, and hope; by predestination. With moderate fasting, orderly waking and watching, as well as passionate praying (the true masterful regimen of the spiritual, philosophical fire), it only has to be nourished, augmented, and continually kept in the fire, until its proper time and perfection.'[41] The practices of spiritual alchemy Franckenberg described—fasting, waking, praying—were similar to those of Paul Nagel's 'Our *Azoth* Turned to Gold.' In the second extant letter to König, dated 18/28 August 1649, Franckenberg doubled down on the interiority of this spiritual alchemy when contrasted against laboratory activity: 'One does not need any other fire, vessel, or oven beyond a pure, faithful heart and a new, certain spirit, in which God and the Word dwell and effect his work.'[42] Breaking down the doctrinal content of his spiritual alchemy to the everyday life of his disciples, the ascetic lifestyle of fasting, waking and watching, and praying—carefully maintained throughout their entire lives—was the fire in which the physico-spiritual new birth would mature to perfection.

Playing on a passage in the Rosicrucian *Fama Fraternitatis* (News of the Fraternity) that Franckenberg had first encountered during his student days in Jena between 1613 and 1617, he exhorted König to focus on the chief work.[43] As vividly illustrated in Daniel Mögling's pseudonymous *Speculum sophicum rhodo-stauroticum* (Sophic Rosicrucian Mirror) of 1618, this took place in the *oratorium* and mostly consisted in prayer:[44]

> in sum, one should faithfully focus on the chief work (*Ergon*), which is to earnestly pray for the Holy Spirit, to seek the kingdom of God within oneself, and to knock at the door of life. Then the subordinate work (*Parergon*)—the light of nature, which receives its lustre from the light of grace, as the moon from the sun—will also be found in due course.[45]

Franckenberg reiterated this notion in the second letter. In addition, he stressed that König would have to embark on his own spiritual process without relying on 'artisanal habits, tools, or hands-on skills (*Handgriffen*), for these belong to the mechanical *parergon*, which only afterwards comes forth out of the main work and becomes manifest.'[46]

Since Franckenberg's letters to König survive because Seidenbecher copied them, there are tangible connections between them and the ones that the Thuringian traveller later addressed to his teacher. If Franckenberg prescribed daily devotions as an alchemical regimen to König, there is a closely related passage in one of Seidenbecher's letters. In it he described his religious edification in alchemical terms and alternately construed himself as the matter or the adept:

the philosophers' stone may be used by those who have it. For my part, as a beginner still, I work towards the stone of which Psalm 118, Isaiah 8 and 28, Daniel 2, and other passages treat. I am still in putrefaction. I have to pray daily: 'Mortify me through your goodness,' etc., and 'Break my will,' etc. This ought to be handled carefully, also industriously and diligently. It means a lot to me to be taught a spiritual artifice (*ein Geistlich Handgriefl.*) by you, in order to correctly direct the work. Yet everything depends on the grace of our Thrice-Greatest (του τρισμεγίστου): we have to seek it daily in humility and content ourselves with whatever is given us from above.[47]

As alchemical matter in God's furnace, Seidenbecher viewed himself as currently undergoing an early but most significant stage of the great work; as a novice in spiritual alchemy, he sought further instruction on how to successfully progress in it. On the whole, Seidenbecher's words appear very similar to Nagel's spiritual alchemy and its emphasis on daily prayer. His request for a new 'spiritual artifice' is particularly fascinating: in alchemical literature, the German word Seidenbecher used (*Handgriff*) commonly referred to the most practical instructions that could be difficult to communicate in writing. In the most literal sense, these moves would require hands-on dexterity. In a way, then, Seidenbecher was requesting spiritual exercises that were specifically alchemical (within the context of spiritual alchemy). Distancing himself from the adepts who possessed the *lapis* in ways reminiscent of Franckenberg's advice to König, Seidenbecher emphasised his spiritual rather than laboratory alchemy.

In addition, the young disciple exhibited familiarity with various tropes on the relation between alchemy and Christianity. He used the *lapis-Christus* analogy when describing his quest for the heavenly cornerstone and established a parallel between Hermes Trismegistus and Christ as the pioneers of laboratory and spiritual alchemy, respectively.[48] Seidenbecher played on Hermes' 'Thrice-Greatest' epithet, for which different explanations had been proposed. A century and a half earlier, for instance, the Florentine philosopher Marsilio Ficino had famously described Hermes as 'the greatest philosopher, and the greatest priest, and the greatest king.'[49] Franckenberg furnished a similar explanation to show that Christ equally deserved it: 'KING in the Resurrection: *Mem.* PRIEST in the Passion: *Shin.* PROPHET in the Institution: *Ḥet.*'[50] The three Hebrew letters form the root of the verb 'to anoint,' from which 'messiah' (*mashiaḥ*) is derived. While both Jesus and Hermes were kings and priests, they distinguished themselves through their third role: although alchemical literature also occasionally hailed Hermes as a prophet, he was much more commonly described as a leading philosopher.[51]

Having instructed König and, by the same token, Seidenbecher in the basics of his spiritual alchemy, Franckenberg also pointed them to literature through which they would be able to learn more. The Silesian mystic made the following recommendations:

> on this subject, one might also read Gerard Dorn's booklet out of Trithemius on the supersensible and supernatural magistery, as well as the *Wasserstein der Weysen* (which the Teutonic Jacob Boehme recommended in a letter to Valentin Thirnes [Tschirness], to be found with Mr Joachim Polemann) and other similarly foundational writings.[52]

At the time the Boehme epistle to which Franckenberg referred in his letter to König was only available in manuscript; its actual recipient had been the Striegau physician Jonas Daniel Koschwitz.[53] Although König's share of the epistolary exchange has been lost, it would seem that he expected more specific guidance on laboratory matters from Franckenberg: both he and Joachim Polemann, his son-in-law, who probably first introduced him to the Silesian nobleman, were skilled practitioners.[54] In this respect, they can be contrasted against Seidenbecher, who readily admitted his ignorance in laboratory alchemy but gradually became more familiar with alchemical literature, as Franckenberg requested information on the holdings of the ducal library at Gotha.[55] Not distracted by the subordinate work, the young disciple found it easier to grasp Franckenberg's spiritual alchemy as the main work.

Regarding further issues raised in an additional letter from König that arrived while Franckenberg was writing to him, the Silesian mystic indicated that more insights would be found in his own '*RaphaEL*, copied by Joachim Polemann, as well as J. B. T.'s treatise on rebirth and *Signatura rerum*, as well as in *The Way to Christ* and *On the Threefold Life*.'[56] Polemann thus emerges as an important collector of works by Boehme and Franckenberg in manuscript. More significantly, however, the very list itself (to which we might add the *Emerald Tablet*, attributed to Hermes Trismegistus, and the Rosicrucian manifestos) confirms how widely read Franckenberg had become by the late 1640s. Several of these texts and authors had not yet appeared in the *Conclusiones* or the *Theophrastia Valentiniana*. In addition, the strong presence of Boehme in Franckenberg's reading recommendations confirms that, specifically regarding spiritual alchemy, he continued to attribute great importance to the theosopher even more than two decades after he had composed the *Theophrastia Valentiniana*.

The Journey of Friedrich Gallus and the *Kabbalistic Regimen*

In addition to the two letters Franckenberg had written to König, Seidenbecher also copied several short texts with material on alchemy and other arcane subjects. Seidenbecher's biographer, Verpoorten, printed them under the header 'Other [Texts] Pertaining to the Rosicrucians,' presumably with the intention of showing to what questionable material—skirting the boundaries of credulity, superstition, and heterodoxy—Franckenberg had introduced the young Seidenbecher. Two among these merit closer scrutiny, the longest one, *Reise Frieder[ich] Galli* (The Journey of Friedrich Gallus), and the most cryptic one, *Reg[imen] Cabal[isticum]* (Kabbalistic Regimen). According to Seidenbecher's closing statement, he had copied the former text 'in the month of August 1649 out of A. V. F.'s manuscripts (which had been communicated to the same out of the very own handwritten itinerary of Friedrich Gallus in 1638).'[57] Franckenberg thus claimed familiarity with the work a decade before its first printed edition of 1648. Philological comparison has confirmed this: Didier Kahn holds that the version harking back to Seidenbecher's copy is more reliable than any other edition.[58] Since Johann Fabel in Amsterdam had published a number of works by the Silesian mystic since 1646, Franckenberg was most likely aware of the 1648 Gallus edition.[59] Yet the nobleman continued to prefer the manuscript over the print. This testifies to the importance Franckenberg attached to manuscripts and the practices surrounding them.

Indeed, it would seem that Franckenberg consciously used the medium of the handwritten page to promote Seidenbecher's spiritual progress. There were good reasons for doing so. On a more superficial level, Fabel's product (like Beyerland's Boehme editions) may not have met Franckenberg's high philological standard. Joachim Telle remarks that Franckenberg, for all his mystical aspirations, was also a keen philologist who greatly appreciated reliable texts.[60] At a deeper level, though, Franckenberg's decision to let Seidenbecher work with the manuscript might have had to do with the psychology of textual acquisition as well as the intensity of working with that medium. One of Franckenberg's closest friends, the Silesian courtier and poet Johann Theodor von Tschesch, explicitly stated that he copied texts from which he hoped to derive significant devotional benefit.[61] From his perspective as a teacher and spiritual guide, Franckenberg would have wanted to communicate certain materials in a way that would enhance their impact. His ownership of the source and the effort Seidenbecher had to invest in order to literally make the text his own would have greatly contributed to the importance and relevance it held for the disciple. Conversely, if Franckenberg had merely given him the print, it is conceivable that Seidenbecher might not even have found the time to read it. Considering how deeply Seidenbecher cared for his manuscripts, it is safe to assume that he would also have paid close attention to *The Journey of Friedrich Gallus* and the other texts Franckenberg had shared with him in Danzig. By recommending that his disciple copy *The Journey of Friedrich Gallus*, Franckenberg made sure that Seidenbecher would absorb its lessons.

As the title suggests, the text details Friedrich Gallus's quest for the philosophers' stone, which led him from Seidenbecher's native Thuringia across the Alps to what is now Italy. The German wayfarer finally found a true adept at a monastery near Trent. The scion of a noble family, Von Trautmannsdorf, he propagated a very high-minded ideal for the true alchemist: 'in sum, his entire life, whatever he does and does not do, is inclined towards God and righteousness.' Due to his strong iatrochemical focus, Trautmannsdorf held transmutational alchemists in contempt. 'Always remember this as a touchstone,' he admonished Gallus, 'those alchemists or supposed philosophers who wager whatever is given to them on the transmutation of metals build but golden mountains within heads, persuade, promise much, make expenses, demand to be published—these are false cheats.' They were the noisy alchemical charlatans who advertised their skills, whereas those who really had the tincture considered it less important than their right standing with God and kept quiet about it. Furthermore, the adept also posited two kinds of medicine, resembling Nagel's twofold *azoth*. 'For since God has prescribed medication for the soul through Christ,' Trautmannsdorf asked, 'would he not also provide the least thing for the body, that is, righteous medicine within nature, by which it [the body] could fend off accidents and turn away illnesses until the appointed time, which it cannot and may not transcend?'[62] The adept proved this point through his own extreme longevity: having met Gallus in 1602, he supposedly died in 1609, at the biblical age of 147 years.

Another notable text copied by Seidenbecher merits closer scrutiny, too: the *Kabbalistic Regimen*, an exceedingly cryptic piece of writing even by

Franckenberg's high standard of opacity. It begins by expressing the desire to transcend the binary division and quaternary matter of the four elements in order to return, by way of the ternary—the three principles but also the Trinity—'to the simplicity... of the divine monad.'[63] Since numbers figure so prominently in the *Kabbalistic Regimen*, Franckenberg's unprinted *Sephiriel* can shed light on the associations they carried for its author (see fig. 5.1). The number two was closely associated with separation from God and opposition generally: 'for whatever is split in two or divided... is an exit and departure from the ONE, as in divorce and opposition, through which discord is born in the reflection or counterpart.' Three, by contrast, was the number of the divine Trinity, surpassed only by one: 'the ONE or number ONE is not normally in and of itself a NUMBER, for it belongs to GOD who is not contained by any number.' Regarding the number four, Franckenberg wrote that it was 'the first physical number of the outward, worldly regime or natural, bodily ELement.'[64] Only by overcoming contrariety and the physical world through the Trinity would the believer be able to achieve the distinctly mystical goal of oneness with the divine.

In its use of challenging language and the ideas expressed through it, the *Kabbalistic Regimen* resonated with Franckenberg's angelic treatises *Sephiriel* and *Raphael*, as well as Gerard Dorn's *De spagirico artificio Jo. Trithemii sententia* (Johannes Trithemius' Theses on the Spagyric Art) and the circular engravings of Khunrath's *Amphitheatrum sapientiae aeternae*. At the very end of his *Raphael*, Franckenberg himself quoted remarkably similar statements from the pseudo-Paracelsian *Aurora philosophorum* (Dawn of the Philosophers), which Dorn had translated into Latin.[65] Prior to the Flemish alchemist, the English magus John Dee had also used similar language, and his *Monas hieroglyphica* of 1564 came to be widely read among alchemists.[66] Thus, there was ample precedent for Franckenberg's combination of alchemy and numerological mysticism.

Somewhat more accessibly, Franckenberg continued to extemporise on the same notion of mystical union in two German stanzas, playing on alchemical tropes and language. Like alchemists baffled by the simplicity of their work in theory and the immense difficulties they faced when putting it into practice, Franckenberg described the process of uniting with the One as 'a difficult and easy work' both at the same time. Once the One was attained, or once the 'temporal *One*' (*Ain*) was made 'an eternal 1,' it 'gives us all power on earth, / Even though the fool ridicules it.'[67] Franckenberg used the unusual spelling 'Ain' instead of 'Ein' in order to allude to its Hebrew meaning as

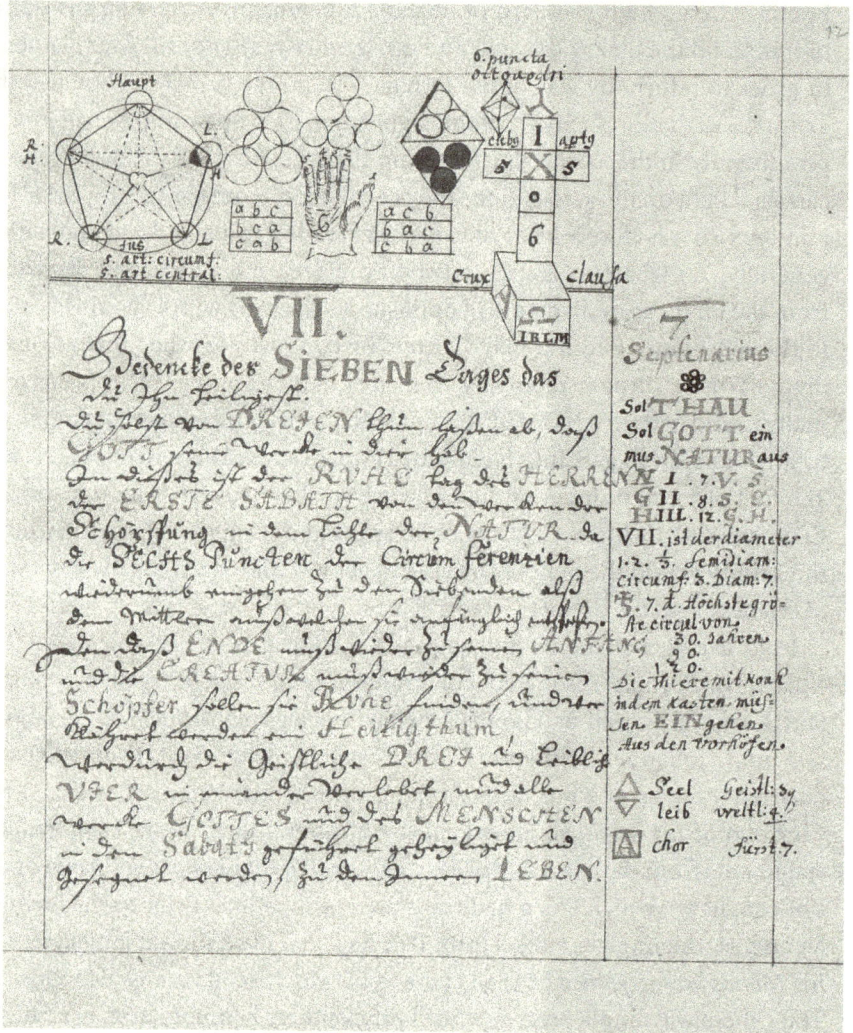

Fig. 5.1 Abraham von Franckenberg, *Saephiriel*. One of the most carefully executed *Sephiriel* manuscripts, this copy uses three different colours and contains elaborate marginalia and diagrams. Zurich, Zentralbibliothek: SCH R 809 (Bibliothek Oskar R. Schlag), f. 12r. © ZB Zurich, Digitalisierungszentrum.

a possible transliteration of the words *'ayin* (eye) or *'ayin* (nothing). With a different pronunciation, the latter formed part of the kabbalistic key term *'en soph* (without end). Franckenberg used this expression to furnish Boehme's *Ungrund* with the credentials of ancient wisdom.[68] This return to the One, to God in his primordial state, is a central topic of Franckenberg's mysticism as expressed subtly throughout *Sephiriel*.⁶⁹ As it bestows power on earth, the celestial stone that is attained in the process corresponds to Jesus and recalls the words of his Great Commission: 'all authority has been given to me in heaven and on earth.'⁷⁰ In discussions of the *lapis-Christus* analogy, not least in pseudo-Weigelian alchemy, the worldly rejection of Jesus as the cornerstone and the humble appearance of the philosophers' stone were frequently aligned.

Reverting to Latin, Franckenberg instructed Seidenbecher to perform an alchemical marriage. Alchemists spoke of marriage when they so thoroughly united two contrary substances that they could not (or hardly) be separated anymore. The prime example for this was the intimate union of sulphur and mercury in gold.⁷¹ According to Franckenberg, heaven and earth had to be joined together to form a single matter:

> MAKE
> Out of the celestial sea and the terrestrial feminine
> The CIRCLE of a simple BODY:
> Thence the kabbalistic quadrangle
> Of the four-elementary colours.⁷²

Franckenberg had also used the language of alchemical marriage and the union of opposites in his letter to Werdenhagen, dated 13 August 1637 and published as the final part of *Trias mystica*. In that context, the Silesian mystic wrote of 'that most holy and great MYSTERY and Sacrament of the MARRIAGE (of the sun and moon), . . . of THINGS divine and human, spiritual and corporeal, celestial and terrestrial.'⁷³ This suggested that the alchemical marriage of gold and silver was analogous to the unification of God and man, just as in Paul Nagel and Jacob Boehme.

Indeed, beyond alchemy, the ultimate exemplar for the union of opposites was Jesus Christ, the 'God-man' (Θεάνθρωπος) uniting within himself deity and humanity.⁷⁴ As already observed with regard to Johann Siebmacher, alchemical hermaphrodites could be viewed as reflecting this in the laboratory. Ultimately, it was Christ's example that believers had to emulate and re-enact. Already in the *Theophrastia Valentiniana*, Franckenberg had expressed this notion in unmistakably alchemical terms: 'this yoke, this syzygy is thus a great work, in which—by descent or distillation—the superior [things] flow into the inferior ones and—by ascent or sublimation—the inferior [things] rise up to the superior ones; and like a new birth, [they] sprout, flourish, grow, blossom in GOD's paradise.'⁷⁵ In a process analogous to alchemical weddings, then, believers had to attain 'the eternal con- and deiformity,' following the tracks of Christ's Incarnation in reverse: if God the Son had to become human, humans had to become god.⁷⁶

Although Franckenberg did mention the four elements, the four colours he had in mind here were not those usually associated with them but with the great work of alchemy. In this regard, the inclusion of black is telling. The Silesian nobleman first mentioned black (*nigra*), white (*alba*), and yellow (*citrina*), which he associated with body, spirit, and soul, respectively. As the context and progression indicate, he had in mind the alchemical colour stages *nigredo*, *albedo*, and *citrinitas*. Ultimately, these would culminate in the red stage, *rubedo*, strongly associated with the philosophers' stone: 'through the fiery Redness (*Rubedine*), once again the unchangeable gold of the most singular MONAD.' Franckenberg concluded: 'and you shall have the secret Light of the Philosophers: the most excellent MEDICINE for the corrupted intellect,' restoring this fallen capacity to its primordial state.⁷⁷ Not to be confused with our modern notion of intelligence, the term 'intellect' referred to a more elevated form of understanding that made meditation possible and could grasp matters divine, among other things.⁷⁸ In a way, this was Franckenberg's rather heady restatement of the *lapis-Christus* analogy between the highest medicine for the body and the soul: according to him, the Fall not only affected the body but, perhaps more importantly, also the spirit and the soul.⁷⁹ Only the heavenly cornerstone could cure the spiritual malaise of fallen humankind and allow it to commune with the divine.

Franckenberg's *Kabbalistic Regimen* was thus the description of a process of, or a recipe for, spiritual alchemy. This tied in with the way he associated kabbalah with the cure for the spirit throughout *Raphael*.⁸⁰ At the very end of the *Kabbalistic Regimen*, a table detailed its threefold aim:⁸¹

	True	G	is to be Known		the Blessing	of the ONE
Aim: The	Good	O	is to be Loved	B Y	the Knowledge	of the TRUTHFUL
	One	D	is to be Blessed		the Enactment	of the GOOD.

In a similar vein, a short text in two columns, titled *In Schola ☉rientali* (In the ☉riental School), listed a number of spiritual adepts, commonly known as patriarchs, prophets, and apostles throughout the Bible, and provided a general description: 'men, evidently, within God (*Enthei*) and contemplative: who were likewise resigned and crucified to the world; in denial and dead to themselves; dedicated to and buried in CHRIST; reborn and brought to life by the Spirit. Thus, skilled in mystical theology and harmonic philosophy, having left behind the dark prison of the body, they commended their illuminated soul to GOD.'[82] With these words, Franckenberg gave Seidenbecher an ideal to which he could aspire, and through their conversations and the manuscripts he shared with his disciple, he instructed him in the spiritual alchemy that would allow him to attain this goal himself.

In this way, during his final years, Franckenberg actively passed on his spiritual alchemy to Seidenbecher, thanks to whom several important sources survive. One of these is *The Journey of Friedrich Gallus* according to a copy Seidenbecher made in 1649, which is superior to other printed editions. The young traveller wrote it out by hand and, by the same token, absorbed its high-minded ideal of the alchemist and the corresponding moral lessons. In addition to this accessible story, Franckenberg had Seidenbecher copy an obscure text titled *Kabbalistic Regimen*, which turned out to be a veritable recipe for the aspiring spiritual alchemist. Perhaps it was in view of this very text that Seidenbecher requested further practical instructions that would allow him to mature beyond *nigredo*, the black stage in which he found himself. Seidenbecher's later works exhibit little concern with alchemy, yet we need to consider that his life was cut short. Both regarding longevity and spiritual alchemy, the same cannot be said of his associate Friedrich Breckling, to whom I shall now turn.

6
Friedrich Breckling, the 1682 Boehme Edition, and Spiritual Alchemy

After Abraham von Franckenberg's death, his disciple Georg Lorenz Seidenbecher spent the final decade of his life cultivating contacts with numerous religious dissenters. To a significant extent, the Silesian mystic had laid the foundation for his acolyte's network of heterodox associates. Facilitated by Franckenberg's letter of introduction, the encounter with Christoph Hirsch was exemplary in this regard. But during his travels upon leaving Danzig in 1649 and afterwards, Seidenbecher also made new acquaintances beyond those of the more sedentary Franckenberg. In the long term, these associates greatly contributed to Seidenbecher's millenarian convictions but also rendered his employment as a Lutheran minister precarious. Eventually, it was the heterodox anticipation of the millennium that brought him into contact with the young Friedrich Breckling, who had been merely twenty-three years old when Franckenberg passed away in 1652. Although only a handful of Seidenbecher's letters to Breckling survive, they corresponded, exchanged ideas on millenarianism, and even met in person repeatedly. This chapter begins by probing their acquaintance and shared convictions.

Over recent years, there has been great interest in Breckling, an exiled networker among religious dissenters, and several scholars have engaged with his papers, preserved mostly in Gotha.[1] While Paul Estié has meticulously researched Breckling's years in Zwolle from 1660 to 1672 and Guido Naschert has vividly portrayed his time in The Hague from 1690 to 1711, we know little about Breckling's long residence in Amsterdam during the intervening years.[2] This thriving city was the leading centre of the book trade at the time.[3] Breckling's livelihood depended on the publishing business: he worked as a proofreader and took a very active role in disseminating heterodox literature in print. Particularly the way Breckling included Boehme's complete works—alongside a number of his own writings—in a chronological account of his life suggests that he may have contributed to the project in some capacity.

Spiritual Alchemy. Mike A. Zuber, Oxford University Press. © Oxford University Press 2021.
DOI: 10.1093/oso/9780190073046.003.0007

Immediately afterwards, Breckling published two short treatises with promising titles: *Christus mysticus, sol et sal sapientiae* (The Mystical Christ, Sun and Salt of Wisdom) and *Pseudosophia mundi* (The Fake Wisdom of the World). Both of these pamphlets were published in 1682, just like Boehme's complete works. In a concise, condensed manner, Breckling used these two works to outline his spiritual alchemy.

The Shared Millenarianism of Seidenbecher and Breckling

Seidenbecher and Breckling had a significant number of mutual acquaintances, such as the controversial preacher and writer Joachim Betke and the virtually forgotten school teacher Johann Sarnov of Hamburg.[4] In later life, Breckling recalled that his studies had taken him to Hamburg in 1654, 'to consult the beautiful library there.'[5] In the Hanseatic trading city, he first seriously engaged with various religious dissenters, including Sarnov, 'who set me straight through the writings of Tauler, Joachim Betke, and Christian Hoburg.'[6] Seidenbecher and Breckling also had shared contacts in the circle of the ageing prophet Ludwig Friedrich Gifftheil. Breckling had temporarily joined him in Amsterdam during his travels in 1656. This encounter with Gifftheil, facilitated by the publisher Heinrich Betke, would prove defining for much of Breckling's later life. Indeed, he often looked back to the days or weeks he had spent with Gifftheil, who became his role model in a spiritual mentorship. The encounter with Gifftheil in Amsterdam was to Breckling's life what the one with Franckenberg in Danzig had been for Seidenbecher. In Gifftheil, 'an old confessor and faithful witness of the truth,' Breckling found 'the true, living word and oracle of God,' as he 'had come to know it from the prophets and longed to find it again.'[7] Gifftheil must have been an awe-inspiring figure, with an aura of prophetic grandeur.

Even after Franckenberg had distanced himself from Gifftheil, he saw him in a vision. Franckenberg later related this experience to Seidenbecher as they talked about biblical patriarchs and prophets.[8] From 1649 onwards, Seidenbecher was therefore aware of the controversial prophet. Although it is unclear whether Seidenbecher ever personally met Gifftheil, one of the prophet's associates later facilitated Seidenbecher's contact with Breckling. Seidenbecher's first extant letter to Breckling dates from 16 November 1660. After his sojourn in Holland during 1656, Breckling returned to his parents in Danish-ruled Handewitt, where he succeeded his father as the local minister following a stint as army chaplain. The young firebrand quickly alienated his ecclesiastical superiors and was forced to flee his native town in March 1660. He initially found refuge in Amsterdam but transitioned to Zwolle as a minister before the year ended.[9] It was probably there that Seidenbecher's letter eventually found him. The missive began by mentioning that Johann Friedrich Münster, Gifftheil's faithful amanuensis, had passed on Breckling's greetings as well as 'the booklet *Truth's Triumph* (*Veritatis triumphus*), by which I sufficiently grasp your special affection towards me and that we are of one mind in Christ.'[10] Based on one of Breckling's early publications sent to him as a gift, Seidenbecher noted that they shared the same understanding of Christianity.

From that time onwards, Seidenbecher and Breckling corresponded until the former's death on 30 August 1663. The last of Seidenbecher's five extant letters dated from the first day of that month.[11] As Breckling soon ministered to the Lutheran congregation of Kampen as well as that of Zwolle, his correspondence with Seidenbecher lapsed for a relatively long time.[12] A little less than two years later, having been removed from office towards the end of 1661, Seidenbecher travelled to the Low Countries from 24 April to 26 June 1662 (Old Style). He visited Breckling in Zwolle on the way to Holland as well as on the way home.[13] During Seidenbecher's two sojourns in Zwolle, he and Breckling likely discussed millenarianism and perhaps alchemy. At the very least, we know that Breckling gave his visitor a letter intended for Nicolaus Stumm, a chymist in Erfurt.[14] The vagaries of the ministry would also have loomed large in their conversations. Having been forced into exile himself, Breckling would have been a sympathetic listener who had gone through turmoil similar to that of Seidenbecher. More trouble was already looming for Breckling: the Lutheran consistory of Amsterdam, the most powerful in the Low Countries, had opposed his appointment and sought to counteract him at every turn.[15]

Despite the limited number of letters Breckling received from Seidenbecher, he attached great importance to their epistolary contact. A volume of correspondence addressed to Breckling contains not only the original of Seidenbecher's letter dated 10 November 1662 but also two copies of it.[16] Responding to Breckling's intention to write a millenarian treatise, Seidenbecher encouraged him to do so but also urged him to discuss the matter with Petrus Serrarius, the son of Walloon refugees, in Amsterdam, so they could all put up a unified front.[17] Privately, as his own letter to Serrarius shows, Seidenbecher was hedging his bets: 'I learnt that Breckling wanted to author a certain public writing, on the glorious mystery of the reign of Christ on earth. It remains to be seen whether he embarks on the right path, because the mind of men is prone to go astray in such matters.'[18] Subsequently, Breckling must have asked for clarification on Seidenbecher's own approach, prompting the latter to include a lengthy passage on millenarianism in the following letter dated 10 May 1663. Seidenbecher briefly summarised the eight arguments with which he supported his millenarian conviction. Breckling promptly seized upon these for his *Christus iudex* (Christ the Judge), published the same year, quoting Seidenbecher's introductory formulations in sequence and, for the most part, word for word.[19] Seidenbecher thus played an important role in cultivating Breckling's millenarian views, which he was to profess until his dying day almost half a century later.[20] Seidenbecher's untimely death meant that the seeds of spiritual alchemy Franckenberg had imparted to his disciple failed to germinate. Eventually, the kindred spirit of Breckling took Seidenbecher's place in this regard.

Long before that came to pass in the 1680s, Gifftheil's influence made itself felt. It was particularly the hospitality the prophet extended to those who had become poor for the sake of Christ that inspired Breckling until his death in 1711.[21] As the minister of Zwolle developed a reputation for hospitality in the 1660s, his parsonage came to be home to a significant number of young men, all of them exiled, removed from office, or both: early in 1667, Breckling listed no fewer than six of them by name. Their sheer number greatly contributed to the scandal that erupted when the minister decided to also take in a young woman, who experienced visions and whose parents were no longer able to provide for her: Elisabeth Crouse, aged twenty-four.[22] To remove all grounds for suspicion that anything untoward was taking place at the minister's house, Breckling decided to marry Elisabeth. On 8 February 1667, just after the minister had publicly announced this intention (and turned thirty-nine), his former maidservant, Anna Schutten, claimed that he had previously promised to marry her.[23] Furthermore, she asserted that he had entertained sexual relations with her. Though Breckling denied intercourse, he reluctantly admitted to sleeping in the same bed and touching Anna once. Opponents then spread the scandalous rumour that these encounters had taken place within the church, and more specifically on the communion table. Numerous female churchgoers promptly refused to receive the Eucharist from Breckling's sullied hands. He married Elisabeth despite the backlash. Even after he was forced out of his ministry, he remained in Zwolle for several years and only left for Amsterdam in mid-1672.

In 1667, around the time Breckling married Elisabeth and lost his ministry, one among his roommates was Johann Georg Gichtel, who would later be involved with the publication of the 1682 edition of Boehme's complete works.[24] After he had been imprisoned at Nuremberg for his outspoken activism, this trained lawyer found refuge at Breckling's home in Zwolle. In a letter he wrote to Breckling on 2 February 1660, before his final departure from his native Regensburg, Gichtel expressed nothing but admiration and fraternal love for the exiled minister.[25] Yet before the 1660s were over, their relationship had soured. Throughout his life, Gichtel fervently opposed marriage as a matter of principle. Breckling had expressed similar views earlier, yet he never attached the same importance to celibacy as his former *protégé*.[26] Rather than making exceptions for his friends, Gichtel tended to view their getting married as personal betrayals and chastised Breckling for his decision, just as he would famously criticise Gottfried Arnold decades later. In one of the few surviving letters he wrote to Breckling, sent from Amsterdam to Zwolle on 4 September 1669, Gichtel—a misogynist even by the low standards of his day—cast aspersions on Elisabeth's character and denied her the authority to prophesy publicly.[27] The formerly close, even cordial relationship between Breckling and Gichtel thus gave way to a strained and conflicted one that would yet continue for decades as they lived in Amsterdam as neighbours.

The Boehme Edition as a Collaborative Project

During the early 1680s, the first complete edition of Boehme's works inspired Breckling's spiritual alchemy. It was a project that thrived on the efforts of numerous contributors, though most of them have largely been forgotten. Indeed, it is a common assumption that Gichtel more or less singlehandedly saw the Boehme edition through the press. This view reflects the manner in which the former lawyer and his disciples portrayed the events after they had fallen out with their erstwhile allies, whom they effectively consigned to oblivion.[28] For a long time, consequently, scholarship only remembered Gichtel and paid scant attention to any other potential coworkers. By drawing attention to them and Breckling's possible involvement, I argue that it is highly unlikely that Gichtel was solely responsible for this massive project: in fact, he was merely one collaborator among others, likely with a comparatively minor role, even though he did negotiate with the printers.[29] Breckling played an important part in the events leading up to this accomplishment: despite the fact that they were no longer close, he introduced Gichtel to a circle of Dutch friends who discovered Boehme for themselves around 1680. They subsequently acquired the most important collection of the theosopher's works in manuscript and saw to the publication of his oeuvre. Gichtel and Breckling were both part of close-knit circles of religious dissenters in Holland, particularly active during the last third of the seventeenth century.

Back when Gichtel first moved to Amsterdam in March 1668, there was not the slightest hint that he would eventually become known as a leading authority on Jacob Boehme. A telling episode early on in Gichtel's long residence in Amsterdam shows his lack of interest in the theosopher and his writings at the time. Down on his luck and flat broke, Gichtel experienced God's provision through various unexpected gifts. The most consequential of these involved Benedict Bahnsen, a German mathematician and bibliophile. Increasingly lonely towards the end of his life, he had formerly been well-connected among religious dissenters; his associates included both Seidenbecher and Breckling.[30] Now he offered to use his remaining contacts to get Gichtel a job as a translator and corrector at the famous Blaeu publishing firm. The exiled lawyer declined, preferring to await God's guidance.[31] In 1669, not too long after meeting Gichtel, Bahnsen fell ill, sent for the younger man, entreated him to ensure a decent burial, and named him 'heir over his books and household.' Soon afterwards, upon Bahnsen's death, the destitute exile thus became the owner of a wealth of choice books.

On this occasion, the lofty contemplative acted rather like a savvy businessman and auctioned off the collection at the first opportunity: he 'compiled a catalogue of the books' of Bahnsen's library 'and sent it abroad' in preparation for the auction that was to take place on 9 April 1670. Gichtel's clever strategy generated many bids and fetched high prices for books that 'could well have been bought at the flea-market' for small change.[32] Bahnsen's library was catalogued and auctioned jointly with books formerly owned by Petrus Serrarius; it remains unclear why. The sole surviving copy of the catalogue is incorrectly bound; restored to proper order, Bahnsen's collection emerges as the much more significant of the two.[33] While Dietrich Hakelberg and others have recently discussed the printed books listed in the catalogue, Bahnsen's manuscript collection merits a few remarks here.[34] It encompassed particularly rare items, including several manuscripts with texts by Boehme and Franckenberg as well as a copy of pseudo-Weigel's *Azoth and Fire*. Unfortunately, the current whereabouts of these important documents remain unknown. The point here is that Gichtel did not care much for Boehme manuscripts in 1669 and was anything but poised to become the theosopher's self-proclaimed heir and successor.

The train of events through which Gichtel gradually discovered the role for which he was to become famous began several years later. In 1674 Breckling facilitated Gichtel's encounter with the Dutch theologian Alhardt de Raadt, formerly professor at Leiden and then Harderwijk.[35] Gichtel's 1722 biography vividly described the scene with the hindsight of half a century. Back in March 1674, the rich Dutch millenarian Johannes Rothé had marched on Hamburg to conquer it in the same way Joshua had captured Jericho.[36] Most of Rothé's faithful and he himself were arrested, yet De Raadt escaped prison and quickly returned to Amsterdam. Bitterly disillusioned that the millennial rule of Christ on earth had failed to materialise, he visited Breckling and noticed an unbound treatise lying around. De Raadt leafed through it, 'and his devastated spirit found nourishment.'[37] He asked Breckling where the author might be found. After momentary confusion, Breckling realised that De Raadt was asking for Gichtel. Breckling and Gichtel were no longer on cordial terms but also unable to avoid each other: for most of the 1670s, they were basically neighbours on an Amsterdam canal, the Egelantiersgracht: Gichtel lived 'in the Elephant, on the southern side,' and Breckling lived at the house of the printer Christoffel Cunradus, for whom he also worked as a proofreader. Breckling sent his almost four-year-old son, Johann Friedrich Immanuel, to guide De Raadt to Gichtel's abode.[38]

The friendship between Alhardt de Raadt and Gichtel that formed after this first encounter was very close for a decade. Its rupture in 1684 rattled the German lawyer: until his dying day, Gichtel's letters frequently alluded to this ultimate betrayal, as he viewed it. Yet there were no signs of conflict in 1680, when De Raadt and his Dutch friends precipitated Gichtel's familiarity with Boehme. This year saw Willem Gozewijn Huygens, mayor of Arnhem and a close friend of De Raadt from the 1660s onwards, purchase the Beyerland collection of Boehme manuscripts, some of which had formerly been owned by Franckenberg. To pay for them, Huygens used funds left by his sister, Louise, who had joined the sect of the Labadists and died in their community at Wieuwerd in Frisia on 30 January 1680.[39] The younger Johannes Goethals, who would later inherit the collection of Boehme manuscripts, was the third member of their circle. Gichtel's biography relates that his 'fellow brethren,' meaning De Raadt, Huygens, and Goethals, 'became interested in the writings of Jacob Boehme and, at first sight, gained considerable understanding of them, while he [Gichtel] himself was not yet deeply grounded in them.'[40] This passage comes close to an admission of ignorance on Gichtel's part and attributes agency to these fellow brethren even as the biography is notoriously reluctant to name them in positive contexts. De Raadt and particularly Huygens were instrumental in acquiring Beyerland's collection of Boehme manuscripts, and it was only due to Breckling's introduction that Gichtel had become involved with them.

Gichtel was embedded in a network of friends and allies, and the Boehme edition was very much a large-scale project only conceivable in such an environment. Yet Gichtel's biography basically attributed the monumental effort of editing Boehme's works to him alone, only to note 'the deep foundation of the unity' between Gichtel and De Raadt in the following paragraph.[41] An early letter by Gichtel, dated 1 September 1681, appears more honest in this regard: 'we are currently busy with Boehme's works (which have all been revised according to the manuscripts, purified of a great many glaring errors).'[42] The use of the first-person plural and the passive voice is telling: clearly Gichtel by himself would have been unable to complete this monumental project in such a short time. In this context, we should also note that the exiled lawyer eschewed work in all its forms: he viewed labour as punishment for the Fall, which no longer afflicted regenerate believers, and supported himself through the donations of wealthy correspondents.[43] Moreover, Gichtel quite obviously tried to take the credit for someone else's work in another case more than a decade later: he falsely claimed to have translated the writings of the widowed English prophetess Jane Leade into German.[44] This grand effort was unambiguously that of Loth Fischer, another German exile who had found refuge in Holland. Shirking efforts at all costs, Gichtel instead adorned himself with borrowed plumes.

In view of Gichtel's stance regarding work and his unfounded claim regarding the Leade translations, we should be wary of ascribing too much credit to him when it comes to the Boehme project. The more sophisticated accounts in scholarship acknowledge that he would have been but one among quite a number of collaborators.[45] Indeed, Frank van Lamoen has suggested that De Raadt was, at the very least, responsible for part of the actual philological work on the Boehme edition of 1682.[46] Some of the other known collaborators were Johannes Goethals, Willem Gozewijn Huygens, Gichtel's roommate Georg Christian Fuchs, and the calligrapher Michael

Andreae, who contributed the designs of the twenty-two popular engraved frontispieces.[47] Incidentally, the first tensions with the Dutch theologian De Raadt occurred during this time: while the collaborators were discussing issues surrounding the printing of Boehme's works, 'Satan drove into De Raadt.'[48] The former professor's very presence during this meeting shows that he was intimately involved with the project. Johann Wilhelm Überfeld, who would become Gichtel's favoured disciple, later consigned the Dutch theologian to divine punishment: 'the editors (*Editores*) of both prints (*Drucken*) of 1682 and 1715,' by which he presumably meant De Raadt and the Hamburg scholar Johann Otto Glüsing, 'had been found to be evil before God, and therefore they had to die in their sins.'[49] Überfeld would never have said such things about Gichtel. We can only guess what kinds of disagreements among the collaborators led to such enduring enmity, yet it should now be clear that Gichtel's role in publishing the 1682 edition was a minor one.

The partisan accounts of the Gichtelians not only amounted to a *damnatio memoriae*, they also obscured the fact that there were important role models in Gichtel's life before he found his niche as Boehme's self-proclaimed heir and interpreter. His biography routinely presented him as a charismatic leader, helping poor associates—spiritually or, more commonly, financially—who then became his pliable disciples. In important ways, Gichtel thus appropriated the strategy of Gifftheil and Breckling, while seeking to introduce a significant trade-off between material support and spiritual submission. In this vein, Gichtel referred to Michael Andreae as 'my first poor companion here' in Holland, and Gichtel's biography relates in detail how he extended financial support to Andreae.[50] However, if we consider this account critically, we might question why even a former professor of theology, such as De Raadt, or an elder religious dissenter who owned and produced precious manuscripts, like Andreae, should bow to the guidance of Gichtel. Read in this light, there are hints in Gichtel's biography that specifically the virtually forgotten Andreae proved an important rival. Fuchs, one of the collaborators who roomed with Gichtel, reconciled with the exiled lawyer on his deathbed, and their disagreement was attributed to the fact that Fuchs had 'cleaved to Michael Andreae.'[51] The Gichtelians equally blamed De Raadt's estrangement on Andreae, 'who had promised him the *lapis philosophorum*.'[52] Arguably, both De Raadt and Andreae would have been commanding and charismatic figures in their own right, and Gichtel's differences with them may have been grounded in their very reluctance to accept his authority—or his to accept theirs. Überfeld and his associates—who collectively became known as the

Angelic Brethren—retrospectively portrayed Gichtel as Boehme's sole legitimate heir and glossed over many former friends and enemies who considerably complicate that image. Much research remains to be done on the tangled and conflicted networks of so-called Boehmists in the Low Countries.

In addition to De Raadt and Michael Andreae, Breckling himself was yet another competitor in this struggle for dominance among Boehme enthusiasts. In a manuscript passage written around 18 November 1684, the obscure chymical practitioner Peter Moritz claimed that 'F. B. [Friedrich Breckling] . . . appoints himself pope of the Boehmists.'[53] It was perhaps in this context of a struggle for priority that Breckling's later autobiographical documents claimed that he had first encountered both alchemy and the writings of Jacob Boehme during his student days in Gießen back in the early 1650s. He credited professor of medicine Johann Tackius with having introduced him to both.[54] Yet for almost thirty years the seeds of Breckling's interest in alchemy and theosophy lay dormant, only to bud and bear fruit as Boehme's complete works went to press in Amsterdam. All things considered, it seems that Breckling overstated his case when he backdated his engagement with both Boehme and alchemy.

Written in or before 1688, Gichtel's disparaging letter on the subject of Breckling's *Anticalovius*, a controversial defence of Boehme probably first composed around 1685, also indicates deeply felt rivalry.[55] As a corrector working for Cunradus, Breckling could well have become intimately acquainted with Boehme's writings several years prior to Gichtel and his Dutch friends: after all, Cunradus printed eleven Boehme titles between 1676 and 1678 alone.[56] Also known under the Dutch name Hendrick Beets, Heinrich Betke—a friend of Breckling's who had introduced him to Gifftheil back in 1656—financed this impressive string of publications.[57] In fact, through their many Boehme editions going back to the 1660s, Betke and Cunradus provided important groundwork for the complete works of 1682. In 1678, the second edition of the *Mysterium magnum* was the crowning achievement of their collaboration. Unlike the corrupt first edition, this one was based on the personal copy of Franckenberg, who had carefully compared it to Boehme's autograph.[58] This is crucial, because it means that both Betke and Cunradus, and possibly Breckling as well, had access to the Beyerland collection before Huygens purchased it in 1680. Indeed, during those very years Breckling was living at Cunradus' house, and a catalogue of projected writings he published in 1678 already contains possible allusions to Boehme and his writings.[59] Among all the people closely connected to this network, Gichtel may have been among the very last to take an active interest in Boehme and his manuscript writings.

Breckling's *Christus Mysticus* and *Pseudosophia Mundi*

For the year 1682, Breckling's chronological account of his own life records that he had 'printed the writings of Jacob Boehme' (*gedrücket Jacob Boemen Schrifften*) and a string of publications authored by himself.[60] Breckling most commonly used this wording for his own output. This renders it quite remarkable that he mentioned Boehme's complete works in the same breath as a whole list of his writings—among his yearly accomplishments, as it were. For 1686 he also used the same phrase for Bartholomaeus Sclei's *Theosophische-Schrifften*, in which project he was to play an important role. The precise nature of Breckling's involvement with the Boehme edition remains unknown, yet there was clearly no shortage of pages that needed to be proofread as the theosopher's copious writings went to press. Simultaneously, Breckling showed himself well-acquainted with Boehme's theosophy from 1682 onwards. Some of the earliest dated proofs of Breckling's familiarity with Boehme can be found in the very same treatises that outline his spiritual alchemy: *Christus mysticus, sol et sal Sapientiae* and *Pseudosophia mundi*, both published in 1682. The theosopher appeared in both texts: *Christus mysticus* listed him as 'Teutonicus' among a whole range of near-contemporaneous prophets, and the *Pseudosophia* discussed the three principles according to Boehme's writings.[61] For Breckling, exposure to the theosopher of Görlitz appears to have finally quickened the seed of interest in natural philosophy and alchemy or chymistry allegedly planted by Tackius almost thirty years earlier.

If Breckling thus succeeded in earning more than he usually did thanks to his work on the Boehme edition, he immediately financed a string of his own publications. In 1681, he had two treatises printed together for 12 *Reichsthaler*, and many more titles followed throughout the following year.[62] Due to a chronic shortage of funds, Breckling used paper sparingly both when writing and printing: his chief publishing strategy consisted in cramming the greatest amount of small type onto as little paper as possible, and he employed a parallel approach in most of his autograph manuscripts (see fig. 6.1). Despite their humble appearance, then, his octavo treatises—many of them printed on a single sheet or sixteen pages only—contained tolerably

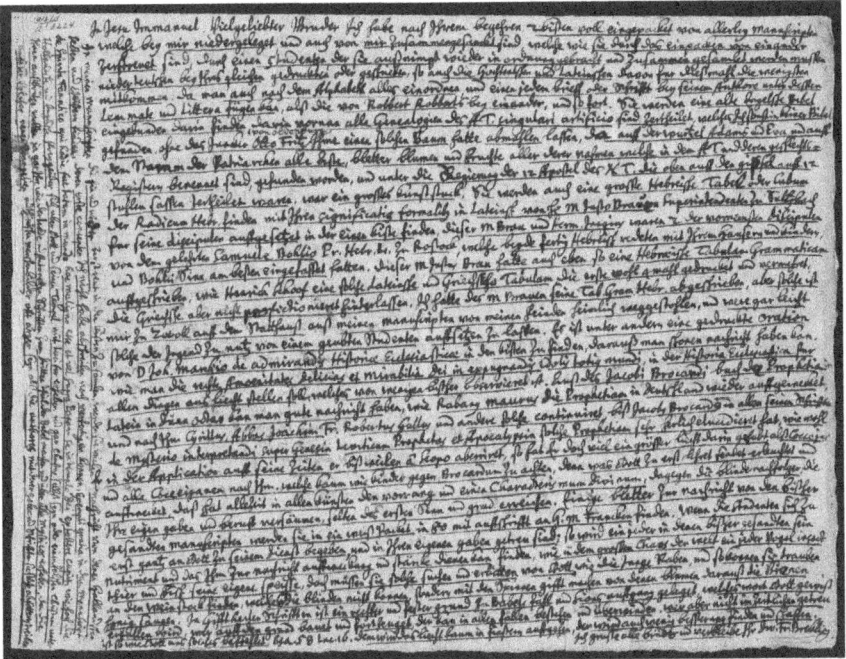

Fig. 6.1 Friedrich Breckling, undated autograph letter. Breckling typically sought to fill every last piece of blank space of paper with his minute hand. In this letter he announced that he had sent 'two crates full… of all sorts of manuscripts,' accompanied by a user manual on how to reassemble them in a separate package 'addressed to Mr Francke MA.' On the back, Breckling wrote 'your orphanage,' making it highly likely that the famous August Hermann Francke himself was his addressee. The Hague, Koninklijke Bibliotheek—National Library of the Netherlands: 72 E 14, unpaginated. © KB Beeldstudio.

long sermons and diatribes. Due to Breckling's scandalous past and controversial views, most of his publications appeared without a publisher's or printer's imprint. Apparently, he often worked with his long-term landlord and employer, Christoffel Cunradus, whose productions contributed significantly to the deluge of heterodox German literature printed at Amsterdam throughout the seventeenth century.[63] Furthered by shared views on religion, Breckling's collaboration with Cunradus began in 1660 and extended beyond his death in 1684 to the involvement of his widow in later projects.[64] It seems reasonable to assume that Breckling self-published and that Cunradus was the printer of most of his works.

Already the packed title pages of Breckling's *Christus mysticus, sol et sal sapientiae* and *Pseudosophia mundi* contain a striking mixture of mystical and alchemical language. Redolent with scriptural allusions, the 'mystical Christ' portrayed as 'the sun and salt of wisdom' had a distinctly alchemical ring.[65] In a firmly entrenched correspondence, the sun stood for gold, and salt was one of the three Paracelsian principles. This mystical Christ was 'inviting all mystics and the greatest theologians, philosophers, adepts, magi, and pansophers' to accomplish distinctly alchemical goals: 'so that the highest would be conjoined to the least and so that, through the true and mystical path, the volatile would become fixed and the fixed volatile; and thus the work of God, begun on earth, would be completed, for the glorious exaltation of the only God and the truly infinite multiplication of the faithful.' The language used here is saturated with alchemical terms, though these are also playfully reinterpreted, for instance when 'exaltation' (sublimating or purifying a substance) comes to refer to the adoration of God and 'multiplication' (increasing the potency of the tincture) to the spread of the Gospel.[66] Breckling's spiritual alchemy thus involved a practice of worship that simultaneously exalted God and the believer, and the limbs of Christ's body on earth multiplied as the divine tincture did its work.

Probably the earlier treatise of the two, *Christus mysticus* ends with a section that contains much spiritual alchemy in its few pages. Appropriately, it is titled 'The Mystical Path (*Via Mystica*) beyond the veil and to the hidden treasures of wisdom, opened and made level for the mystics and magi, so that the stone and mystical tincture (*Lapis et Tinctura Mystica*) could be revealed to them.'[67] By taking up key statements and phrases from 'The Mystical Path,' the *Pseudosophia* essentially picks up the thread where the shorter text left off. The exhortation to 'seek God more than gold,' for instance, appears on the final page of *Christus mysticus* and again in the *Pseudosophia mundi*.[68] The second treatise seeks to overthrow the false learning of the world and to replace it with 'true theosophy' and promised to outline 'the true path to the Christian, universal, internal, and central pansophy.' Among its various other stated aims, we find the following two, couched in alchemical language: 'so that . . . the tree of life, the panacea, the stone and universal, mystical tincture would evangelise everyone . . . and all adepts, magi, and theosophers would be invited to the communion of everyone with Christ and his mystical members and poor from heaven.'[69] Through spiritual alchemy, Breckling held, believers would become part of the body of Christ.

The exiled networker began 'The Mystical Path' in *Christus mysticus* with an appeal to several alchemical authors. These included Heinrich Khunrath and the English physician Robert Fludd, both of whom were famous for lavishly illustrated tomes of arcane lore. Breckling emphasised that such authorities all attributed crucial importance to self-knowledge: to the extent that 'we deeply know and enter into ourselves and are unlocked, to the same extent we will also perceive and unlock all the hidden mysteries, treasures, and powers of Holy Writ, nature, and all creatures.' Breckling here paraphrased a passage in Robert Fludd's 'beautiful' *Clavis philosophiae et alchymiae* (Key of Philosophy and Alchemy) of 1633.[70] Yet the English would-be Rosicrucian had put it precisely the other way around: 'Geber,' an authoritative writer commonly believed at the time to be an Arabic alchemist, 'teaches that someone cannot attain to the perfection of true chymistry unless he first recognises its principles within himself.'[71] Intimately familiar with the heterodox literature of the seventeenth century and cursorily acquainted with alchemical writers, Breckling drew attention to a shared trait: both featured numerous exhortations along the lines of 'Know thyself.' Johann Siebmacher's *Introductio hominis* was, in effect, an extended meditation on this subject. Breckling's approving reference to Fludd's *Clavis* is important: according to Hereward Tilton, it is here that 'the phrase "spiritual alchemy" itself . . . occurs in an esoteric context' for the very first time.[72] Indeed, Fludd used the Latin *alchymia spiritualis* at least twice, one of which instances is on the very same page as that quoted by Breckling.[73] Fludd's *Clavis* thus contained an extended passage on 'spiritual alchemy' that Breckling must have read. It is therefore no coincidence that he included Fludd in a list of 'witnesses of the truth among physicians and chymists.'[74] As there is little reason to believe that the Englishman would have known Boehme's writings by the early 1630s, Fludd's example shows that it was possible to independently arrive at very similar notions of spiritual alchemy.

The aim of Breckling's own spiritual alchemy was for the believer to become a mystical adept. But to achieve this, the believer first needed to undergo transmutation. Rather than the *parergon* of laboratory alchemy, Breckling emphasised the *ergon* of spiritual alchemy in strictly mystical terms and alluded to the three paths of *purificatio*, *illuminatio*, and *unio*: 'first and above all things, see to it that—through the path of purification, illumination, and union . . . you may be transmuted into pure gold in Christ and renewed, so that you could in turn prepare, perfect, and tinge others with the tincture of light, by which you were first transformed and deified.'

Once mystical union and spiritual transmutation had been attained, deified believers would be able to transmute others. In this regard, they could be construed as spiritual adepts or 'living stones,' as opposed to 'the rich of this world' and fraudulent 'alchemists, sellers of processes, and dead stones.'[75]

Only through knowing one's own self, mystically reliving Christ's Passion, and enduring the abuse of the world could this state of deification be attained. The spiritual adepts 'first let themselves be prepared, purified, tinged, and united with Christ, before they search the tincture towards the perfection of metals beyond themselves, thus learning the correct process as it applies to themselves and Christ's process on the cross—suffering, dying, and rising in him.'[76] In terms reminiscent of Boehme's *Signatura rerum*, Breckling described Christ's Passion itself as chymical:

> those who will yet lose themselves and wholly surrender to Christ's chymical process of the cross, they will yet find much more eye ointment and purified gold with Christ than with all physicians and philosophers, by which they may be renewed, fixed, and tinged so that they would withstand the great judgements by fire that are impending and, like a fixed tincture, endure all trials by fire, in which the world with its pharisees, sophists, and alchemists must waste away and be devoured.[77]

Breckling had in mind a passage from Paul's First Epistle to the Corinthians, which described how worldly works would be burnt but godly works would withstand God's fire.[78] Having become fixed tinctures at the end of the great work of spiritual alchemy, true believers would prove themselves when assayed; they would not be found wanting during the Last Judgement.

Once the *ergon* had been completed, the *parergon* would follow as a matter of course. Recalling a common trope often repeated in alchemical literature, these spiritual adepts would then use the philosophers' stone to alleviate the plights of their neighbours. Having entered into 'this imitation of Christ, when they ask God for the *lapis* as support and medication for their poor brethren and elaborate it, they use it to this end in a Christian and careful manner.'[79] For a true spiritual chymist or adept, the philosophers' stone of laboratory alchemy was not much more than a nice extra. There is much that sounds familiar here, and Breckling sometimes lucidly distilled into a single passage what had remained mostly implicit in authors like Abraham von Franckenberg. At the same time Breckling considerably expanded spiritual alchemy to also encompass ecclesiology: rather than describing the spiritual resurrection body, he was more concerned with the invisible church of the true believers as Christ's 'spiritual body'.[80] Yet in view of the Lutheran doctrine of Christ's ubiquitous body, we can assume that Breckling took this literally rather than figuratively, in keeping with spiritual alchemy proper.

In addition, Breckling viewed false teachers as fraudulent alchemists, extending analogies in a negative direction. Indeed, Breckling frequently employed the term 'alchemists' (*Alchymisten*) with distinctly negative associations, contrasting them against adepts and chymists (*Chymici*). A similar distinction already occurred in Siebmacher's *Wasserstein*, a work Breckling knew well.[81] Yet unlike Siebmacher, who had in mind actual frauds pretending mastery of laboratory alchemy, the former minister extrapolated the common differentiation between fraudulent charlatans and true alchemists with great insights in natural philosophy from the realm of laboratory alchemy to spiritual alchemy. In no uncertain terms, he expressed his wish 'that the spirit of Christ and Elijah would drive all the false goldmakers, calf-servants' worshipping Aaron's golden idol, 'sellers of processes, peddlers of absolution, comforters of Adam'—the old, unredeemed human, as opposed to the new birth—'theolongians,' who appear tall but lack God's word, 'sophists, simonists, and servants of Babel-Baal-book-letters and [their own] belly from the temple of God and nature with Christ's sword and whip'.[82] This reflected two closely related core elements of his theology and practice: his scathing criticism of the clergy within the institutional churches of all confessions and, conversely, his profound sympathy for the persecuted dissenters suffering due to the former. This significant development was therefore intimately tied to Breckling's devoted support of exiled brethren and his perennial feud with orthodox clergy, respectively.

Breckling contrasted the true spiritual adept against both laboratory alchemists who pursued worldly gain and false spiritual alchemists— religious teachers and preachers who led believers astray by lightly made promises of salvation. A passage of the *Pseudosophia* described in some detail these 'false, terrestrial, carnal, antichristian, lying, deceptive, and satanic teachers, prophets, priests, theologians, lawyers, physicians, magi, kabbalists, alchemists, soothsayers, interpreters of omens, astrologers, philosophers, and seducers.' Instead of dying to themselves in Christ, alchemists as the less harmful of the two groups 'live for themselves . . . and seek themselves and gold more than God, or they become pious and seek God for the sake of gold, so that they might find the *lapis*. They read the writings of the philosophers more than God's word and want to steal God's secrets with Lucifer in this manner.' Instead of focusing on spiritual alchemy, their aims were limited to those of *chrysopoeia* and iatrochemistry: 'They rather want to cure and tinge metals and the stinking maggot-bag,' that is, the human body, 'than their eternal soul.' By looking outward, they sought shortcuts to goals that could only rightfully be reached through introspection and mystical identification with Christ: 'they learn and buy many false processes out of books or from alchemists and pass over the process of Christ through cross, fire, and death. They want to recognise and think through nature and its hidden secrets, centres, and treasures outside of themselves, before they investigate themselves.... For this reason, they stray from the hidden wisdom and indwelling of Christ within us (*Einwohnung Christi in uns*) entirely.'[83] Alchemists who focused their entire attention on the outward world and the laboratory tended to neglect introspection, rebirth, and the cultivation of *Christus in nobis*. Rather than harming others, they mainly hindered their own spiritual progress.

In contrast, the false spiritual alchemists seemed much more dangerous to Breckling. They were the more villainous antagonists as they endangered not only the purses of the credulous but also their immortal souls. For Breckling, the defining feature of true mystical adepts was saving faith, grounded in mystical identification with Christ. This contrasted with a faith that remained limited to words and assent to specific beliefs, which false spiritual alchemists sought to impress upon their audience. Consequently, they were ministers and teachers who provided a prime example of the blind leading the blind: 'such pseudo-theologians, sophists, alchemists, and builders of Babel must lead themselves and all who follow them astray on a thousand wrong tracks, thus deceiving and ruining the world and all the confessions (*Secten*) along with themselves.'[84] Rather than the true, saving faith, 'worth more than refined gold tried in the fire,' these false preachers taught merely historical belief and performed outward rituals, offering 'false gold that receives the greatest lustre, praise, and esteem among the people.' They related to the persecuted faithful as did the haughty pharisee to the repentant tax collector: Christ's assessment inverted the standard of the world.[85] In Breckling's spiritual alchemy, false teaching became identified as false spiritual gold, for which churchgoers, by supporting their ministers financially, unfortunately paid in hard currency.

Breckling exhorted his readers, the 'true children, magi, adepts, and theosophers chosen by God,' to beware of the false spiritual alchemists as well as their worthless merchandise. Instead, rather than looking up to the minister on his pulpit, they ought 'to keep themselves down to Christ's humble and poor members sharing in his cross.' In other words, the true believers who formed Christ's invisible church shared the fate of the unseemly matter of the philosophers' stone, as described in alchemical literature, and Christ, the 'stone that the builders rejected.' Everyone 'trampled them underfoot like stones, in which a noble tincture and treasure often lies hidden.'[86] Breckling contrasted this against how spiritual adepts treated the true believers. Using all means in their possession (such as the *lapis philosophorum*), spiritual adepts 'thus nourish, clothe, shelter, visit Christ in his spiritual body and members, caring for them in life and in death.' This was precisely what Breckling did with his meagre means, and he buried many of his poor associates during his long career.[87]

Just as the most despised substance contained the potential for the tincture of laboratory alchemy, these persecuted believers also had something crucially important to give. Only very few people, however, sought to collect their spiritual insights as Breckling did: 'the true theologians, lawyers, physicians, chymists, magi, kabbalists, mystics, mysteriarchs, philosophers, astrologers, diviners, doctors, and pansophers born from God or recognised, sent, blessed, and taught by God ... seek the best and whatever is most necessary, and they often find it in those who are the least and most despised, in whom God has hidden it most deeply from the high-minded.'[88] It is precisely in this sense that Breckling could also present himself as a bookish alchemist of knowledge, spagyrically 'differentiating all writers as good, better, and best, as well as separating ... what is evil.'[89] In collecting the documents left behind by living stones as 'God's librarian,' Breckling was equally an adept who recognised their potential to become tinctures, something to which so many others were blind.[90] By combining his bookish alchemical quest with the hospitality he extended to religious dissenters over decades, Breckling was able to create one of the richest repositories of sources on German religious dissent throughout the seventeenth century.[91]

Inspired by Boehme's use of alchemical language, Breckling outlined his distinctive spiritual alchemy in two tiny pamphlets published in 1682: *Christus mysticus, sol et sal sapientiae* and *Pseudosophia mundi*. Breckling's statements are exceptional for how explicitly they draw attention to the mysticism underlying much of spiritual alchemy. He innovated by adapting the distinction between fraudulent alchemists and true adepts to spiritual alchemy. This provided him with an alchemical variation on the contrast between the clergy practising their priestcraft and the truly faithful who suffered persecution. In addition, Breckling viewed these witnesses of the truth, as he called them, both as members of Christ's body and as unsightly, oft-rejected stones that nevertheless contained the tincture. The final transmutation of the bodies of individual believers into a state corresponding to Christ's resurrection body played a less important role for him. To recover this aspect of spiritual alchemy, we need to explore Breckling's unmarked contributions to the work of an obscure author who had been active in the late sixteenth century.

7
Collaboration, Counterfeit, and Calumny in Amsterdam

After the diminutive treatises of 1682 with their grandiose titles, *Christus mysticus* and *Pseudosophia mundi*, Friedrich Breckling's spiritual alchemy went underground. The exiled minister hid it in unacknowledged contributions to the works of the virtually unknown Bartholomaeus Sclei. This author allegedly lived in Lesser Poland during the late sixteenth century. Originally, Sclei may have written his treatises as a reaction against the 'Minor Reformed Church' or Polish Brethren, defined by their endorsement of Socinianism.[1] Named after sixteenth-century theologians Lelio and Fausto Sozzini, this school of unitarian theology also became fashionable in Holland during the late seventeenth century.[2] In this context, Sclei's forgotten mystical and trinitarian works were suddenly relevant again and duly published in 1686. They appeared under the title *Theosophische-Schrifften* (Theosophical Writings) or, according to the frontispiece, *Theologia universalis* (Universal Theology). It had been almost one hundred years since Sclei wrote in the 1590s and a little less than half a century since Abraham von Franckenberg had published Sclei's *Pater Noster* (Our Father) in 1639, based on what appears to have been a shortened version.[3]

In a brief text on Sclei's life, Breckling proudly noted that his writings 'were all published at Amsterdam, corrected very thoroughly, and purified from some human chaff, along with a beautiful preface in which the foremost mystical authors are named.'[4] What Breckling did not acknowledge here was that he himself had been deeply involved with this publication. Elsewhere he claimed that he had 'printed (*gedrucket*) the *Universal Theology* of Dr Bartholomaeus Sley.'[5] While the scholarly consensus views Breckling as the editor of this volume, it has largely been overlooked that others also contributed to the project. A mere few years after Boehme's *opera omnia* had gone to press, Breckling and several associates, some of whom were also close to Johann Georg Gichtel, worked together to publish Sclei's writings. Contemporaneous documents and annotated copies of the *Theosophische-Schrifften* show that there were disagreements among the collaborators regarding the textual integrity of Sclei's writings. Very soon there were accusations and rumours that Breckling had considerably altered the text presented in the 1686 Sclei edition. This chapter describes how the project became controversial, identifies some of Breckling's collaborators, probes his unacknowledged role as editor, and shows that the former minister hid important elements of the spiritual alchemy of rebirth in Bartholomaeus Sclei's *Theosophische-Schrifften*. Finally, documents from the last phase of Breckling's life once again discuss spiritual alchemy more openly. During his final decade, the networker even actively engaged with the laboratory experiments of his associates.

Breckling's Accomplices and the Adulterated Sclei Edition

Within a few years of the publication of Sclei's *Theosophische-Schrifften*, gossip regarding Breckling's alterations circulated among religious dissenters. Eventually, the republic of letters at large accused Breckling of having considerably adulterated Sclei's works with textual contributions of his own.[6] The first to raise such accusations in print was the poet and prophet Quirinus Kuhlmann. In a treatise dated to 4 April 1688, he alleged that Breckling had 'counterfeited the work of Sclei,' thus causing 'the greatest offence and prejudice against other writings, which are subject to doubt because of this.'[7] In his attempt to purify the spiritual gold of Sclei's writings, Breckling had become a false alchemist himself—a counterfeiter, the kind of alchemical practitioner that harmed the reputation of the art.[8] If Breckling moulded written testimonies left behind by witnesses of the truth according to his own theological views, Kuhlmann argued, that severely undermined their validity. On 4 May 1688, exactly a month after Kuhlmann had made his objections public, Breckling defended himself in a letter to the merchant Marcus Arnoldi: 'the garden book of B. Sclei is not entirely free from weeds, and I have provoked much displeasure among the enthusiasts (*fladdergeistern*), because I chopped down the weeds here and there, trimming this vine as much as possible.'[9] Breckling was unrepentant and simply dismissed Kuhlmann, who had even uttered death threats against him, as a misguided heretic.[10] Evidently, Breckling was proud of the hard work he had put in as a corrector of not only linguistic but also theological flaws. That was a view not everyone shared.

Even though Kuhlmann singled out Breckling for criticism, he was far from the only one who had been involved with publishing Sclei's writings. In fact, the obscure Polish author posthumously commanded the attention of a number of religious dissenters in the orbit of Gichtel and Breckling. They quarrelled among themselves about who would contribute prefatory material and to what extent Sclei's writings ought to be edited. As Frank van Lamoen has pointed out, Gichtel's letters to his disciple Johann Wilhelm Überfeld show that the latter was involved with the Sclei project in early 1686.[11] In a letter dated 4 February 1686, Gichtel encouraged Überfeld to go ahead: 'the preface for Sclei's *Theosophia* may remain, I like to read such lessons, for it is a mirror and wake-up call for me to beware of such evil.'[12] Apparently, Überfeld found himself doubting the merits of the venture generally and his contribution specifically.

From his home in Amsterdam, Gichtel was able to report on various tensions affecting the collaborators, whereas Überfeld in Leiderdorp was less directly involved in these conflicts. In his next letter, dated 10 February, Gichtel mentioned the reclusive physician Isaac Schmidberger. Apparently, Schmidberger had complained about Breckling to Gichtel, who immediately proceeded to gossip about Schmidberger in his letter to Überfeld: 'Schmidberger judges Breckling's addition (*Zugabe*) to be but blind zeal, and his own thorny preface itself is not worth a bean.'[13] We might read Gichtel's verdict on Schmidberger's preface as an unfavourable comparison to Überfeld's alternative, which he had praised in the previous letter. Unfortunately, it remains unclear whether 'Breckling's addition' refers to a separate text or interspersed extrapolations.

Schmidberger was a fickle character in every sense of the word. His acquaintance with Breckling is first documented in 1675, when he likely visited the former minister in Amsterdam.[14] Formerly a court physician in Sulzbach, Schmidberger travelled frequently; on a journey to Frankfurt, he established contact with Überfeld, who was to help with the distribution of two hundred copies of the 1682 Boehme edition.[15] By October 1683, Schmidberger had moved to the Dutch metropolis himself.[16] A 1686 letter to Breckling gave his address as Schmidberger's house 'on the Prinsengracht, near the Labyrinth.'[17] This could imply that Breckling and his family were living under Schmidberger's roof during the very time they collaborated on publishing Sclei; at the very least, it indicates that they were in frequent contact. The physician also owned a magnificent library and zealously restricted visitors' access to it. Despite minor disagreements, he and Breckling remained close for a number of years but finally parted ways irrevocably in 1703.[18]

Gichtel's letter mentioned yet another collaborator, whose contribution was much more conspicuous than Breckling's or Schmidberger's: Michael Andreae. He designed the frontispiece for the Sclei edition, in the same style as the cycle of images he had created for Boehme's complete works, and the Amsterdam artist Joseph Mulder prepared the copperplate engraving (fig. 7.1).[19] Gichtel intimated that Breckling and Andreae were engaged in a struggle over a manuscript copy of Sclei's works and, by extension, the text it contained: 'since he [Breckling] thinks Brother Michael [Andreae] wants to wage war against him, one had better have another copy (*Copey*) made in Riga so that this wrathful brother [Breckling] can keep his copy, for he would only become more obdurate if one challenged him much.'[20] This remark suggests that the collaborators of the 1686 edition used several different Sclei manuscripts. With his far-ranging network and predilection for otherwise unappreciated heterodox manuscripts, Breckling seems to have had his own copy of Sclei's writings. Andreae may have helped Breckling obtain it through contacts in Riga, Andreae's former home. His disapproval of Breckling, as recorded by Gichtel, may have prompted Andreae to scribe a calligraphic Sclei manuscript under the title *Instantis universalis theologiae partes III* ('Three Parts of an Urgent Universal Theology'). Similar headings appear in the 1686 edition. This manuscript likely presented Sclei's works without Breckling's interventions. Last documented in 1867, its present location is unknown.[21]

In the absence of such manuscript witnesses for the original text of Sclei's works, we can currently only rely on annotated printed copies. As rumours regarding Breckling's editorial liberties spread beyond networks of religious dissenters to the republic of letters, the most diligent readers of Sclei's *Theosophische-Schrifften* sought to learn exactly how the exiled networker had manipulated Sclei's works. On 29 April 1703, for instance, the Helmstedt orientalist Hermann von der Hardt showed the Silesian traveller Gottlieb Stolle—whose diary recorded the learned world's gossip—his neatly annotated copy of the Sclei edition in which Breckling's changes were highlighted.[22] The present location of Von der Hardt's Sclei exemplar is unknown, but three other annotated exemplars of the 1686 edition shed light on Breckling's interventions.

Hermann Geyer has drawn attention to one such copy of the *Theosophische-Schrifften* that survives in Nuremberg.[23] An explanatory remark at the beginning states in unflattering terms that the annotations

Fig. 7.1 Bartholomaeus Sclei, *Theosophische-Schrifften* (Amsterdam: [Christoffel Cunradus' widow], 1686), frontispiece. The frontispiece for Sclei's works—designed by Michael Andreae just like the twenty-two engravings for Boehme's complete works and executed by engraver Joseph Mulder—served to visually connect Sclei to Boehme's theosophy. The Hague, Koninklijke Bibliotheek—National Library of the Netherlands: PH2762 (Ritman Kerncollectie). © KB Beeldstudio

highlight Breckling's contributions: 'note well—everything that is covered in brown or sooty colour throughout the entire book is not the author's, but the adulterating additions (*eingemischter zusatz*) of Friedrich Breckling.'[24] Considering the limited distribution of the said colour throughout, the annotator clearly did not complete the laborious task. More than for marking the extent of Breckling's contributions, the manuscript annotations are valuable for corroborating Gichtel's statements concerning Schmidberger's involvement. Comments in this exemplar attribute two specific passages, including the preface praised by Breckling, to Isaac Schmidberger.[25] This suggests that Gichtel's advocacy for Überfeld's preface failed. On the basis of the Nuremberg annotations, Breckling's interventions seem mostly restricted to adding references to Bible verses and making justifiable changes to render the work more accessible.[26] Notable exceptions to this general practice can be found on some twenty pages only, situated near the beginning of a bulky work running to more than eight hundred pages. The first longer addition is marked by Breckling's distinctive paratactic style, attained by listing synonymous words or expressions.[27] Elsewhere, Breckling integrated one of his favourite scriptural commonplaces: that God's wisdom appears as foolishness to the world.[28] He also emphasised the mystical identification with Christ, crucial to Breckling's theology as well as spiritual alchemy generally.[29]

A second annotated copy may be found in The Hague. In contrast to the Nuremberg exemplar, the highlighted passages here carry on until the very end of the book, attributing the postscript to Breckling. An explanatory note on the rear flyleaf adopts a more neutral tone than the Nuremberg copy: 'note well—whatever is marked (*außgestrichen*) with green colour in the present book is Fr. Breckling's addition (*additamenta*).' Another hand immediately continues: 'which Mr Secretary Straube thus crossed out (*durchstrichen*) according to his exemplar. Mylius.'[30] Due to the absence of first names, neither Straube nor Mylius can be identified: at the time, several people bearing these surnames were active in Pietist correspondence networks.[31] More importantly, Mylius' remark implies that the annotations of the Hague copy in turn derived from another annotated Sclei edition. Together with the evidence regarding Von der Hardt's exemplar, this suggests that numerous annotated Sclei exemplars circulated soon after 1686.

Finally, there is a third annotated copy in Amsterdam that broadly agrees with the Hague exemplar. There is neither any previous owner's name nor explanatory remark as in the other annotated copies, and the markings can only be identified as highlighting Breckling's contributions through comparison with the Hague copy. Written in a Dutch hand, the annotations of the Amsterdam exemplar are slightly less comprehensive than in that other copy.[32] However, the Amsterdam volume's annotator also paid attention to another kind of intervention by Breckling: rather than only focusing on additions, the annotator also noted some of the deletions and supplied missing words or phrases. In addition, this annotator pointed out that a separate portion of text derived from Weigelian writings and attributed another one to an unknown writer not identical to 'this authority' or Sclei.[33] Taken together, the three annotated Sclei copies provide important information on Breckling's interventions. Contrary to Breckling's claim that he had mainly cut questionable material, the annotations in these three copies emphasise his additions. Sclei's *Theosophische-Schrifften* presented a hybrid text that indiscriminately linked the late sixteenth and seventeenth centuries. This undermines the assessment of previous scholarship, which has approached Sclei's writings as dating to the 1590s.[34]

Vintage Spiritual Alchemy from the 1590s with Ingredients from the 1680s?

Since we now know that Breckling considerably altered the text of Sclei's works in the 1686 edition, the spiritual alchemy contained in this volume needs to be explored with caution. The three annotated copies provide important support towards achieving that goal. Yet we should be wary of assuming that these exemplars contain a complete record of Breckling's additions: several relevant passages have a distinctly Brecklingian ring to them even in the absence of highlighting in any of the three exemplars. In many cases, it is impossible to tell where Sclei ends and Breckling begins, yet I contend that the spiritual alchemy encountered throughout Sclei's *Theosophische-Schrifften* largely dates from the 1680s, rather than the 1590s, and therefore should be attributed to Breckling. Regarding the broader story of spiritual alchemy, the 1686 Sclei edition also contains statements on the physical aspect of alchemical rebirth and spiritual transmutation that are otherwise largely absent in Breckling's papers and printed works. Thus, Breckling's Sclei edition contains a necessary element that completes the picture regarding Breckling's spiritual alchemy.

Given the potentially incomplete record of the annotated copies and the sheer length of Sclei's *Theosophische-Schrifften* at more than eight hundred pages, deciding where to begin the investigation is a challenge in itself. Fortunately, there is an index—clearly datable to 1686—that provides a point of entry to Sclei's voluminous works. Its very presence is remarkable, as indices were not commonly included in early-modern devotional publications. Yet there was one person among Breckling's contacts whose productions habitually included elaborate indices: Loth Fischer.[35] As an important precedent, the 1682 edition of Boehme's works also featured a substantial index, but it predated Fischer's arrival in the Low Countries. In his first documented contact with the Holland Boehmists, Fischer became a distributor of the 1682 edition and supplemented his meagre livelihood in this manner.[36] Soon after, in 1683, Fischer collaborated with Überfeld and Andreae on *Der Weeg zum Ewigen Leben* (The Way to Eternal Life).[37]

After his banishment from Nuremberg on 29 April 1684, Fischer moved to Holland and took up residence in Utrecht. He soon began to work on a series of large translation projects. Published from 1687 to 1704, Fischer's editions of the sixteenth-century Dutch spiritualist Hiël, the Philadelphian prophetess Jane Leade, and her erstwhile mentor John Pordage all feature indices that are remarkably similar to the one in Sclei's *Theosophische-Schrifften*.[38] As documented in a 1691 letter, from 1688 Breckling worked closely with Fischer regarding the distribution of his controversial *Anticalovius*.[39] In addition, Fischer's interest in spiritual alchemy is documented for later years. In 1698 he translated Pordage's *Ein Gründlich Philosophisch Sendschreiben* (A Thorough Philosophical Epistle) into German. This epistolary treatise identified the process of spiritual rebirth with that of the *opus magnum* in laboratory alchemy.[40] When the travelling diarist Gottlieb Stolle visited Fischer in Utrecht on 10 August 1703, Fischer shared his views on spiritual alchemy with his guest.[41] All of this presents a wealth of circumstantial evidence suggesting that Fischer compiled the index for Sclei's *Theosophische-Schrifften*.

Even without conclusive proof for Fischer's involvement, it is striking that many index entries reflect a concern with spiritual alchemy. Under the first letter of the alphabet alone, we find entries such as 'adept of the mystical stone' (*Adeptus Lapidis Mystici*), 'mystical alchemy' (*Alchymia Mystica*), and 'godly spagyric anatomy' (*Anatomia Divino-Spagyrica*). Further keywords throughout the index include 'sophic stone' (*Lapis Sophicus*), 'matter of the mystical stone' (*Materia Lapidis Mystici*), 'universal panacea' (*Panacaea universalis*) or 'universal tincture' (*Tinctura Universalis*), and 'mystical process towards rebirth' (*Processus Mysticus zur Wiedergeburt*).[42] Indices rarely attract scrutiny in their own right, yet this one appears to be anything but a neutral signpost. In fact, the index to Sclei's writings reflects a hidden agenda revolving around spiritual alchemy. Some of the entries could even be viewed as attempts to steer readers' interpretations by referring to passages under specific keywords. Many of the alchemical terms point to a single section: the preface to the second part of Sclei's *Theologiae universalis instans*. Unlike the 'Preface of the Author' to the first part, it is not explicitly marked as Sclei's. Yet the annotated copies also do not attribute it to Breckling as a whole, though two of them highlight individual snippets or passages of the preface as his. Since this preface recalls several themes he had previously employed in *Christus mysticus* and *Pseudosophia mundi*, I suspect that both the annotated copies underestimate Breckling's contribution. Given Breckling's activist work as Sclei's editor, it appears likely that he, at least, rewrote Sclei's preface extensively. To reflect this, I use the phrase 'Breckling's Sclei' to refer to the text's indistinct authors.

The preface begins by extolling 'God, the highest artist' as well as 'the one and only *spagyrus*,' who 'placed his son, his unutterable word into such a marvellous visible and invisible ANATOMY.' God here combined the two roles—artist and *spagyrus*, a term often associated with Paracelsianism—linked to the highest goals of transmutational and medical alchemy. In an oblique reference to Breckling's notion of the spiritual body and members of Christ, God's Son 'rejuvenated himself so wonderfully, spread, reproduced, and made himself grow in this marvellous ANATOMY,' always remaining 'the only One' in the course of 'this manifold multiplication.'[43] Though this specific passage remains unmarked, elsewhere throughout Sclei's works Breckling subtly inserted this notion through small interventions.[44] The term *multiplicatio* refers to the potency of tinctures in alchemy, or rather the process by which that potency is increased: prior to undergoing multiplication (repeatedly), one part of tincture might be able to transmute an equal amount of a lesser metal, perhaps ten parts, yet this proportion could potentially be increased to one thousand or more.[45] Even the spread of Christianity was thus conceivable in alchemical terms for Breckling's Sclei. Breckling had used *multiplicatio* in the very same unusual sense on the title page of his *Christus mysticus*.

On this view, the entire world becomes 'but an ATHANOR, fiery furnace, and workshop of God, in which he digests his ternary into the quaternary and instantly transmutes it through this into true unity.' God 'thus prepares, cooks, purifies, rejuvenates, multiplies, and brings to light his eternal heavenly, independent TRUTH itself.' Such language already occurred in the works of Dorn, Khunrath, and Dee; Franckenberg used it for purposes of spiritual alchemy in his 'Kabbalistic Regimen' a few decades later. It would not have been utterly impossible for Sclei to have used the same sources as Franckenberg, but his composition of a text on spiritual alchemy during the 1590s does seem exceptionally early. Instead, the use of bombastic terms and phrases, as well as their rapid succession, is typical of Breckling's style, though neither annotator identified Brecklingian additions this far into the preface. As it continues, we read that God had hidden his heavenly wisdom 'among the simple, ignorant laypeople, in which he placed his ore of gold, therein to make it shine and reveal it, thereby bringing to light his wonderful wisdom and great power.'[46] A passage expressing a very similar idea, with Boehme as an exemplary layman bringing forth 'golden wisdom' like labourers working in 'gold mines,' occurs in Breckling's *Anticalovius*, probably written in 1685 but only printed in 1688.[47] It is quite unlikely that Breckling would have found such a lucid presentation of his own theology and project as God's librarian in Sclei. Rather, we have to assume that Breckling hid these gold nuggets of insight in Sclei's textual mine.

After a small number of minor additions marked mostly in the Hague copy, Breckling also integrated one of his favourite notions: that the 'terrestrial wisdom of those highly learned' is wrongly advertised as 'heavenly wisdom.'[48] Elsewhere, a Breckling addition marked by both the Amsterdam and Hague copies reads: 'for God has turned the wisdom of this world into folly.'[49] Further on in the preface, Breckling's Sclei referred to the purveyors of such learning (in terms reminiscent of the *Pseudosophia mundi*) as 'the false, seductive alchymists,' by which Breckling meant the university-educated theologians who promised salvation without the arduous process of rebirth and pretended to have divine authority as they preached from their pulpits. The entire speech that is attributed to them is marked as Breckling's contribution in the Hague and Amsterdam copies. If this passage is removed, the introductory sentence does not cohere with the text around it, so it must be assumed that Breckling either added it as well or replaced Sclei's original text with his own. In view of the similarity of the phrase to other ones encountered in Breckling's 1682 treatises, *Christus mysticus* and *Pseudosophia mundi*, the former option appears more likely.

The preface posited that 'this greatly powerful treasure and such pure ore of gold never yet entered into the poisonous heart of any false, deceptive, godless alchymist; much less did it come into their impure hands, and least of all into their hellish athanor of the academic schools.' In contrast to the false learning of the universities, Breckling's Sclei emphasised 'a supernatural, heavenly alchemy' (hereafter, underlined text is marked as Breckling's contribution in annotated exemplars of Slei's work): 'celestial alchemy is true magic. True magic is nothing other than the commutation of Christ, <u>that is, the transmutation of man into god (*Transmutatio Hominis in Deum*). Which can be attained and put into practice by no human on earth whatsoever, but only by the Son of God, CHRIST, as the highest *spagyrus*.</u> And it will have to remain like this, however foolishly and thoughtlessly our false alchymists, pseudo-magi, and shapeshifters (*falsche Alchymisten, Pseudo Magi und Transformatores*) pretend, who pride themselves on, and endeavour to do, something impossible and inhuman.'[50] The deification of the believer is tantamount to her spiritual transmutation wrought by Christ, the only one able to succeed at this kind of alchemy.[51]

Breckling's Sclei presented Christ not only as an adept but also as the transmuting agent. In parentheses, God's Son was described as 'true tincture, <u>panacea, *lapis*, and magnesia</u>,' and the annotator of the Hague copy highlighted all but the first two words as Breckling's. A passage arguing that believers have gained the tincture implicitly alludes to the notion of *Christus in nobis*: 'he [Christ] has given us the tincture [Christ] into our hand, so that everyone can forthwith tinge, transform, and rejuvenate himself towards the Son of God through faith on and in Christ Jesus.' Nothing else was needed beside this tincture, yet the clergy tried to insert themselves and various rituals into the true process of spiritual alchemy. In so doing, they corrupted it: the false alchymists 'boast that they alone have this tincture in their hand, and consequently they falsely attempt to tinge others—although they cannot even tinge themselves, because they do not know the same [tincture] <u>but seek the gold of all the world more than God</u>.'[52] Particularly the final phrase sounds familiar; it echoes Breckling's 1682 treatises. As false teachers who sought to usurp Christ's unique role as the mediator between God and humanity, ministers of the confessional churches became fraudulent alchymists who peddled an ineffective tincture to earn their keep. True teachers pointed believers to the saving grace and transmuting agent of *Christus in nobis* instead.

Breckling's Sclei vigorously asserted that the tincture (Christ) alone could bring about salvation and that the 'pseudo-alchymists' (the clergy) sought to 'steal God's glory' by arguing otherwise and seeking their own profit. Recalling Breckling's 1682 treatises, Breckling's Sclei asserted that 'the pseudo-alchymists' failed to recognise 'the matter of this heavenly *lapis*, which tinges all ore into gold, is found plenteously and overflowingly, lying around in one heap beside another, upon all streets, in front of all doors, even in all houses.' In their priestcraft, 'instead of the true matter, the pseudo-alchymists took a false, fraudulent, fictitious matter, acting and gesturing much by way of strange marvels and fools' work.'[53] Breckling's Sclei thus unflatteringly compared the clergy to the charlatans and mountebanks who advertised their potions and nostrums on streets and town squares.[54] Not only did they lack 'the true *mumia*,' 'the blood of Christ,' and the 'fixed matter that can withstand fire,' they also did not have 'the practical skill' (*des rechten Handgriffs*) required or the ability to master different degrees of heat used in the work of spiritual alchemy: 'they also do not know <u>the hidden, heavenly, and central</u> fire and the four kinds of fire of true regeneration, without which four degrees nobody can be born again. First he has to pass through all of these four fires, for only in the fourth creation is man made perfect and entirely transformed and born towards the kingdom of God. <u>As the fourth man became a Seth (*ein Seth*). Malachi 3:4</u>.'[55] By the four kinds of fire, Breckling could have alluded to an expanded scheme of four mystical paths (the final one being *unio* or *deificatio*), though he preferred the more traditional scheme of three paths in other situations. What is decisive is that Breckling's Sclei contrasted the process of rebirth with the antics of priests and fraudulent alchemists against the 'adept of the mystical *lapis*,' much as Breckling's 1682 treatises did.[56]

Believers were possessors of the philosophers' stone, not transmuting agents themselves. They had received that for which alchemists strove, yet its application required wisdom and discretion: 'because God the Father showed and gave us the matter of the *lapis*, in which the tincture lies hidden, he wants us to use it according to his disposition.' This entailed that believers were the matter that needed to be transmuted, which—in a departure from laboratory alchemy noted previously—had to suffer in the process of transmutation. Breckling's Sclei rendered this explicit: 'for we ourselves are not the tincture, but we have it from God the Father, who alone is and remains the same, according to Scripture: "I am the Lord who sanctifies you."'[57] Like pseudo-Weigel and other writers on spiritual alchemy, Breckling's Sclei insisted that nobody should fool himself into believing 'that his salvation and transmutation would or could take place without fire, without great danger, and without mighty sorrow. For if the tincture [Christ] had to first pass through these and taste the most intense suffering, how much more so the parts that need to be tinged? <u>Which from impure metals ought to be tinged and thus deified into truly, finely purified gold in Christ?</u> . . . For

Christ's appearance in us is like the fire of a goldsmith to melt, cleanse, and purify—who will stand the day of his return? Malachi 3.'[58] With its emphasis on purification rather than transmutation, the passage is reminiscent of Franckenberg's *Theophrastia Valentinana*, and Breckling would later count Johann Overbeek, the owner of the manuscript source Gottfried Arnold used for his 1703 edition of that work, among his acquaintances.[59] Furthermore, the part marked as Breckling's in both the Amsterdam and Hague copies recalled his *Christus Mysticus* of 1682.[60]

As presented in Breckling's 1682 treatises, his spiritual alchemy seemed to lack a crucial component: its physical, bodily consequences. Among other things, Breckling's Sclei quoted the Pauline proof text for these: 'in order to confirm this truth of God, Paul speaks thus: "Our way of life or community is in heaven, from whence we await our saviour, our Lord Jesus Christ, who will transform the body of our lowliness so that it will be like unto the body of his clarity, according to the effect by which he is able to conquer all things." Philippians 3.'[61] According to the New Testament, then, the human body would be transmuted into a heavenly one, akin to Christ's resurrection body. In addition, under the lemma 'mystical process towards rebirth,' the Sclei volume's index guides readers to this passage: 'afterwards, Sodom and Gomorrah and all terrestrial being in us must be devoured by fire from heaven and wholly ground to powder, before the young phoenix with his crystalline body can appear from the charred ashes.... For our God is a consuming Fire. Hebrews 12.'[62] The anticipated resurrection of the body necessitated its prior calcination and purified reconstitution in a highly subtle, spiritual matter.

The fact that this aspect does not occur in Breckling's 1682 treatises or the preface to the second part of Sclei's *Theosophische-Schrifften* raises an important question: was it too obvious or too esoteric for inclusion in these contexts? The answer, I suspect, would have to be both at once: Paul's Letter to the Philippians clearly spelt out the future bodily transmutation of believers for all to see. Yet not everyone had eyes to see or ears to hear, just as most people continued to trample the precious cornerstone and heavenly tincture underfoot while looking for it in all the wrong places. The findings presented in this chapter indicate that Breckling likely contributed considerably more to the spiritual alchemy found in the *Theosophische-Schrifften* of 1686 than even the copious annotations in the Amsterdam and Hague copies would lead us to believe. Though unlikely, it is possible that Sclei may have independently arrived at discussing spiritual rebirth in the same alchemical terms as pseudo-Weigel already during the 1590s. However, it is all but impossible that Sclei would have shared Breckling's agenda as God's librarian, used *multiplicatio* in his idiosyncratic sense, or described the fraudulent alchemy of the clergy in the very same terms Breckling used during the 1680s.

Breckling's Mature Spiritual Alchemy and Interest in the Laboratory

After 1686 it becomes much easier to find sources on Breckling's spiritual alchemy and professions of allegiance to Jacob Boehme. Breckling's continued interest in both appears much more frequently in documents dating from the last quarter-century of his life. A particularly important example is his letter to the Berlin patrician Levin Schardius, composed on 22 November 1691. Here Breckling claimed that Boehme had surpassed all other authorities on alchemy: 'in his book *Signatura rerum*, Jacob Boehme detailed the signatures and harmony of all things out of the inward root and spiritual central world and elaborated them to the highest philosophical work as suitably short and central as none before him.'[63] Though they did not attain Boehme's lucidity and faced clear limits, 'the chymists (*Chymici*) unfold the mystical philosophy best, surpassing others.'[64] It was probably no coincidence that Breckling alluded to the title of the 1618 volume *Philosophia mystica*, which included Johann Siebmacher's *Introductio hominis*.

The very same letter also contains a particularly apt restatement of Breckling's spiritual alchemy. Breckling succinctly summarised it for the benefit of Schardius: 'but when God restores us to the lost image of omnipotence, goodness, and all-wisdom in Christ and newly forms, tinges, transmutes, makes, and recreates within us philosophers by the supercelestial fire and cross of Christ, the whole concentrated concatenation and Christian pansophy comes to the one who first seeks the kingdom of God and the one thing necessary in Christ and lets himself be super-chymically (*super chymicé*) calcinated, putrefied, purified, cohobated, solved, perfected, and coagulated.'[65] The new birth (or the restoration of the divine likeness lost in the Fall) transmuted believers into spiritual adepts, rather than mere laboratory alchemists or 'philosophers by the fire.'[66] In analogy to the material philosophers' stone, such a born-again believer had, super-chymically or spiritually, undergone the seven stages of the great work: while individual alchemists might disagree about the precise terms or sequence, Breckling clearly alluded to this traditional concept as he described the core elements of spiritual alchemy in an exceedingly succinct manner.[67]

Around 1695, Breckling composed a short treatise titled *De studio universalissimo et pansophico* (On the Most Encompassing and Pansophic Education). Here he described how Boehme stood head and shoulders above all the many notable authors whose works he had read: 'among all these, I found none who explained to me more thoroughly and better than Jacob Boehme in his writings—before which I had to stand still in awe and thank God—how the divine reveals itself out of the inward root and spiritual world in the human, worldly, and terrestrial, and through which hidden paths and principles God continues to daily create, sustain, illuminate, perfect, and concentrate everything.' Only Luther and Johannes Tauler equalled the theosopher of Görlitz: 'all chymists and physicians, theologians and philosophers could learn much, if they wanted to become the disciples of this cobbler [Boehme], Luther, and Tauler.'[68] Coming from a Lutheran, no matter how heterodox, this was an exceptional statement.

In the second half of the 1690s, Breckling regularly corresponded with August Hermann Francke, the famous founder of the Halle Orphanage and a leading figure of the Pietist movement.[69] In one such letter to Francke, the exiled networker described Boehme as the key authority on the *lapis-Christus* analogy. In Breckling's estimation, Boehme's writings surpassed Johann Siebmacher's *Wasserstein* in this regard:

> what the true central chymists teach with good reason on the analogy of the true medicine, tincture, panacea, and *lapis philosophorum* with Christ and his incarnation, passion, death, and resurrection, that [teaching] can also stand the light of truth and be found in it, as the author of the *Wasserstein der Weysen* and others, many divine magi and kabbalists . . . assert [in classic collections of alchemical texts]. However, in his books and profound writings, especially the *Aurora, Mysterium magnum*, and *Signatura rerum*, Jacob Boehme specifically wrote most sublimely and deeply of the analogy between the inner, spiritual and the outer, visible world and [the analogy] of these two with God, their proper origin and root, as well as [the analogy] of the philosophers' stone with Christ, for the benefit of the children of light.[70]

As Boehme averred particularly in *Signatura rerum*, the alchemical process of the great work corresponded to Christ's life on earth. What alchemical writers could but dimly apprehend, the theosopher of Görlitz presented with great depth of insight.

After the publication of Gottfried Arnold's *Impartial History* at the turn of the century, Breckling achieved a degree of fame due to his contributions to that widely read work. Soon he found himself contacted by aspiring adepts, such as the Swabian Pietist Gottlieb Hoffstetter, who had lost his position as a school teacher due to his millenarian convictions.[71] Although Hoffstetter's alchemy largely exhausted itself in his quest for rare manuscripts and books, including Franckenberg's *Raphael*, Breckling also made the acquaintance of actual laboratory practitioners. He learnt much from them and sought to support their endeavours as best he could. An unnamed Saxon, who had worked for Dorothea Juliana Wallich and thus gained considerable insights into her alchemy, explained her anonymously published works to Breckling sometime in 1706 or 1707.[72] A few years later, he took a close interest in a mysterious adept called De Stahan, whom he described 'as a genuine disciple and adept son of Paracelsus.'[73] Ever wary of what powerful rulers might do to gain his secrets, De Stahan turned down a tempting offer from Elector Palatine Johann Wilhelm to join his Düsseldorf court. Instead, De Stahan decided to 'pass into the community of Christ and his angels to work for the common good of the poor and miserable members of Christ.'[74] In so doing, De Stahan showed himself an adept after Breckling's own heart, who did his best to recommend De Stahan to Francke and the Halle Orphanage.[75] Inspired by his engagement with Wallich's assistant and De Stahan, Breckling took notes on alchemical works they deemed important and even wrote a short, incomplete text on alchemy.[76]

In summary, Breckling's spiritual alchemy was not limited to *Christus mysticus* and *Pseudosophia mundi*, the two diminutive treatises published in 1682. Rather, he developed it further in unmarked additions to an earlier writer's works, the *Theosophische-Schrifften* of Bartholomaeus Sclei, and in his own later documents. I have described the 1686 Sclei volume as a collaborative project involving various German exiles and religious nonconformists in a circle of acquaintances throughout Holland. Kuhlmann's calumny exposed the edition as a controversial case of counterfeit, and several early readers marked Breckling's interventions in their exemplars. Three annotated copies currently known provide a record of Breckling's contributions, yet it still appears incomplete: most passages relevant in the context of spiritual alchemy bear Breckling's mark and must date to the 1680s. Even the bodily, physical aspect of rebirth and spiritual alchemy reappears in Breckling's additions and changes to Sclei's text. Ringing endorsements of Boehme as a key authority on the art of the philosophers' stone abound in documents by Breckling dating from the later decades of his life, which also poignantly summarises his spiritual alchemy. And during his very last years, Breckling even developed a strong interest in laboratory alchemy, which he believed could be mastered by born-again believers and harnessed for the benefit of the godly.

8
Dionysius Andreas Freher, Boehme's Apostle to the English

Shortly before Breckling, Schmidberger, Andreae, and Überfeld saw Sclei's collected works through the press, Dionysius Andreas Freher of Nuremberg appeared among them around Christmastide 1685. Attracted to Amsterdam by the reputation of those responsible for the 1682 edition of Boehme's complete works, he went on to live together with Johann Wilhelm Überfeld in Leiderdorp from early 1686. During the following nine years, Freher meditated on the writings of the theosopher and received the stimuli for his own oeuvre. In the first half of 1695, he left for London to escape his strained relationship with Überfeld and to make contact with Jane Leade and her budding Philadelphian Society.[1] Though short-lived itself, the Philadelphian Society and its literary productions continued to exert great influence particularly in the German-speaking world, spreading an ideal of brotherly love and undogmatic toleration of other creeds.[2] When he left Holland, Freher took Boehme's spiritual alchemy of rebirth across the North Sea to England, with far-reaching consequences for modern interpretations of the art of the philosophers' stone.

During Freher's time in London, where he spent the remainder of his life, associates perceived him as a resourceful authority on Boehme's opaque writings. Partly responding to requests, he composed a considerable body of works elucidating these writings' secrets as well as resolving perceived tensions. To this day posterity remembers Freher as a faithful expositor of Boehme's writings, and he is even more widely known as the creator of fascinating images. These he presented throughout his virtually unknown writings but also in concentrated form, with works largely consisting of figures, such as the cosmogonical *Hieroglyphica sacra* (Sacred Hieroglyphics), the anthropological *Three Tables*, and the emblematic *Paradoxa, emblemata, aenigmata, hieroglyphica de uno, toto, puncto, centro* (Paradoxes, Emblems, Riddles, Hieroglyphics on the One, Whole, Point, Centre).[3] While these visual creations may be more popular today, the main fruit of Freher's long engagement with the theosopher of Görlitz was the *Fundamenta mystica Jacobi Behmen, explicata* (The Mystical Foundations of Jacob Boehme Explained). Marked with the letters A through H rather than numbers, its eight volumes contain treatises that are as long as books or as short as a few pages.[4] After summarising what is known about Freher's early life and describing his transition to England, this chapter turns to an investigation of spiritual alchemy within the *Fundamenta mystica* and shows how part of it, 'The Process in the Philosophical Work,' became well-known in the nineteenth century.

Freher's Years in Holland

We know little about Freher's mature years in London and even less about his early life on the Continent. The scion of a long line of educated men in a family claiming noble descent, Dionysius Andreas Freher was born in Nuremberg on 12 September 1649.[5] He matriculated at the nearby University of Altdorf in 1663, around the age of fourteen.[6] Such an early start in academic education was not unheard of at the time, yet Freher would have been among the youngest students in his peer group. Prior to embarking on a *peregrinatio academica*, he would likely have continued his university studies in Altdorf for a number of years. During these student days and from a remarkably early age, he contributed small pieces to publications commemorating events in his family or circle of friends.[7] In 1667, he matriculated at the University of Heidelberg and decided to focus on theology two years later.[8] This choice is remarkable: whereas Nuremberg cultivated a proudly Lutheran identity, this particular university was one of the most important seats of Reformed learning and famous for the Heidelberg Catechism of 1563, a foundational document for the confession.[9] According to Roland Pietsch, Freher lived in Muscovy from 1677 until 1684.[10] In later documents, Breckling and Überfeld confirmed that Freher had spent time in Moscow and harboured a strong dislike for Russian cuisine.[11]

Scholarship routinely mentions Gichtel in connection with Freher, yet his association with the less famous Johann Wilhelm Überfeld was much closer. With support from Gichtel, Freher had initially looked for accommodation in Amsterdam around Christmas 1685. As Gichtel's biography records, it was customary to conclude annual rental contracts in Amsterdam on St Stephen's Day (26 December).[12] Finding suitable rooms apparently proved too difficult. By 4 February 1686, it seems, Freher had moved in with Überfeld in Leiderdorp. For almost nine years, Freher and Überfeld lived under the same roof in that small village on the outskirts of Leiden. Both of them frequently corresponded with Gichtel. In a letter that also touched upon Sclei's *Theosophische-Schrifften* as a work in progress, Gichtel requested the prayerful intercession of Überfeld 'as well as Brother Freher.'[13] The Nuremberg native initially got along well enough with Überfeld, and Gichtel was pleased that 'God gives unity of the spirit,' as he noted on 19 July 1687.[14] Yet by 15 November 1688, there were signs of serious tension between Freher and Überfeld, who would later look back on the years with Freher as an epic struggle against the learned world as a whole.[15]

That struggle continued for years with ups and downs. Finally, on 9 February 1695, Gichtel obliquely referred to Freher's departure and shed no tears at the report: 'I have received your small letter of the first of this month and perceived your love in it. The Most High be praised eternally, who has revealed his great compassion and liberated us from the unbelieving, false brethren.'[16] In a 1707 letter, more than a decade after the fact, Überfeld vividly recounted the event that precipitated his companion's departure. With Freher's help Überfeld was filling 'a large wheelbarrow with bags of apples for Loth Fischer.' Yet suddenly, 'the evil spirit fell upon' Freher, and he stopped dead 'without saying a word.' When Überfeld asked if Freher would help him still, he refused because 'Loth Fischer had not sent him greetings.' So Überfeld tried to carry on alone, 'but having reached the gate of our garden, I could not possibly pass the threshold without assistance.' He turned and commanded Freher, 'by virtue of the fraternal community which we have with one another in Christ,' to help him pass the threshold. Yet even when Überfeld repeated his command a second time, Freher refused to be ordered around. The third time, Überfeld added the fateful words: '"and if you will not help me, you cannot be my brother any longer. Therefore, you must help me now or depart." Which latter he subsequently chose, . . . and transferred to Leade in London.'[17] An omitted greeting on the part of Fischer and a cartload of apples thus brought years of simmering conflict to a head and sealed the permanent rupture between Überfeld and Freher.

There was no further direct contact between them, so Gichtel and Überfeld had to rely on what others related of Freher. He left Leiderdorp at the beginning of February 1695, almost exactly nine years after he had moved there, and remained in Holland for another few months. By 17 May he had left for England, by way of Rotterdam.[18] Freher's transition to London thus took place in or shortly before May 1695. This is an important corrective to the date given as 1694 in earlier accounts.[19] Instead, the significant development of 1694 was Freher's first encounter with Leade's writings. On the basis of Gichtel's published correspondence, Lucinda Martin has drawn attention to Holland-based intermediaries between German Pietists and English Nonconformists, establishing that Gichtel himself was familiar with Leade from 1694 at the latest.[20] From the same year onwards, Loth Fischer—a long-term associate not only of Gichtel and Überfeld but also of Breckling— published Leade's writings in German translations. With a transparent play on his initials, he signed the translator's postscript for *The Heavenly Cloud Now Breaking* as 'Loving Friend' (*Liebwilliger Freund*) on 6 April 1694.[21] While still in Holland, Freher was firmly embedded in Gichtel's network and therefore among the first to encounter Leade in a continental context.

After his exposure to Leade's writings, they fascinated Freher so much that he decided to leave Holland for London. Upon arriving in the English metropolis, he shared rooms with one Scheller and the future secretary of the Philadelphian Society, Johann Heinrich Deichmann. Scheller eventually visited Gichtel in Amsterdam and told him about Freher's early days in London. Gichtel then relayed Scheller's account to Überfeld in a letter dated 30 January 1696. To introduce himself, Scheller reported, Freher 'wrote a Latin letter to Leade, spanning an entire sheet,' in which he 'confessed that he had been awakened through her writings and was unable to rest until seeing her face to face.' As the elderly widow was, of course, entirely unable to read Latin, Scheller had to translate the long-winded letter into English: brevity was never Freher's strong suit. Deichmann and Scheller together then took Freher to meet Leade. During this much-anticipated meeting, the prophetess agreed to write an individual letter to each of them. Scheller received the lion's share of Leade's praise, leaving Freher offended that she had failed to recognise his own superiority.

He promptly admonished her in a reply, yet Leade cut him down to size by responding that 'even if he had Solomon's wisdom, there would yet be more with her, which instantly lessened Freher's affection' for her. Disappointed in his high hopes for the encounter with Leade, the former disciple of Gichtel and Überfeld sought to emulate them and found his own spiritual community. However, Deichmann and particularly Scheller showed no enthusiasm. As Freher proved an unpopular roommate, his would-be disciples soon left him, one after the other.[22] Following this initial disappointment with Leade and her followers, it appears that Freher adopted the pose of a confident, perhaps even independent-minded associate, who maintained close contacts with the Philadelphians until the elderly widow's death and beyond. After the dissolution of the Society, Freher also engaged with the Quaker congregation of Bow Lane, which he addressed in letters written between 1712 and 1715.[23] It seems that he met most of his close friends in the context of that religious community, and some of them—notably Jeremias Daniel Leuchter and Allen Leppington—became productive copyists of Freher's works.[24] Much remains unclear about Freher's later life in London, yet that should not keep us from engaging with his writings.

Freher's *Fundamenta Mystica Jacobi Behmen Teutonici, Explicata*

The peculiar *Fundamenta mystica* represent the most impressive fruit of Freher's long-standing intellectual engagement with the theosopher of Görlitz. In the only monograph on Freher so far, Charles A. Muses has hailed the work as a most faithful exposition of Boehme's theosophy.[25] Freher likely thought of his work in a similar way, although he modestly acknowledged his limitations, 'saying plainly, that I do not Understand him [Boehme] any further, than According to the small Measure of my own Progress.'[26] For an Anglophone audience, Freher played the important role of a cultural intermediary. In this capacity, he communicated his own understanding of Boehme to people who, by and large, read Boehme's works in English translation. In the process, Freher commented upon choices made by earlier translators and occasionally translated Boehme passages himself.[27]

Moreover, Freher's writings often addressed specific interlocutors, though in many cases it is no longer possible to establish their identities. Yet two whole volumes of the *Fundamenta mystica* are significant exceptions to this rule. The first of these, volume F, remained incomplete as Freher's antagonist, one Mr Pierce, found himself prematurely convinced; the second, volume H, specifically dealt with the objections and queries of Rev. Edward Waple.[28] After initially 'instructing children in Latin' and thus sharing the lot of Franckenberg in Danzig half a century earlier, it seems likely that Freher offered his skills and insights into Boehme in exchange for room and board.[29] He may have found patrons among his wealthier acquaintances, most notably Waple, whose questions also prompted Freher to write *The Substance of a Conference betwixt a German Theosophist, and an English Divine*. His writing thus earned his keep or at the very least contributed to augmenting the meagre livelihood he gained through teaching. In this peculiar situation, Freher at times appeared to write as a Boehme expert on demand: he expanded on topics and digressed 'according to what was lately desired,' as a rare admission reveals.[30]

The following survey of Freher's *Fundamenta mystica* focuses on the manner in which he appropriated Boehme's spiritual alchemy and communicated it to an English audience. The theosophical jargon Boehmists employed around 1700 made excessive use of alchemical terms, yet only a few instances actually harked back to transmutational alchemy. Despite this, the 'outward Process of the Philosophical Work' of alchemy played an exceptional role, supplying as it did the 'similitude . . . which would be the nearest and most proper' to the mysteries Boehme sought to convey.[31] Nonetheless, the situation remained tangled even in Freher's expositions. In *The Substance of a Conference*, for instance, Freher himself all but admitted that the theosophical use of the transmutational key term 'tincture' was nearly impenetrable.[32] Fortunately, Freher defined and used some words in a more systematic manner. For instance, he employed alchemical language to express the key idea (borrowed from Aristotle) that the creation of one thing is the undoing of another. To provide two simple examples, the birth of the new man is the death of the old Adam, and the transmutation of gold is the annihilation of lead—that Freher would use precisely this parallelism is, of course, highly significant. To express this general notion, he employed the terms 'transmutation' and 'annihilation.'[33] In their dynamic interplay, Freher asserted, 'lyeth the true and only Key to the Understanding [of] Behmen's Writings.'[34] Just like Freher, 'I shall say nothing more' of annihilation, but transmutation certainly merits further discussion due to its distinctly alchemical origin. Ultimately, Freher's own perceptive commentary on Boehme's writings actually succeeded in bringing out several hidden connections between the meanings involved in alchemical terminology and their theosophical appropriation.

Throughout his monumental work, Freher—like Boehme—often relied on alchemy and its terms. Yet the German expatriate appears to have had an even more limited grasp of alchemy than Boehme, Franckenberg, and Breckling, deriving his knowledge from Boehme's writings and his own mentors in Holland, Gichtel and Überfeld. Though Freher never referred to many authors other than the omnipresent Boehme, it does not seem that he engaged with alchemical literature, let alone the actual practice of alchemy in the laboratory. Nevertheless, and in stark contrast to Gichtel and Überfeld, Freher's attitude towards alchemy remained positive: like Breckling, he did not turn his back on the physical world and its investigation.[35] In this he truly did remain more faithful to the theosopher of Görlitz than either Gichtel or Überfeld. Throughout what follows, I have chiefly relied on the collection of Freher manuscripts at the British Library, established in 1973 from the collections of the British Museum and based at St Pancras since 1997. These twenty-seven volumes come closest to providing a *textus receptus*, as they have been publicly available ever since Edward Fisher of Bath donated them to the British Museum on 30 September 1801.[36] There is reason to believe that an interested audience soon became aware of the public availability of Freher's works at the British Museum.[37]

Tincture and Transmutation

Alchemy and its terminology appear throughout almost all volumes of Freher's *Fundamenta mystica*.[38] Due to the peculiar nature of volume H, it provides the best point of entry. The title page promises 'Miscellaneous Observations occasioned by Mr. Waple's own Writings about J. B. which he desired me to correct and to compleat.'[39] In practice, volume H takes the form of a series of questions and answers on the more recondite aspects of Boehmist theosophy, which Freher sought to clarify for Waple, his long-term patron and interlocutor. One of the questions discussed is the following: what is it that Boehmist theosophers 'teach concerning the Philosophical Work?' 'They teach in Substance,' Freher explained, 'that the Process of the Universal Tincture, for Transmuting Metalls, and Healing the Body, (attainable, if all the requisites are truely in the Artist found) is the very same, with the Process of the Holy Spiritual Tincture, for the Soul of Man; attainable in the Regeneration.' Freher held that spiritual and laboratory alchemy were not only analogical but in fact identical. Through this conflation he paved the way for Mary Anne South's approach to alchemical literature.

Put simply, the transmutations of metals and of human souls share a single process, which 'in itself is very short.' This can be accounted for by the fact that 'the Life of Man, and so of Mettals, as also of the whole Nature,' is based on the '7. Properties.' When referring to these properties, Freher meant Boehme's seven source spirits. These in turn derive from the seven planets or metals, and Freher's use of the traditional symbols in his imagery emphasised this heritage. However, 'these 7. Properties are now under the Curse, and stand in meere Strife and Contrariety.' This state of affairs cannot be mended and restored to harmony, 'except there come such a Death into these 7. Properties, as... may be first a Death unto them, and then also able, to raise them up again, into One Harmonious Life and Will.' Only through death and resurrection could the Curse be lifted. Once this is accomplished 'in the Philosophical Work' of alchemy, 'the Universal Tincture is prepared, the Curse is removed, Earth is turned in, and Heaven out. And this therefore is able also, to Reharmonize all the 7. Disorder'd Properties, both in the Metals of the Earth, and in the Distemper'd Bodies of Men.'[40] Just as laboratory alchemy had profound effects on the physical attributes of metals, so spiritual alchemy completely transformed the bodies of born-again believers.

Both spiritual and laboratory alchemy worked on the very fabric of the universe. Freher distinguished between two different kinds of matter, associated 'with the One-Elementary Paradise' and 'this four-Elementary World,' respectively.[41] Freher further described the one element while discussing the matter out of which Adam was first created: 'it was the Light's Essence or Materiality; It was the one, pure, Eternal Element, which is the Materiality of Eternity, wherein the Growing, greening or Flourishing Life is Paradise: It was Paradisical Earth, wherein there was a Celestial Qualification: It was the matrix of the Earth: It was a quint-Essence of Stars and Elements: It was a threefold Substance of all the 3. Worlds: It was an External and Internal, a Celestial and Terrestrial Substance etc.'[42] The one element was a subtle matter, and Freher correspondingly spoke of a 'Spiritual Materiality.'[43] For his part, Boehme had simply called it 'the element' or, less often, 'the holy element.'[44] Freher asserted that it 'is Unquestionable, that the first Adam had before his Fall a Pure, Æthereal, Holy Body, able to dwell in Paradise,' which 'Body... must have been a particular Microcosm, or Compendium of that whole Universe, or Universal Body of the One-Elementary World.'[45]

Freher's one element was closely related to the ether or quintessence in cosmology and alchemy.[46] The statement that the sun and stars could not be without the 'finest and purest Æther in this World' represented a clear nod to traditional conceptions of superlunary matter, of which the heavenly bodies were formed.[47] The one element was eternal, like the quintessence of Aristotelian cosmology, and exhibited a perfectly harmonious balance of all qualities. In contrast, the four elements were imperfect derivates, in which opposing qualities struggled for dominance. What applied to the macrocosm equally held true for the microcosm. Freher described Adam's prelapsarian body as 'holy, pure and perfect, Clear and Crystalline' or as a 'Crystalline One Elementary Body'.[48] In a contrast reminiscent of Franckenberg, Freher spoke of 'Man's Corrupt 4 Elementary Body, or Flesh and Blood, which cannot inherit the Kingdom of God' because it was 'beast-like.'[49] The same deterioration affected the 'One Elementary World,' which became one consisting of four elements marked by strife. As I shall show in due course, Freher held that both laboratory and spiritual alchemy played a role in restoring the earlier, harmonious state, both within nature and within the believer.

Despite his lack of familiarity with laboratory practice and its literature, Freher took the reality of alchemy, as well as its adepts and fabled transmuting agent, for granted, if only as lesser instances of processes that ultimately took place within the mysterious deity of Boehme's theosophy. Foreshadowing the current scholarly consensus, Freher described his authority's references to alchemy as follows: 'seeing that he [Boehme] never made it his Business to teach us that Curious Art [of alchemy], which he also understood not himself, as to the outward Handling and Practice thereof; but intended always some other thing of deeper Consideration, and greater Necessity; which, he sayth, All the like Descriptions shall only be subservient unto.'[50] Perhaps this statement even more aptly describes Freher himself, as Boehme likely had a somewhat greater understanding of alchemy than his expositor. However, both of them referred to laboratory alchemy strictly in order to adumbrate loftier goals. Elsewhere, Freher specified two general requirements for success in laboratory alchemy: '1. An Experimental Understanding, from the Artist's Process in his own Regeneration, and 2. a Divine Call for this Undertaking.' Boehme and, by extension, Freher himself had the former, though not the latter: 'but there is also required an Especial Calling thereunto, which he [Boehme] had not.'[51] Practitioners needed to be both reborn and called by God to pursue the great work: Boehme and Freher agreed in making rebirth a crucial precondition for alchemical success.[52] Like Boehme, Freher neither grasped laboratory alchemy nor was called to pursue it. As a born-again believer, he construed alchemy as mirroring the process of regeneration and treated it as subservient to this more sublime ambition.

Both Boehme and Freher viewed the physical world as a lesser reflection of the two invisible worlds of fire and light. On this understanding, alchemical transmutation reflected processes within what Boehme called 'Eternal Nature,' a distinct plane also described as God's body, situated between the deity and the material world and mediating between them through the seven forms or properties.[53] On this plane, the '3. first Forms of Eternal Nature' (Saturn, Mercury, and Mars) were associated with the principle of fire; these needed to be transmuted into the forms linked to light (Luna, Jupiter, and Venus).[54] In Freher's understanding, the change of the first, fiery principle's properties into those tied to the second principle of light was the prototypical instance of transmutation. Even in the physical world, this did not entail that the fiery or dark properties ceased to exist, a notion that would not make any sense in eternal nature.[55] According to Freher, all properties were inextricably mixed in the third principle; whether a piece of metal appeared as lead or gold depended on whether the dark or light properties attained dominance (and, indeed, the eye of the beholder).[56] The actual alchemical transmutation of base metals into gold in the physical world thus mirrored processes taking place within eternal nature.

Between the extremes of divine becoming and metallic transmutation lies another parallel process, centred on the believer's spiritual rebirth: 'let us consider attentively the Process of our own Restoration or Regeneration, which is, (in short, and chiefly) nothing else, but an Essential Reconciliation, and most Intrinsecal Transmutation of the harsh, rough, bitter, fierce, Stinging, hating, fighting, whirling and Anguishing Properties of our own Immortal Soul.'[57] Consequently, Freher's chief concern was the transmutation taking place within Eternal Nature, always with a view to spiritual rebirth but hardly ever to alchemical *chrysopoeia*. This had fundamental implications for Freher's understanding of alchemy: in the layered cosmology he espoused, the material plane was a mere outgrowth of the spiritual plane. Just as it had been for Boehme, the visible world and its laboratory alchemy were but lesser reflections of the divine realm and spiritual alchemy. Due to Freher's almost complete lack of familiarity with alchemical literature and laboratory practice, this tendency was heightened further.

When Adam fell into transgression, he also fell 'under the Dominion of the 3. first Forms of Eternal Nature, divorced from their Eternal Light and Love.' Consequently, to restore Adam's prelapsarian state, God—as a mastermind alchemist—'must then . . . bring forth such a Renovation and Transmutation in time, upon Man's Immortal Soul, as was wrought out from Eternity in Eternal Nature itself.' Through this as yet unspecified process, Adam and his descendants would be reintroduced 'into Paradise again, nay even into a higher and more glorious State, than his first Paradise hath been.' The prelapsarian condition would not merely be restored but surpassed. 'But by what means,' Freher asked rhetorically, 'could there be effected such a Transmutation of our Souls?' The required agent was missing: 'Here was no Transmuting Tincture, neither in Heaven nor upon Earth. Our Loving Father in Heaven was not changed in his Love by our Transgression; but still he loved us, no less thereafter than before. But his Love could not yet be our Transmuting Tincture.'[58] Human souls were in need of transmutation, yet even God's love could not effect this by itself. By virtue of his divine attributes, God simply could not 'take into Paradise such a Degenerated, Disharmonious Soul, without Renovation and Transmutation, by a meere Pardoning from without.'[59] Just like pseudo-Weigel, Freher held that forensic justification was not sufficient to accomplish this restoration of humankind.

The solution to this quandary lay in the Incarnation of Christ or, more specifically, the process of redemption he enacted throughout his life on earth, from the Virgin Birth until Ascension and Pentecost. In other words, the Incarnation was crucial, yet at the same time it was only the beginning of a process that involved all of Christ's life and actions on earth: '[God's] Eternal Love ... must itself come down from Heaven, in Order to prepare a Transmuting Tincture for our Souls; And for this End it must enter actually into Conjunction with our Degenerated Nature. Which was also done accordingly, in the Womb of the Virgin Mary. But that Holy thing which was born of her, was not then Immediately the perfected or Consummated Tincture, but stood as then in the beginning Process only, by the Consummation of which it was to be made a Transmuting Tincture for our Souls.'[60] Freher was adamant that even the fact of the Word made flesh was not enough: 'in all his Life upon Earth He could not yet Tincture One single Soul,' as the disciples only became representatives of Christ both convinced and convincing after Pentecost: only then were they willing to die for their faith and able to convert many others to it.[61] Prior to completing 'the Process of his own Personal Transmutation' through his passion and resurrection, Christ had not yet acquired the ability to tinge others, and 'only after all this, when he could be called the First begotten from the Dead, when his whole Process was fully Consummated ... then He was and is the only Transmuting Tincture of our Souls.'[62] As for the theosopher of Görlitz, the spiritual alchemy of rebirth depended on the Incarnation as the crucial event of salvation history.

'The Process in the Philosophical Work' between Boehme and Atwood

Building on Boehme's *Signatura rerum*, Freher went on to describe this alchemical process of redemption at length in volume G of the *Fundamenta mystica*. As the title for the resultant treatise, he chose 'The Process in the Philosophical Work, Considerd as thoroughly Analogical with that in Man's Redemption through Jesus Christ.' Throughout, Freher presented a close reading of part of Boehme's *Signatura rerum*, of which he owned the 1682 edition.[63] It dwelt at length on Boehme's analogy between the Incarnation, passion, and resurrection of Jesus Christ and the spiritual rebirth of the individual believer. Unlike the bulk of Freher's writings, which remains unpublished to this day, a shortened version of 'The Process in the Philosophical Work' found inclusion in *The Lives of Alchemystical Philosophers*, a popular work on alchemy first published under a different title in 1814 and reissued in 1815. As such this was the first ever fragment of Freher's mature works that appeared in print with proper attribution to its author.[64] Freher's 'Process' tangibly links early-modern spiritual alchemy to its modern descendant. Indeed, perhaps more than any other work discussed in this study, this one epitomises the claim for continuity from Boehme to Atwood.[65] If Freher's 'Process' was thus primarily encountered in isolation, the following account presents it within the context of Freher's *Fundamenta mystica*, while drawing out the lines back to Boehme and forward to the 1815 edition, as well as the *Suggestive Inquiry*.

Unfortunately, it is unknown who was responsible for compiling *The Lives of Alchemystical Philosophers*.[66] We would likely have to look for someone in circles where Nonconformist religion combined with interest in occult lore. Due to the prominence accorded to Freher and Boehme, it appears likely that the editor was a member of Behmenist networks.[67] The alchemical texts in the volume include one titled 'First Principles, According to the Writings of Jacob Behmen,' and there is an account of Boehme's life among the biographies of adepts. The book concluded with a panegyric on the theosopher 'copied from MS. in a volume of his works.'[68] Walton identified the author of these lines as the playwright Henry Brooke, who had composed them in 1769, and the young Mary Anne South in turn included some of them in her *Suggestive Inquiry*.[69] In addition, the anonymous editor of *The Lives* prominently placed Freher's 'Process' as the very first of numerous 'Alchemic Treatises.'[70] This drastically shortened edition of Freher's text omits entire passages and shortens all retained paragraphs, reducing them to key statements while modernising Freher's accented English. The editor's source was the copy held at the British Museum, at the time a comparatively recent acquisition.[71] Although Mary Anne South may also have had access to the complete text there or through Walton's edition, likely read by her father, she repeatedly quoted this 1815 edition of Freher's 'Process' throughout her *Suggestive Inquiry*.[72]

In an extended passage of his *Signatura rerum*, Boehme had established parallels between the *opus magnum* of alchemy and Christ's redemptive work. Freher seized upon the same project, though he approached it considerably more systematically. At first glance, Freher's 'Process' might thus appear as a mere exercise in the *lapis-Christus* analogy. For both Boehme and Freher, however, the issue was more complex than that and involved a three-way analogy between alchemy, Christ's biography, and *Christus in nobis* or the believer's spiritual rebirth. It comes as no surprise, then, that both Boehme and Freher employed variations on a formula to establish specific *lapis-Christus in nobis* analogies. 'Thus also is the process of the wise with the noble stone,' Boehme wrote of the *proto-evangelium*, promising the victory of the woman's seed over the serpent.[73] Yet more important was the striking fact that he then proceeded to further identify that *lapis* as 'the noble stone of the new rebirth in Christ Jesus,' construing the born-again believer as a spiritual adept.[74] For his part, Freher employed the formula 'so also in this Philosophical Work' (with slight variations) no fewer than twelve times, which number further increases if other equivalent phrases are included in the count.[75]

Particularly salient are the more elaborate, less formulaic variations that establish analogies by moving from alchemy to something else. 'So it was also in the Process with the Lord Christ,' Freher claimed with regard to a transient, not yet fixed transmutation.[76] Elsewhere, he stated that 'the Process in the Regeneration of Man runs Parallel exactly' with the alchemical *coniunctio oppositorum* of heaven and earth.[77] Intriguingly, in phrasing it the way he did, Freher purposely retained ambiguity as to whether he meant Christ's life or the individual process of rebirth. Elsewhere, he had been very explicit in this regard: 'In all the Description of the Philosophical Work' contained in Boehme's *Signatura rerum*, 'both the Process of Christ through this World, Death and Hell, and the Process of Man's Regeneration also is declared.'[78] In fact, Freher even used the technical phrase 'the Incarnation of Christ' in this latter sense, explaining on one occasion that it was 'not Consider'd as that particular History, happened so many Ages ago, which is not hereby Undervalued; but Consider'd as that great perpetual Business, where every Christian Soul ought actually to be engaged in.' This was entirely in keeping with the spiritualist heritage that chastised the orthodox clergy for teaching a merely historical faith centred on past events. The incarnation of Christ in the believer dovetailed with *Christus in nobis*: 'he that hath Christ in him Incarnated, or he that is Regenerated, in that most proper Sense, . . . needs not to be told what Christ is in him'—he intimately knows it already.[79] The *lapis-Christus in nobis* analogy was thus not isolated or an end unto itself; rather, it was firmly embedded into the drama of the Fall and redemption, as it unfolded on the cosmic plane and within the life of the individual believer.

Although Freher's 'Process' is clearly evocative in its own right, many implications only become clearer in view of his understanding of alchemy and its terms. Already the first paragraph, for instance, alludes to the alchemical work as the redemption of matter: 'for if Man understandeth not his own Corrupted Nature, and that Curse which he himself now lyeth under, . . . upon what Ground can he presume to deliver such or such a Particular thing from that Curse; or to be Instrumental in this Deliverance? Which yet is the true Artist's chiefest, nay only Business.'[80] A shortened rendering very similar to this quotation would have greeted readers of *The Lives of Alchemystical Philosophers* at the very outset of their foray into alchemical literature, defining the 'deliverance' of 'matter from that curse' as 'the true artist's only business.'[81] Elsewhere, Freher claimed that the alchemist's 'design is nothing less than to fetch out a Body from the Curse, and to raise it from the Dead; which never can be done by him, that is still dead himself, both in his understanding, and as to his Internal Life,' which equally found its way into the 1815 edition and even the *Suggestive Inquiry*.[82]

In Freher's 'Process' and the *The Lives of Alchemystical Philosophers*, we encounter very strong statements on the soteriological potential of alchemy. Freher held that the shared objective of alchemy and rebirth was the restoration of an earlier, harmonious state of affairs that would lead the conflicted four elements back to the serenity of the one element. This hints at a crucial shift: for Freher 'the Process of the Holy Spiritual Tincture' had implicitly become the model for 'Transmuting Metalls.'[83] Put another way, if Siebmacher in his *Wasserstein* had construed sinful human beings as lesser metals in need of transmutation, Freher now thought of lesser metals as sinful human beings in need of redemption. For him, who may never have studied alchemical literature, much less set foot in a practitioner's laboratory, alchemy was, in effect, more abstract than spiritual rebirth. If Boehme used alchemy to make rebirth more tangible, Freher's knowledge of alchemy was so limited that rebirth appeared to make alchemy more palpable. In this sense, even beyond mere chronology, Freher was already considerably closer to nineteenth-century readers who approached alchemical literature with baffled fascination. This is a striking reversal, as all the figures and texts hitherto discussed viewed rebirth as something that needed to be made less abstract by illustrating it with recourse to alchemical transmutation in the laboratory.

Freher consistently discussed alchemy through the lens of salvation history. The exotic contours alchemy took on in the process ultimately inspired those who engaged with it in the nineteenth century, such as the anonymous editor of *The Lives of Alchemystical Philosophers* in 1815 and Mary Anne South in 1850. In the twentieth century, the Swiss psychiatrist C. G. Jung articulated a vision of the alchemist as concerned with the salvation of the material world that continues to hold great intuitive appeal even among specialist scholars.[84] It should be noted that it is one thing to say that alchemy provides a glimpse of the ultimate restoration of nature and quite another to claim that the alchemist is actively working towards it: there are certainly early-modern examples of the former, weaker claim, but almost none of its stronger, more emphatic version.[85] Apart from Heinrich Khunrath, whose analogy of the *lapis* as the 'son of the macrocosm' with the Son of Man (or microcosm) could be taken to imply as much, but no more than that, the salient exceptions to this rule are Boehme and Freher.[86]

In his *Signatura rerum*, Boehme emphasised that the Fall affected humanity and all of creation equally, claiming that 'mankind and the earth, with its secrets, lie sealed under the same curse and death and require one and the same restoration.'[87] Underlining and marking passages in pencil, C. G. Jung carefully perused the chapter of *Signatura rerum* in which this statement occurred.[88] In so many words, Freher repeatedly expressed the idea that the alchemist's aim was the redemption of nature: 'we know that we live, and lye in this time, together with the whole Creation, under the Curse, and that the whole Business in all this Philosophical Work is only this, that the Curse may be taken from the Creature, as far as it can be done during this Time.' According to Freher, 'all the Chymists, . . . if they be true Understanding Artists,' labour towards freeing creation from the consequences of Adam's Fall.[89] His is 'an Understanding of this Philosophical Work, wherein the Cursed Nature is restored, from the Strife of its Seven Disharmonized Properties, into their Paradisical Union.'[90] The prelapsarian harmony of the natural world could therefore be restored through alchemy. Freher also expressed this view in 'The Process in the Philosophical Work,' whence it was transmitted to the nineteenth and twentieth centuries by way of *The Lives of Alchemystical Philosophers* and the *Suggestive Inquiry*.[91]

In comparison to Freher's emphasis of paradisiacal union, some of Boehme's formulations were more daring because they employed the language of deification. A time-honoured variant of *unio mystica* that dominated in the Eastern Orthodox churches, deification focused on regaining the divine likeness of the prelapsarian state rather than attaining marital intimacy with the divine. 'God must become human, human must become god,' Boehme wrote; 'heaven must become one thing with the earth, the earth must become heaven.'[92] These juxtaposed statements drew equally on the German mystics, much esteemed in Boehme's circles, and on the *Tabula smaragdina*, attributed to Hermes Trismegistus, the mythical inventor of alchemy. Believed to contain all secrets of the art, this short text discussed how the attributes of heaven and earth could be united through alchemy. Elsewhere, Boehme reiterated that 'God became human and made the human god.'[93] While avoiding deification here, Freher did not shy away from it elsewhere in the *Fundamenta mystica*: 'it is known sufficiently, that the Mystical Writers commonly use the Expressions of God Incarnated, and Man Deified, or of God-Man and Man-God; Applying them not only to Christ the Head . . . but als[o] unto the Christians his members.'[94] One of the writers he had in mind here was among the apprentices of Franckenberg's spiritual alchemy, Angelus Silesius or Johannes Scheffler: a rare instance of an author whom Freher mentioned by name.[95] Instead of focusing on deification, Freher expanded upon the unification of heaven and earth, better suited to the alchemical theme of his treatise: 'the whole Work consists Summarily therein, that two things must be reduced back into One . . . as they were from the Beginning. . . . A Heavenly thing and an Earthly one are to be joined. . . . Earth must be turned in, and Heaven out.'[96] The language and underlying concepts clearly derive from alchemy, though Freher discussed them without any recourse to its literature.

In a passage ruthlessly shortened for the 1815 edition, Freher sought to clarify the union of heaven and earth further. He alluded to topics he had developed elsewhere throughout the *Fundamenta mystica*: 'consider only with thy self the Heavenly Humanity of the Regenerator, and the Earthly [humanity] of poor falln man, that is to be regenerated: Consider, that the former must be received or taken in by the latter, and that this must suffer itself to be subdued, changed, kept under, and turned in by that.' By becoming joined to Christ's heavenly humanity or his one-elementary body, the terrestrial body—consisting of, and subject to, the four elements—loses its dominance. At the Last Judgement, 'as in the Compleatest Period of the

Regeneration,' this will cause the body to be raised up again, 'which then shall no more be Earthly, but Heavenly, and Conformable unto his [Christ's] own Glorified Body.'[97] As we have come to expect, this corresponded to 'that which disappear'd in Man, by his Fall, and in the Earth, by the Curse.'[98] Subsequently, Freher partially made up for his omission of deification by quoting John's Gospel: 'As many as Received him [Christ], to them gave he Power to become the Sons of God.' In addition, he used the related phrase 'Child of God.'[99] Unfortunately, along with the material just discussed, this entire passage fell victim to the nineteenth-century editor.

In contrast to Boehme's overt expressions of mysticism, his emphasis on the *proto-evangelium* reverberated through the centuries. Extended passages of *Signatura rerum* closely associated the great work of alchemy with the crushing of the serpent, both through Christ and within the believer: 'now in this lies the *lapis philosophorum*, how the woman's seed may crush the head of the serpent; this takes place in spirit and being, temporally and eternally.'[100] Freher quoted Genesis at greater length, yet his words appear to be a direct, if extrapolating, translation of the Boehme passage: 'immediately after the Fall of Man God said unto the Serpent: I will putt Enemity between thee and the woman, and between thy Seed and her Seed: Her Seed shall bruise thy Head, and thou shalt bruise his Heel. And herein the Philosopher's Stone or Tincture lyeth implicitely. For tho' this primarily concerneth Man, yet secundarily it concerneth the whole Creation also; and this Bruising of the Serpent's Head is done both Spiritually and Corporeally, and both in time and in Eternity; And tho' in different Degrees, yet in a Parallel Process or Method, both here and there.'[101] A related passage more explicitly interiorises the crushing of the serpent as the subjugation of selfishness.[102] In noteworthy exceptions to his usual approach, the anonymous editor retained both of these passages virtually without shortening them.[103] One of them also fed wholesale into the *Suggestive Inquiry*, in which Mary Anne South included the entire beginning of Freher's treatise. In addition, she also paraphrased a part towards the end of Freher's 'Process,' thus including more than 10 per cent of the 1815 edition in her *magnum opus*.[104]

By taking the spiritual alchemy of rebirth from Holland and introducing it to an English audience for the first time, Freher played a most crucial role in this story of how spiritual alchemy reached the Victorian age and, specifically, the young Mary Anne South. I have expanded on Freher's sojourn in Holland based on previously ignored documents harking back to the Angelic Brethren, the sect founded by his erstwhile roommate, Johann

Wilhelm Überfeld. If his life in London still remains largely obscure, this can be put down to his consciously quiet lifestyle with few friends, most of whom shared his desire to avoid public attention. Freher's eight-volume *Fundamenta mystica* primarily served the purpose of interpreting and explaining Boehme's theosophy to an Anglophone audience. In the course of this grand project, Freher also employed several alchemical terms, derived from Boehme, rather than any independent encounter with alchemical literature, and related them to the overarching concern he shared with the theosopher of Görlitz: spiritual rebirth. Particularly in 'The Process in the Philosophical Work,' Freher detailed the three-way analogy between alchemy, Christ's Incarnation, and the regeneration of individual believers. As a rare exception among his mostly unprinted work, a drastically shortened version of Freher's 'Process' found its way into *The Lives of Alchemystical Philosophers*, likely compiled by an English Behmenist. 'The Process in the Philosophical Work' guarantees the continuity of spiritual alchemy from Boehme to Atwood.

9
Mesmerists and Alchemists in Victorian London

Eventually better known as Mrs Atwood, Mary Anne South was born in 1817, only a few years after the publication of *The Lives of Alchemystical Philosophers*. Dionysius Andreas Freher was the youngest author whose work found inclusion in that volume, alongside his contemporary, mining expert and alchemist Georg von Welling.[1] This reflected a prevailing sense that the age of the adepts of old had passed with the likes of Welling and Freher. In the first quarter of the eighteenth century, alchemy swiftly became marginalised under an onslaught of Enlightenment polemicists. Leading practitioners in London, Paris, Leiden, and Halle distanced themselves from the gold-faking charlatans of old.[2] The 'Golden Age' of alchemy, as Lawrence M. Principe describes it, had come to an end.[3] Yet the history of alchemy continued into the modern period, and it was only after 1850 that spiritual interpretations of the *opus magnum* gradually shifted from the margins to becoming a mainstream view of alchemy. Mary Anne South played a pivotal role in this development. In her early thirties, around the middle of the nineteenth century, she became an avid reader of *The Lives of Alchemystical Philosophers* and relied on it while composing *A Suggestive Inquiry into the Hermetic Mystery*.[4]

As the story goes, the author and her father, Thomas South, withdrew the *Suggestive Inquiry* after publication and burnt all the copies they could buy. Over time, fascination with the book's story gradually replaced actual engagement with its content. Beyond the Victorian verbiage and occasional references to magnetism, its views are quite traditional and in many ways aligned with Christian mysticism and Boehme's theosophy of rebirth. Correspondingly, South gestured towards the time around 1700 as a crucial period for the revelation of alchemy's *arcana*: 'when, however, the writings of Jacob Böhme appeared in Germany, some century and a half ago,' she held, 'the Alchemists who lived at that period, write as if they supposed their art could no longer remain a secret.'[5] After this whirlwind of revelations, it seemed that the adepts no longer needed to speak: Boehme and his disciples had already revealed all the secrets. The widespread availability of the theosopher's works (guaranteed by the three complete editions of 1682, 1715, and 1730) and the immense attention they attracted both on the Continent and across the Channel made sure of this. Yet Freher's posthumous reputation as a great expositor of Jacob Boehme's theosophy co-existed uneasily with the neglect accorded to Freher's manuscript works. Perhaps it was precisely the strictly limited availability of his papers that added to their mystique and appeal.

Freher's writings caused precious few ripples for more than a century after his death. Those who encountered his papers chiefly contented themselves with handing them down for the remainder of the eighteenth century as well as the first half of the nineteenth. The very transmission of these manuscripts, however, testifies to continuity in circles of English Behmenists from the early eighteenth to the second half of the nineteenth century.[6] Nevertheless, several Anglophone Boehme devotees testified to Freher's lasting impact among insiders: eighteenth-century devotional writer William Law was succeeded by the Methodist silk-mercer-turned-jeweller Christopher Walton as well as Anne Judith Penny (née Brown), whose writings on Boehme were eventually published in book form.[7] Thomas South and especially his daughter Mary Anne must equally be mentioned in this context. They both corresponded with Walton, and Thomas intently discussed Freher in his letters. The young woman kept these connections to English Behmenists alive until her death: even as an old widow in 1907, Mrs Atwood still corresponded with one 'Mrs. Johnson' who was 'a great niece... by her mothers side, of Dr. William Law—the great promoter of our Jacob Böhme.'[8] To establish the context in which Mary Anne wrote the *Suggestive Inquiry*, this chapter explores the correspondence between Walton and the Souths. It then outlines a new interpretation of that work which places it in the context of Boehmist spiritual alchemy.

The Souths' Correspondence with Christopher Walton

Thomas South and his daughter Mary Anne exchanged letters with Christopher Walton in the years surrounding the publication and subsequent withdrawal of her *Suggestive Inquiry*. Walton's missives do not survive, as he requested that South destroy them: 'be assured all your correspondence is burnt,' South confirmed.[9] Despite their brevity, South's letters document the great interest in Boehme and Freher he shared with Walton. If anything, South briefly even surpassed Walton in this regard, as Walton initially wholly focused on William Law and only gradually engaged more seriously with Freher. Joscelyn Godwin has suggested that an informal circle of Behmenists around James Pierrepont Greaves, the self-styled 'sacred socialist,' could have played a role in facilitating their acquaintance.[10] For her part, Mary Anne Atwood reminisced in 1903 that she and her sister had been involved with 'Christian Socialism' in her 'early youth,' mentioning Robert Owen and John Minter Morgan but not Greaves, though she may well have encountered him in similar contexts.[11] Greaves is indeed a possible source for the Souths' keen interest in regeneration. In the early 1830s, he wrote about his religious views, which encompassed *Christus in nobis*, mystical union, mystical death, deification, regeneration, the restoration of the prelapsarian state, and even transmutation.[12] These excerpts were then published in 1847, five years after Greaves's death, as *New Theosophic Revelations*, a title that could well be viewed as a nod to Boehme.

Alternatively, South and Walton could have established contact as reticent authors whose shared interests bridged their age gap of almost thirty years. Using a pseudonym, South had published *Early Magnetism* in 1846, Walton his rare and anonymous *On the Present, Past and Future* in 1847.[13] South's oldest datable letter—it must have been written on 29 April 1848—correspondingly opens with an expression of gratitude 'for your pamphlet... which it gave me pleasure to peruse.'[14] Walton's publication included an announcement of projected editions of the works of Boehme, Law, Freher, and Louis-Claude de Saint-Martin, in this unchronological sequence.[15] Among these, the little-known Freher especially intrigued South. He clearly expressed his admiration for Freher: 'I like the mind that could illustrate and comment upon Behmen.' South wrote further that the 'intended publication' of a new Boehme edition 'interests me, but more particularly a translation of Frehers works, which I should much desire to possess.'[16] South likely spoke of a translation because Walton's brief prospectus mentioned two works Freher had composed in German.[17] In addition, South also returned 'the small work edited by [Pierre] Poiret' and inquired whether Walton might have advice on where the 'writings of [Jane] Leade and [John] Pordage' could be bought, as he had tried to obtain them 'in vain these last three years.'[18] South had thus been interested in these Boehme disciples of the late seventeenth and early eighteenth centuries since around 1845 at the latest. This helps to account for the great esteem in which his daughter held the same authors and the relevance she attached to the period during which they were active.

The discussion of early-modern theosophical writers formed a frequently recurring topic throughout the correspondence between Walton and South. While they both agreed on the importance of the literature these authors had produced, they differed on their individual merits. South, for instance, could not comprehend Walton's adulation of William Law, and Walton apparently thought dismissively of Leade, which assessment South repeatedly tried to correct. Most strikingly, South was full of admiration for Freher and repeatedly urged Walton to prioritise him. On 6 May 1848, South wrote: 'it appears that you possess in Frehers MSS. a most valuable treasure, but you are without the Key otherwise you would not speak of Leade as you have done. . . . Would it were in my power to persuade you in the sacred cause of truth to edit Freher solely and alone, apart from the others[.] My opinion is that if you undertook this well . . . you perhaps by publishing these *cum notis* [with commentary], would do more than Behmen or than Freher himself have done, you would enlighten the world without mystification.'[19] Yet Walton was not swayed and told South as much. In the next letter, dated 26 August, South wrote: 'I cannot but conclude without again regretting that Freher should not have stood No. 1. in your Series.'[20] Due to Freher's great insight and clarity, South thought that Walton could have rendered the world an inestimably greater service by focusing on him rather than Law, many of whose works had been published in print.

Within the space of the next year, roughly, South appears to have considerably enlarged his familiarity with Freher's writings. It is possible that he made use of his stay in London to consult the Freher manuscripts at the British Museum or in Walton's private collection. Godwin has pointed out that some of Walton's acquaintances well knew that a collection of Freher manuscripts was available at the British Museum.[21] The lodgings of South and his daughters—Mary Anne had a sister named Louisa, about whom virtually nothing is known—in the metropolis enabled easy access to that institution.[22] In November 1848 the young ladies stayed at 15 Great Coram Street near Russell Square, which was but a pleasant stroll of half a mile from the British Museum.[23] Most likely during the winter of 1848 and 1849, their father resided at 18 Albany Street, a little bit further away near Regent's Park but still within easy reach using a coach.[24] Unfortunately, complete records on readers who studied Freher's manuscripts at the British Museum during the nineteenth century have not been preserved.[25]

Be that as it may, we do know that Walton shared his Freher extracts with South as they were printed. These texts spanned more than two hundred pages of small print in Walton's *Notes and Materials*.[26] A note appearing alongside printers' marks indicates that a specific sheet, 'AAA,' was printed on 29 December 1848.[27] A considerable body of Freher's writings, including all of 'The Process in the Philosophical Work,' thus would have gradually become available to South from 1848 onwards.[28] Only in January 1850 did the printing of the Freher excerpts finally reach its conclusion.[29] In view of this, simply stating 1854 as the date of publication for Walton's sprawling work is thoroughly misleading: parts were printed in the 1840s already, while bits and bobs in print as well as manuscript additions still accrued into the 1860s. It is therefore possible that Walton's edition of Freher's 'Process in the Philosophical Work' triggered the Souths' engagement with alchemy. Any evidence there once may have been for this must be presumed lost along with Walton's side of the correspondence.

Whether or not South read anything beyond Walton's printed extracts, his initial fascination with Freher soon matured into profound admiration. He penned the following assessment on 18 July 1849: 'Freher tells you of an art (not a trick remember) most holy, most divine far surpassing any revealments I ever met with in Law[.] Whether he knew Alchemy at all, I do not pretend to know, but have met with no passage in his writings which convince me that he did so. Freher is profoundly skilled and your extracts from his works are indeed most valuable truly philosophic, and very enlightening.'[30] Considering that rebirth is the main topic of Freher's works, it is likely that this was what South had in mind. His conclusion regarding Freher's knowledge of alchemy is apposite. Yet more importantly, alchemy now became a topic in the South-Walton correspondence, after Freher had already been discussed for some time. Even years later, the pre-eminent collector of Freher manuscripts relied on South's expertise once more, approaching him with 'questions on Freher.' South responded to them on 19 September 1853 but also complained that his interlocutor had neither ears to hear nor eyes to see: 'you are so apt to go off so in a tangent upon Behmen that I never can get a continuous conversation with you upon our Hermetic philosophy.' South suggested that Walton failed to perceive the art of alchemy, invented by Hermes Trismegistus, as central to Boehme's writings and instead focussed on minor matters. Clearly, the jeweller was not as receptive to South's new interest in alchemy as South would have liked.

After this tirade, South went on to explain that 'Freher as well as others had knowledge of a practice in common with Behmen, which and *which only* raised them where they were not regenerate but on the road to be so.' In each generation, 'there is but one, one only was, no one ever dared to reveal it openly, never in print never in writing, and never personally but after long experience of character.' South found himself in a different position because 'it was never discovered to me in this way, I am under no oaths but those which conscience sealed my lips with.' Instead, Mary Anne's father claimed that he had experienced an independent revelation: 'the light burst on me as it has rarely burst on others, I tell you, as my honest friend this holy light, has surely beamed on my unworthy self, after a long course of intense worldly suffering mental and bodily, that beam that kindled Behmen [and] Freher also fell on the humble head that now directs this pen.'[31] The ageing South thus viewed himself as someone who had independently attained knowledge of a secret practice towards regeneration, previously passed down orally from one spiritual adept to another. In their respective generations, Boehme and Freher were the only ones who had known of it. Thomas South explicitly presented himself as their successor during his own age.

Mysticism, Magnetism, and Alchemy

Throughout the correspondence between South and Walton, there are repeated references to a disjuncture that prevented them from communicating as smoothly as they would have liked. At the outset, commenting on his reading of Walton's *On the Present, Past and Future*, South wrote that 'the kind of light you mystics have always surprises me.' He thus classed Walton as a mystic. However, 'in my view of things,' South continued, 'there is still one [light] more direct, and tangible.'[32] Similarly, he construed both himself and Walton as travelling towards the same destination but at vastly different velocities. 'We are evidently in different spheres of mind,' South wrote on 27 November 1848, 'I cannot help viewing it as tho you travel by rail, and that our school passes you in the electric telegraph. . . . We shall meet on the platform for we both travel for truths sake.'[33] Walton was evidently offended by this unflattering comparison, which saw him trudging towards the highest summit of mysticism at a snail's pace. South apologised profusely on 11 December, although he continued to insist that his assessment was accurate.³⁴ South reiterated that he would only be able to clarify this difference in a personal encounter.³⁵

If Walton was a mystic, South must have thought of himself as pursuing something related to, but different from, mysticism. Initially, in 1848, he had in mind magnetism, but gradually alchemy took its place as the fast track towards mystical union with the divine. To better understand this development, we need to consider the 1846 publication *Early Magnetism*, in which alchemy did not yet play any role.³⁶ Published under the anagram 'ΘΥΟΣ ΜΑΘΟΣ,' it is usually attributed to Thomas South. However, Mary Anne's biographer Walter Leslie Wilmshurst asserted that she had written *Early Magnetism* in its entirety.³⁷ She herself did not claim this and more precisely identified her contribution as 'the first part of that little book' in a hitherto overlooked letter, dated 1 April 1903, to her trusted friend Isabelle de Steiger (*née* Lace).³⁸ In her portion of *Early Magnetism*, South argued that magnetism provided a technique to attain the same exalted state of mind as the pious heathens of antiquity and the early disciples 'of the Divine Founder of Christianity.'³⁹

The religious subtext of the Souths' interest in magnetic trance is apparent throughout and gradually intensifies towards the conclusion of *Early Magnetism*, composed by Thomas South. As his closing words make clear, he was reluctant to speak openly and explicitly about the implications of his realisation, for fear of offending prevalent religious sensibilities.⁴⁰ The same reticence also surfaced repeatedly in his dealings with Walton. Godwin notes that many Anglicans and Catholics 'looked on the magnetic phenomena—dangerously close to those of certain saints and of Jesus himself—with terror disguised as contempt.'⁴¹ Similarly, it appears that Walton the Methodist found it hard to overcome his initial misgivings towards 'all the pretences of Alchemy or Occult Science.'⁴² Ultimately, after many years, the Souths finally convinced him: in 1855 he included '*Popular Experimental Transcendentalism*, or *Animal Magnetism*' as a section in his reading list, and he even received communications from Freher's ghost in the early 1860s.⁴³

According to Thomas South, magnetic techniques could induce a trance he described as 'the sabbath of the senses,' through which it became possible 'to feel, to see and know the yet unstirred, unapproached, unappreciated, unbelieved, unrevered *Divinity* within us.'⁴⁴ This language is remarkably similar to what earlier protagonists, from pseudo-Weigel to Freher, would have described as *Christus in nobis*. In addition, South lamented the Fall and longed for the restitution of the prelapsarian state: 'were we not fallen, or could we still regain the high estate!'[45] This could be achieved through 'a new birth,' whose goal was 'the purification and perfection of human life,' as his daughter put it.[46] Even before the Christian era, the sages had found ways to attain 'regenerate purity,' among other things through initiatory rites that effected 'a re-birth and purification not dissimilar in idea from our baptismal form.'[47] Having attained union with the divine and regeneration, the human being became 'the divinized Epitome,' the deified microcosm.[48]

The Souths thus viewed magnetism in terms of older notions, which could be labelled as ancient wisdom (*prisca sapientia*) and Christian mysticism. However, they carefully veiled the latter aspect with language that avoided overtly Christian doctrines. In the exalted state attained through either magnetism or rebirth, 'the Absolute' could be known 'by the experience of co-essence in union, . . . by becoming it,' as Mary Anne South put it in *Early Magnetism*.[49] In their striving for *unio mystica*, the mystics pursued the very same goal; they merely took much longer to attain it, as her father repeatedly implied in letters to Walton. Consequently, Thomas South tried to encourage Walton to explore Mesmerism and magnetism. Mesmerism reached London in 'the late 1830s,' writes J. Jeffrey Franklin, upon which it 'rapidly became a subject of intense public and medical interest in the mid-1840s, and had saturated popular culture by the 1850s.'[50] South and his daughters were evidently very much caught up in these developments.[51]

South's letter dated 2 November 1848 explicitly presented the Mesmeric approach as the fast track to mystical and theosophical insights. He invited Walton to contact his 'daughters, now in London 15. Great Coram Street Russell Square,' who 'are quite in the magnetical world' and would introduce him to it. The jeweller was to 'witness the Trance and its phenomena of clairvoyance etc.' South claimed that if Walton thoroughly reflected upon these as he himself had done, he would 'get more light into Behmen in one week, than thru a whole lifes speculation without this Key.' Surpassing the theosopher of Görlitz, 'Freher goes a step beyond,' yet 'magnetism as it is now revealed strides before them both, and unlocks treasures and truths such as you have an inward yearning to behold.'[52] South's personal approach to theosophical writings consisted in reading them through the lens of Mesmerism and its phenomena. Animal magnetism was the telegraph wire on which the Souths were travelling, while Walton was stuck with bookish mysticism and devotional literature as his first-class train carriage.

In reaction, Walton wrote to South's daughters in London, and Mary Anne responded to his letter. Her brief missive is undated but was most likely written during November 1848, from the same address her father had mentioned at the beginning of the month. Walton had high hopes of Mesmerism, which Mary Anne South sought to moderate somewhat. She wrote that it was not in her 'power to offer you all the experimental satisfaction you desire— I do not believe that the verification of true science is in the power of any sleepwaker or mesmerize[d] Clairvoyant now living certainly not any of those I am, or have been, acquainted with hitherto.'[53] In other words, Walton would not find the conclusive proof of the supernatural for which he longed. Mary Anne invited the jeweller to a *séance* in Camden Town the next day, but he was unable to use this opportunity to witness the magnetic phenomena.

Even at this early stage, father and daughter held divergent views on animal magnetism and its phenomena. Whereas he thought of them as exceedingly important, she saw them as intriguing but ultimately very limited, a view she further accentuated in her old age. On 6 May 1903, for instance, she wrote to a close friend that there 'is too much importance ascribed to the ordinary Mesmeric trance in "Early Magnetism" written in a fit of enthusiasm.'[54] Despite this later reconsideration, in the early 1850s Mary Anne South viewed these phenomena 'as an example or forecast of a superior condition of life, and of the power of artificial means for inducing a state of self contemplation, by entrancing the senses,' and it was in this regard that 'Mesmerism appears to me now principally interesting.'[55] Abraham von Franckenberg had also claimed to intermittently experience a similar foretaste of the life to come, unencumbered by the burdens of the Fall. This elevated state of being was the same as the prelapsarian state of the human being, attained through spiritual rebirth, a notion developed in more detail throughout the *Suggestive Inquiry*. Though to vastly different extents, both father and daughter thus viewed magnetism as intimately connected to the age-old pursuit of mystical deification.

Between 1849 and 1855, that is, from the first mention of alchemy to the end of the Walton-South correspondence, alchemy gradually superseded magnetism as the surest path to rebirth. Most likely in 1853, on 4 January, South placed them on an equal footing when he inquired after Walton's progress in his 'search for truth, in the profounder study of practical Magnetism, in alighting the veil of Isis in Alchemy.'[56] Yet soon alchemy surpassed magnetism. The following year, on 5 January 1854, South pressed Walton to take 'Alchemy (the Key be assured to all you love)' seriously.[57] A few months later, on 18 May, South praised Walton's 'Summary of Questions' while cautioning that 'none but a practical Alchemist could answer' them.[58] Another year passed until South insisted on 30 March 1855 that 'none but the Alchemist' would be able to help: 'without him believe me little progress to Regeneration can be made.'[59] The alchemist, as conceived by South, was the most reliable guide to rebirth, and he relied on a more ancient, more disciplined form of the theory and practice of magnetism to achieve this goal much faster than ordinary mystics.

The correspondence of father and daughter South with Christopher Walton documents that particularly Mr South expressed great interest in Freher in the late 1840s. Specifically, he encouraged Walton to focus his editorial efforts on Freher rather than William Law and Boehme himself, whose works were quite readily available. Furthermore, whether through Walton's excerpts, the Freher manuscripts at the British Museum, or both of these, South also acquired a degree of knowledge of Freher's writings that even Walton, as the leading Freher collector, took seriously. Considering the close companionship of father and daughter in their intellectual pursuits, he surely would have highlighted Freher to her, and the quotes she integrated into the *Suggestive Inquiry* may have been merely the most superficial element of her own acquaintance with Freher. As Mary Anne South's *Suggestive Inquiry* must in turn have played a key role in furthering her father's interest in alchemy, I now turn to this milestone in the story of spiritual alchemy.

The Alchemy of Mystical Death and Rebirth in the *Suggestive Inquiry*

Despite the passage of time, the intriguing narrative surrounding the *Suggestive Inquiry* remains highly compelling. It has inspired not only C. G. Jung's 'description of the importance of the *soror mystica*' in his 1944 *Psychologie und Alchemie* (Psychology and Alchemy) but also Lindsay Clarke's enthralling novel *The Chymical Wedding* of 1989.[60] Freemason and lawyer Walter Leslie Wilmshurst related the story in his lengthy introduction to the second edition of 1918, subsequently reprinted many times.[61] According to Mrs Atwood's biographer, father and daughter South were engaged in a friendly competition to reveal the secrets of alchemy in verse and prose, respectively. Whereas Thomas South never completed his poem, Mary Anne wrote a substantial treatise.[62] It was published anonymously on Monday, 18 November 1850, and priced at 16 shillings.[63] As the printed book arrived at Bury House, Alverstoke (today Gosport), the Souths were awestruck by the implications of having revealed the secrets contained in the *Suggestive Inquiry* to the public at large. They quickly bought up all the exemplars that had not yet been sold and burnt them, preserving only a small number of personal copies. The first edition thus quickly became a rare collector's item: in the early twentieth century, Arthur Edward Waite, a well-informed occultist writer, estimated that 'there were only 15 copies in existence, and one was rarely offered for sale under £10.'[64]

The *Suggestive Inquiry* is a layered and voluminous book that has largely escaped scholarly attention, despite its wide audience beyond academia.[65] With its reception of classical or alchemical sources and the contemporaneous fascination with Mesmerism, various approaches could usefully be brought to bear upon it. However, I argue that the spiritual alchemy of Mary Anne South is a direct descendant of Boehme's theosophy and its focus on rebirth. For all the obscurantism of the *Suggestive Inquiry* and the fascination it engendered in occultist circles around 1900, one cannot emphasise enough that what the young Mary Anne South sought to propagate were traditionally Christian views, merely dressed up in esoteric garb. In many ways, hers was not a modern project but one defined by earlier understandings of ancient wisdom and religion, predicated on spiritual rebirth. Incidentally, these notions achieved dominance particularly throughout the early-modern period. Among the authors previously surveyed, Abraham von Franckenberg stands out for the weight he attached to ancient authorities, such as Valentinus, long denounced as a gnostic heretic, and even older pagan sages (Zoroaster and Hermes Trismegistus, among others), whose sayings found inclusion in his *Via veterum sapientum*.[66] Like Franckenberg two centuries earlier, Mary Anne South stressed a shared piety and common goal as the thread that connected the wisdom of the ancients to the teachings of the Christian church: mystical union with the divine through rebirth.

According to South, the 'Theurgic Art' of the pagan sages surpassed all others in how nearly it approached 'a fulfilment of the perfect doctrine of regeneration preached by Jesus Christ and his apostles.'[67] Christ came to reform old rites rather than establish new ones: 'thus the Mysteries of Antiquity changed their form only to appear more resplendent when Christianity came to be the prevailing religion; when baptismal regeneration was an effectual rite, and the Eucharist a true initiation; when Faith by humiliation under the exemplary cross of Christ, brought him forth anew in each regenerate life.'[68] In other words, in the days of primitive Christianity the rites of baptism and the Eucharist carried actual efficacy, which helped the believer to become born again and, by the same token, to give birth to Christ within, closely approximating the notion of *Christus in nobis*. This contributed to the rapid spread of the Gospel, which South described in terms reminiscent of Breckling's *multiplicatio*. Elsewhere, South lamented how, during the Reformation, 'our Reformers, mistaking these things for superstitions, ... turned them all out of doors; retaining indeed little more of the mystery of regeneration than a traditional faith.'[69] Pagan sages and the first Christians alike practised their rituals to attain 'the mystical death and regeneration' that were also at the heart of Franckenberg's *Theophrastia Valentiniana*.[70]

It is not entirely clear what South meant by her dismissive reference to traditional faith. Among other things, she probably had in mind the Christian church's rituals as practised without a sense of their actual efficacy and a corresponding disregard for the bodily side of the spiritual alchemy of rebirth. From Boehme to Freher and beyond, rebirth also had physical implications for the born-again believer. According to Freher, it triggered the dormant seed that would flower to become a one-elementary body akin to Christ's resurrection body. Freher's one element was based on earlier notions of the quintessence or ether, and it is precisely the latter term that received new life in the wake of Mesmerism and animal magnetism. According to the *Suggestive Inquiry*, then, there was a 'divine germ of humanity,' though it found itself in 'a deplorable condition' and 'said to be beheld under the thousand evils of its birth.'[71] In more overtly theological language, this germ could have been called the divine image afflicted by original sin.

Following her father's lead, Mary Anne South wrote that Mesmerism 'of all modern arts' was the most pertinent to the material process of rebirth, since it was 'working in the same matter.'[72] A closer look reveals that the role she accorded to Mesmerism was actually quite limited: it was an attention-grabbing primer, nothing more. The ancient mysteries were 'immeasurably superior to ... modern Mesmerism.'[73] Indeed, 'the best effects of Mesmerism, if we connect it with the ancients' Sacred Art, appear as trifles in comparison.'[74] Though father and daughter were initially fascinated with Mesmerism, they both became disillusioned with the perceived ignorance and immorality of practitioners, as well as the predominantly random, uncontrollable effects of the magnetism they unleashed. Mary Anne South already recorded this assessment in her *Suggestive Inquiry*.

In contrast, through the alchemists' controlled, ritual manipulations of the ether, the new birth would be nourished and grow stronger: the intention behind 'theurgic rites, by the medium of the passive Ether,' was to 'unfold the embryo vigour of her [the soul's] newly conceived life.'⁷⁵ In South's spiritual alchemy, physically enacted rituals thus helped to nourish the new birth growing within the believer. An earlier passage expanded on the material basis of these doctrines in more traditional terms: 'for though the material [ether] is one throughout [the mineral and animal kingdoms], ... in him [the human being] it assumes an Image that is Divine ... which is in this life yet an embryo, but when unfolded through a new birth ... transcends the limits of this nether sphere, and passes into communion with the highest life, power, science, and most perfect felicity.'⁷⁶ Through a process starting with spiritual rebirth, this germ could develop its full potential and allow believers to participate in heaven while still on earth. It was this process that culminated in mystical union with the divine.⁷⁷

Nourishing the new birth through prayer and ritual, all the sages were occupied with cultivating 'the Divine Light within' or, as *Early Magnetism* expressed the matter, the '*Divinity* within us.'⁷⁸ Through these expressions, South articulated her modern version of what her predecessors would have called *Christus in nobis*. Implicitly, that very notion underlies several crucial statements throughout the *Suggestive Inquiry*. On various occasions, Christ within obliquely appeared, for instance, as the *lapis angularis*, the stone formerly rejected that came to be the cornerstone. Drawing on a passage in one of South's favourite books of the Bible, Paul's First Epistle to the Corinthians, she described the human body as 'that living temple wherein alone the wise of all ages have been securely able to raise their rejected Corner Stone,' that is, to resurrect Christ within themselves.⁷⁹ Among other things, they did so by using certain ritual practices: 'the evil of the Original Sin being overcome by so many subtle stratagems, the New Life thence arises, whose quintessential virtue, imperishable and perpetually victorious, is the Corner Stone or first Material foundation of the Hermetic Art.'⁸⁰ Having vanquished sin and death, the risen Christ is the defining trait of the new birth, and the use of the word 'quintessential' again hints at the materiality of rebirth and, in keeping with Boehme and Freher, the saviour himself.

If Mesmerism plays a subordinate role and much of the *Suggestive Inquiry* boils down to traditional mysticism, what is novel is mainly that Mary Anne South emphatically identified alchemical adepts as heirs and especially clear exponents of this 'Divine Art.'⁸¹ Incidentally, Breckling had made a similar claim when he wrote that 'chymists' best explained 'the mystical philosophy.'⁸² In so doing, she was guided by authorities that were far from prototypical alchemists, although they have become familiar to readers of the present book. 'The most pious and experienced amongst the Adepts do not demur either to compare the phenomena of their work to the Gospel tradition of the Life of Christ and our human redemption,' she wrote, making the three-way *lapis-Christus in nobis* analogy explicit before mentioning names: 'Khunrath, Böhme, Freher, Grasseus, and various others amongst the more modern, agree with the early Adepts; pointing out too how, in every minute respect, their magistery not only corresponds, but is in very deed a type, and promise, and foundation of our Christian Creed.'[83]

Among the four names mentioned, Boehme and Freher clearly had not practised laboratory alchemy. By Grasseus, South here meant 'the reputed author of the *Water Stone*' (which she more commonly quoted by its Latin title as *Aquarium sapientum*) and further described him as 'a personal friend of Böhme's.'[84] It is unclear how she came to identify Johann Grasse, sometimes called Grasshoff, another contemporaneous writer on alchemy, as the author of the *Wasserstein der Weysen*. Yet this mistaken attribution together with Boehme's ringing endorsement of the treatise must have led her to the unfounded conclusion that they had been close friends. Apart from the *Wasserstein* and its actual author, Johann Siebmacher, Boehme and Freher certainly emphasised the three-way analogy between the alchemical work, Christ's Incarnation, and the salvation of the individual believer, implicitly based on *Christus in nobis*. Just as her father had styled himself as the successor of Boehme and Freher in his letter to Walton, his daughter also placed herself in the lineage of Siebmacher, the theosopher of Görlitz, and his expatriate expositor.

According to Mary Anne South's understanding, alchemists—with Boehme and Freher among her prototypical examples—were explicit about the bodily side of rebirth, more so than any of their predecessors or contemporaries who pursued the same goals by different strategies. Based on the common insistence throughout alchemical literature that the adepts were not handling common substances, South became convinced that they were occupied with manipulating the ether itself, that subtle substance which pervaded the whole world and condensed to form the new bodies of reborn believers. (As the later notes included in the 'Appendix' of subsequent editions indicate, Mrs Atwood was aware of the identity of ether and quintessence.)[85] When alchemists wrote of the lead of the philosophers or their water, this is what they really meant: 'this water they speak of is not the fluid with which in this life we are conversant, either as dew, or of clouds, or air condensed in caverns of the earth, or artifically distilled in a receiver out of sea fountains, either of pits, or rivers, as the empirical chemists formerly imagined; but it is *the ethereal body of life and light* which they profess to have discovered.'[86] Though common chemists missed out on this insight, the real adepts also knew that the *lapis philosophorum* consisted of this substance.

Playing on the *lapis-Christus* analogy as well as Scripture, South claimed that it was 'this Stone, which, as a halo or crown of light, the regenerate soul puts on as a new body, wherein it can rule over the elementary world and pass through it, overcoming evil and falsehood, and ignorance and death.'[87] Through putting on the Stone, akin to putting on Christ, believers took on a subtle body that shared key attributes with Christ's resurrection body.[88] Thus, the 'worshipper' or adept was to be transmuted 'into that Harmony and Beauty, which, in the dim beholding, he venerated and loved.'[89] Just as God had become human, the human being was at last deified. Theurgy, mysticism, and alchemy were but differing instances of one and the same art, which South called divine because its purpose was the unification of humanity and deity.[90]

In the years leading up to the publication of the *Suggestive Inquiry*, Thomas South and Christopher Walton corresponded. Freher and his writings formed a recurring topic throughout South's extant letters, and alchemy gradually became central to his understanding of rebirth. It was in this intellectual context that his daughter Mary Anne composed the *Suggestive Inquiry*. Although her work abounds with unwieldy verbiage, I have shown how it nevertheless contains the core elements of the spiritual alchemy associated with Boehme's name throughout this study. Qualifying her youthful enthusiasm for Mesmerism and other magnetic techniques, she came to view them as mere primers that could not compete with age-old wisdom. Like Franckenberg more than two hundred years earlier, Mary Anne South closely associated pagan piety and early Christianity. In the teachings of Christ, his apostles, and particularly the Epistles of Paul, she saw the continuation and culmination of ancient theurgy, to which rebirth was central. Stretching the boundaries of the adepts' self-imposed secrecy, Boehme and particularly his disciples around 1700 (Gichtel, Freher, and the Philadelphian Society, among others) provided particularly clear expositions that presented spiritual rebirth as the actual work of alchemy. Mary Anne South perceived the relevant literature to be discussing the physical side of the regenerative process, the cultivation of the spiritual body of the new birth so often disregarded by the institutionalised churches. This bodily aspect of spiritual alchemy involved the manipulation of the ether, although in ancient, superior, and much more controlled ways than Mesmerism.

10
Mary Anne Atwood and Her First Readers

Despite the bonfire at Bury House that devoured most copies of the *Suggestive Inquiry*, the Souths kept several exemplars for themselves and occasionally entrusted them to associates and friends. Beyond direct contact with the Souths, determined readers would have been able to consult individual copies the publisher had sold or expedited before the withdrawal of the remaining print run. One such book became the subject of a rather baffled review that appeared in the *Athenaeum* on 10 May 1851, half a year after the publication of the *Suggestive Inquiry*.[1] In addition, there were legal deposit copies at the British Museum in London and the Bodleian Library in Oxford. Whereas many pages in the latter remain uncut and hence unread to this day, the former was well-thumbed and eventually rebound in two volumes: there is evidence that occultists shared its precise shelf-mark among themselves.[2] The South family's copies, renegade exemplars, and legal deposits allowed a small but determined readership to study the *Suggestive Inquiry* from the time of its first publication in 1850.

This chapter contextualises the interpretation of the *Suggestive Inquiry* presented in chapter 9 with an exploration of the work's early reception and its author's mature views. Early readers of the *Suggestive Inquiry*, many of whom knew its author as Mrs Mary Anne Atwood since the 1880s, correctly perceived the central importance it accorded to Christian mysticism and the doctrine of rebirth. Those who engaged with the *Suggestive Inquiry* include Arthur Edward Waite, the prolific occultist writer; Isabelle de Steiger, Atwood's most trusted friend; and Walter Leslie Wilmshurst, who became the first Atwood scholar. They all agreed in viewing mysticism and rebirth as central to understanding the *Suggestive Inquiry*. Despite this, these earlier readers and allies—most notably Waite—developed their own interpretations and, in so doing, gave rise to a plethora of divergent approaches to alchemy that lie beyond the scope of this book. After discussing De Steiger as Atwood's disciple, I turn to the later papers of the *Suggestive Inquiry*'s author, preserved due to the loving care of De Steiger and partly printed by Wilmshurst in the book's 1918 reissue. Even in her later years, Atwood continued to engage with Boehme and the spiritual alchemy of rebirth, expressing her views much more succinctly than in her youthful *Suggestive Inquiry*.

The Early Reception of the *Suggestive Inquiry*

Two of Mary Anne South's extant letters mentioning individual copies of the *Suggestive Inquiry* document how closely she monitored the circulation of her work. Both missives suggest that they were intended as temporary loans, although the two copies in question also show that the books were unlikely to be returned.[3] One otherwise unidentified John Preston received a copy from the author on 24 August 1852, as a note in her hand glued to the flyleaf at the back indicates (fig. 10.1). Mary Anne South noted 'with real regret' that it could not be given 'in the way of a free gift,' as two 'conditions (unavoidable however) are interposed.' Preston received this copy for the limited duration

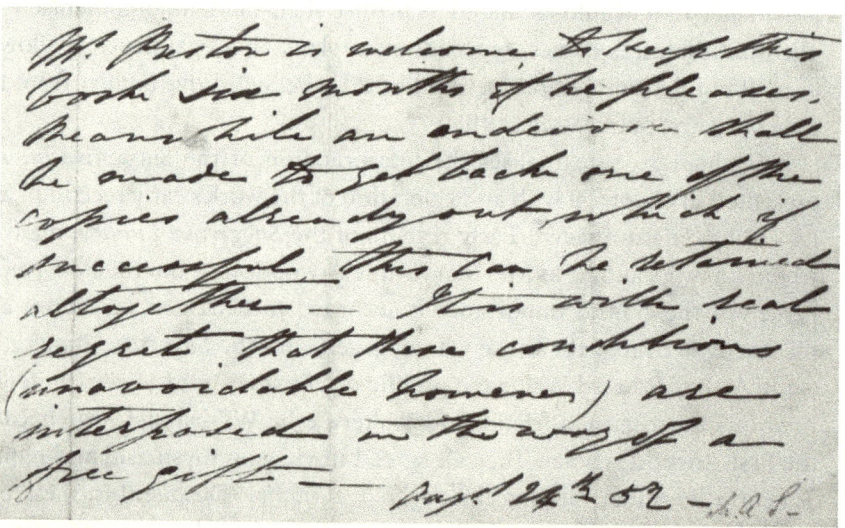

Fig. 10.1 [Mary Anne South], *A Suggestive Inquiry into the Hermetic Mystery* (London: Trelawney Saunders, 1850), letter glued to back flyleaf. With brief communications such as this one to John Prestond, dated 24 August 1852, Mary Anne South sought to establish the terms according to which the rare surviving copies of her *Suggestive Inquiry* were lent to select readers. London, Wellcome Collection Library, EPB/B/49072. © Author.

of 'six months if he pleases' and had 'to get back one of the copies already out which if successful, this can be retained altogether.'[4] In other words, should Preston succeed in facilitating the discovery of another renegade copy, he would be able to keep this one as a reward. Perhaps he did accomplish that task, but it is more likely that he conveniently forgot to return the book to its author and rightful owner. South's request indicated her own lifelong quest for those copies of the *Suggestive Inquiry* that had escaped destruction, one she was to pursue for more than half a century.[5]

Slightly earlier than Preston, Christopher Walton had received a copy of the *Suggestive Inquiry*, and he apparently requested an extension of his initially finite loan period. 'With respect to the "Hermetic Enquiry" you are welcome to retain it as long as you may desire,' Mary Anne South replied on 11 June 1852; 'I can replace the loan to my sister at any time and am truly sorry that there are any restrictions about the matter at all.' Nonetheless, she insisted 'that the scruples' which had prompted the withdrawal of the book 'are real, I do again assure you, and [they] exist not only in my fathers mind, as you appear to believe, but in my own likewise very vexatingly.'[6] Her sister Louisa had thus given Walton her personal copy for a limited time, but Mary Anne could provide her with a substitute to allow the jeweller to keep the exemplar he already had. Walton retained this exemplar of the *Suggestive Inquiry* until his death in 1877, since which time it has been publicly available at Dr Williams's Library.[7]

In the meantime, the circumstances of Mary Anne South had changed considerably. Her father, Thomas, died on 7 June 1858, 'in the 78th year of his age, deeply deplored by his family.'[8] A little over a year later, Mary Anne married the widowed minister Thomas Alban Atwood on 4 August 1859.[9] Atwood took his wife to his remote Yorkshire vicarage at Knayton, Thirsk; their union remained childless. He had graduated from Worcester College, Oxford, in 1836, after which he was ordained as deacon and subsequently priest over the next two years. In July 1852 he became vicar of Leake, in which capacity he served for thirty-three years, concurrently also acting as rural dean of Thirsk for fifteen years. He died on 2 August 1883.[10] Apart from his interest in the Swedish visionary Emanuel Swedenborg, it is unclear to what extent he shared his wife's intellectual proclivities. After being widowed and as surviving copies of the *Suggestive Inquiry* changed hands throughout the second half of the nineteenth century, Mrs Atwood's approach to the withdrawn book did not remain the same.

In 1886, after a hiatus of three decades, she suddenly became comparatively more forthcoming regarding her work. On the occasion of her last journey to London in the same year, she gave away several copies of the *Suggestive Inquiry* as gifts. Charles Carleton Massey, a leading member of the Theosophical Society, founded in 1875, received his personal copy on 22 February 1886. Upon his death in 1905, the book returned to Atwood, as noted in a posthumous catalogue of her choice library.[11] According to Wilmshurst, the classicist Walter Moseley also received a copy in 1886. From late 1885, Anna Kingsford (*née* Bonus), together with her close associate Edward Maitland, were also familiar with the *Suggestive Inquiry*, and Atwood confirmed in a letter to Maitland, dated 19 September 1886, that she had 'sent it for you to keep, please.'[12]

Kingsford had previously been the president, and Maitland the vice president, of the British Lodge of the Theosophical Society. Kingsford lost that position due to an internal conflict that saw the Society's Christian wing pitted against a rival one that privileged non-Christian Eastern religions such as Buddhism. Most of Atwood's associates who received copies of the *Suggestive Inquiry* represented the Christian party within the Theosophical Society. As they all had significant network among occultists, the *Suggestive Inquiry* and a concomitant interest in alchemy spread through these circles within only a few years.[13]

Atwood gave the same milieu an even larger gift in early 1888. Around that time she contacted Alfred Percy Sinnett, formerly a journalist who had by then succeeded Kingsford as president of the London Theosophical Society. In his autobiographical notes, Sinnett recalled that 'I had never met her,' that is, 'Mrs. Atwood—the authoress of "A suggestive enquiry into the Hermetic Mystery."' Rather than due to personal acquaintance or mutual contacts, 'she had written to me on the strength of having read my books.' Sinnett's notable publications of the early 1880s included *The Occult World* and *Esoteric Buddhism*. Atwood was concerned that the 'considerable library of books relating to occult subjects collected by her father, Dr. [sic] South, and late husband and herself,' would be 'dispersed at her death. She was already far advanced in life and her days of study were over.' Atwood therefore offered the collection to Sinnett, who eagerly accepted. In March 'the books came together with a very beautiful bookcase that held the most important of them.' Ironically, Sinnett's custodianship already ended in 1908—two years before Atwood's death—when he gave 'the whole collection to Mr. Scott Elliot' of 'Arkleton in Scotland.'[14] Moreover, even prior to that Atwood herself had grown disillusioned with 'Mr. Sinnett, whose subsequent teachings ... have not interested me.'[15]

Back in 1888, though, soon after Sinnett had received Mrs Atwood's gift, he allowed his friend and fellow occultist Arthur Edward Waite to consult the collection. Waite described it as 'her admirable library of alchemical texts. They were mostly in Latin and not much use to him [Sinnett], but I went over all the treasures.' Waite also discussed '*The Suggestive Enquiry*' with his host.[16] This was the context in which Waite first encountered the suppressed work of 1850 and learnt about its author. Over the following decades, he devoted a considerable portion of his efforts as a writer and translator to alchemy. Very soon after encountering the late Thomas South's library, Waite published his first enthusiastic reaction to the *Suggestive Inquiry* on 15 September 1888. It appeared as a letter to the editor in the occultist journal *Light*.[17] Titled 'A New Light of Mysticism,' Waite's contribution summarised his insights in twenty-two theses and announced a book project, *Azoth; or, The Star in the East*, that was eventually completed in 1893. The theses clearly derived from the *Suggestive Inquiry*, though Waite did not highlight this explicitly. He observed that 'alchemists, in common with other mystics, were in possession of a secret theory' or 'esoteric art, which may be denominated psychic chemistry.'[18]

Along with copies shared among hand-picked readers, knowledge regarding the author of the *Suggestive Inquiry* spread inevitably. In published writings, however, it remained shrouded in polite secrecy. In preparation for writing *Azoth*, Waite reissued the 1815 *Lives of Alchemystical Philosophers* in December 1888. For this third edition of the *Lives*, he expanded on the number of biographies but removed the alchemical texts, including Freher's 'Process in the Philosophical Work.' Boehme's expositor no longer appeared, yet he had done his part by passing on the spiritual alchemy of rebirth to his audience. Identifying himself as an 'English mystic,' Waite included an 'Introductory Essay.' He used this opportunity to express his admiration for the *Suggestive Inquiry* and the 'lady of high intellectual gifts' and 'unparalleled woman' who had authored it.[19] A few years later, in the first issue of his journal *The Unknown World*, published on 15 August 1894, he similarly alluded to the identity of the 'anonymous writer' who 'is now known to be a woman, whose name also is now well known in certain circles, though it would be bad taste to mention it.'[20] Yet a year earlier, Waite had shown no compunction about skirting the boundaries of impropriety when he had publicly mentioned 'the daughter of Mr. South' in connection with the *Suggestive*

Inquiry.²¹ Writing in 1894, Patience Sinnett, Alfred Percy's wife, also knew perfectly well who the anonymous author was yet politely refrained from the least allusion to Mrs Atwood's identity.²² Simultaneously, other occultists who did have some knowledge about the book and its story remained in the dark regarding that identity.²³

By the late 1880s and early 1890s, the *Suggestive Inquiry* had found a number of readers, and for some of them its author's name was an open secret. As Atwood's readers grappled with her book, they perceived its mystical bent and contrasted it with rival interpretations such as those of the American major general Ethan Allen Hitchcock and the French occultist Eliphas Lévi. In contrast to the high praise Waite showered on Atwood's *Suggestive Inquiry*, he gave a considerably less favourable verdict on the moralist approach to alchemy that Hitchcock had independently outlined during the 1850s.²⁴ Waite also criticised 'the showiness of merely suggestive interpretations' of 'metallic alchemy,' specifically 'that of Eliphas Levi.'²⁵ Patience Sinnett concurred in an essay published in the Theosophical journal *Lucifer* on 15 May 1894. According to her, alchemists 'were really for the most part the Occultists of their period.' In other words, they were the worthy predecessors of the Theosophical Society, as Sinnett explicitly stated later in her piece. This understanding of alchemy had conclusively been established as the correct one by Hitchcock and, more insightfully still, by 'the anonymous writer of a profoundly interesting and remarkable book called *A Suggestive Enquiry into the Hermetic Mystery*, a treatise replete with Occultism of the most exalted order.'²⁶

More importantly, Sinnett argued that the 'superiority' of the *Suggestive Inquiry* over Hitchcock's *Alchemy and the Alchemists* hinged on Atwood's deeper grasp of 'the double mystery of Alchemy.' The art of the sages was not reducible to a quest for moral rectitude, as Hitchcock suggested: 'although the genuine alchemist set out with the primary purpose of exalting his own nature to high spiritual levels, when he had actually done this he was in a position to accomplish on the physical plane the very task' of transmuting metals, 'which he began by speaking of in its purely symbolical aspect.'²⁷ This accorded well with the emphasis on spiritual rebirth as a necessary precondition for successful alchemical practice, a view shared by notably Boehme and Freher. Both Waite and Sinnett thus discussed Hitchcock in terms very similar to the manner in which Atwood herself had discussed him in an obscure publication of 1868: she criticised his approach as 'an ethical theory' of alchemy with clear limits.²⁸

In 1894, just a few months after Sinnett's publication, Waite once again presented Atwood's understanding of alchemy as follows: 'the interpretation of the *Suggestive Inquiry* was spiritual and "theurgic" in a very highly advanced degree: it was indeed essentially mystical, and proposed the end of Mysticism as that also of the Alchemical adepts.'[29] In doing so, he perceptively summed up the main thrust of Atwood's work. Waite clearly articulated the close identification of alchemy and mysticism posited by Atwood. He still summarised Atwood's views succinctly on 14 November 1913: 'The ancient alchemists . . . were concerned with the same work as the mystics within the Church living the life of contemplation; but they had carried the experiment a stage further, and embodied the results of their experiences in symbolic texts.'[30] It was this interpretation, mediated through acquaintance with Waite and his work, that led Evelyn Underhill to include passages on spiritual alchemy in her classic *Mysticism* of 1911.[31]

However, due to the enormous impact of Charles Darwin's work *On the Origin of Species* and its attendant controversies from 1859 onwards, Waite himself developed a different spiritual alchemy. It had a distinctly evolutionary slant through which it was to help humanity to collectively attain a higher state of consciousness.[32] This tendency can already be perceived in his 1888 letter in *Light* and introduction to the *Lives*. When Waite finally published *Azoth* in 1893, five years after announcing it, the book included a fully-fledged account of alchemy's role in the evolution of humanity. Indeed, Waite portrayed Darwin as a latter-day prophet: 'when Darwin discovered evolution he discovered God's intention towards man.'[33] Waite's theologically inflected and highly teleological conception saw humanity consciously working towards the 'perfection of the supreme summit of evolution' in the spiritual, intellectual, moral, and even physical order.[34] For him, 'the first thing that must strike a modern reader of the old books is that every true alchemist . . . was, in fact, an undisguised evolutionist.'[35] Thus, Waite rendered spiritual alchemy subservient to evolution.

In so doing, he departed from the tradition that linked Boehme to Atwood, a lineage of which he was well aware. Under the header 'The Spiritual Interpretation of Alchemy', Waite wrote that it 'began openly with Jacob Böhme, but it was first systematically developed in the *Suggestive Inquiry into the Hermetic Mystery and Alchemy*.' Yet even Atwood's slightly exaggerated 'hundred and one successors in the "spiritual hermeneutics" of transmutation literature' had so far ignored that the same 'principles which work mystically in the soul can be applied outwardly to the body of man' and reveal to us 'the mystery of our physical evolution.'[36] Waite went so far as to recommend vegetarianism as part of the 'suitable regimen' that would allow for the production of 'a perfect body.'[37] On his view humanity strove towards greater physical beauty, whereas all the other exponents of spiritual alchemy I have discussed saw the mortal body as beyond redemption.

Since Waite imposed such a new, evolutionary narrative, he simultaneously relegated the biblical account of the Fall to a minor role. While admitting that there were lessons to be learnt from it, he adopted an agnostic or indifferent position towards this older narrative: 'did ever this fabled time have a place in fact is a barren enquiry. It at least has a place in the future; we must either work up to it or back to it; the desire of all the world spurs us on to achieve perfection.'[38] Hints of the distinction between humanity's prelapsarian and postlapsarian states remain throughout *Azoth*, yet Waite's focus lies squarely on future perfection rather than the restoration of a former one that has been lost. The displacement of the Fall narrative by that of evolution and the emphasis on physical beauty are two important fault lines that separate Waite from spiritual alchemy in Boehme's wake. Atwood's later judgements on Waite reflected this, for instance when she wrote in 1902 that 'Mr. W. has no real appreciation of J. B. [Jacob Boehme] being of a different make of mind poetical and intuitive as was my dear Father rather than reflective.'[39] In early 1907, she criticised Waite's 'dispa[ra]gement of J. B.,' and in late 1908 she observed that 'Mr. Waite dilutes every thing he touches and this spoils the deepest suggestive writings and writers.'[40] Perhaps she included herself among them as her *Inquiry* was, after all, a suggestive one, too.

Nonetheless, a lot of common ground remained. Waite continually spoke of union with the divine and 'regeneration—that New Birth for which also the Alchemists worked.'[41] Like others before him, he emphasised the parallelism of alchemy and spiritual rebirth: 'there is a close connection between the philosophical process . . . and our mystery of the New Birth, for the property of alchemical putrefaction is to destroy the old, original nature of a thing, after which ensues the introduction of a new nature, and occasionally it is stated in the words of the Adepts themselves, that the process has the same result as a second generation.'[42] Waite also played on the mystical incarnation of Christ within the believer, for instance when he wrote that the accomplishment of the 'work of Regeneration' coincided with the birth of 'the Christ . . . into the soul.'[43] Moreover, Waite even used expressions that harked back to *Christus in nobis* when treating of 'The Evolution of the Christ in Man' or 'the Christ abiding within us.'[44] In easing spiritual alchemy's transition from the individual plane to that of humanity generally, Waite paved the way for further variations spelled out by Rudolf Steiner, the founder of anthroposophy, and C. G. Jung, among others. The stage was set for a proliferation of spiritual alchemies as the twentieth century dawned. Early readers correctly perceived that Christian mysticism and rebirth were at the centre of the *Suggestive Inquiry*, yet they soon developed their own divergent interpretations.

Atwood's Disciple Isabelle de Steiger

Atwood observed these developments largely in silence, yet she did have a faithful deputy in Isabelle de Steiger, who increasingly spoke up on her behalf. During the final decades of Atwood's life, De Steiger—a widow of means, a painter, and an occultist of constantly shifting allegiances—became her closest confidante and correspondent. Their acquaintance reached back to the time of Atwood's marriage: as a regular contributor to *Light* in 1879, De Steiger had drawn the attention of Atwood's close friend Anne Judith Penny by mentioning 'a dog I had, all of us being dog-lovers.' Apart from a shared interest in canines, De Steiger was well-placed in London and 'a personal member of the then newly formed Theosophical Society.' Mistaking the meaning of this term to refer to the theosophy of Boehme, Penny and Atwood were greatly interested: 'this name was reminiscent of the days when, before their respective marriages, they were pupils and students in . . . Mr. Grieves' [*sic*] circle.'[45] James Pierrepont Greaves had died in 1842, when Mary Anne South was twenty-five and Anne Judith Burton merely seventeen years old. Although De Steiger's remark is currently the only known evidence for this, Greaves may have been the first to introduce these young women to Boehme's theosophy.[46] It was not until after Atwood had given large parts of her father's library to these new Theosophists that she fully grasped how little they had in common with the cobbler of Görlitz.

We do not know much about the earliest phase of Atwood's acquaintance with De Steiger, although they first met in person on the occasion of Atwood's last journey to London in 1886. Perhaps during that meeting, perhaps some time later, Atwood invited De Steiger 'to pay her a visit at her home in Yorkshire,' and the artist accepted. Subsequently, she visited Atwood at least once a year and spent almost every summer in Knayton, even though her description painted it as a less than appealing location.[47] Only individual letters from the years prior to 1893 survive, yet their correspondence intensified considerably during that year and continued almost until Atwood's death on 13 April 1910, by which time she had 'long since ceased to write to any one else,' as her final letter indicated.[48] Indeed, after Penny's death in 1893, the younger woman took her place as Atwood's 'chief and only correspondent.' To her dismay, acquaintances were quick to identify her as heiress designate not merely in the intellectual sense. Perhaps as a token of this special relationship, De Steiger received 'Mrs. Atwood's own original copy of *The Suggestive Enquiry*,' which in August 1900 narrowly escaped the flames of an Edinburgh fire that consumed most of De Steiger's belongings and art.[49]

During her elderly friend's lifetime but largely independently, De Steiger wrote her own study of alchemy and mysticism. Titled *On a Gold Basis: A Treatise on Mysticism*, it was published in 1907 against the backdrop of economic crisis and the failing of the gold standard.[50] When Atwood eventually read the copy De Steiger had given her, she commended the work and expressed but one minor criticism—the discussion of 'the Abraxas which were the foundation and resultants of the Idolatry that the Bible so strongly inveighs against.'[51] Although De Steiger's book engaged with many distinctively modern discussions, trends, and terms, the spiritual alchemy it articulated remained faithful to Atwood and her predecessors. Boehme was the dominant authority: the original theosopher appeared throughout De Steiger's book, and its prologue largely consisted of quotations from Boehme's works, especially his *Signatura rerum*.[52] After appealing to that same treatise yet again, De Steiger explained that the 'mystics fully believe ... that the process by which regeneration is attained is portrayed in its various degrees in the different events in the life of Christ'—the core idea of the process of Christ as Boehme described it in *Signatura rerum*.[53] Indeed, that 'same interior process, or the history of the events in the life of the Arch Man, Jesus the Christ, is the experience of all regenerate or sanctified men.'[54] She explicitly linked the seven degrees of the regenerative process to 'seven degrees of transmutation,' that is, 'solution, distillation, putrefaction, calcination, coagulation, sublimation, and tincturation.'[55] Although other cultures and religions expressed the same truth differently, the spiritual alchemy of rebirth provided a sure path to immortality in a Christian context.

There was, nonetheless, one important difference: if the historicity of Christ and the events of his life having actually taken place were crucial for

Boehme and his early-modern followers, this was not the case for De Steiger and Atwood. Yet that is not to say that they thought little of the biblical accounts of Christ's life. In a turn not entirely alien to the theological tradition of spiritualism, they viewed the Gospels as true on a much deeper level than mere history and hence described them as 'arch-history.'[56] On this understanding, 'it is indeed folly to dispute concerning' the New Testament's 'letter, its historical or any other accuracy.'[57] Consequently, Christ was the 'Archetypal Son,' 'the Lord and Archetype of all life and perfection' who had to be emulated, as Atwood's own usage confirms.[58] By following in the footsteps of Jesus Christ, born-again believers prepared their hearts to become the habitation of the indwelling divinity—the mystical incarnation of Christ within the believer. De Steiger put it in these terms: 'the son of man' (a phrase with which Christ referred to himself in the Gospels) 'or the New man, must, as mystics teach, be born in the cradle of the heart at Bethlehem.'[59]

By the same token, believers obtained 'a permanent spiritual new body.'[60] The 'alchemists' spoke of its matter as 'ether,' yet it was 'not common ether' but a superior one that De Steiger linked to 'the Quintessence.' Redemption took place through 'the recovery of the Quintessence,' that is, the primordial matter out of which the four elements 'emanated.'[61] In De Steiger's hierarchy of ethers, unregenerate souls were 'composed . . . of carnal and adulterous ether—that is, mixed with the lower Cosmic Ether.'[62] This impure ether was a direct consequence of the Fall and could be described as postlapsarian. De Steiger contrasted it against both 'virgin' ether, which would be prelapsarian and uncorrupted, and 'free ether,' which she associated with spirit and assigned to the divine.[63] In a trichotomous anthropology, the human spirit remained unaffected by the Fall and the body could not be saved. This left the soul as that component which had to be purified and spiritualised, as it were:

> man therefore in his spirit is in eternity, in his soul in the middle region which joins time with eternity, and in his body in the kingdom of time. In his spirit he knows only unity or eternity. His soul, which longs to join his spirit, at the Fall entered voluntarily the middle region, and thence into time. Ever since that voluntary act, man's soul has longed to leave the dominion of time, as an inferior one, and regain that of eternity. But as it was a voluntary act in which all mankind share, and due to a *desire to experience*, henceforth the soul must go back through that experience; and hence comes all the difficulty of the return to Paradise.[64]

All of this closely resembles Boehme's doctrine of the body consisting of the one element that Adam and Eve had lost in the Fall and needed to regain through rebirth.

Elsewhere, De Steiger described the new, subtle, and regenerate corporeality more fully as 'the spiritual body and the glorified sensorial (astral) body, transmuted by identic union with the Aurific spirit.' It had to be 'formed by man himself during life, and sealed afterwards with the new name of the New Humanity.'[65] As Boehme had already explained, the formation of the new birth's subtle body took place in this life and prepared believers for the life to come. The gold-making spirit De Steiger mentioned was none other than Jesus Christ, who was 'sanctified and transmuted at His mystical re-birth,' the 'God-man' who became 'Himself the Elixir Vitæ and the Philosopher's Stone,' just as Freher had summarised it following Boehme.[66] Christ had thus laid the groundwork for reversing the Fall: 'as in Adam all men fell, so in Adam can all men rise.'[67] De Steiger described regenerate humanity as 'the *new Adamic race, the first-fruits of which was Jesus Christ*, the perfect Man.'[68] It was 'the hope of this immortality' that prompted 'the alchemists ... so earnestly to find out what this stone was,' to regain 'that sound and pure matter' out of which '*originally* man had been created.'[69]

Throughout her *Gold Basis*, De Steiger criticised the Darwinian theory of evolution and stressed its incompatibility with the biblical narrative of the Fall that undergirded the spiritual alchemy of rebirth. In this regard, her spiritual alchemy differed sharply from Waite's, which embraced evolution. For De Steiger, humans were not the apex of evolution but instead creatures afflicted with postlapsarian degradation: 'mystic writers oppose the doctrine of evolution by *theirs*—that man *has* fallen from his original high estate.'[70] Conversely, 'the fall of man' was 'a hateful phrase to modern evolutionists.'[71] De Steiger did not shrink back from the polemical: 'the present doctrine of evolution ... is a lie that masquerades gaily as a modern truth.'[72] Instead, the 'mystic holds that mankind never evolved from the Simian kingdom, but that the ape world is degraded, ruined humanity, never to be restored as before until a future calamity and a re-created nature after a Crisis would end the "curse," and "this middle-ape realm" would be no more.'[73]

Just as 'the Fall of Man' and 'the Fall of the Planet' (or Curse) had occurred in tandem, so their restorations were equally linked. Due to the prayerful efforts of born-again believers, De Steiger expressed hope that some of the effects of the Curse under which creation laboured would be undone. 'The noblest work,' she explained, is 'to co-operate with God's laws' and to 'follow the Divine Pattern' of Christ. In so doing, 'he [man] will raise himself and the planet from its present condition.'[74] Specifically, De Steiger believed that the tilt of the earth's axis would give way to a perfectly upright position and thus restore a perfect, temperate climate to the British isles: 'as the mass of mankind raise their minds and desires upwards, so likewise will the axis of this earth rise too, and Paradise will be regained.'[75] Accomplishing this lay squarely within the purview of regenerate alchemists, as De Steiger implied by using the art's terminology: 'The great work, the *magnum opus* of the world in general, and of man in particular, is therefore to re-instate the world in its upright position, to restore Paradise!'[76] Born-again humanity thus actively participated in the divine work of redeeming creation, an idea I have previously identified in the works of Boehme and Freher.

After Atwood's death, De Steiger called out Waite in the *Occult Review* of December 1911 for criticising the *Suggestive Inquiry* and adopting an approach to alchemy that was explicitly independent of Atwood's in his book *The Secret Tradition in Freemasonry*.[77] Atwood's disciple sought to shield the *Suggestive Inquiry* against Waite's critique and drew attention to his earlier praise for that work.[78] Waite defended himself in the next issue, January 1912, by noting that his earlier statements 'in 1888 and 1893' reflected his 'knowledge at those dates; that which I have recorded since has been under a fuller and clearer light.'[79] Later in 1912, H. Stanley Redgrove, author of *Alchemy: Ancient and Modern*, published in 1910, approached De Steiger with the idea of founding an alchemical society to bring together chemists and occultists. Alongside astrologer Walter Gorn Old, and despite their public airing of differences, De Steiger and Waite became the inaugural 'Vice-Presidents' of the Alchemical Society in November 1912.[80]

Competing against a number of alternative conceptions, De Steiger campaigned for Atwood's spiritual rebirth both in a talk of her own and by presenting an unpublished essay by her late friend. Unfortunately, this piece was never printed: due to World War I gradually engulfing Europe, the Alchemical Society ceased publishing its journal after only three volumes in late 1915.[81] De Steiger's own lecture emphasised Mesmerism to a considerable extent that coexisted uneasily with Atwood's views: during her lifetime, Atwood had repeatedly downplayed her youthful enthusiasm for animal magnetism in letters to De Steiger.[82] Strangely enough, in her *Gold Basis*, De Steiger herself had denounced the grave wrongdoing 'constantly perpetrated by the psychical vivisector, when he uses his brother or sister simply for mere inquisitorial mesmeric experiment!'[83] She thus likened the practices of Mesmerists to those of the vivisectionists, whose gruesome animal experiments gave rise to significant controversy in the late Victorian era.[84] The underlying idea seems to have been that Mesmerists dabbled with etherial forces they failed to understand and place in the proper context of spiritual development. In contrast, alchemists as construed by Atwood cultivated a highly disciplined and responsible approach to the subtle matter that pervaded the universe.[85]

In her lecture, De Steiger also announced her intention to reissue the *Suggestive Inquiry*.[86] It seems that her continued enthusiasm for Atwood's spiritual alchemy prompted her to contravene her friend's own wishes. As far as one can tell from her letters to De Steiger, Atwood herself continued to believe that the suppression of the *Suggestive Inquiry* had been the right course of action. On 8 February 1903, for instance, she had written to her confidante in no uncertain terms that she had 'never regretted the withdrawal of the "Enquiry" needs must that offences come but woe to them by whom they come.'[87] In a similar vein, in 1908, less than two years before her death, Atwood requested that De Steiger 'please destroy all letters,' an expectation the artist fortunately did not fulfil.[88] Undeterred, the disciple pressed on with her project of reissuing the *Suggestive Inquiry*. She drew on the notes and corrections of Atwood herself, as well as those of the skilled classicist Moseley, to improve the text of the sprawling work.[89] Moreover, she enlisted the support of Freemason William Leslie Wilmshurst, who wrote the introduction to the work's second edition of 1918. With these collaborators, De Steiger brought to an end the early phase of the *Suggestive Inquiry*'s reception.

Wilmshurst's comprehensive introduction expanded at length upon rebirth as central to the *Suggestive Inquiry*, and in support of this he also adduced a short text Atwood had published in an obscure journal in 1868.[90] This text and the more explicit appendix, titled 'Table Talk and Memorabilia' and included in later editions, both suggest that Atwood herself became more concise in describing her understanding of alchemy as she matured. In 1919, just a year after the second edition of Atwood's *opus* was in print again, Wilmshurst published an article in two parts, 'The Later Mysticism of Mrs. Atwood.' In it he gave an accurate summary of her views in the *Suggestive Inquiry*. However, he also attributed later notions to her that seem to have sprung rather from a Freemason's mind than that of a contemplative as solitary as Atwood. It appears that Wilmshurst occasionally pandered to the occultists and Theosophists who provided the main audience for his new edition of her work.[91] In the absence of the full range of documents on which

Wilmshurst drew, it is difficult to assess the validity of his presentation in some respects. Yet even if some of these sources may have been lost, there is sufficient documentation to allow for a new investigation of Atwood's mature views.

Atwood's Later Views on Boehme, Alchemy, and Rebirth

De Steiger likely split up the collection of Atwood's papers she inherited and gave part of them to Wilmshurst, who relied on these sources for the 'Table Talk and Memorabilia' appendix, his introduction, and his later studies on her mysticism.[92] He presumably had recourse to De Steiger as a witness of Atwood's conversation and claimed that some of the documents he used dated back to as early as 1860. The whereabouts of these sources remain unknown, yet De Steiger's portion of the Atwood papers survives and can usefully be collated with excerpts Wilmshurst published in the appendix. In extant notes and papers dating to Atwood's life as an isolated widow between 1883 and 1910, there are several shifts of emphasis compared to her *Suggestive Inquiry*. First, Freher receded into the background despite the fact that, at an unknown point in time during her married life, she acquired Freher manuscripts corresponding to volume A of the *Fundamenta mystica* (see fig. 10.2). The unknown copyist notes that she or he 'began' copying these manuscripts in 'January 1802.' Now part of a private collection in the United States, both volumes are marked 'AT&MAAtwood' on the front flyleaves.[93] The initial enthusiasm for Freher, fuelled by her father, Thomas South, and Christopher Walton, may have worn off, yet Boehme took on ever greater importance. Indeed, Atwood came to view him as an unequalled authority. As late as 1908, she schemed with others, including 'Archdeacon [Basil] Wilberforce,' whom she had known since he was 'a little curly headed boy' in the early 1840s, to bring about 'the republication of Böhme's works,' although this endeavour ultimately came to nothing.[94] To phrase this more positively, it could be said that she graduated to studying the master rather than his disciple Freher.

It is particularly in the appendix compiled by Wilmshurst that the incomparable status Atwood accorded to Boehme finds expression. According to her, he easily surpassed not only later visionaries, such as Emanuel Swedenborg, who had been esteemed highly by her husband, but also the high-water marks of ancient and modern philosophy, represented by

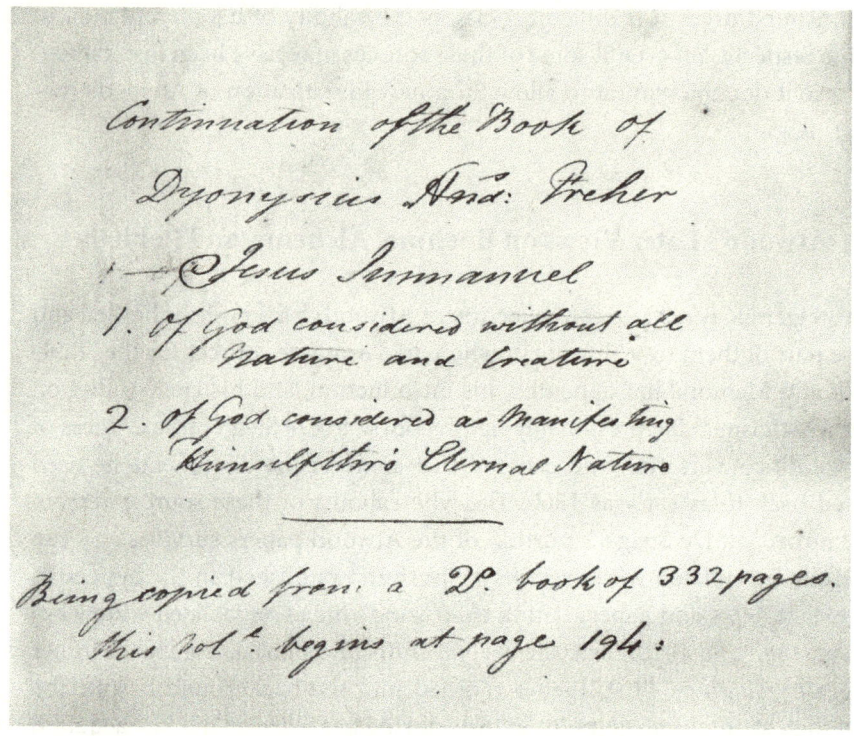

Fig. 10.2 Dionysius Andreas Freher, *Jesus Immanuel*, 2 vols. This nineteenth-century copy of writings by Freher contains the text of volume A of the *Fundamenta mystica* in two volumes. Both volumes indicate their former owners as 'AT&MAAtwood' (Alban Thomas and Mary Anne Atwood) in pencil. Private Collection of S. Brown, vol. 2, title page. © Owner.

Hellenic neo-Platonists and German Idealists.[95] In an intriguing analogy, Atwood likened mystical theosophy to science. This reflected a more widespread concern among those engaging with occultism in the Victorian era who sought to present their interests as scientifically sound and thus legitimate.[96] The neo-Platonists had provided the basis, but Boehme formed the apogee 'so that their theosophy bears the same relation to Behmen's as the astronomy of Ptolemy would to that of Newton.'[97] Boehme was to Plotinus as Newton to Ptolemy, and it is difficult to imagine higher praise flowing from the pen of an erudite Englishwoman. Just as Breckling had placed Boehme on a par with Luther, Atwood elevated him to the same status as Newton. Indeed, 'Sir Isaac Newton,' she claimed, 'should be named amongst the admirers of J. Böhmen.'[98] She could have said the same of Georg Wilhelm

Friedrich Hegel, and she indeed viewed the situation as similar with regard to the German Idealists.[99] 'Many modern metaphysicians,' she wrote, 'I mean Fichte, Schelling, Hegel, Kant, and others of kindred mind ... worked hard on the margin of intellectual intuition of truth.' Like Boehme, they shared 'their starting point' with 'the Mystics'; unlike him, they never achieved mystical union with the divine.[100] The German Idealists could see and perhaps even intuit the scientific corollaries better than Boehme, yet he was able to completely enter into the divine mystery they contemplated. In other words, the theosopher of Görlitz had achieved mystical union with the divine. Elsewhere, Atwood captured the same thought more tersely: 'Kant saw it, Hegel saw it, Fichte knew it, Schelling saw it, Bohme knew it and proved it by his experienced *in-seeing* whereby he became it,' that is, he attained deification.[101] Even if the modern Idealists shared the same point of departure with 'Böhme amongst the rest of mystics,' it was only he who actually made it past the finish line and accomplished 'the philosophic work of regeneration or divine evolution,' which 'is spiritual, ... self-reparative and radically disruptive'—the alchemy of rebirth and deification.[102]

Despite Boehme's exceeding merits, his words fell on deaf ears in the late nineteenth and early twentieth centuries. Among Atwood's unpublished papers, a draft letter dated 23 May 1902 notes that 'Bohme's writings can never be popular,' since they are at odds with modern society: 'the doctrine of regeneration implied throughout, is inimical to this life[;] no one wants to be reformed but thinks the more he needs it—the less desirable such a process, as is involved, would be. It is not possible to popularise Bohme without shortcoming of the bare Truth. But this you will object is common to all Xtian (Christian) teaching and there are always a few ready and willing to accept—it was indeed for them that Böhme wrote and the old Alchemists taught and recited their most arcane and intimate experiences.'[103] The theosopher of Görlitz and the alchemists alike wrote for the few rather than the many, those who were willing to follow in their footsteps on the arduous path of the new birth.

Indeed, Atwood was convinced that 'our Böhme' could 'never become popular ... for cogent reasons as I very well know and which had their part in my reasons for withdrawal of "the Enquiry" and will interfere with the success of your book [De Steiger's *Gold Basis*] in the West at all events—where no one is wishing at all to be improved off the face of the earth!'[104] Most people simply were not interested in the transformation the spiritual alchemy of rebirth entailed: 'will they seek self knowledge? and discern the need of human regeneration[?] "Verily I say unto you ye must be born again."' Atwood here paraphrased the words of Jesus Christ in the *locus classicus* of rebirth, a passage she quoted frequently. Afterwards she repeated the catchphrase of her final decade: 'improved or reformed off the face of the earth.'[105] For her the pursuit of the spiritual alchemy of rebirth could only be alluring to more than a handful of people if they thoroughly misconstrued what it entailed.

Indeed, Atwood held that most of those who engaged with her work did so in a misguided manner, confusing alchemy with occultism. As she stated in a text titled 'The Stone,' a fair manuscript copy scribed in someone else's hand, she viewed 'Alchemy' as 'the reverse of what is now called "Occultism" if by such a barbarous term is meant a discursive dealing with the cosmic aether on the astral plane where folly meets confusion by mediumistic venture, finding no truth.'[106] Atwood clearly had little patience for those Spiritualists whose attention-grabbing performances were not grounded in ancient wisdom and were devoid of higher purpose. Alternatively, instead of positing the art of the philosophers' stone as the opposite of occultism, she could portray alchemy as its whole point, which almost all those who pursued occult interests missed: 'apart from this Alchemy all Occultism so called, is rubbish and worse.'[107] Statements such as these clearly show the disdain she harboured for Mesmerist and Spiritualist *séances*. When she wrote the *Suggestive Inquiry*, this opposition was not yet as pronounced, but its basics were already in place.

Considered from this angle, her eventual falling-out with the 'psudo theosophists' of the Theosophical Society was inevitable.[108] Among other things, she accused them of 'doing away with Christianity and . . . watering [down] the old Mystics by their renderings, in fact emasculating their remains by eliminating the tradition of baptismal regeneration.'[109] The charge is highly similar to that of Franckenberg, who had alleged that the Jesuits castrated devotional, mystical, and spiritualist writings. In contrast to the momentary thrill of occultism, alchemy entailed a 'process of vital purification' that 'is lifelong,' and this 'process of regeneration is never perfected here,' only in the life to come. Engaging with this almost appeared to be a prerequisite to attaining a significant level of wisdom: 'Many profound thinkers and those well experienced in the process of regeneration have been thorough Christians in the fullest meaning of the term.'[110]

Atwood consciously placed herself in a decidedly Christian lineage that stretched all the way from the Apostle Paul to her, by way of Boehme and the alchemists. Although expressions differed throughout the ages, she and all of these predecessors shared a common goal: 'St. Paul would never have written so[,] neither Böhme or Saint Martin though these equally recognise and celebrate the divine germ in each member of the human family—'heirs of god and joint heirs with Christ' truly but not without Him who is their absolute Whole, bond, focus, root and offspring without Whom these would all perish as branches separated from the parent stem.'[111] All of these profound seekers agreed on the crucial importance of literally and physically becoming members of Christ's body through rebirth. Indeed, 'St Pauls doctrine and that of all the apostles' concerned not 'reincarnation' but 'resurrection by a new body coordinated to the Divine Basis and archetype of all Truth,' Jesus Christ.[112]

According to her, the Christian faith properly understood entailed not merely moral but bodily transmutation. For Atwood this was not an evolution towards greater physical beauty, as Arthur Edward Waite had it, but a process of purifying and spiritualising the soul. In keeping with Boehme's views on the close connection between rebirth and resurrection, 'the Hermetic Art' established 'a nexus' on which God would ultimately act to effect such a transformation: 'divine wisdom knows how by crucifixion or differentiation of our Karma to prepare the way of redemption so that the "body of sin" in the blood may become circularly transmuted and by degrees built up into a new spiritual concrete organism: which, superceding the need of the gross body or "coat of skins," will survive the wreck of antecedents and continuously thereafter feeding on its Intercessory Universal Accomplishment, belong to an everlasting Kingdom and recreated life eternal.'[113] The language is, of course, thoroughly rooted in Atwood's own age and reflects a growing interest in Eastern religions. Intriguingly, in her *Gold Basis* De Steiger used the term 'Karma' as synonymous with sin: 'the sublimest Hierophant, that Adeptus [Christ], ... took upon Himself the sin—the Karma of the world,' an allusion to the words of John the Baptist.[114]

This strongly suggests that the ideas Atwood and De Steiger expressed and shared nonetheless still corresponded to the spiritual alchemy of Boehme or Franckenberg and its distinctly Christian framework. Mystical death on the cross and rebirth paved the way for a transmutation of the mortal body into a spiritual one, eucharistically feeding on Christ as the divine intercessor and thereby participating in the kingdom of Heaven. For Atwood, mercury was the substance of the spiritual body, and the philosophers' stone foretold that body's ultimate completion: 'all is in *Mercury* that the wise men seek: i.e. in the cosmic ether which under certain conditions was taken in hand.... Such is the Philosophers' Stone, an adamantine achievement, foreshadowing the future and the destiny[,] origin and final cause of mankind.'[115] Particularly Franckenberg had also described the heavenly body in crystalline terms, for which 'adamantine' provided Atwood's equivalent.

Despite what she viewed as the failure of many to read Boehme and alchemical literature properly, Atwood also found material of interest in new scholarship that both confirmed her views and allowed her to hone them further. In an excerpt from a book on Boehme by the Danish theologian Hans Lassen Martensen, Atwood found a statement on alchemy quite similar to her own understanding but also subtly distinct: 'the legitimate Alchymist... regards it [his art] as closely akin to the transmutation which is to be effected in man by Regeneration in Christ; and, indeed, views it in connection with the history of the Kingdom of God, the consummation of which is brought about through processes of *Digestion, Fermentation, Putrefaction* (corruption of all that pertains to the old, dead, sinful nature), and *Sublimation* (refinement and exaltation of the good that had been buried beneath the earthly cerements).... The elements of all this are found in Böhme.'[116] Atwood, of course, had taken this a considerable step further by identifying alchemical transmutation with spiritual regeneration. In a passage published by Wilmshurst that drew on this very excerpt, she criticised Martensen for describing alchemical terms, such as '*salt, sulphur, mercury*,' as 'barbarous.' Despite his uncommon insight, Martensen was not 'practically conversant with the subject,' since the very same terms had been 'found to be scientifically appropriate by students in the schools who have accepted them for continuous instruction in the Divine Art of prototypic Assimilation.'[117] In other words, the alchemical novices who used such terminology as a matter of course sought to be conformed to Christ. Martensen had no business criticising their arcane language and, in so doing, only revealed the limits of his own understanding.

In addition to dwelling on rebirth at length in his introduction, Wilmshurst also chose for inclusion in the appendix a statement that is remarkable for its overtly Christian language. In her old age, Atwood succinctly explained that rebirth was central to her understanding of Christianity:

> the Christian scheme is the bringing of the whole of our life into the Sonship by regeneration; it is an eternal marriage-union between man and God in Christ, as is hinted by St. Paul and in the Book of Revelation. No doubt the state of it, when thoroughly achieved, is one of perfect beautitude; the mind then revels as it were in the appreciation of its Maker, its Source. Man is so

a child of God, regenerated or born again as an offspring of his own will, given up in passivity to the Divine Will. It is the death to sin with a new birth awakened in us, and until that takes place we know little or nothing of the sinfulness of this life.[118]

Through regeneration, deification took place in an inseparable mystical union: human was to become god, just as God had become human in the Incarnation. The 'beautitude,' rather than mere beatitude, could be taken to imply the restoration of the prelapsarian state, whereas the mind's revelling in God would amount to its awakening to the second principle of love and light, to use Boehme's terms. Mysticism and theosophy (in the pre-modern sense) are thus inextricably linked in Atwood's spiritual alchemy of rebirth.

While theology occupies a large share of her papers, Atwood's continued engagement with alchemy shines through frequently as she restated her views on the subject. The appendix compiled by Wilmshurst contains several attempts at definition. 'Alchemy,' she stipulated, 'is an universal art of vital chemistry, which by fermenting the human spirit, purifies, and, finally dissolving it, opens the elementary germ into new life and consciousness.'[119] Another definition further specifies what is meant by 'spirit' and identifies the ensuing process as regeneration, that is, rebirth: 'alchemy is the art of fermenting the human vital spirit in order to purify it and finally to dissolve it, so that the principle be re-constructed through a regeneration.'[120] Although much remains unclear in this statement, it is evident that the art entailed a practice that affected and transformed the spirit. In a letter to De Steiger dated 26 May 1908, Atwood explained alchemy in similar terms and linked it to Christ: 'Alchemy was a process of fermentation and by mental fermentation the Archetypal Light or Logos was evolved which leavens the Whole of human life and recapitulates It and immortalises that which is recapitulated by our sensorial life,' upon which she apologised for 'writing badly and expressing my thoughts imperfectly.'[121] That may be true, yet it is sufficiently clear that the underlying notion was that of Christ's mystical incarnation within the believer.

The vital spirit tied the soul to the body, yet the problem was, in the words of the Apostle Paul as quoted in the *Suggestive Inquiry*: 'flesh and blood cannot enter into the kingdom of heaven.'[122] Therefore, this bond needed to be severed, so that a reborn spirit and spiritual body fit for heaven could arise. A further definition spells out the consequence for the former body: 'we must remember that Alchemy is Divine Chemistry, and the transmutation of Life; and therefore that which is the medium between soul and body is changed, and the soul freed from the chains of corporeity, and the body is left as a mere husk. These people put on their bodies as mere coats.'[123] The soul linked spirit—the divine spark—and body, and it had to be released from its corporeality. Beneath the husk of the body, the new birth of spiritual alchemy would be nourished.

Curiously, Freher wrote of regeneration in strikingly similar terms: 'a Person may be still surrounded Outwardly, or may have Cleaving unto him as a Shell or Huske from without, a 4. Elementary Body and may yet have attained within to that Perfection, which is in the one Elementary Body, hid under this outward.'[124] Eventually, the one-elementary body would be folded out and subdue the four-elementary one. As if with Boehme and Freher's views in mind, Atwood wrote: 'our present state is one of inversion,' implying that it needed to be reversed so the original state would be restored.[125] In letters to De Steiger, Atwood explicitly stated that it took a conscious act of the will—a conversion, in other words, leading on to regeneration—to do so, 'a voluntary return of the creature reversing the Fall,' with 'the promise of immortality' being 'conditional by conversion to our Principle in Christ Jesus.'[126]

If there can still be any lingering doubt as to the spiritual alchemy opaquely expounded in the *Suggestive Inquiry*, one of Atwood's late letters put it in so many words. As plainly as she could manage, she explained it to De Steiger on 2 April 1908: 'the Alchemists understood and taught that regeneration (by which the *fall* which to *them* was made apparent) was the only way of real *recovery*—a corrupt root could not bring forth good fruit—"Ye must be born again"—by *ablation* of this sensorial *life* and by the fermentation thereof by its Principle finding a new Foundation and building up *anew* in coordination with its Archetypal Mandate, a *resurrection* body.'[127] Just a week earlier, on 24 March, Atwood could not have been clearer either: '"Ye must be born again" and get a resurrection body. . . . The old Bible is radically consistent from beginning to end.'[128] As Atwood's later papers reveal with particular clarity, true alchemy amounted to the fermentation of the vital spirit in order to loosen it from the mortal, sinful body, thus making room for a new birth to grow inside. The last line she ever wrote to De Steiger summed up the message of her life's work: 'don't forget what I [s]ay of regeneration being essential to the fabrication of the new rectified life.'[129] From the early seventeenth century to World War I, individuals believed they could regain that prelapsarian state from which Adam and Eve had fallen and prepare themselves for the heavenly life to come through the spiritual alchemy transmitted from Boehme to Atwood.

Epilogue

Having surveyed the development of spiritual alchemy from its inchoate beginnings in pseudepigraphic writings attributed to Valentin Weigel to the mature notes of Mary Anne Atwood, we might do well to return to the question with which this book began: what is alchemy? And what is *spiritual* alchemy? Recent historiography has given us a good sense of that with which pre-modern alchemy and its later revivals were typically concerned: hands-on work with material substances, using laboratory equipment and different degrees of heat to accomplish a variety of goals. Included among them was the aim of making gold (*chrysopoeia*), which over time became the prototypical aspiration.[1] Indeed, by the 1720s, the term 'alchemy' was largely synonymous with what had earlier been but one more restricted aim, that of turning lesser metals into gold. Throughout this book, I have shown that, in parallel, there existed a specific kind of spiritual alchemy that came into its own in the wake of Jacob Boehme, the theosopher of Görlitz, and eventually reached the Victorian era. This Boehmist spiritual alchemy of rebirth did not come anywhere near dominating the conception of alchemy until the late nineteenth century, yet that was also the point in time at which it rapidly began to unravel. What had once been a definable, if somewhat idiosyncratic, school of alchemy that co-existed with its laboratory practice became an overarching interpretation of alchemy itself and very soon gave way to many competing, similar yet distinct interpretations.

There are two crucial points to make regarding this complex situation and the continuity I have documented. First, the less obvious but more important one is that this spiritual alchemy was more than just a literary conceit or purely religious metaphor. Although spiritual alchemy undeniably originated in such rhetorical devices, it did not remain so but instead took on independent reality. This was possible because it was grounded in Scripture and firmly embedded in an early-modern cosmology infused by Lutheran theology, specifically the doctrine of Christ's ubiquity. To a significant extent, this transition can be attributed to the notion of *spiritus*, a subtle matter pervading the universe. Variously called the holy element, quintessence, or ether, it defies the hard and fast modern distinction between spirit and matter, whether we encounter it in the writings of Boehme or in the context of the Victorian vogue for Mesmerism.

Although it is very difficult for us to fathom this in the twenty-first century, it is my contention that, from Boehme at the latest, the representatives of spiritual alchemy discussed throughout this book were convinced that their spiritual rebirth implanted within them a new body consisting of a subtle, imperceptible, and unquantifiable matter. Writing in a Lutheran context, the theosopher of Görlitz went as far as identifying this subtle matter with the ubiquitous body of Christ that suffused all of creation. Through mystical identification with Christ and physical participation in his ubiquitous body, as well as a regimen of spiritual alchemy (watching and waking, fasting, prayer, introspection, and anticipation of the life to come), believers actively nourished this new birth and its heavenly bodiliness. In so doing, they believed they were preparing themselves for the resurrection of the dead at the Last Judgement. We might take this spiritual alchemy as a fascinating hybrid of what we are wont to contrast as science and religion. It is a striking example of 'science' (if we may identify late sixteenth-century alchemy as having a tenuous connection to our modern notion) being appropriated to develop 'religion' (if the Weigelian heretics of the time may represent it).

The second and perhaps more obvious point is that, rather than being merely a modern, anachronistic misinterpretation, spiritual alchemy had its origins in a period during which laboratory alchemy thrived. This is a surprising and important finding given that a number of older conceptions proposed in scholarship were based on mistaken dichotomies, such as physical/spiritual, exoteric/esoteric, and outer/inner alchemy, or indeed chemistry/alchemy. Laboratory alchemy and spiritual alchemy were anything but mutually exclusive: although it would have led too far afield to study this aspect in detail, all protagonists from pseudo-Weigel and Paul Nagel to Friedrich Breckling (with the minor exception of Georg Lorenz Seidenbecher) actively engaged with the literature and practice of laboratory alchemy. I have explored this matter in more detail elsewhere concerning Jacob Boehme.[2] In this book, I have briefly sketched how Abraham von Franckenberg was still tracking down alchemical texts just before his death and how Friedrich Breckling—in his seventies—enthusiastically followed the gold-making experiments of some acquaintances, hoping that they would be able to fund charitable activities with their gains. In tendency, the subjects of this book found spiritual alchemy more accessible to begin with and used it as a springboard to also explore laboratory alchemy, although pseudo-Weigel, Paul Nagel, and Johann Siebmacher took the opposite route.

All of this goes to show that the relation between laboratory alchemy and spiritual alchemy was not one of enmity or mutual exclusion until the late nineteenth century. To the contrary, their relation was a beneficial one, certainly for spiritual alchemy at the time. After the fortunes of laboratory alchemy declined and various spiritual, religious, moral, or psychological interpretations of its literature became dominant, these later understandings in turn inspired a considerable portion of the modern reception of alchemical writings. In fact, it could be said, then, that the continuity of spiritual alchemy was preserved for such a long time precisely because it could still be anchored in, or at least related to, the laboratory practice of alchemy. This only began to change with Dionysius Andreas Freher, who was perhaps the author least familiar with alchemical literature among all the ones studied in this book.

In contrast, Mary Anne South had access to many old books on alchemy yet lacked familiarity with the tradition of laboratory work. Around the middle of the nineteenth century, it was the perceived absurdity of *chrysopoeia* from the perspective of contemporaneous chemistry that contributed to decisively changing the situation. In 1855, South's American contemporary Ethan Allen Hitchcock expressed this thought in so many words: 'the very absurdity ... on their face' of the works of 'the Alchymists' should prompt one to consider 'the possibility of a concealed purpose' that has nothing to do with foolish attempts at turning base metals into gold.[3] The nearly total eclipse of *chrysopoeia* in the age of Enlightenment brought about changed circumstances in which spiritual alchemy ceased to be an identifiable, cosmologically embedded article of faith with bodily consequences and practical repercussions, documented in certain historical sources. Instead, it could now potentially take on much greater significance and provide a general framework for the interpretation of alchemical literature altogether. Yet spiritual alchemy, unmoored from its grounding in laboratory alchemy, quickly lost its internal cohesion and gave way to a proliferation of 'spiritual alchemies,' or rather, as A. E. Waite put it, numerous '"spiritual hermeneutics" of transmutation literature,' interpretive lenses applied to older works on alchemy.[4] That is not to say that, prior to the late nineteenth century, there were no alternative conceptions or traditions competing with, or developing in parallel to, the Boehmist spiritual alchemy explored throughout this book. It merely remains to be seen whether some of these modern interpretations equally had more or less continuous antecedents reaching back to the early-modern or even medieval periods.

South's *Suggestive Inquiry into the Hermetic Mystery* occupied a liminal position with regard to this transition. For South, the one lingering foundation that guaranteed continuity was Boehmist theosophy, and she was in close contact with representatives of English Behmenism throughout her life. This allowed her to largely remain true to the spiritual alchemy of rebirth, which the works of the theosopher and Freher, his London-based disciple, had conveyed to her. Yet this continuity was hanging by a thread by that time and did not hold much longer. Beginning in the 1880s, the widowed Mrs Atwood engaged with current and former members of the London Theosophical Society. Recruited from that occultist milieu and its widespread fascination with Eastern religions such as Buddhism and Hinduism, early readers of the *Suggestive Inquiry* soon developed their own understandings of alchemy. Indeed, towards the end of Atwood's life, a plethora of diverging interpretations completely divorced from the laboratory sprouted forth. It was during that very time—beyond the scope of this book—that spiritual alchemy dissociated itself from its distinctly Christian heritage and thereby became something different, or rather: many different interpretations of alchemy.

An old and oft-repeated adage of alchemical literature claims that 'all the sages agree' (*omnes philosophi consentiunt*).[5] Arguably, though, this stance is not conducive to the careful analysis of sources in their particularity. Indeed, most of what little serious scholarly work has been done on 'spiritual alchemy'—as an umbrella term rather than as referring to the precise tradition investigated here—has inevitably tended to lump together, rather than split apart, any evidence that could be presented to prop up a vague idea of 'spiritual alchemy.' Similarly, although some scholars have followed one leading modern interpreter more closely than another, the same approach seems to undergird engagement with those who developed their own spiritual interpretations of alchemy. A similar tendency can be observed even in critics of such interpretations. In their seminal article 'Some Problems with the Historiography of Alchemy,' Lawrence M. Principe and William R. Newman make clear that there are important differences between, for instance, the psychologising approach of C. G. Jung and the vitalist emphasis of Mircea Eliade.[6] Yet at a deeper level, Principe and Newman, as well as the advocates of Jung and Eliade, have considered the general similarity more important than the subtle differences.[7] As the academic study of esotericism continues to emancipate itself from its religionist heritage that traditionally sought to perceive a singular universal truth through history's thicket, it is the small differences that matter and that will help us move beyond the claim that 'all the sages agree.'[8]

This book has focussed on one particular kind of 'spiritual alchemy,' a Boehmist variety whose potential existence writers and scholars have flagged for more than a century.[9] For the first time, this book has gathered and presented comprehensive evidence for its continuity into the nineteenth century. For most of that time, it did not provide a general, overriding interpretation of all texts on laboratory alchemy. That only began to change in the late nineteenth century, and the speed and extent of this development are nothing short of astonishing. It is every researcher's well-worn *cliché* that more research is needed. Yet the proliferation of 'spiritual alchemies' from the late nineteenth century onwards would indeed merit closer scrutiny: it appears that the basic idea of interpreting alchemy in ways detached from the laboratory was one whose time had come. Such 'spiritual' or non-laboratory interpretations of alchemy themselves now deserve careful study, historicisation, and contextualisation. Significantly, this proposed approach presumes that modernity's 'spiritual' interpretations are no longer rivals to be debunked by the New Historiography of Alchemy. Instead, they become legitimate topics for research not only for scholars working on esotericism but also for historians engaging with alchemy from a variety of disciplinary angles.

Put another way, if laboratory alchemy has now ceased to be a 'wretched subject' and experienced a comprehensive rehabilitation among historians, the time has come to extend the same rehabilitation to a host of divergent modern conceptions of alchemy.[10] These came to be detached from the laboratory not least due to the successful afterlife of Boehmist spiritual alchemy inaugurated during the late nineteenth century. That is not to say, however, that these 'spiritual' or non-laboratory interpretations are potential alternatives to the New Historiography of Alchemy when it comes to historical research on the subject. By virtue of its very success, the New Historiography need no longer be defensive regarding 'spiritual' interpretations of alchemy and can instead historicise them just as it previously historicised laboratory alchemy. If there was once a need to establish that these interpretations fell short as attempts at historiography, it is simply no longer necessary to view them as ill-founded or perniciously misleading misunderstandings. In other words, these different modern interpretations of alchemy can now be investigated as complex historical phenomena in their own right, whose specific contours are currently hardly discernible, due to a lack of rigorous studies. This anticipated shift could be viewed as reflecting a much larger trend in the history of science that has recently seen it expand its scope to encompass the humanities and even non-academic knowledge. It is now possible to envision future studies fruitfully approaching other modern proponents of non-laboratory conceptions of alchemy, exploring their historical antecedents or parallels, and establishing whether there were continuities that linked them.

Notes

Introduction

1. See Tara Nummedal, 'The Alchemist,' in *A Companion to the History of Science*, ed. Bernard Lightman (Chichester: Wiley Blackwell, 2016), 58–70, on 58–59. For Rowling's interview admission that she wanted to be 'an alchemist' and had 'learned a ridiculous amount about alchemy,' see Anne Simpson and J. K. Rowling, 'Casting a Spell over Young Minds,' *Herald* (Edinburgh, 7 December 1998).
2. For an illuminating discussion of the problematic terms 'superstition' and 'magic,' as well as the observation of a widely shared 'tacit acceptance of the triad "magic—religion—science" as universal concepts,' see Wouter J. Hanegraaff, *Esotericism and the Academy: Rejected Knowledge in Western Culture* (Cambridge: Cambridge University Press, 2012), 156–77, on 166.
3. Lawrence M. Principe, 'The End of Alchemy? The Repudiation and Persistence of Chrysopoeia at the Académie Royale des Sciences in the Eighteenth Century,' in *Chemical Knowledge in the Early Modern World*, ed. Matthew D. Eddy, Seymour H. Mauskopf, and William R. Newman (Chicago: Chicago University Press, 2014), 96–116. See also Lawrence M. Principe, 'A Revolution Nobody Noticed? Changes in Early Eighteenth-Century Chymistry,' in *New Narratives in Eighteenth-Century Chemistry: Contributions from the First Francis Bacon Workshop, 21–23 April 2005, California Institute of Technology, Pasadena, California*, ed. Lawrence M. Principe (Dordrecht: Springer, 2007), 1–22; Lawrence M. Principe, 'Transmuting Chymistry into Chemistry: Eighteenth-Century Chrysopoeia and Its Repudiation,' in *Neighbours and Territories: The Evolving Identity of Chemistry*, ed. José Ramón Bertomeu-Sánchez, Duncan Thorburn Burns, and Brigitte van Tiggelen (Leuven: Mémosciences, 2008), 21–34.
4. Bruce T. Moran, 'Introduction,' *Isis* 102 (2011): 300–4, on 301.
5. Walter Pagel, 'The Vindication of "Rubbish,"' in *Religion and Neoplatonism in Renaissance Medicine*, ed. Marianne Winder (London: Variorum Reprints, 1985), 1–14; O. Neugebauer, 'The Study of Wretched Subjects,' *Isis* 42 (1951): 111.
6. Herbert Butterfield, *The Origins of Modern Science 1300–1800* (London: G. Bell, 1949), 115.
7. Ethan Allen Hitchcock, *Remarks upon Alchemy and the Alchemists, Indicating a Method of Discovering the True Nature of Hermetic Philosophy* (Boston: Crosby, Nichols, and Company, 1857), 76; viii, 224; see also Ethan Allen Hitchcock, *Remarks upon Alchymists, and the Supposed Object of Their Pursuit; Showing that the Philosopher's Stone is a Mere Symbol* (Carlisle: Herald Office, 1855). For more on Hitchcock, see I. Bernard Cohen, 'Ethan Allen Hitchcock: Soldier—Humanitarian—Scholar.

Discoverer of the "True Subject" of the Hermetic Art,' *Proceedings of the American Antiquarian Society* 61 (1951): 29–136. Hitchcock's collection of alchemical literature has been preserved at the University of Missouri–St. Louis, St. Louis Mercantile Library, M-108: The Ethan Allen Hitchcock Alchemy Collection.

8. Herbert Silberer, *Probleme der Mystik und ihrer Symbolik* (Vienna: Heller, 1914), e.g. 97–100, 211–12. On Silberer, see Karl Fallend, '"Über den Wolken": Herbert Silberer—"Führer erster Classe" und Mitglied der Wiener Psychoanalytischen Vereinigung,' *Zeitschrift für Psychoanalyse und Gesellschaftskritik* 5 (1988): 67–86; Bernd Nitzschke, 'Herbert Silberer—Luftschiffer und Halluzinationsforscher—Stichworte zu seinem Leben und Werk,' in *Aus dem Kreis um Sigmund Freud: Zu den Protokollen der Wiener Psychoanalytischen Vereinigung*, ed. Ernst Federn and Gerhard Wittenberger (Frankfurt a.M.: Fischer-Taschenbuch-Verlag, 1992), 170–75.

9. Mircea Eliade, ed., *The Encyclopedia of Religion*, 16 vols. (New York: Macmillan, 1987), vol. 1, s.v. 'Alchemy,' on 183. See also Mircea Eliade, *The Forge and the Crucible*, trans. Stephen Corrin (London: Rider, 1962).

10. This is emphasised by Hereward Tilton, *The Quest for the Phoenix: Spiritual Alchemy and Rosicrucianism in the Work of Count Michael Maier (1569–1622)* (Berlin: De Gruyter, 2003), 2–9; Hanegraaff, *Esotericism and the Academy*, 288–95.

11. C. G. Jung, *Psychologie und Alchemie*, 2nd ed. (Olten: Walter-Verlag, 1972), 265–67. Jung even characterised the alchemical process as 'an essentially (*an sich*) chemical investigation' on 542. This aspect is also highlighted by Tilton, *The Quest for the Phoenix*, 11–15; Hanegraaff, *Esotericism and the Academy*, 289–91.

12. C. G. Jung, 'The Bologna Enigma,' *Ambix* 2 (1946): 182–91, on 185.

13. Lawrence M. Principe, 'Reflections on Newton's Alchemy in Light of the New Historiography of Alchemy,' in *Newton and Newtonianism: New Studies*, ed. James E. Force and Sarah Hutton (Dordrecht: Kluwer, 2004), 205–19, on 213–16. Compare B. J. T. Dobbs, *The Foundations of Newton's Alchemy: Or, 'The Hunting of the Greene Lyon'* (Cambridge: Cambridge University Press, 1975); B. J. T. Dobbs, *The Janus Faces of Genius: The Role of Alchemy in Newton's Thought* (Cambridge: Cambridge University Press, 1991). A new study is now available in William R. Newman, *Newton the Alchemist: Science, Enigma, and the Quest for Nature's 'Secret Fire'* (Princeton: Princeton University Press, 2019).

14. Barbara Obrist, *Les débuts de l'imagerie alchimique (XIVe–XVe siècles)* (Paris: Editions le Sycomore, 1982), 11–36. On the significance of Obrist's critique, see Tilton, *The Quest for the Phoenix*, 8–9; Hanegraaff, *Esotericism and the Academy*, 293, n. 124. For an exemplary early review of Jung's work on alchemy, balancing lavish praise with mild criticism, see e.g. Walter Pagel, 'Jung's Views on Alchemy,' *Isis* 39 (1948): 44–48.

15. Obrist, *Les débuts de l'imagerie alchimique*, 35–36, on 35.

16. For the most important essays in this regard, see William R. Newman, '"Decknamen or Pseudochemical Language"? Eirenaeus Philalethes and Carl Jung,' *Revue d'histoire des sciences* 49 (1996): 159–88; William R. Newman and Lawrence M. Principe, 'Alchemy vs. Chemistry: The Etymological Origins of a Historiographic Mistake,' *Early Science and Medicine* 3 (1998): 32–65; Lawrence M. Principe and William R. Newman, 'Some Problems with the Historiography of Alchemy,' in *Secrets of*

Nature: Astrology and Alchemy in Early Modern Europe, ed. William R. Newman and Anthony Grafton (Cambridge: MIT Press, 2001), 385–431. To my knowledge, the first use of the term 'new historiography of alchemy' occurs in a 2004 essay by Principe, 'Reflections on Newton's Alchemy,' esp. 207, 210.

17. Qtd. Newman, '*Decknamen*,' 160. For an early study using this approach, see Lawrence Principe, '"Chemical Translation" and the Role of Impurities in Alchemy: Examples from Basil Valentine's *Triumph-Wagen*,' *Ambix* 34 (1987): 21–30. See also Lawrence M. Principe, 'Alchemy Restored,' *Isis* 102 (2011): 305–12, on 310; Lawrence M. Principe, *The Secrets of Alchemy* (Chicago: University of Chicago Press, 2013), 10–11.

18. In German scholarship, for instance, the New Historiography can still be sidestepped, as in the contributions by Anne-Charlott Trepp and Heinz Schott to a recent collective volume and exhibition catalogue: Petra Feuerstein-Herz and Stefan Laube, eds., *Goldenes Wissen: Die Alchemie—Substanzen, Synthesen, Symbolik* (Wiesbaden: Harrassowitz, 2014), 67–72, 99–110, resp. Trepp summarises findings first presented in her earlier monograph: Anne-Charlott Trepp, *Von der Glückseligkeit alles zu wissen: Die Erforschung der Natur als religiöse Praxis in der Frühen Neuzeit* (Frankfurt a.M.: Campus Verlag, 2009). Schott's essay reiterates Jungian positions without due consideration of the New Historiography.

19. Newman and Principe, 'Alchemy vs. Chemistry,' 34–35. For the place of this essay in current historiography, see Marcos Martinón-Torres, 'Some Recent Developments in the Historiography of Alchemy,' *Ambix* 58 (2011): 215–37, on 220–22. For an early critical reaction, see e.g. Ferdinando Abbri, 'Alchemy and Chemistry: Chemical Discourses in the Seventeenth Century,' *Early Science and Medicine* 5 (2000): 214–26.

20. E.g. A. J. Rocke, 'Agricola, Paracelsus, and "Chymia,"' *Ambix* 32 (1985): 38–45, on 38; Owen Hannaway, *The Chemists and the Word: The Didactic Origins of Chemistry* (Baltimore: Johns Hopkins University Press, 1975), x. See also the discussion in Newman and Principe, 'Alchemy vs. Chemistry,' 44–47. For a full-length study on Libavius, see Bruce T. Moran, *Andreas Libavius and the Transformation of Alchemy: Separating Chemical Cultures with Polemical Fire* (Sagamore Beach: Science History, 2007).

21. Newman and Principe, 'Alchemy vs. Chemistry,' 64.

22. Principe and Newman, 'Some Problems,' 388, 397.

23. Abbri, 'Alchemy and Chemistry'; Brian Vickers, 'The "New Historiography" and the Limits of Alchemy,' *Annals of Science* 65 (2008): 127–56; George-Florin Călian, '*Alkimia Operativa* and *Alkimia Speculativa*: Some Modern Controversies on the Historiography of Alchemy,' *Annual of Medieval Studies* 16 (2010): 166–90; Tilton, *The Quest for the Phoenix*, 1–34, 253–56; Hereward Tilton, '*Alchymia Archetypica*: Theurgy, Inner Transformation and the Historiography of Alchemy,' *Quaderni di studi indo-mediterranei* 5 (2012): 179–215; Hanegraaff, *Esotericism and the Academy*, 191–207. For shorter discussions, see e.g. Peter J. Forshaw, 'Subliming Spirits: Physical-Chemistry and Theo-Alchemy in the Works of Heinrich Khunrath (1560–1605),' in *Mystical Metal of Gold: Essays on Alchemy and Renaissance Culture*, ed. Stanton J. Linden (New York: AMS Press, 2007), 255–75, on 261–65; Bruce Janacek, *Alchemical Belief: Occultism in the Religious Culture of Early Modern England* (University

Park: Pennsylvania State University Press, 2011), 12–15; Antonio Clericuzio, 'William R. Newman and Lawrence M. Principe, *Alchemy Tried in the Fire: Starkey, Boyle, and the Fate of Helmontian Chymistry*' (review), *Annals of Science* 62 (2005): 406–8; Anna Marie Roos, 'The Experimental Approach towards a Historiography of Alchemy (Reviewing L. M. Principe, *The Secrets of Alchemy*),' *Studies in History and Philosophy of Biological and Biomedical Sciences* 44 (2013): 787–89. As a representative of the old historiography that views alchemy as inalienably occult, Vickers has been refuted twice: William R. Newman, 'Brian Vickers on Alchemy and the Occult: A Response,' *Perspectives on Science* 17 (2009): 482–506; Hanegraaff, *Esotericism and the Academy*, 184–91.

24. Hanegraaff, *Esotericism and the Academy*, 196–97.
25. For an account tracing the development of our modern notion of religion as a set of beliefs and the ensuing conflict with science, see Peter Harrison, *The Territories of Science and Religion* (Chicago: University of Chicago Press, 2015).
26. Tara Nummedal, 'Alchemy and Religion in Christian Europe,' *Ambix* 60 (2013): 311–22, on 312, 322.
27. Principe, *The Secrets of Alchemy*, 15–24. See also Kyle A. Fraser, 'Zosimos of Panopolis and the Book of Enoch: Alchemy as Forbidden Knowledge,' *Aries* 4 (2004): 125–47; Michèle Mertens, ed., *Zosime de Panopolis: Mémoires authentiques* (Paris: Les Belles Lettres, 1995).
28. Pamela H. Smith, 'Preface to the New Paperback Edition,' in *The Business of Alchemy: Science and Culture in the Holy Roman Empire*, 2nd ed. (Princeton: Princeton University Press, 2016), xi–xxv, on xiii.
29. Petrus Bonus, *Introductio in artem chemiae integra, ab ipso authore inscripta margarita preciosa novella* (Montbéliard: Apud Jacobum Foillet, 1602), 141 (emphasis added). See also Chiara Crisciani, 'The Conception of Alchemy as Expressed in the *Pretiosa Margarita Novella* of Petrus Bonus of Ferrara,' *Ambix* 20 (1973): 165–81. For more on the medieval context, see e.g. Zachary A. Matus, 'Alchemy and Christianity in the Middle Ages,' *History Compass* 10 (2012): 934–45.
30. See Joachim Telle's entry in Kurt Ruh et al., eds., *Verfasserlexikon: Die deutsche Literatur des Mittelalters* (Berlin: De Gruyter, 1978–2008), s.v. 'Ulmannus.' For a study of the work's imagery, see Obrist, *Les débuts de l'imagerie alchimique*, ch. 3.
31. *Rosarium philosophorum* (Frankfurt a.M.: Ex officina Cyriaci Jacobi, Mense Junio, 1550), f. a4r. On the German *alchemia picta* that led to the *Rosarium*, see Joachim Telle, *Sol und Luna: Literar- und alchemiegeschichtliche Studien zu einem altdeutschen Bildgedicht* (Hürtgenwald: Pressler, 1980).
32. Examples can be found from the early 1980s onward until 2013, the year of his death; see e.g. Joachim Telle, 'Zum *Opus mago-cabbalisticum et theosophicum* von Georg von Welling,' *Euphorion* 77 (1983): 359–79, on 371, 374; Joachim Telle, *Alchemie und Poesie: Deutsche Alchemikerdichtungen des 15. bis 17. Jahrhunderts*, 2 vols. (Berlin: De Gruyter, 2013), 151, n. 14.
33. E.g. Italo Ronca, 'Religious Symbolism in Medieval Islamic and Christian Alchemy,' in *Western Esotericism and the Science of Religion*, ed. Antoine Faivre and Wouter J. Hanegraaff (Leuven: Peeters, 1998), 95–116, on 95–96; Karen-Claire Voss, 'Spiritual

Alchemy: Interpreting Representative Texts and Images,' in *Gnosis and Hermeticism from Antiquity to Modern Times*, ed. Roelof van den Broek and Wouter J. Hanegraaff (New York: State University of New York Press, 1995), 147–82, on 151. Voss's study is heavily indebted to Eliade and exemplary of what Principe and Newman argue against.

34. Principe, *The Secrets of Alchemy*, 98.
35. The former understanding is dominant for Principe and Newman, who use the phrase as shorthand for 'the "spiritual" interpretation of alchemy'; Principe and Newman, 'Some Problems,' 388. Other scholars instead describe certain contents of historical sources as spiritual alchemy. This distinction is not found in Călian, 'Alkimia Operativa and Alkimia Speculativa,' 166, 174.
36. Schleswig, Landesarchiv Schleswig-Holstein (LASH): Abt. 7, Nr. 2059:3, f. 2v counting from the title (no foliation); Robert Fludd, *Clavis philosophiae et alchymiae Fluddanae* (Frankfurt a.M.: Prostat apud Guilhelmum Fitzerum, 1633), 75, 83; Angelus Silesius, *Cherubinischer Wandersmann: Kritische Ausgabe*, ed. Louise Gnädinger (Stuttgart: Reclam, 2000), bk. 1, no. 102; Bartholomaeus Sclei, *Theosophische-Schrifften: Oder Eine Allgemeine und Geheime, jedoch Einfältige und Teutsche THEOLOGIA*, ed. [Friedrich Breckling] (Amsterdam: [Christoffel Cunradus' widow], 1686), index, s.v. 'Alchymia Mystica'; Thomas Hooker, *The Application of Redemption, By the effectual Work of the Word, and Spirit of Christ*, 2 vols. (London: Printed by Peter Cole at the sign of the Pringting-press [sic] in Cornhil, neer the Royal Exchange, 1656–57), 2:218; Johann Philipp Maul, *Zahav mi-zafon sive medicina theologica, chymico irenica, et christiano-cabbalistica, Vorgestellet in der Ersten Continuation curioser und erbaulicher Gespräche Vom Gold von Mitternacht*, 2nd ed. (Wesel: Bey Jacobus von Wesel, Buchh., 1713), 590, 600; Johann Heinrich Haug, ed., *Die Heilige Schrift Altes und Neues Testaments, Nach dem Grund-Text aufs neue übersehen und übersetzet*, 8 vols. (Berleburg, 1726–42), vol. 8, 'Haupt-Register,' s.v. 'Chymie wahre geistliche.' On the fascinating project of the Berleburg Bible, see e.g. Douglas H. Shantz, *An Introduction to German Pietism: Protestant Renewal at the Dawn of Modern Europe* (Baltimore: Johns Hopkins University Press, 2013), 219–29. The occurrence of such terms is also noted by Principe and Newman, 'Some Problems,' 398. For mentions of 'Spiritual Chemists' or a 'spiritual alchemist' in the seventeenth and eighteenth centuries, respectively, see also Thomas Willard, 'Two Early References to "Spiritual Chemists,"' *Cauda Pavonis* 3 (1984): 3–4; Jeff Bach, *Voices of the Turtledoves: The Sacred World of Ephrata* (University Park: Pennsylvania State University Press, 2002), 177.
37. Boaz Huss, 'The Sacred Is the Profane, Spirituality Is Not Religion: The Decline of the Religion/Secular Divide and the Emergence of the Critical Discourse on Religion,' *Method and Theory in the Study of Religion* 27 (2015): 97–103, on 101.
38. This state of affairs could also give rise to discussions concerning spiritual bodiliness or subtle bodies; e.g. Christine Göttler and Wolfgang Neuber, eds., *Spirits Unseen: The Representation of Subtle Bodies in Early Modern European Culture* (Leiden: Brill, 2008), esp. xv–xxv. See further Geoffrey Samuel and Jay Johnston, *Religion and the Subtle Body in Asia and the West: Between Mind and Body* (London: Routledge, 2013).

On the meaning of anthropology throughout the early-modern period, see Tricia M. Ross, 'Anthropologia: An (Almost) Forgotten Early Modern History,' *Journal of the History of Ideas* 79 (2018): 1–22.

39. D. P. Walker, 'The Astral Body in Renaissance Medicine,' *Journal of the Warburg and Courtauld Institutes* 21 (1958): 119–33, on 120. See also D. P. Walker, *Spiritual and Demonic Magic: From Ficino to Campanella* (Notre Dame: University of Notre Dame Press, 1975).

40. Katharine Park, 'The Organic Soul,' in *The Cambridge History of Renaissance Philosophy*, ed. Quentin Skinner, Eckhard Kessler, and Jill Kraye (Cambridge: Cambridge University Press, 1988), 464–84, on 469.

41. Edward N. Zalta, ed., *The Stanford Encyclopedia of Philosophy*, Summer 2015 ed. (Stanford: Stanford University, 2015), s.v. 'Marsilio Ficino,' 4. (Legacy) and 3.4 (Ethics, Love).

42. Sylvain Matton, 'Marsile Ficin et l'alchimie: Sa position, son influence,' in *Alchimie et philosophie à la Renaissance: Actes du colloque international de Tours (4–7 Décembre 1991)*, ed. Jean-Claude Margolin and Sylvain Matton (Paris: Librairie philosophique J. Vrin, 1993), 123–92, on 142–48. See Marsilio Ficino, *Three Books on Life: A Critical Edition and Translation with Introduction and Notes*, ed. and trans. Carol V. Kaske and John R. Clark, 3rd ed. (Tempe, AZ: Renaissance Society of America, 2002), 254–57 (bk. 3, ch. 3). See also Hiro Hirai, 'The World-Spirit and Quintessence in the Chymical Philosophy of Joseph Du Chesne,' in *Chymia: Science and Nature in Medieval and Early Modern Europe*, ed. Miguel López Pérez, Didier Kahn, and Mar Rey Bueno (Newcastle: Cambridge Scholars, 2010), 247–61.

43. *Artis auriferae, quam chemiam vocant, volumen primum: quod continet Turbam Philosophorum* (Basel: Excudebat Conr. Waldkirch, Expensis Claudii de Marne, et Joan. Aubry, 1593), 'In Turbam Philosophorum exercitationes,' ch. 14, on 180.

44. Marielene Putscher, *Pneuma, Spiritus, Geist: Vorstellungen vom Lebensantrieb in ihren geschichtlichen Wandlungen* (Wiesbaden: Steiner, 1973), 72. On Paracelsus' fluctuating use of this vocabulary, see Ernst Wilhelm Kämmerer, *Das Leib-Seele-Geist-Problem bei Paracelsus und einigen Autoren des 17. Jahrhunderts* (Wiesbaden: Steiner, 1971), 27–40.

45. The triad of body, soul, and spirit occurs in alchemical texts predating Paracelsus, yet he formalised their analogy with salt, sulphur, and mercury while elevating the latter three to great importance as fundamental principles; Reyer Hooykaas, 'Chemical Trichotomy before Paracelsus?,' in *Selected Studies in History of Science* (Coimbra: Por ordem da Universidade, 1983), 105–19.

46. Throughout the seventeenth century, several academic disputations attacked this position from the perspective of Lutheran orthodoxy: e.g. Johann Winckelmann and Balthasar Werner, *Disputatio theologica de partibus hominis, contra novam opinionem quorundam tres partes substantialiter differentes constituentium* (Gießen: Ex officina Typographica Casparis Chemlini, 1623); Theodor Thumm, Georg Hehl, and Marcus Hailand, *Brevis consideratio trium quaestionum, nostro seculo maximè controversiarium* (Tübingen: Typis Theodorici Werlini, 1624); Heinrich Wiedeburg and Christoph Tobias Wiedeburg, *Disputatio theologica inauguralis qua*

theologiae fanaticae fundamentum de tribus partibus hominis corpore anima et spiritu (Helmstedt: Typis Georgii Wolfgangi Hammii, Acad. Typogr., 1695). See also Nicolaus Hunnius, *Christliche Betrachtung Der Newen Paracelsischen und Weigelianischen Theology* (Wittenberg: Gedruckt bey Johan Gorman, In verlegung Caspar Heiden Buchh., 1622). For important pointers in scholarly literature, see e.g. Kristine Hannak, *Geist=reiche Critik: Hermetik, Mystik und das Werden der Aufklärung in spiritualistischer Literatur der Frühen Neuzeit* (Berlin: De Gruyter, 2013), 61–62, 104–5, 191–93, 205–6, 210; J. J. Poortman, *Vehicles of Consciousness: The Concept of Hylic Pluralism (Ochēma)*, trans. N. D. Smith, 4 vols. (Utrecht: Theosophical Society, 1978), 1:43–45, 55; 2:76–77, 101, 130–31; 3:7–12.

47. Winckelmann and Werner, *Disputatio theologica de partibus hominis*, f. A2v; Wiedeburg and Wiedeburg, *Disputatio theologica inauguralis*, f. A2v.

48. On Luther's doctrine of the ubiquity of Christ's body, see the monograph-length chapter by Jörg Baur, 'Ubiquität,' in *Creator est Creatura: Luthers Christologie als Lehre von der Idiomenkommunikation*, ed. Oswald Bayer and Benjamin Gleede (Berlin: De Gruyter, 2007), 186–301.

49. Ehregott Daniel Colberg, *Das Platonisch-Hermetisches Christenthum, Begreiffend Die Historische Erzehlung vom Ursprung und vielerley Secten der heutigen Fanatischen Theologie*, 2 vols. (Frankfurt a.M./Leipzig: Bey Moritz Georg Weidmann, Druckts Joh. Köler, 1690–91), 1:3–4. On Colberg, see Hans Schneider, 'Das *Platonisch-hermetische Christenthum*: Ehre Gott Daniel Colbergs Bild des frühneuzeitlichen Spiritualismus,' in *Hermetik: Literarische Figurationen zwischen Babylon und Cyberspace*, ed. Nicola Kaminski et al. (Tübingen: Niemeyer, 2002), 21–42; Sicco Lehmann-Brauns, *Weisheit in der Weltgeschichte: Philosophiegeschichte zwischen Barock und Aufklärung* (Tübingen: Niemeyer, 2004), ch. 3; Wouter J. Hanegraaff, 'The Birth of Esotericism from the Spirit of Protestantism,' *Aries* 10 (2010): 197–216; Hanegraaff, *Esotericism and the Academy*, 107–14.

50. Throughout this book, I frequently talk of rebirth, born-again believers, and the process of being born again. This is not to suggest any direct link between my book's protagonists and that political force in recent US history associated with 'born-again Christianity.' Elsewhere, however, I do suggest that a tenuous link of intellectual ancestry connects the two: Mike A. Zuber, 'Surely Born-Again Christianity Has Nothing to Do with Occult Stuff Like Alchemy?,' in *Hermes Explains: Thirty Questions on Western Esotericism*, ed. Wouter J. Hanegraaff, Peter Forshaw, and Marco Pasi (Amsterdam: Amsterdam University Press, 2019), 252–60.

51. The phrase and concept is older than this, appearing also in German mysticism and Reformation debates (often opposed to *Christus pro nobis*), but it came to be defining for spiritualist dissent throughout the seventeenth century; see Hannak, *Geist=reiche Critik*, 128, 154, 215–16. The most elaborate attack on the spiritualist understanding of Christ is mounted by Colberg, *Das Platonisch-Hermetisches Christenthum*, vol. 2, ch. 5: 'Von Christo'; 1:109. See also Martin Schmidt, 'Christian Hoburg and Seventeenth-Century Mysticism,' *Journal of Ecclesiastical History* 18 (1967): 51–58, on 53; Lehmann-Brauns, *Weisheit in der Weltgeschichte*, 140, 164; Wilhelm Schmidt-Biggemann, *Philosophia Perennis: Historical Outlines of Western Spirituality in*

Ancient, Medieval and Early Modern Thought (Dordrecht: Springer, 2004), 190–92, 202–7.

52. Daniel Schneider, *Gläubiger Christen Hertzens-Freude. . . . Bey ansehnlicher Leichbestattung Des . . . Benedicti Hinckelmanns, . . . Welcher im Jahr 1659. den 17. Aprilis . . . eingeschlaffen* (Dresden: Gedruckt durch Melchior Bergen, Churfürstl. Sächs. Hoff-Buchdr., 1662), f. G1r. For Luther's *locus classicus* and a recent discussion, see Martin Luther, *Werke: Kritische Gesamtausgabe* (Abt. Tischreden), 6 vols. (Weimar: Böhlau, 1912–21), vol. 1, no. 1149; Nummedal, 'Alchemy and Religion,' 311–12. For more on alchemical bodies and Lutheran eschatology, see Tara Nummedal, *Anna Zieglerin and the Lion's Blood: Alchemy and End Times in Reformation Germany* (Philadelphia: University of Pennsylvania Press, 2019).

53. For important remarks on how modern Western preconceptions concerning ritual reach their limits in the context of spiritual bodiliness, see Crystal Addey, 'In the Light of the Sphere: The "Vehicle of the Soul" and Subtle-Body Practices in Neoplatonism,' in Samuel and Johnston, *Religion and the Subtle Body*, 149–67, on 156–63.

54. Ronald K. Rittgers and Vincent Evener, eds., *Protestants and Mysticism in Reformation Europe* (Leiden: Brill, 2019). Throughout this book, I have sought a compromise between overly restrictive and exceedingly broad definitions of mysticism. Basically, I refer to mysticism when the sources exhibit a striving for greater proximity to the divine, usually through *unio* or *deificatio*, however construed, and place themselves in a lineage of mystical literature through explicit references, allusions, or shared content.

55. An earlier precursor could be seen in the *Opusculum de bombyce* (c. 1492–94), a poem of 254 lines by Lodovico Lazzarelli, particularly the passage discussed by Wouter J. Hanegraaff and Ruud M. Bouthoorn, *Lodovico Lazzarelli (1447–1500): The Hermetic Writings and Related Documents* (Tempe, AZ: Arizona Center for Medieval and Renaissance Studies, 2005), 54–56. For a modern edition, see Georg Roellenbleck, 'Lodovico Lazzarelli, Opusculum de bombyce,' in *Literatur und Spiritualität: Hans Sckommodau zum siebzigsten Geburtstag*, ed. Hans Rheinfelder, Pierre Christophorov, and Eberhard Müller-Bochat (Munich: Fink, 1978), 213–31. In this respect, the specific context in which the doctrine of rebirth gained traction and the Boehmists, among whom spiritual alchemy thrived, are key: in contrast to Lazzarelli, Boehme succeeded in forming something that might be called a school of early-modern alchemy.

56. 1 Corinthians 12:12–27.

57. Patrick Curry, *Prophecy and Power: Astrology in Early Modern England* (Princeton: Princeton University Press, 1989), 2.

58. Tara Nummedal, *Alchemy and Authority in the Holy Roman Empire* (Chicago: University of Chicago Press, 2007), 16. See also Bruce T. Moran, 'The Alchemist's Reality,' *Halcyon* 9 (1987): 133–48.

59. F. Sherwood Taylor, *The Alchemists: Founders of Modern Chemistry* (New York: Arno Press, 1974), 227–28.

60. Principe and Newman, 'Some Problems,' 400.

Chapter 1

1. *Deutsches Wörterbuch von Jacob Grimm und Wilhelm Grimm*, http://woerterbuchnetz.de/DWB (Trier: Universität Trier, 1998 ff.), s.v. 'Wi(e)dergebären,' 'Wi(e)dergebärung,' and esp. 'Wi(e)dergeburt.' The *locus classicus* is John 3:1-8. While English Bible translations from John Wycliffe on use the phrase 'born again' and 'reborn' first appears in 1598, the earliest example listed for the noun 'rebirth' stems from the very late eighteenth century (1790); *Oxford English Dictionary: The Definitive Record of the English Language*, http://www.oed.com (Oxford: Oxford University Press, 1992 ff.), 'born, adj.' (2. b.); 'reborn, adj'; 'rebirth, n.'
2. Examples are listed and briefly discussed in Michael Egerding, *Die Metaphorik der spätmittelalterlichen Mystik*, 2 vols. (Paderborn: Schöningh, 1997), 2:220, 228-29 (Meister Eckhart); 230, 234 (Johannes Tauler); 235, 239-40 (Heinrich Seuse); 240-41 (Heinrich von Nördlingen). On 2:239, Seuse's definition of rebirth as the restoration of a fallen human being to the prelapsarian state is very similar to that of Boehme.
3. For an English full-length study on the most influential medieval German mystic, Meister Eckhart, see e.g. Bernard McGinn, *The Mystical Thought of Meister Eckhart: The Man from Whom God Hid Nothing* (New York: Crossroad, 2001). German scholars have proposed the term *Alchemoparacelsismus*, which I translate here; e.g. Wilhelm Kühlmann and Joachim Telle, *Der Frühparacelsismus (Corpus Paracelsisticum)*, 3 vols. (Berlin: De Gruyter, 2001-13), 1:16, 26. An exemplary survey may be found in Julian Paulus, 'Alchemie und Paracelsismus um 1600: Siebzig Porträts,' in *Analecta Paracelsica: Studien zum Nachleben Theophrast von Hohenheims im deutschen Kulturgebiet der frühen Neuzeit*, ed. Joachim Telle (Stuttgart: Steiner, 1994), 335-406. In Anglophone scholarship, the futility of separating purer from less pure forms of Paracelsianism has been noted by Stephen Pumfrey, 'The Spagyric Art; or, the Impossible Work of Separating Pure from Impure Paracelsianism: A Historiographical Analysis,' in *Paracelsus: The Man and His Reputation, His Ideas and Their Transformation*, ed. Ole Peter Grell (Leiden: Brill, 1998), 21-51.
4. Charles Webster, *Paracelsus: Medicine, Magic and Mission at the End of Time* (New Haven: Yale University Press, 2008). For earlier studies, see e.g. Andrew Weeks, *Paracelsus: Speculative Theory and the Crisis of the Early Reformation* (Albany: State University of New York Press, 1997); Walter Pagel, *Paracelsus: An Introduction to Philosophical Medicine in the Era of the Renaissance*, 2nd, revised ed. (Basel: Karger, 1982).
5. Dane T. Daniel, 'Paracelsus on Baptism and the Acquiring of the Eternal Body,' in *Paracelsian Moments: Science, Medicine, and Astrology in Early Modern Europe*, ed. Gerhild Scholz Williams and Charles D. Gunnoe (Kirksville: Truman State University Press, 2002), 117-34; Dane T. Daniel, 'Paracelsus' *Astronomia magna* (1537/38): Bible-Based Science and the Religious Roots of the Scientific Revolution' (PhD thesis, Indiana University, 2003), 214-28.
6. Newman, *Newton the Alchemist*, 66; further, 73-82.
7. Urs Leo Gantenbein, 'The New Adam: Jacob Böhme and the Theology of Paracelsus (1493/94-1541),' in *Jacob Böhme and His World*, ed. Bo Andersson et al. (Leiden: Brill,

2019), 166–96, on 193; see also Urs Leo Gantenbein, 'Cross and Crucible: Alchemy in the Theology of Paracelsus,' *Ambix* 67 (2020): 88–99. In addition, it bears noting that transmutation, a notion central to spiritual alchemy, played only a negligible role in Paracelsus' authentic writings: Otto Nowotny, 'Paracelsus und die Transmutation,' in *Rosarium litterarum: Beiträge zur Pharmazie- und Wissenschaftsgeschichte*, ed. Christoph Friedrich, Sabine Bernschneider-Reif, and Daniela Schierhorn (Eschborn: Govi-Verlag, 2003), 251–58. For an alternative view, see Andrew Sparling, 'Paracelsus, a Transmutational Alchemist,' *Ambix* 67 (2020): 62–87.

8. E.g. Wilhelm Zeilfelder, *Ungetauffter kinderlein Predigt* (Gera: Durch Martinum Spiessen, 1611), title page. Such phrases hark back to Titus 3:5.
9. Zuber, 'Born-Again Christianity,' 254.
10. Urs Leo Gantenbein, '"Himmlische Philosophia" bei Paracelsus und Caspar Schwenckfeld,' *Daphnis* 48 (2020): 296–318.
11. E. J. Furcha, 'Key Concepts in Caspar von Schwenckfeld's Thought: Regeneration and the New Life,' *Church History* 37 (1968): 160–73; Paul Gerhard Eberlein, *Ketzer oder Heiliger? Caspar von Schwenckfeld, der schlesische Reformator und seine Botschaft* (Metzingen: Franz, 1998), 165–68. See also Horst Weigelt, *Spiritualistische Tradition im Protestantismus: Die Geschichte des Schwenckfeldertums in Schlesien* (Berlin: De Gruyter, 1973), esp. 36–46; Horst Weigelt, *Von Schlesien nach Amerika: Die Geschichte des Schwenckfeldertums* (Cologne: Böhlau, 2007).
12. Siegfried Wollgast, *Philosophie in Deutschland zwischen Reformation und Aufklärung 1550–1650*, 2nd ed. (Berlin: Akademie-Verlag, 1993), ch. 9, esp. 522–34, 576–600; Siegfried Wollgast, 'Zur Wirkungsgeschichte des Paracelsus im 16. und 17. Jahrhundert,' in *Resultate und Desiderate der Paracelsus-Forschung*, ed. Peter Dilg and Hartmut Rudolph (Stuttgart: Steiner, 1993), 113–44.
13. In contrast to the technical, theological meaning, the term 'spiritualist' carries very different associations in Victorian Britain, where it referred to attempts at communicating with the spirits of deceased persons. It is comparatively rare that this polysemous term could be appropriately used in both senses within a single monograph. Similarly, the theosophies of Boehme and the Theosophical Society have very little in common. To subtly note these differences in meaning, I shall capitalise both terms (Theosophy and Spiritualism) when used in their nineteenth-century senses.
14. David C. Fink, 'Was There a "Reformation Doctrine of Justification"?,' *Harvard Theological Review* 103 (2010): 205–35; Olli-Pekka Vainio, *Justification and Participation in Christ: The Development of the Lutheran Doctrine of Justification from Luther to the Formula of Concord (1580)* (Leiden: Brill, 2008).
15. Andreas Osiander, *Disputationes duae: Una, de lege et evangelio, habita nonis Aprilis. 1549. Altera, de iustificatione, habita 9. Cal. Novembris. 1550* (Königsberg: Ex officina haeredum Joannis Lufftii, 1550), f. B3v. For more on Osiander and the ensuing theological debate, see Vainio, *Justification and Participation*, ch. 4; Timothy John Wengert, *Defending Faith: Lutheran Responses to Andreas Osiander's Doctrine of Justification, 1551–1559* (Tübingen: Mohr Siebeck, 2012).
16. Ralf Bröer, 'Friedenspolitik durch Verketzerung: Johannes Crato (1519–1585) und die Denunziation der Paracelsisten als Arianer,' *Medizinhistorisches*

Journal 37 (2002): 139–82, on 152; Carlos Gilly, 'On the Genesis of L. Zetzner's *Theatrum Chemicum* in Strasbourg,' in *Magic, Alchemy and Science 15th–18th Centuries: The Influence of Hermes Trismegistus*, ed. Carlos Gilly and Cis van Heertum, 2 vols. (Florence: Centro Di, 2002), 1:417–67, on 451; Kurt Goldammer, 'Paracelsus, Osiander and Theological Paracelsism in the Middle of the 16th Century: Some Remarks Concerning a Paracelsian Pseudepigraphon on the Ten Commandments,' trans. Victor J. Gustitus, in *Science, Medicine and Society in the Renaissance: Essays to Honor Walter Pagel*, ed. Allen G. Debus, 2 vols. (London: Heinemann, 1972), 1:105–20.

17. On Weigel's engagement with Paracelsus, see Horst Pfefferl, 'Valentin Weigel und Paracelsus,' in *Paracelsus und sein dämonengläubiges Jahrhundert*, ed. Sepp Domandl (Vienna: Verband der Wissenschaftlichen Gesellschaften Österreichs, 1988), 77–95. For a concise summary of Weigel's views on rebirth, see Hans-Joachim Schoeps, *Vom himmlischen Fleisch Christi: Eine dogmengeschichtliche Untersuchung* (Tübingen: Mohr, 1951), 56–62. On Weigel generally, see Andrew Weeks, *Valentin Weigel (1533–1588): German Religious Dissenter, Speculative Theorist, and Advocate of Tolerance* (Albany: State University of New York Press, 2000); Douglas H. Shantz, 'Valentin Weigel,' in Rittgers and Evener, *Protestants and Mysticism*, 243–64.

18. Kämmerer, *Das Leib-Seele-Geist-Problem*, 70–77.

19. E.g. Valentin Weigel, *Schriften: Neue Edition*, ed. Horst Pfefferl, 14 vols. (Stuttgart-Bad Cannstatt: Frommann-Holzboog, 1996–2015), vol. 8: *Der Güldene Griff*, ch. 15, on 64.

20. P. Gennrich, *Die Lehre von der Wiedergeburt, die christliche Zentrallehre in dogmengeschichtlicher und religionsgeschichtlicher Beleuchtung* (Leipzig: Deichert, 1907), 159, 161 (Weigel), 161–64 (Arndt). Gennrich does not mention Boehme at all.

21. Johann Arndt, *Vier Bücher Von wahrem Christenthumb*, 4 vols. (Magdeburg: Durch Joachim Böel, In verlegung Johan Francken, 1610), e.g. vol. 1, 'Vorrede,' f. A3r; 23, 52; ch. 11. These expressions are largely synonymous, though individual writers may exhibit a preference for one over the other. See also Hermann Geyer, *Verborgene Weisheit: Johann Arndts 'Vier Bücher vom Wahren Christentum' als Programm einer spiritualistisch-hermetischen Theologie*, 3 vols. (Berlin: De Gruyter, 2001), 2:97–182. On the controversial early reception of Arndt, see Martin Brecht et al., eds., *Geschichte des Pietismus*, 4 vols. (Göttingen: Vandenhoeck & Ruprecht, 1993–2004), 1:142–51.

22. Sibylle Rusterholz, 'Zum Verhältnis von *Liber Naturae* und *Liber Scripturae* bei Jacob Böhme,' in *Gott, Natur und Mensch in der Sicht Jacob Böhmes und seiner Rezeption*, ed. Jan Garewicz and Alois Maria Haas (Wiesbaden: Harrassowitz, 1994), 129–46, on 136, 145.

23. Jacob Boehme, *Theosophische Send-Schreiben* (Amsterdam: Verlegt durch Henrico Betkio, 1658), 149 (ET 12:60).

24. Brecht et al., *Geschichte des Pietismus*, 1:212.

25. W. R. Ward, *Early Evangelicalism: A Global Intellectual History* (Cambridge: Cambridge University Press, 2006), ch. 1; Douglas H. Shantz, 'The Origin of Pietist Notions of New Birth and the New Man: Alchemy and Alchemists in Gottfried Arnold and Johann Heinrich Reitz,' in *The Pietist Impulse in Christianity*, ed. Christian T. Collins

Winn et al. (Eugene: Pickwick, 2011), 29–41; Shantz, *An Introduction to German Pietism*, ch. 6, esp. 154–58. See also Zuber, 'Born-Again Christianity.'

26. Despite C. G. Jung's enthusiasm, Dorn has received little scholarly attention; see, however, Didier Kahn, 'Les débuts de Gérard Dorn d'après le manuscrit autographe de sa *Clavis totius Philosophiæ Chymisticæ* (1565),' in Telle, *Analecta Paracelsica*, 59–126; Jean-François Marquet, 'Philosophie et alchimie chez Gerhard Dorn,' in Margolin and Matton, *Alchimie et philosophie*, 215–21. On Khunrath, see Peter J. Forshaw, 'Ora et Labora: Alchemy, Magic, and Cabala in Heinrich Khunrath's *Amphitheatrum sapientiae aeternae* (1609)' (PhD thesis, 2 vols., Birkbeck, University of London, 2003); Peter Forshaw, '"Alchemy in the Amphitheatre": Some Considerations of the Alchemical Content of the Engravings in Heinrich Khunrath's *Amphitheatre of Eternal Wisdom* (1609),' in *Art & Alchemy*, ed. Jacob Wamberg (Copenhagen: Museum Tusculanum Press, 2006), 195–220. On Croll, see Hannaway, *The Chemists and the Word*, chs. 1–3; Oswald Crollius, *Alchemomedizinische Briefe 1585 bis 1597*, ed. Wilhelm Kühlmann and Joachim Telle (Stuttgart: Steiner, 1998).

27. Forshaw, 'Ora et Labora,' 2:222–3. I have adapted Forshaw's transcription and translation in a variety of ways, most notably by translating *regeneratio* as 'rebirth.' The string of consonants 'JHSVH' stands for Jesus; it is the pentagrammaton of Christian kabbalah, first formed by Johannes Reuchlin. On him, see Joseph Dan, 'The Kabbalah of Johannes Reuchlin and Its Historical Significance,' in *The Christian Kabbalah: Jewish Mystical Books and Their Christian Interpreters*, ed. Joseph Dan (Cambridge: Harvard University Press, 1997), 55–84; Charles Zika, 'Reuchlin's *De verbo mirifico* and the Magic Debate of the Late Fifteenth Century,' *Journal of the Warburg and Courtauld Institutes* 39 (1976): 104–38. Cf. Wisdom 7:30.

28. For examples, see Forshaw, 'Ora et Labora,' 2:52, 170, 206, 214, 222, 240, 280, 318, 448, 452, 462, 464, 472 (with translations on facing pages). See also Johann Arndt, *Das große Geheimniß der Menschwerdung des ewigen Worts. In einem Sendschreiben an seinen guten Freund Erasmum Wolfartum, Notar. Publ. Caes. etc.* (n.p., 1676), esp. 12–13. Arndt has become the subject of several recent studies; e.g. Geyer, *Verborgene Weisheit*; Hanns-Peter Neumann, *Natura sagax—Die geistige Natur: Zum Zusammenhang von Naturphilosophie und Mystik in der frühen Neuzeit am Beispiel Johann Arndts* (Tübingen: Niemeyer, 2004); Hans Schneider, *Der fremde Arndt: Studien zu Leben, Werk und Wirkung Johann Arndts (1555–1621)* (Göttingen: Vandenhoeck & Ruprecht, 2006); Thomas Illg, *Ein anderer Mensch werden: Johann Arndts Verständnis der imitatio Christi als Anleitung zu einem wahren Christentum* (Göttingen: V&R unipress, 2011).

29. Weeks, *Valentin Weigel*, 75. For more on this subject, see Martin Žemla, 'Valentin Weigel and Alchemy,' in *Latin Alchemical Literature of Czech Provenance: Proceedings from the Centre for Renaissance Texts Conference (16–17 October 2014)*, ed. Tomáš Nejeschleba and Jiří Michalík (Olomouc: Univerzita Palackého, 2015), 21–49.

30. Lee Stavenhagen, ed., *A Testament of Alchemy: Being the Revelations of Morienus, Ancient Adept and Hermit of Jerusalem to Khalid ibn Yazid Muʿawiyya, King of the Arabs of the Divine Secrets of the Magisterium and Accomplishment of the Alchemical Art* (Hanover: Brandeis University Press, 1974), 52. The term occurs on 14 (with

transcription in n. 14), 20, 24, 32; it is translated as 'quicksilver' on the facing pages. See also Kühlmann and Telle, *Der Frühparacelsismus*, 3/1:607–8. In the nineteenth and twentieth centuries, the term was taken up, among others, by Eliphas Lévi, *Dogme et rituel de la haute magie*, 2nd expanded ed., 2 vols. (Paris: Germer Baillière, 1861), 2:298; Arthur Edward Waite, *A New Light of Mysticism: Azoth; or, The Star in the East. Embracing the First Matter of the Magnum Opus* (London: Theosophical Publishing Society, 1893); Aleister Crowley, *777 and Other Qabalistic Writings*, ed. Israel Regardie (Boston: Weiser Books, 1973), 47. For important studies on these figures, see e.g. Julian Strube, *Sozialismus, Katholizismus und Okkultismus im Frankreich des 19. Jahrhunderts: Die Genealogie der Schriften von Eliphas Lévi* (Berlin: De Gruyter, 2016); R. A. Gilbert, *A. E. Waite: Magician of Many Parts* (Wellingborough: Thorsons, 1987); Marco Pasi, *Aleister Crowley and the Temptation of Politics* (Durham: Acumen, 2014).

31. To my knowledge, there are five extant manuscript versions predating the printed editions available from 1701, here listed by (partly conjectural) dating from oldest to youngest: Berlin, Staatsbibliothek—Preußischer Kulturbesitz (SB-PK): Ms. germ. fol. 1070, ff. 21r–23r, ff. 21r–23r; Heidelberg, Universitätsbibliothek (UB): Cod. Pal. Germ. 782, ff. 177r–79v; Halle, Universitäts- und Landesbibliothek (ULB): 23 B 11, vol. 1, ff. 289v–90v; Karlsruhe, Badische Landesbibliothek (BLB): Cod. Allerheiligen 3, pp. 397–402; Berlin, SB-PK: Ms. germ. quart. 1525, ff. 2r–5v. Some of these are mentioned in Berthold Kress, *Divine Diagrams: The Manuscripts and Drawings of Paul Lautensack (1477/78–1558)* (Leiden: Brill, 2014), xxiv–xxv; Joachim Telle, 'Jakob Böhme unter den deutschen Alchemikern der frühen Neuzeit,' in *Offenbarung und Episteme: Zur europäischen Wirkung Jakob Böhmes im 17. und 18. Jahrhundert*, ed. Wilhelm Kühlmann and Friedrich Vollhardt (Berlin: De Gruyter, 2012), 165–82, on 169, n. 17. The remainder are listed in an unpublished portion of Horst Pfefferl's 1991 PhD thesis (Philipps-Universität Marburg), alongside two later manuscripts irrelevant in this context.

32. The first printed editions are [Johann Anton Söldner], *Fegfeuer der Chymisten, Worinnen Für Augen gestellt die wahren Besitzer der Kunst; Wie auch Die Ketzer, Betrieger, Sophisten und Herren gern-Grosse* (Amsterdam, 1701), ff. B1r–B4r; [Johann Anton Söldner], *Keren Happuch, Posaunen Eliae des Künstlers, oder Teutsches Fegfeuer der Scheide-Kunst* (Hamburg: Bey Gottfried Libernickel, im Dohm, 1702), 75–83. *Keren Happuch* was likely an expanded reprint of the *Fegfeuer*. Both of these editions have largely been ignored by scholarship in favour of the 1787 edition: pseudo-Weigel, *Himmlisch Manna, Azoth et Ignis, das ist: güldenes Kleinod, handelnde von dem köstlichen Eckstein der Natur und desselben wunderbaren unaussprechlichen Kräften und Tugenden* (Amsterdam, 1787), 37–42. Pfefferl also mentions an edition allegedly dating from 1700: Andreas Glorez, *Des Mährischen Albertus Magnus . . . Eröffnetes Wunderbuch von Waffensalben* (Regensburg/Stadtamhof, 1700 [1850?]), 565–71. Closer scrutiny reveals that the date on the title page must be misleading; the book is almost certainly a nineteenth-century reprint of the 1787 edition. On the attribution of the *Fegfeuer* to Söldner, see Rafał T. Prinke and Mike A. Zuber, ' "Learn to Restrain Your Mouth": Alchemical Rumours and Their Historiographical Afterlives,' *Early Science and Medicine* 25 (2020): 413–52, on 434, n. 54.

33. Berlin, SB-PK: Ms. germ. fol. 1070, f. 23r; Heidelberg, UB: Cod. Pal. Germ. 782, f. 179v.
34. Horst Pfefferl, 'Die Überlieferung der Schriften Valentin Weigels (Teildruck)' (PhD thesis, Philipps-Universität Marburg, 1991), pt. 1, 18–22, 53, 56, 70 (n. 42); pt. 3, 380–83; pt. 4, 37.
35. [Benedict Biedermann], *Theologia Weigelii. Das ist: Offentliche Glaubens Bekändtnüß* (Newstatt [Magdeburg]: Bey Johann Knuber [Johann Francke], 1618), e.g. ff. 8r/v, 9v, 24v, 25v, 27v, 38r, 41r, 42v, 47r. Alchemy is mentioned on ff. 3v, 42r, 47v.
36. Horst Pfefferl, 'Christoph Weickhart als Paracelsist: Zu Leben und Persönlichkeit eines Kantors Valentin Weigels,' in Telle, *Analecta Paracelsica*, 407–23.
37. Karlsruhe, BLB: Cod. Allerheiligen 3, p. 397.
38. Kress, *Divine Diagrams*, 263.
39. Berlin, SB-PK: Ms. germ. fol. 1070, ff. 22v–23r. The year 1599 is given on ff. 1r, 10r.
40. The middle portion is especially Lautensackian: Berlin, SB-PK: Ms. germ. fol. 1070, ff. 10v–20v. Nevertheless, Weigel is mentioned e.g. on f. 17v.
41. Halle, ULB: 23 B 11, vol. 1, f. 289v. For a description of these manuscripts, see Kress, *Divine Diagrams*, 339–45.
42. Heidelberg, UB: Cod. Pal. Germ. 782, ff. 176v–77r.
43. Karlsruhe, BLB: Cod. Allerheiligen 3, pp. 397–402. On Nagel, see Leigh T. I. Penman, 'Climbing Jacob's Ladder: Crisis, Chiliasm, and Transcendence in the Thought of Paul Nagel (†1624), a Lutheran Dissident during the Time of the Thirty Years' War,' *Intellectual History Review* 20 (2010): 201–26.
44. Penman, 'Climbing Jacob's Ladder,' 206; Armin Schlechter and Gerhard Stamm, *Die kleinen Provenienzen* (Wiesbaden: Harrassowitz, 2000), 187–94, on 188. On Sendivogius, see the work of Rafał T. Prinke, e.g. 'New Light on the Alchemical Writings of Michael Sendivogius (1566-1636),' *Ambix* 63 (2016): 217–43; 'Beyond Patronage: Michael Sendivogius and the Meanings of Success in Alchemy,' in López Pérez et al., *Chymia*, 175–231; 'The Twelfth Adept: Michael Sendivogius in Rudolfine Prague,' in *The Rosicrucian Enlightenment Revisited*, ed. Ralph White (Hudson: Lindisfarne Books, 1999), 143–92.
45. Karlsruhe, BLB: Cod. Allerheiligen 3, pp. 395–96, 403–5; for a Croll excerpt, see pp. 60–61.
46. Karlsruhe, BLB: Cod. Allerheiligen 3, p. 397. In contrast to Nagel's interpretation, pseudo-Weigel likely understood *azoth* to refer to the philosophical matter (mercury), and fire to the alchemist's most important tool—the carefully regulated furnace.
47. Bruce T. Moran, 'Alchemy, Prophecy, and the Rosicrucians: Raphael Eglinus and Mystical Currents of the Early Seventeenth Century,' in *Alchemy and Chemistry in the 16th and 17th Centuries*, ed. Piyo Rattansi and Antonio Clericuzio (Dordrecht: Kluwer, 1994), 103–19, on 113. For more on Egli, see J. Wälli, 'Raphael Egli (1559-1622),' *Zürcher Taschenbuch* 28 (1905): 154–92.
48. Karlsruhe, BLB: Cod. Allerheiligen 3, p. 397. See Heidelberg, UB: Cod. Pal. Germ. 782, f. 178r; Berlin, SB-PK: Ms. germ. quart. 1525, f. 2v.
49. Heidelberg, UB: Cod. Pal. Germ. 782, ff. 177r–78r.

50. Karlsruhe, BLB: Cod. Allerheiligen 3, pp. 397–98. See Psalm 118:22; Matthew 21:42; Mark 12:10; Acts 4:11.
51. Revelation 13:18; Matthew 26:2.
52. Halle, ULB: 14 B 22, f. 10r.
53. E.g. Andrew Weeks, 'Valentin Weigel and Anticlerical Tradition,' *Daphnis* 48 (2020): 140–59; Carlos Gilly, 'Das Sprichwort "Die Gelehrten die Verkehrten" oder der Verrat der Intellektuellen im Zeitalter der Glaubensspaltung,' in *Forme e destinazione del messagio religioso: aspetti della propaganda religiosa nel Cinquecento*, ed. Antonio Rotondò (Florence: Olschki, 1991), 229–375.
54. Heidelberg, UB: Cod. Pal. Germ. 782, f. 178r.
55. Karlsruhe, BLB: Cod. Allerheiligen 3, p. 400.
56. Karlsruhe, BLB: Cod. Allerheiligen 3, p. 401. Other manuscripts have 'diabolical' instead of 'from the devil'; compare Berlin, SB–PK: Ms. germ. fol. 1070, f. 22r; Heidelberg, UB: Cod. Pal. Germ. 782, f. 179r.
57. Karlsruhe, BLB: Cod. Allerheiligen 3, p. 400.
58. Karlsruhe, BLB: Cod. Allerheiligen 3, p. 401. In contrast, another version omits the sentence on the born-again human: Heidelberg, UB: Cod. Pal. Germ. 782, f. 179r.
59. This is also the case in the most recent edition, prepared by Pfefferl; Weigel, *Schriften*, vol. 13. The classic study on the authenticity of Weigelian writings is Winfried Zeller, *Die Schriften Valentin Weigels: Eine literarkritische Untersuchung* (Berlin: Ebering, 1940). Pfefferl's survey of extant Weigelian manuscripts is indispensable: Pfefferl, 'Die Überlieferung der Schriften Valentin Weigels.' On the shared fortunes of pseudo-Weigelian and pseudo-Paracelsian works specifically, see also Pfefferl, 'Weigel und Paracelsus.' Previous discussions of *Ad dialogum de morte* can be found in William R. Newman, *Promethean Ambitions: Alchemy and the Quest to Perfect Nature* (Chicago: University of Chicago Press, 2004), 229–32; Will-Erich Peuckert, *Pansophie: Ein Versuch zur Geschichte der weissen und schwarzen Magie*, ed. Rolf Christian Zimmermann, 2nd, rev. ed. (Berlin: Erich Schmidt, 1973), 300–1. At times, the text is mistakenly attributed to Alexander von Suchten, who died more than ten years before Weigel composed his *Dialogus;* see Oliver Humberg, 'Die Verlassenschaft des oberösterreichischen Landschaftsarztes Alexander von Suchten,' *Wolfenbütteler Renaissance-Mitteilungen* 31 (2007): 31–50.
60. Peuckert, *Pansophie*, 301.
61. Valentin Weigel, *Dialogus de Christianismo: Das ist, Ein Christliches, hochwichtiges, nothwendiges Colloquium oder Gespräche, dreyer fürnembsten Personen in der Welt* (Halle: In verlegung Joachim Krusicken, 1614), 99–104.
62. Geyer, *Verborgene Weisheit*, 1:34-39; Leigh T. I. Penman, 'Paraluther: Explaining an Unexpected Portrait of Paracelsus in Andreas Hartmann's *Curriculum Vitae Lutheri* (1601),' in *Religion, the Supernatural and Visual Culture in Early Modern Europe: An Album Amicorum for Charles Zika*, ed. Jennifer Spinks and Dagmar Eichberger (Leiden: Brill, 2015), 161–84, on 176; Leigh T. I. Penman, *Hope and Heresy: The Problem of Chiliasm in Lutheran Confessional Culture, 1570–1630* (Dordrecht: Springer, 2019), 69–71.
63. E.g. Weigel, *Schriften*, 13:69–158, on 76.

64. Weigel, *Schriften*, 13:74. See also Alfred Ehrentreich, 'Valentin Weigels religiöser "Dialogus" als literarische Schöpfung,' *Zeitschrift für Religions- und Geistesgeschichte* 21 (1969): 42–54, on 48.
65. Weigel, *Dialogus de Christianismo*, 99. Compare Schleswig, LASH: Abt. 7, Nr. 2059:3, f. 1v. The manuscript lacks foliation; the indications given are my own.
66. Schleswig, LASH: Abt. 7, Nr. 2059:3, f. 1v. The verse quoted is John 3:3.
67. Weigel, *Dialogus de Christianismo*, 100.
68. Luther, *Tischreden*, vol. 1, no. 1149.
69. See Luther's 1545 translation of the Greek *palingenesia* (παλιγγενεσίᾳ) in Matthew 19:28.
70. Schleswig, LASH: Abt. 7, Nr. 2059:3, ff. 2v–3r. Compare Revelation 12:1.
71. Heinrich Khunrath, *Von Hylealischen, Das ist Pri-Materialischen Catholischen, oder Algemeinen Natürlichen Chaos, Der Naturgemessen Alchymiae und Alchymisten* (Magdeburg: Durch Andreas Genen Erben, 1597), 121.
72. Claus Priesner and Karin Figala, eds., *Alchemie: Lexikon einer hermetischen Wissenschaft* (Munich: Beck, 1998), s.v. 'Basilius Valentinus'; Principe, *The Secrets of Alchemy*, 138–55; Lawrence M. Principe, 'The Development of the Basil Valentine Corpus and Biography: Pseudepigraphic Corpora and Paracelsian Ideas,' *Early Science and Medicine* 24 (2019): 549–72.
73. Hans Schmauch, 'Neue Funde zum Lebenslauf des Coppernicus,' *Zeitschrift für die Geschichte und Altertumskunde Ermlands* 28 (1943): 54–99, on 68–69. For more on Suchten, see Humberg, 'Verlassenschaft des . . . Alexander von Suchten'; Włodzimierz Hubicki, 'Alexander von Suchten,' *Sudhoffs Archiv* 44 (1960): 54–63; W. Haberling, 'Alexander von Suchten, ein Danziger Arzt und Dichter des 16. Jahrhunderts,' *Zeitschrift des Westpreussischen Geschichtsvereins* 69 (1929): 177–230.
74. Schleswig, LASH: Abt. 7, Nr. 2059:3, f. 7r.
75. Schleswig, LASH: Abt. 7, Nr. 2059:3, ff. 8v–9r. Compare Weigel, *Dialogus de Christianismo*, 103–4.
76. Weigel, *Dialogus de Christianismo*, 103. Compare Schleswig, LASH: Abt. 7, Nr. 2059:3, f. 8r.
77. Heidelberg, UB: Cod. Pal. Germ. 782, f. 178r.
78. Psalm 118:22.
79. Bernardus Trevisanus, *Von der Hermetischen Philosophia, das ist, von dem Gebenedeiten Stain der Weisen* (Strasbourg: Bey Christian Müller, 1574), f. L6r. Cf. Schleswig, LASH: Abt. 7, Nr. 2059:3, f. 8r/v. Trevisanus is frequently confused with an Italian namesake who lived during the fourteenth century; see Didier Kahn, 'Recherches sur le *Livre* attribué au prétendu Bernard le Trévisan (fin du XVe siècle),' in *Alchimia e medicina nel Medioevo*, ed. Chiara Crisciani and Agostino Paravicini Bagliani (Firenze: Sismel—Edizioni del Galluzzo, 2003), 265–336; Kühlmann and Telle, *Der Frühparacelsismus*, 2:283–85; Wilhelm Kühlmann, ed., *Killy Literaturlexikon: Autoren und Werke des deutschsprachigen Kulturraumes*, 2nd, completely reworked ed., 13 vols. (Berlin: De Gruyter, 2008–11), s.v. 'Bernardus Trevisanus.'

80. Schleswig, LASH: Abt. 7, Nr. 2059:3, f. 9r. Compare Weigel, *Dialogus de Christianismo*, 104. The print edition omits the symbol.
81. Schleswig, LASH: Abt. 7, Nr. 2059:3, f. 10r. Compare Weigel, *Dialogus de Christianismo*, 104.
82. Jacob Böhme, *Werke: Morgenröte. De signatura rerum*, ed. Ferdinand van Ingen (Frankfurt a.M.: Deutscher Klassiker Verlag, 1997), 740–41 (SR 14:29).

Chapter 2

1. Mike A. Zuber, 'Jacob Böhme and Alchemy: A Transmutation in Three Stages,' in *Jacob Böhme and His World*, ed. Bo Andersson et al. (Leiden: Brill, 2019), 262–85.
2. Hermann Fictuld, *Des Längst gewünschten und versprochenen Chymisch-Philosophischen Probier-Steins Erste Claß*, 2nd, expanded ed. (Frankfurt a.M./Leipzig: Bey Veraci Orientali Wahrheit und Ernst Lugenfeind, 1753), 161–62 (no. 172); Hermann Fictuld, *Des Längst gewünschten und versprochenen Chymisch-Philosophischen Probier-Steins Erste Classe*, 3rd ed. (Dresden: In der Hilscherschen Buchhandlung, 1784), 156–57 (no. 172). The first edition mentions only Ambrosius Siebmacher; see Hermann Fictuld, *Der längst gewünschte und versprochene Chymisch-Philosophische Probier-Stein* (Frankfurt a.M./Leipzig: Bey Michael Blochberger, 1740), 106 (no. 153). For Wolfgang Siebmacher, see Paulus, 'Alchemie und Paracelsismus um 1600,' 382–83.
3. Reinhard Breymayer, ed., *Johann Valentin Andreae: Ein geistliches Gemälde. Entworfen und aufgezeichnet von Huldrich StarkMann Diener des Evangeliums* (Tübingen: Noûs-Verlag Thomas Heck, 1991), XIX–XXII; Carlos Gilly, '"Theophrastia sancta": Paracelsianism as a Religion, in Conflict with the Established Churches,' in Grell, *Paracelsus*, 151–85, on 171–72, n. 48; Gilly and Van Heertum, *Magic, Alchemy and Science*, 2:151–53. Compare Žemla, 'Valentin Weigel and Alchemy,' 37; Harald Haferland, 'Eine kurze Theoriegeschichte der alchemistischen *multiplicatio* und der *Vorbothe der am philosophischen Himmel hervorbrechenden Morgenröthe* des Johannes de Monte Raphaim (Amsterdam 1703),' in *Magia daemoniaca, magia naturalis, zouber: Schreibweisen von Magie und Alchemie in Mittelalter und Früher Neuzeit*, ed. Peter-André Alt et al. (Wiesbaden: Harrassowitz, 2015), 393–417, on 410, n. 51.
4. Paulus, 'Alchemie und Paracelsismus um 1600,' 340, 404. See also the brief entry in Christian Gottlieb Jöcher, *Allgemeines Gelehrten-Lexicon*, 4 vols. (Leipzig: In Johann Friedrich Gleditschens Buchhandlung, 1750–51), s.v. 'Siebmacher (Johann).'
5. Telle noted as early as 1978 that these diverging titles actually refer to the same work: Joachim Telle, 'Alchemie II. Historisch,' in *Theologische Realenzyklopädie*, ed. Horst Balz, Gerhard Krause, and Gerhard Müller, 36 vols. (Berlin: De Gruyter, 1978), 2:199–227, on 209. See also his more recent entry in Kühlmann, *Killy Literaturlexikon*, s.v. 'Wasserstein der Weisen.'

6. John Ferguson, *Bibliotheca Chemica: A Bibliography of Books on Alchemy, Chemistry and Pharmaceutics*, 2 vols. (London: Derek Verschoyle, 1954), s.v. 'Siebmacher (Johann Ambrosius).'
7. [Johann Siebmacher], *Das Güldne Vließ, Oder Das Allerhöchste, Edelste, Kunstreichste Kleinod, und der urälteste verborgene Schatz der Weisen* (Leipzig: Bey Samuel Benjamin Walthern, 1736), title page. The following year, a reprint appeared in Nuremberg.
8. [Siebmacher], *Das Güldne Vließ*, f.):(6r.
9. [Siebmacher], *Das Güldne Vließ*, 201.
10. Breymayer, *Ein geistliches Gemälde*, XIX–XXII; Gilly, 'Theophrastia sancta,' 171–72, n. 48.
11. Breymayer, *Ein geistliches Gemälde*, XX–XXI. For Siebmacher's Weigel publication, see pseudo-Weigel, *Zwey schöne Büchlein, Das Erste, Von dem leben Christi, . . . Das Ander, Eine kurtze außführliche Erweisung*, ed. [Johann Siebmacher] (Newstatt [Frankfurt a.M.]: [Lucas Jennis], 1618/21?). Most extant copies feature manuscript corrections of the year of publication from 1618 to 1621, which makes the later date appear more likely. On the *Philosphia mystica*, see Martin Žemla, 'From Paracelsus to Universal Reform: The (Pseudo-)Paracelsian-Weigelian *Philosophia Mystica* (1618),' *Daphnis* 48 (2020): 184–213.
12. The Hague, Koninklijke Bibliotheek (KB): Ritman Kerncollectie, PH404 M315, ff. 61v–62r. (Note that the Ritman Kerncollectie, otherwise known as the state-owned part of the Bibliotheca Philosophica Hermetica, has been transferred to the Allard Pierson Collections of the University of Amsterdam since the research for this book was completed.) Compare [Johann Siebmacher], 'Introductio Hominis, Oder Kurtze Anleitung zu einem Christlichen Gottseligen Leben,' in *Philosophia Mystica, Darinn begriffen Eilff unterschidene Theologico-Philosophische, doch teutsche Tractätlein, zum theil auß Theophrasti Paracelsi, zum theil auch M. Valentini Weigelii*, ed. [Benedictus Figulus] (Newstadt [Frankfurt a.M.]: Zu finden bey Lucas Jennis, Buchhändler, 1618), 228–72, on 269–70.
13. The Hague, KB: PH404 M315, f. 61v; [Siebmacher], 'Introductio Hominis,' 269. Compare [Siebmacher], *Das Güldne Vließ*, title page.
14. E.g. pseudo-Weigel, *Dritter Theil Deß Gnothi Seauton Oder Cognosce Teipsum genandt* (Newstadt: Bey Johan Knuber, 1618), ff. 12r–14r. Compare [Siebmacher], 'Introductio Hominis,' 246–47. On the date of composition, see Pfefferl, 'Teildruck,' pt. 1, 69, 73.
15. Bonus, *Introductio in artem chemiae integra*, ch. 6. The first edition of 1546, published by the famous press of Aldus Manutius, features a version of the text heavily redacted by Janus Lacinius; Petrus Bonus, *Pretiosa margarita novella de thesauro, ac pretiosissimo philosophorum lapide: Artis huius divinae typus, et methodus*, ed. Janus Lacinius (Venice: Apud Aldi Filios, 1546).
16. The Hague, KB: PH404 M315, ff. 2v–3v.
17. The Hague, KB: PH404 M315, f. 60r.
18. The Hague, KB: PH404 M315, f. 60v. See Revelation 13:18.

19. [Siebmacher], 'Introductio Hominis,' 269.
20. [Johann Siebmacher], *Wasserstein der Weysen, Das ist, Ein Chymisch Tractätlein, darin der weg gezeiget, die Materia genennet, und der Proceß beschrieben wird, zu dem hohen geheymnuß der Universal Tinctur zukommen* (Frankfurt a.M.: Bey Lucas Jennis zufinden, 1619), 17.
21. [Siebmacher], *Wasserstein*, e.g. 87, 132, and 134–35, resp.
22. [Siebmacher], *Wasserstein*, 89, 108, 111, 133, 136.
23. [Siebmacher], *Wasserstein*, 111; see also 108.
24. [Siebmacher], *Wasserstein*, 88–89.
25. *Rosarium philosophorum*, f. G4r; Tara Nummedal and Donna Bilak, eds., *Furnace and Fugue: A Digital Edition of Michael Maier's* Atalanta fugiens *(1618) with Scholarly Commentary*, https://doi.org/10.26300/bdp.ff (Charlottesville: University of Virginia Press, 2020), emblem 33. For scholarly discussions of alchemical hermaphrodites, see e.g. Leah DeVun, 'The Jesus Hermaphrodite: Science and Sex Difference in Premodern Europe,' *Journal of the History of Ideas* 69 (2008): 193–218; Forshaw, 'Ora et Labora,' 1:239–40; Priesner and Figala, *Alchemie*, s.v. 'Hermaphrodit'; Lawrence M. Principe, 'Revealing Analogies: The Descriptive and Deceptive Roles of Sexuality and Gender in Latin Alchemy,' in *Hidden Intercourse: Eros and Sexuality in the History of Western Esotericism*, ed. Wouter J. Hanegraaff and Jeffrey J. Kripal (New York: Fordham University Press, 2011), 209–29.
26. Though images derived from various manuscript versions are frequently reproduced, this important work remains understudied. Essential philological groundwork is lacking, and a published transcription based on a single manuscript is faulty: Uwe Junker, *Das 'Buch der Heiligen Dreifaltigkeit' in seiner zweiten alchemistischen Fassung (Kadolzburg 1433)* (Cologne: Forschungsstelle des Instituts für Geschichte der Medizin der Universität zu Köln, 1986). It has been suggested that Boehme may have been familiar with the *Liber Trinitatis*: W. Ganzenmüller, 'Das Buch der heiligen Dreifaltigkeit: Eine Deutsche Alchemie aus dem Anfang des 15. Jahrhunderts,' in *Beiträge zur Geschichte der Technologie und der Alchemie* (Weinheim: Verlag Chemie, 1956), 231–72, on 271.
27. *Rosarium philosophorum*, f. a4r. On this cycle and the accompanying German poem, see Telle, *Sol und Luna*.
28. [Siebmacher], *Wasserstein*, 99.
29. [Siebmacher], *Wasserstein*, 93–94.
30. [Siebmacher], *Wasserstein*, 123–24.
31. For a quick overview of colours in alchemy, see e.g. Priesner and Figala, *Alchemie*, s.v. 'Farben.'
32. See James 1:2–4
33. [Siebmacher], *Wasserstein*, 128.
34. [Siebmacher], *Wasserstein*, 101; see also 107.
35. [Siebmacher], *Wasserstein*, 100.
36. [Siebmacher], *Wasserstein*, 103–4.
37. [Siebmacher], *Wasserstein*, 111–12.

38. [Siebmacher], *Wasserstein*, 113. For the technical meaning of projection, see Martin Ruland, *Lexicon alchemiae sive dictionarium alchemisticum* (Frankfurt a.M.: Cura ac sumtibus Zachariae Palthenii, Librarii ac D., 1612), s.v. 'Proiectio.'
39. E.g. Johannes Rhenanus, ed., *Dyas Chymica Tripartita, Das ist: Sechs Herrliche Teutsche Philosophische Tractätlein* (Frankfurt a.M.: Bey Luca Jennis zu finden, 1625), 83–117, esp. 108–17.
40. Bonus, *Pretiosa margarita novella*, f. ***4r/v.
41. [Siebmacher], *Wasserstein*, 104.
42. Leigh T. I. Penman, 'The First Appearance of Jacob Böhme's Work in Print,' *Notes and Queries* 57 (2010): 419–21; Leigh T. I. Penman, '"Repulsive Blasphemies": Paul Nagel's Appropriation of Unprinted Works of Jakob Böhme and Valentin Weigel in His *Prodromus astronomiae apocalypticae* (1620),' *Daphnis* 38 (2009): 597–620.
43. Penman, 'Repulsive Blasphemies,' 604. The latter work is also known by the Latin title *De tribus principiis*.
44. Werner Buddecke, ed., *Jacob Böhme: Die Urschriften*, 2 vols. (Stuttgart-Bad Cannstatt: Frommann, 1963–66), 2:373–74 (ET 71:6).
45. The Leipzig manuscript is described in Detlef Döring, *Katalog der Handschriften der Universitätsbibliothek Leipzig: Die neuzeitlichen Handschriften der Nullgruppe*, 4 vols. (Wiesbaden: Harrassowitz, 2000–5), 2:84. For excerpted passages dealing with Boehme, see Carlos Gilly, 'Wege der Verbreitung von Jacob Böhmes Schriften in Deutschland und den Niederlanden,' in *Jacob Böhmes Weg in die Welt: Zur Geschichte der Handschriftensammlung, Übersetzungen und Editionen von Abraham Willemsz van Beyerland*, ed. Theodor Harmsen (Amsterdam: In de Pelikaan, 2007), 71–98, on 73–76.
46. Halle, ULB: 14 B 22, ff. 3r–4v. On August, see e.g. Günther Hoppe, 'Zwischen Augsburg und Anhalt: Der rosenkreuzerische Briefwechsel des Augsburger Stadtarztes Carl Widemann mit dem Plötzkauer Fürsten August von Anhalt,' *Zeitschrift des historischen Vereins für Schwaben* 90 (1997): 125–87. On their first known contact, see Penman, *Hope and Heresy*, 75.
47. Leipzig, Universitätsbibliothek (UB): Ms 0356, f. 32v.
48. Revelation 13:18. For Solomon's gold intake, see 1 Kings 10:14.
49. 1 Kings 10:10; 9:28.
50. Halle, ULB: 14 B 22, ff. 8v–9v.
51. Halle, ULB: 14 B 22, f. 10r.
52. Halle, ULB: 14 B 22, f. 47v.
53. [Biedermann], *Theologia Weigelii*, f. 45r.
54. Halle, ULB: 14 B 22, f. 10v.
55. Ruland, *Lexicon alchemiae*, s.v. 'Incineratio.' For more on Ruland and his work, see Vladimír Karpenko, 'Martin Rulands *Lexicon Alchemiae* im Kontext der chemischen Sprache und Systematik,' *Studia Rudolphina* 11 (2011): 102–26.
56. For studies on this subject, see Jacques Marx, 'Alchimie et palingénésie,' *Isis* 62 (1971): 274–89; François Secret, 'Palingenesis, Alchemy and Metempsychosis in Renaissance Medicine,' *Ambix* 26 (1979): 81–92; François Secret, 'Alchimie, palingénésie et métempsychose chez Guillaume Postel,' *Chrysopœia* 3 (1989): 3–60.

57. Leipzig, UB: Ms 0356, f. 51r. Compare Vergil, *Aeneidos liber sextus*, ed. R. G. Austin (Oxford: Clarendon Press, 1977), v. 129.
58. Halle, ULB: 14 B 22, f. 11r.
59. Munich, Bayerische Staatsbibliothek (BSB): Cgm 4416. 9, f. 11v.
60. Munich, BSB: Cgm 4416. 9, ff. 170v–71r.
61. Munich, BSB: Cgm 4416. 9, ff. 148r–49r.
62. Munich, BSB: Cgm 4416. 9, ff. 148v.
63. Munich, BSB: Cgm 4416. 9, f. 151r. Throughout the Gospels, Christ speaks of 'bad fruit' as tell-tale signs of depravity; e.g. Matthew 7:15–20.
64. Munich, BSB: Cgm 4416. 9, f. 151r.
65. See Genesis 3:14–19.
66. Munich, BSB: Cgm 4416. 9, ff. 153v–54r.
67. Leipzig, UB: Ms 0356, f. 12r/v.
68. Leipzig, UB: Ms 0356, ff. 17v–18r.
69. Munich, BSB: Cgm 4416. 9, f. 157r.
70. Munich, BSB: Cgm 4416. 9, f. 152v.
71. Munich, BSB: Cgm 4416. 9, f. 153v. See [Biedermann], *Theologia Weigelii*, f. 7r/v.
72. Munich, BSB: Cgm 4416. 9, f. 154r/v.
73. Munich, BSB: Cgm 4416. 9, f. 154v.
74. Munich, BSB: Cgm 4416. 9, f. 155r.
75. Munich, BSB: Cgm 4416. 9, f. 155v.
76. Revelation 5:5.
77. Munich, BSB: Cgm 4416. 9, f. 157r/v.
78. Revelation 3:20–21; 2:17.
79. Genesis 3:15. Boehme's *Aurora* contained an incomplete exegesis of the Creation account, and the late *Mysterium magnum* presented a commentary on the entire book of Genesis.

Chapter 3

1. Among the various full-length biographies, I have particularly drawn on the following: Ernst-Heinz Lemper, *Jakob Böhme: Leben und Werk* (Berlin: Union Verlag, 1976); Will-Erich Peuckert, *Das Leben Jakob Böhmes* (Jena: Eugen Diederichs, 1924). For a short biography in English, see Ariel Hessayon, 'Boehme's Life and Times,' in *An Introduction to Jacob Boehme: Four Centuries of Thought and Reception*, ed. Ariel Hessayon and Sarah Apetrei (London: Routledge, 2014), 13–37. Today, Boehme's place of birth is known as Stary Zawidów, Poland. Andrew Weeks notes 'the rudimentary level of his formal education and unfamiliarity with Latin'; Jacob Böhme, *Aurora* (Morgen Röte im auffgang, 1612) *and Fundamental Report* (Gründlicher Bericht, Mysterium Pansophicum, 1620), ed. and trans. Andrew Weeks and Günther Bonheim (Leiden: Brill, 2013), 2.

2. Hessayon, 'Boehme's Life and Times,' 14.
3. Böhme, *Aurora*, 668–69 (A 22:84). For Boehme's *Aurora*, I quote Weeks's translation, although I occasionally depart from it as well.
4. For the seven stages as presented by Leonhard Thurneisser see Böhme, *Werke*, 998–99. For another example, see Leigh T. I. Penman, ed., *Cabala: Mirror of Art and Nature. Editio trilingua: A Critical Edition of the German and Latin Editions 1615–1616, Published by Stephan Michelspacher in Augsburg, together with an Annotated English Translation* (Seattle: Ouroboros Press, 2015), pl. 3,'Mittel: Coniunction'; for commentary and a discussion of the pseudo-Paracelsian source, see 50–51.
5. Lawrence M. Principe and Andrew Weeks, 'Jacob Boehme's Divine Substance *Salitter*: Its Nature, Origin, and Relationship to Seventeenth Century Scientific Theories,' *British Journal for the History of Science* 22 (1989): 53–61; Böhme, *Aurora*, 34–35. See also Prinke, 'New Light.'
6. Böhme, *Aurora*, 674–75 (A 22:105–6). On interactions between alchemy and astrology, see Peter J. Forshaw, '"Chemistry, that Starry Science": Early Modern Conjunctions of Astrology and Alchemy,' in *Sky and Symbol: Proceedings of the Ninth Annual Sophia Centre Conference, 2011*, ed. Nicholas Campion and Liz Greene (Lampeter: Sophia Centre Press, 2013), 143–84.
7. Böhme, *Aurora*, 668–69 (A 22:85–6).
8. Titus 3:5; Böhme, *Aurora*, 374–75 (A 12:122). See Mike A. Zuber, 'Theosophische Spekulation und erbauliche Frömmigkeit: Jacob Böhme, die neue Wiedergeburt und ihre Alchemisierung,' in *Grund und Ungrund: Der Kosmos des mystischen Philosophen Jacob Böhme*, ed. Claudia Brink and Lucinda Martin (Dresden: Sandstein, 2017), 114–29.
9. Matthew 19:28; see e.g. Böhme, *Aurora*, 352–53, 622–23, 664–65 (A 12:50, 21:54, 22:69).
10. Böhme, *Aurora*, 528–29, 666–67, 774–75 (A 18:58, 22:80, 26:77). See Revelation 1:4.
11. Böhme, *Aurora*, 740–41 (A 25:52).
12. Boehme, *Theosophische Send-Schreiben*, 182 (ET 18:13). On the identification of the nobleman, see Hessayon, 'Boehme's Life and Times,' 14.
13. For a ground-breaking study of this phenomenon, see Harold Love, *The Culture and Commerce of Texts: Scribal Publication in Seventeenth-Century England*, 2nd ed. (Amherst: University of Massachusetts Press, 1998).
14. Boehme, *Theosophische Send-Schreiben*, 122 (ET 12:13).
15. Boehme, *Theosophische Send-Schreiben*, 85 (ET 10:26).
16. Leigh T. I. Penman, 'Boehme's Intellectual Networks and the Heterdox Milieu of His Theosophy, 1600-1624,' in Hessayon and Apetrei, *An Introduction to Jacob Boehme*, 57–76. Strictly speaking, the common characterisation of Boehme as a cobbler does not do justice to his various business activities; for a detailed account, see Lemper, *Jakob Böhme*, esp. pt. 1, ch. 2.
17. The earliest letter included in Boehme's correspondence is dated 18 January 1618, yet Buddecke and other scholars before him have emended the year to 1619—even so it remains the theosopher's oldest surviving epistle. For an edition of the autograph

version and comments on the date, see Buddecke, *Die Urschriften*, 2:333–36 (ET, no. 1), 455.
18. Boehme, *Theosophische Send-Schreiben*, 225 (ET 30:6).
19. Böhme, *Werke*, 670, 672 (SR 11: title and 6).
20. Böhme, *Werke*, 600 (SR 7:78).
21. Schoeps, *Vom himmlischen Fleisch Christi*, 56–62; Gantenbein, 'The New Adam'; Pfefferl, 'Weigel und Paracelsus'.
22. According to one study, Boehme was primarily read among Pietists as a devotional writer until his speculative dimension was rediscovered by the Romanticists; Paola Mayer, *Jena Romanticism and Its Appropriation of Jakob Böhme: Theosophy, Hagiography, Literature* (Montreal: McGill-Queen's University Press, 1999), ch. 3.
23. There are many accounts of Boehme's theosophy, ranging from brief summaries to weighty volumes. For a full-length study and a helpful primer in English, respectively, see e.g. Andrew Weeks, *Boehme: An Intellectual Biography of the Seventeenth-Century Philosopher and Mystic* (Albany: State University of New York Press, 1991); Mayer, *Jena Romanticism*, ch. 2. There are also many studies in other languages, particularly French and German; e.g. Alexandre Koyré, *La philosophie de Jacob Boehme* (Paris: Librarie philosophique J. Vrin, 1929); Pierre Deghaye, *La naissance de Dieu ou la doctrine de Jacob Boehme* (Paris: Albin Michel, 1985); Hans Grunsky, *Jacob Böhme*, 2nd ed. (Stuttgart-Bad Cannstatt: Frommann-Holzboog, 1984); Ferdinand van Ingen, *Jacob Böhme in seiner Zeit* (Stuttgart-Bad Cannstatt: Frommann-Holzboog, 2015). On Grunsky and his engagement with Boehme, see Sibylle Rusterholz, 'Jacob Böhme im Spiegel totalitären Denkens: Hans Alfred Grunskys nationalsozialistische Sicht des *Philosophus teutonicus*,' *Böhme-Studien* 3 (2013): 91–116.
24. Wrocław, Biblioteka Uniwersytecka (BU): Ms. Akc. 1975/255, ch. 17, esp. ff. 192r–97r (TP 17:48–69). For a new English translation, see Jacob Boehme, *De tribus principiis, oder Beschreibung der Drey Principien Göttliches Wesens (Of the Three Principles of Divine Being, 1619)*, trans. Andrew Weeks (Leiden: Brill, 2019), which includes a discussion of the manuscript tradition by Leigh Penman on 15–19.
25. Böhme, *Aurora*, 204–5 (A 6:12–13); Wrocław, BU: Ms. Akc. 1975/255, ff. 81v–82r (TP 10:6–7); Jacob Boehme, *Mysterium Magnum, Oder Erklärung über das Erste Buch Mosis*, 2nd, corrected ed. (Amsterdam: Auff Kosten Henrici Betkii, und Consorten, 1678), 121 (MM 19:4–5).
26. Boehme, *Mysterium Magnum*, 121 (MM 19:6).
27. Wrocław, BU: Ms. Akc. 1975/255, ff. 194r and 186r/v (TP 17:58 and 21).
28. Wrocław, BU: Ms. Akc. 1975/255, f. 288r (TP 22:33).
29. Wrocław, BU: Ms. Akc. 1975/255, ff. 286v–87r (TP 22:24–26).
30. See Proverbs 1:20–33. For a recent summary with references to earlier literature, see Lucinda Martin, 'Jakob Böhmes "göttliche Sophia" und Emanzipationsansätze bei pietistischen Autorinnen,' in Kühlmann and Vollhardt, *Offenbarung und Episteme*, 241–57, on 242–43. See also Ferdinand van Ingen, 'Die Jungfrau Sophia und die Jungfrau Maria bei Jakob Böhme,' in Garewicz and Haas, *Gott, Natur und Mensch*, 147–63.

31. Wrocław, BU: Ms. Akc. 1975/255, f. 150r (TP 14:87); Ms. Akc. 1975/271, ff. 50r, 117v (TV 5:41, 44; 11:15); Jacob Boehme, *Von der Gnaden-Wahl, oder dem Willen Gottes über die Menschen* (Amsterdam: Auff kosten Henrici Betkii verlegt, und bey Christoff Cunraden gedruckt, 1665), 73 (EG 5:12).
32. Wrocław, BU: Ms. Akc. 1975/255, f. 297r (TP 22:77). This variation on nuptial mysticism is noted by Ingen, 'Die Jungfrau Sophia,' 147–48, who also observes that Sophia and Christ cannot simply be conflated.
33. Boehme, *Theosophische Send-Schreiben*, 366 (ET 56:12). See Revelation 3:20.
34. Boehme, *Theosophische Send-Schreiben*, 312–13 (ET 46:38 and 40).
35. Jacob Boehme, *Erste Apologia wider Balthasar Tilken. Eine Verantwortung des Authoris* (Amsterdam: Gedruckt bey Christoffel Cunradus, Vor Henricus Betkius, 1677), 83–84 (AT1, para. 314–15).
36. R. Emmet McLaughlin, 'Spiritualism: Schwenckfeld and Franck and Their Early Modern Resonances,' in *A Companion to Anabaptism and Spiritualism, 1521–1700*, ed. John D. Roth and James M. Stayer (Leiden: Brill, 2007), 119–61, on 125–26; Furcha, 'Key Concepts,' 160. Both McLaughlin and Furcha note that Schwenckfeld rejected the Lutheran doctrine of the real presence of Christ in the Eucharist, on which count Boehme did not follow him.
37. Penman, 'Boehme's Intellectual Networks,' 57, 59–62, 64; Leigh T. I. Penman, 'Jacob Böhme and His Networks,' in *Jacob Böhme and His World*, ed. Bo Andersson et al. (Leiden: Brill, 2019), 98–120, on 103, 107–8.
38. Wrocław, BU: Ms. Akc. 1975/255, ff. 307v, 308r (TP 23:11, 14).
39. Baur, 'Ubiquität.'
40. Copenhagen, Kongelige Bibliotek (KB): Thott 49 oktav, f. 46r (TaP, para. 58).
41. Boehme, *Theosophische Send-Schreiben*, 194 (ET 20:8–9). See 1 Corinthians 15:50.
42. Wrocław, BU: Ms. Akc. 1975/271, f. 74r (TV 7:13).
43. Wrocław, BU: Ms. Akc. 1975/271, f. 119v (TV 11:24–25).
44. Wrocław, BU: Ms. Akc. 1975/271, f. 72r (TV 6:96–98).
45. Jacob Boehme, *Von der Menschwerdung Jesu Christi* (Amsterdam: Bey Henrico Betkio, 1660), 8 (IV, pt. 1, 1:5). The work is also known by its Latin title *De incarnatione verbi*.
46. Boehme, *Von der Menschwerdung*, 92 (IV, pt. 1, 8:5).
47. Jaroslav Pelikan and Valerie Hotchkiss, eds., *Creeds and Confessions of Faith in the Christian Tradition*, 4 vols. (New Haven: Yale University Press, 2003), 1:675–77; 2:168.
48. E.g. Boehme, *Erste Apologia wider Balthasar Tilken*, 75–106 (AT1, para. 279–400).
49. Boehme, *Erste Apologia wider Balthasar Tilken*, 82 (AT1, para. 310). See Revelation 1:4.
50. Boehme, *Erste Apologia wider Balthasar Tilken*, 91 (AT1, para. 348).
51. Böhme, *Werke*, 581 (SR 7:25).
52. Boehme, *Von der Menschwerdung*, 112 (IV, pt. 1, 10:1).
53. Jacob Boehme, *Epistolae Theosophicae, oder Theosophische Send-Briefe* ([Leiden?], 1730), e.g. nos. 23, 41 (abbr.).
54. Wrocław, BU: Ms. Akc. 1975/271, f. 77r/v (TV 7:29–30).

55. [Siebmacher], *Wasserstein*, 101–2; Bonus, *Pretiosa margarita novella*, f. ***4v; *Rosarium philosophorum*, f. a4r.
56. Böhme, *Werke*, 585 (SR 7:35).
57. E.g. Böhme, *Werke*, 666 (SR 10:70); see also 679 (SR 11:29).
58. Böhme, *Werke*, 574 (SR 7:1).
59. E.g. Böhme, *Werke*, 670 (SR 11: title).
60. Böhme, *Werke*, 629 (SR 9:26). See Matthew 4:1–11.
61. Principe, *The Secrets of Alchemy*, pl. 3.
62. Böhme, *Werke*, 694 (SR 11:77). See Luke 23:44–45.
63. Böhme, *Werke*, 708 (SR 12:22).
64. Priesner and Figala, *Alchemie*, s.v. 'Opus magnum,' on 262.
65. E.g. Böhme, *Werke*, 684, 685 (as a verb), 750 (SR 11:43, 46; 14:55).
66. Böhme, *Werke*, 591 (SR 7:53); cf. Acts 2:41.
67. Böhme, *Werke*, 591 (SR 7:54).
68. Böhme, *Werke*, 646 (SR 10:10).
69. Böhme, *Werke*, 647 (SR 10:14). See John 2:1–12.
70. On Stiefel, see Ulman Weiß, *Die Lebenswelten des Esajas Stiefel oder Vom Umgang mit Dissidenten* (Stuttgart: Steiner, 2007).
71. Jacob Boehme, *Bedencken Uber Esaiae Stiefels Büchlein: Von Dreyerley Zustandt des Menschen, unnd dessen Newen Geburt. Geschrieben Anno Christi 1621* ([Amsterdam]: [Johannes Janssonius], 1639), 11 (AS1, para. 19).
72. Wolfenbüttel, Herzog August Bibliothek (HAB): Cod. Guelf. 65 Noviss. 4°, f. 88r (AS2, between para. 469 and 470). Printed editions of this work add the pun 'Jacob-Bohemian' (*J. Böhmischen*) between 'Rosicrucian' and 'Brethren,' yet the manuscript quoted here (Michael von Ender's personal copy, based on Boehme's lost autograph) must be considered more reliable: see Werner Buddecke and Matthias Wenzel, *Jacob Böhme: Verzeichnis der Handschriften und frühen Abschriften* (Görlitz: Oberlausitzische Bibliothek der Wissenschaften, 2000), no. 123.
73. Weiß, *Die Lebenswelten des Esajas Stiefel*, 458.
74. Wolfenbüttel, HAB: Cod. Guelf. 65 Noviss. 4°, f. 89r (AS2, para. 473). This work is also known as *Apologia, Betreffend Die Vollkommenheit des Menschen* or *Anti-Stiefelius II*. Although some manuscripts give the date as 26 April 1622, this is unlikely given that Paul Nagel had already discussed it in his letter to Arnold Kerner dated 29 April 1622; Leipzig, UB: Ms 0356, f. 52r/v. Only a single manuscript contains the correct date of 6 April, which Buddecke already tended to prefer; Werner Buddecke, *Verzeichnis von Jakob Böhme-Handschriften* (Göttingen: Dr. Ludwig Häntzschel, 1934), p. XX; no. 124.
75. Boehme, *Bedencken Uber Esaiae Stiefels Büchlein*, 33 (AS1, para. 66); Wolfenbüttel, HAB: Cod. Guelf. 65 Noviss. 4°, f. 55r (AS2, para. 301).
76. Weiß, *Die Lebenswelten des Esajas Stiefel*, 237, n. 237; Penman, *Hope and Heresy*, 146.
77. Boehme, *Theosophische Send-Schreiben*, 199 (ET 20:31–33).
78. Wolfenbüttel, HAB: Cod. Guelf. 65 Noviss. 4°, f. 97r/v (AS2, para. 524, 526–28).

79. Wrocław, BU: Ms. Akc. 1975/255, ff. 311r, 291r/v (TP 23:31 and 22:47), resp.
80. Wrocław, BU: Ms. Akc. 1975/255, f. 311r (TP 23:31).
81. Wolfenbüttel, HAB: Cod. Guelf. 65 Noviss. 4°, f. 96v (AS2, para. 522).
82. Wolfenbüttel, HAB: Cod. Guelf. 65 Noviss. 4°, f. 97r (AS2, para. 524). While the more common term for an alchemist would have been *artista*, Boehme sometimes used the German equivalent; see Ferdinand van Ingen's gloss in Böhme, *Werke*, 563 (SR 5:16).
83. 1 Corinthians 15:35–44.
84. Wrocław, BU: Ms. Akc. 1975/271, f. 90v (TP 8:46).
85. Wolfenbüttel, HAB: Cod. Guelf. 65 Noviss. 4°, f. 97r (AS2, para. 525).
86. Böhme, *Werke*, 688 (SR 11:56).
87. Böhme, *Werke*, 591 (SR 7:53).
88. Böhme, *Werke*, 687 (SR 11:54). In the 1635 edition used by Ingen as well as the *textus receptus* of 1730, the final two words are given as 'im Himmel,' which I take to be a misreading of 'inn Himmel.' Accordingly, the reading 'in Himmel' of the 1682 and 1715 editions is to be preferred; compare Jacob Boehme, *De Signatura Rerum, Das ist: Von der Gebuhrt und Bezeichnung aller Wesen* (Amsterdam, 1682), 139; Jacob Boehme, *Theosophia . . . Oder: Alle Werke*, ed. [Johann Otto Glüsing], 2 vols. ([Hamburg/Altona], 1715), vol. 2, col. 2321.
89. Subsumed under '(Christian) mortalism,' the technical term for Boehme's position is psychopannichism, which is contrasted against the temporary death of the soul (thnetopsychism); see e.g. Nicholas McDowell, 'Dead Souls and Modern Minds? Mortalism and the Early Modern Imagination, from Marlowe to Milton,' *Journal of Medieval and Early Modern Studies* 40 (2010): 559–92, on 559 and 562–63. See Wrocław, BU: Ms. Akc. 1975/252, ff. 80r, 95v (PV 21:10; 29:1).
90. Robin Bruce Barnes, *Prophecy and Gnosis: Apocalypticism in the Wake of the Lutheran Reformation* (Stanford: Stanford University Press, 1988), 37–38.
91. Boehme, *Bedencken Uber Esaiae Stiefels Büchlein*, 38 (AS1, para. 78).
92. Wolfenbüttel, HAB: Cod. Guelf. 65 Noviss. 4°, f. 69r (AS2, para. 381).
93. Decades later, Robert Boyle described the process of degrading gold through transmutation by means of an 'anti-elixir'; see Aaron J. Ihde, 'Alchemy in Reverse: Robert Boyle on the Degradation of Gold,' *Chymia* 9 (1964): 47–57. For more comprehensive studies on Boyle's alchemy, see Lawrence M. Principe, *The Aspiring Adept: Robert Boyle and His Alchemical Quest* (Princeton: Princeton University Press, 1998); William R. Newman and Lawrence M. Principe, *Alchemy Tried in the Fire: Starkey, Boyle, and the Fate of Helmontian Chemistry* (Chicago: University of Chicago Press, 2002), esp. chs. 1 and 5.
94. Böhme, *Werke*, 687 (SR 11:51).
95. Wolfenbüttel, HAB: Cod. Guelf. 65 Noviss. 4°, f. 69r/v (AS2, para. 382).
96. Böhme, *Werke*, 597 (SR 7:68).
97. Wolfenbüttel, HAB: Cod. Guelf. 65 Noviss. 4°, f. 69v (AS2, para. 382).
98. Boehme, *Bedencken Uber Esaiae Stiefels Büchlein*, 22 (AS1, para. 41). Cf. Wrocław, BU: Ms. Akc. 1975/271, f. 82v (TV 8:4).

Chapter 4

1. For recent scholarly assessments, see e.g. Carlos Gilly, 'Abraham von Franckenberg und die Rosenkreuzer: Zur Datierung der Tabula Universalis Theosophica Mystica et Cabalistica von 1623,' in *Rosenkreuz als europäisches Phänomen im 17. Jahrhundert*, ed. Bibliotheca Philosophica Hermetica (Amsterdam: In de Pelikaan, 2002), 212–32; Sibylle Rusterholz, 'Abraham von Franckenbergs Verhältnis zu Jacob Böhme: Versuch einer Neubestimmung aufgrund kritischer Sichtung der Textgrundlagen,' in *Kulturgeschichte Schlesiens in der Frühen Neuzeit*, ed. Klaus Garber (Tübingen: Niemeyer, 2005), 205–41; Sibylle Rusterholz, 'Elemente christlicher Kabbala bei Abraham von Franckenberg,' in *Christliche Kabbala*, ed. Wilhelm Schmidt-Biggemann (Ostfildern: Thorbecke, 2003), 183–97; Wilhelm Schmidt-Biggemann, 'Abraham von Franckenberg als christlicher Kabbalist,' in *Realität als Herausforderung: Literatur in ihren konkreten historischen Kontexten*, ed. Ralf Bogner et al. (Berlin: De Gruyter, 2011), 233–48; Wilhelm Schmidt-Biggemann, 'Abraham von Franckenberg,' in *Geschichte der christlichen Kabbala*, 4 vols. (Stuttgart-Bad Cannstatt: Frommann-Holzboog, 2013), 2:235–57.
2. E.g. Th. C. van Stockum, *Zwischen Jakob Böhme und Johann Scheffler: Abraham von Franckenberg (1593–1652) und Daniel Czepko von Reigersfeld (1605–1660)* (Amsterdam: N.V. Noord-Hollandsche Uitgevers Maatschappij, 1967); John Bruckner, 'Abraham von Franckenberg, Johann Scheffler und Johann Theodor von Tschesch in einem "Quaker-Buche" (1680),' in *Literatur und Volk im 17. Jahrhundert: Probleme populärer Kultur in Deutschland*, ed. Wolfgang Brückner (Wiesbaden: Harrassowitz, 1985), 579–88; Konrad Gajek, 'Georg Philipp Harsdörffers Brief vom 30. Mai 1652 an Abraham von Franckenberg,' in *Studien zur Literatur des 17. Jahrhunderts: Gedenkschrift für Gerhard Spellerberg (1937–1996)*, ed. Hans Feger (Amsterdam: Rodopi, 1997), 403–12; Jan Mohr, 'Konvergenzen in der "poetischen" Böhme-Rezeption Abraham von Franckenbergs und Daniel Czepkos,' in Kühlmann and Vollhardt, *Offenbarung und Episteme*, 93–123. For an art-historical approach, see also Urszula Szulakowska, 'The Alchemical Medicine and Christology of Robert Fludd and Abraham von Franckenberg,' in Linden, *Mystical Metal*, 277–98.
3. E.g. John Bruckner, 'A Bibliography of Abraham von Franckenberg: Problems and Propositions,' *German Life and Letters* 36 (1983): 213–18; János Bruckner, *Abraham von Franckenberg: A Bibliographical Catalogue with a Short-List of His Library* (Wiesbaden: Otto Harrassowitz, 1988); Gerhard Dünnhaupt, *Personalbibliographien zu den Drucken des Barock*, 2nd, improved, and expanded ed., 6 vols. (Stuttgart: Hiersemann, 1990–93), 3:1558–77.
4. Gilly, 'Zur Geschichte der Böhme-Biographie des Abraham von Franckenberg,' in Harmsen, *Jacob Böhmes Weg in die Welt*, 365–81; Mayer, *Jena Romanticism*, 28–34.
5. Boehme, *Theosophische Send-Schreiben*, 266–75 (ET, no. 41). See Telle's remarks in Abraham von Franckenberg, *Briefwechsel*, ed. Joachim Telle (Stuttgart-Bad Cannstatt: Frommann-Holzboog, 1995), 304–7. It has recently been established that Adam von Schweinichen was the most likely recipient: Leigh Penman, 'The Broken

Tradition: Uncovering Errors in the Correspondence of Jacob Böhme,' *Aries* 18 (2018): 96–125, on 115–19.

6. On Valentinus, see e.g. Gilles Quispel, 'The Original Doctrine of Valentinus the Gnostic,' *Vigiliae Christianae* 50 (1996): 327–52; Gilles Quispel, *Valentinus de gnosticus en zijn Evangelie der Waarheid* (Amsterdam: In de Pelikaan, 2003).

7. In the 1920s, facsimiles of the 1676 print and a lavish manuscript copy of *Raphael* made sure that it became the most readily accessible of Franckenberg's works, his biography of Boehme excepted. The facsimile of the 1729 manuscript remains worth mentioning: Heinrich Schneider, ed., *Abraham von Franckenbergs Raphael oder Artzt-Engel (Cod. Guelferbytan. Blancob. No. 160)*, 2 vols. (Wolfenbüttel: Verlag der Freude [Georg Koch und Paul Zieger], 1924). See also Bruckner, *Abraham von Franckenberg*, A 55–57. For a study specifically devoted to *Raphael*, see Maria Paola Scialdone, '"Aller heilsamste MUM IAH": Lebensbalsam (pseudo-)Paracelsiano e *Selbsterlösung* nel *Raphael* di Abraham von Franckenberg,' *Studi Germanici* 39 (2001): 7–35.

8. For the various universities Franckenberg attended, see Mike A. Zuber, 'Franckenberg, Abraham von,' in *Literaturwissenschaftliches Verfasserlexikon: Frühe Neuzeit in Deutschland 1620–1720*, ed. Stefanie Arend et al. (Berlin: De Gruyter, forthcoming), vol. 3: F–H, s.v. On the practice generally, see e.g. Jörg Jochen Berns, 'Peregrinatio academica und Kavalierstour: Bildungsreisen junger Deutscher in der Frühen Neuzeit,' in *Rom—Paris—London: Erfahrung und Selbsterfahrung deutscher Schriftsteller und Künstler in den fremden Metropolen*, ed. Conrad Wiedemann (Stuttgart: Metzler, 1988), 155–81.

9. Franckenberg, *Briefwechsel*, 244, 301.

10. Franckenberg, *Briefwechsel*, 360, 369.

11. Abraham von Franckenberg, *Raphael oder Artzt-Engel* (Amsterdam: Gedruckt bey Jacob von Felsen, wohnhaft in der Utrechtschen Gasse am Reguliers Marckt, 1676), 43.

12. According to the autograph manuscript, Berlin, SB-PK: Ms. germ. fol. 142, ff. 132r–37v, on f. 134r.

13. Abraham von Franckenberg, 'Kurtz- jedoch gründtlich- und warhaffter Bericht, von dem Leben und Abscheid des in Gott seelig ruhenden JACOB BOEMENS,' in *Von Erschaffung des Menschen zu Gottes Ebenbilde... Alles aus J. B. T. Schrifften gezogen: Der IV. Theil*, ed. [Gottfried Richter] ([Toruń]: [Michael Karnall], 1652/53), ff. A2v–C2r, on f. A2v (para. 1). On the many versions in print and manuscript, see Gilly, 'Zur Geschichte der Böhme-Biographie.' Leigh Penman is currently preparing a study of Gottfried Richter and the Toruń 'edition' of Boehme's works.

14. Franckenberg, 'Kurtz- ... und warhaffter Bericht,' f. A8v (para. 20).

15. Franckenberg, 'Kurtze Beschreibung,' f. (O)3r.

16. Franckenberg, *Briefwechsel*, 307–8.

17. Abraham von Franckenberg, 'Kurtze Beschreibung Des Lebens und wandels Jacobi Böhmens,' in Jacob Boehme, *Josephus Redivivus: Das ist Die Uberaus Lehr und Trostreiche Historia von dem Ertzvatter Joseph* (Amsterdam: [Johann and Siegfried

Saccus] zu finden bey Veit Heinrichs Boeckverkoper, 1631), ff. (0)3r–(0)5v, on f. (0)5r.

18. Franckenberg, 'Kurtz- ... und warhaffter Bericht,' f. A8v (para. 21). The work written for the benefit of Schweinichen and Franckenberg is more clearly identified in Franckenberg, 'Kurtze Beschreibung,' f. (0)5r.
19. Günther Bonheim, 'Zur Entstehung und Verbreitung der *Aurora*,' *Böhme-Studien* 4 (2017): 17–49. For remarks on Boehme's unusually clean autographs, see Buddecke, *Die Urschriften*, 2:438.
20. Franckenberg, 'Kurtz- ... und warhaffter Bericht,' f. B3r/v (para. 29).
21. Tobias Kober, 'Umständlicher Bericht ... von der Kranckheit, Absterben und Begräbniß des sel. *Autoris Theosophi*, an die Edlen Herren von Schweinichen,' in Jacob Boehme, *De vita et scriptis* ([Leiden?], 1730), 40–52, on 41, para. 1.
22. Beyerland is the subject of various contributions in Harmsen, *Jacob Böhmes Weg in die Welt*, 39–54 (Gilly), 133–67 (Lamoen), 213–47 (Bouman and Lamoen).
23. Boehme, *Josephus Redivivus*, 1–261 (MM 64:15–78:9); Jacob Boehme, 'Metapsychica de terrestri et coelesti mysterio, ex cognitione mysterii magni concepta, contemplatio,' in Abraham von Franckenberg, *Trias mystica: In quâ 1. Speculum apocalypticum: 2. Mysterium metapsychicum: 3. Epistolium chronometricum: Ad ecclesiam quae est in Philadelphia et Laodiceia* (Amsterdam: Typis Georgii Trigg, 1651), 65–98. Bonheim has prepared an edition of the latter text based on the most accurate manuscripts, published alongside a translation by Weeks, in Böhme, *Aurora*, 793–825. The work is also known by another title: *Mysterium pansophicum*.
24. Gilly, 'Zur Entstehung und Wirkung der Handschriftensammlung Abraham Willemsz van Beyerlands,' in Harmsen, *Jacob Böhmes Weg in die Welt*, 99–132, on 101–5 and 117–19, resp. For more on the deficiencies of the 1634 *Aurora* edition, though without recourse to the full manuscript record, see Ferdinand van Ingen, 'Die Edition von Jacob Böhmes "Aurora" und die Bedeutung eines Variantenapparats,' in *Probleme der Edition von Texten der Frühen Neuzeit: Beiträge zur Arbeitstagung der Kommission für die Edition von Texten der Frühen Neuzeit*, ed. Lothar Mundt, Hans-Gert Roloff, and Ulrich Seelbach (Tübingen: Niemeyer, 1992), 15–25; Böhme, *Werke*, 832–40. Instead of viewing Beyerland's source as deficient, Bonheim recently suggested it harked back to an earlier authorial draft: Bonheim, 'Entstehung und Verbreitung.'
25. Abraham von Franckenberg, *Conclusiones de fundamento sapientiae theorico-practicae. Das ist, Endlicher Beschluß Vom Grunde der Weißheit, Von etlichen Liebhabern der Wahrheit zusammen getragen* (Königstein [Amsterdam]: [Hans Fabel], 1646), 5, no. 11.
26. Franckenberg, 'Kurtze Beschreibung,' ff. (o)4v–5r.
27. On Boehme autographs and other manuscripts, see Wolfram Buddecke, 'Die Jakob-Böhme-Autographen: Ein historischer Bericht,' *Wolfenbütteler Beiträge* 1 (1972): 61–87; Buddecke, *Böhme-Handschriften*; Buddecke and Wenzel, *Verzeichnis der Handschriften*.
28. Carlos Gilly, 'Das Bekenntnis zur Gnosis von Paracelsus bis auf die Schüler Jacob Böhmes,' in *From Poemandres to Jacob Böhme: Gnosis Hermetism and the Christian Tradition*, ed. Roelof van den Broek and Cis van Heertum (Amsterdam: In de

Pelikaan, 2000), 385–425, on 416–422; Rusterholz, 'Franckenbergs Verhältnis zu Jacob Böhme,' 233–37. On the attribution, see Franckenberg, *Briefwechsel*, 33–34, 81–86. The German literature on Arnold is vast; I have found the following account particularly helpful: Lehmann-Brauns, *Weisheit in der Weltgeschichte*, ch. 6. For a concise discussion in English, see e.g. Hanegraaff, *Esotericism and the Academy*, 120–27.

29. Wouter J. Hanegraaff, 'Forbidden Knowledge: Anti-Esoteric Polemics and Academic Research,' *Aries* 5 (2005): 225–54, on 243. In the late 1640s, Franckenberg still sought to avert criticism from the gnostics: Franckenberg, *Briefwechsel*, 358, 367.

30. Sibylle Rusterholz, 'Jacob Böhme im Lichte seiner Gegner und Anhänger: Die zentralen Argumente der Streitschriften von ihren Anfängen zu Lebzeiten Böhmes bis zum Ende des 17. Jahrhunderts,' in Kühlmann and Vollhardt, *Offenbarung und Episteme*, 7–32, on 7; Rusterholz, 'Elemente christlicher Kabbala,' 186–89; Rusterholz, 'Franckenbergs Verhältnis zu Jacob Böhme,' 233–37.

31. Abraham von Franckenberg, '*Theophrastia Valentiniana*. Das ist: Ein unpartheyischer Schrifft- und Natur-mäßiger Bericht Uber ein *Fragmentum* Von der Lehre *Valentini*,' in Gottfried Arnold, *Supplementa, Illustrationes und Emendationes Zur Verbesserung Der Kirchen-Historie* (Frankfurt a.M.: Bey Thomas Fritschen, 1703), 11–49, on 15–16.

32. The symbols, sometimes used for substances such as the regulus of antimony, verdigris, and gold, are arranged around the word 'THEO—SOPHUS'; Franckenberg, 'Theophrastia Valentiniana,' 16. On *fixatio*, see e.g. Priesner and Figala, *Alchemie*, s.v. 'Opus magnum,' on 262; Ruland, *Lexicon alchemiae*, s.v. 'Fixatio.'

33. See Abraham von Franckenberg, *Jordans Steine, welche Einem nach dem Lande der Lebendigen reisenden Mit-Pilgrim, Auß dem Wege zu räumen* (Frankfurt a.M./ Leipzig: Bey Andräe Lupplo [*recte*: Luppio], Buchhändlern in Nimmägen, 1684), 30. The sole surviving exemplar of this publication is preserved in Weimar, Herzogin Anna Amalia Bibliothek: Cat. XVI: 978.

34. Franckenberg, 'Theophrastia Valentiniana,' 21–22. For other examples of 'IAH,' see also 32; The Hague, KB: Ritman Kerncollectie, PH317 M197, ff. 4r, 12r.

35. Franckenberg, 'Theophrastia Valentiniana,' 23–24.

36. See Wouter J. Hanegraaff et al., eds., *Dictionary of Gnosis and Western Esotericism* (Leiden: Brill, 2007), s.v. 'Gnosticism,' esp. 404, 411.

37. Franckenberg, 'Theophrastia Valentiniana,' 24. According to classical and, by extension, early-modern theories of generation, embryos were formed of male semen and female menstrual blood. Already Albertus Magnus drew a parallel to the alchemical sulphur-mercury theory that accounts for transmutation; see Principe, 'Revealing Analogies,' 216–17, 219.

38. Franckenberg, *Theophrastia Valentiniana*, 24.

39. Franckenberg, *Raphael*, 12. See also Scialdone, 'Aller heilsamste MUM IAH.'

40. E.g. Theophrastus Paracelsus, *Sämtliche Werke. 1. Abteilung: Medizinische, naturwissenschaftliche und philosophische Schriften*, ed. Karl Sudhoff, 14 vols. (Berlin: Oldenbourg, 1922–33), 13:344.

41. Martin Luther, *Das dise wort Christi (Das ist meyn leyb etc.) noch fest stehen: widder die Schwermgeyster* (Zwickau: Gedruckt durch Gabriel Kantz, 1527), f. F2v. Compare Franckenberg, 'Theophrastia Valentiniana,' 23.
42. Franckenberg, *Trias mystica*, 15.
43. Berlin, SB–PK: Ms. germ. fol. 142, f. 135v.
44. Genesis 1:7–8.
45. Berlin, SB–PK: Ms. germ. fol. 142, f. 135v.
46. E.g. Abram/Abraham, Sarai/Sarah, Jacob/Israel; Genesis 17:4–6, 15–16; 32:28.
47. Berlin, SB–PK: Ms. germ. fol. 142, f. 136r.
48. Franckenberg, 'Theophrastia Valentiniana,' 23–24.
49. Genesis 18:27 (see also Job 30:19, 42:6); Abraham von Franckenberg, *Notae mysticae et mnemonicae ad Bechinas Olam sive examen mundi R. Iedaia Happenini*, ed. Hilarius Prache (n.p., 1673), ch. 22. Compare Yedayah Ha-Penini, *Beḥinot ha-ʻolam... Examen mundi, R. J. Badreshitae: Latina interpretatione, atque animadversionibus illustratum*, ed. and trans. Allard Uchtman (Leiden: Ex Officina Joannis Maire, 1650), 118–19.
50. Franckenberg, *Notae mysticae*, ch. 31. Compare 1 Chronicles 29:4; Ha-Penini, *Examen mundi*, 168–69.
51. Genesis 2:7; 3:19 (amended for emphasis of 'dust' and 'earth').
52. Franckenberg, *Raphael*, 36.
53. The Hague, KB: PH317 M197, f. 4r.
54. Franckenberg, 'Theophrastia Valentiniana,' 28, 33.
55. Görlitz, Oberlausitzische Bibliothek der Wissenschaften (OLBW): LA III 409, f. 26r.
56. E.g. Matthew 17:2; Mark 9:2–3; Luke 9:29. See also John 20:19 and Luke 24:36–37. Compare Franckenberg, 'Theophrastia Valentiniana,' 39.
57. Franckenberg, 'Theophrastia Valentiniana,' 27. The phrase *himmlische Leiblichkeit* occurs several times throughout the treatise (on 26, 32, 34), so the single instance of *himmlische Lieblichkeit* encountered here appears to be a corruption (*lectio facilior*) that ought to be emended.
58. See also Franckenberg, *Jordans Steine*, 71–72.
59. Franckenberg, 'Theophrastia Valentiniana,' 32–33. See Revelation 21:18–21.
60. 1 Corinthians 15:50.
61. Franckenberg, 'Theophrastia Valentiniana,' 33.
62. [Johann Capito], *Libellus theosophiae de veris reliquiis seu semine Dei in nobis post lapsum relicto* (Newstadt [Frankfurt a.M.]: Zu finden bey Lucas Jennis, 1618), 1, 12. On this attribution, see Hartmut Broszinski, *Manuscripta chemica in quarto* (Wiesbaden: Harrassowitz, 2011), 317–18; Carlos Gilly, 'Khunrath und das Entstehen der frühneuzeitlichen Theosophie,' in *Amphitheatrum Sapientiae Aeternae—Schauplatz der ewigen allein wahren Weisheit: Vollständiger Reprint des Erstdrucks von [Hamburg] 1595 und des zweiten und letzten Drucks Hanau 1609*, ed. Carlos Gilly et al. (Stuttgart-Bad Cannstatt: Frommann-Holzboog, 2014), 9–22, on 16.
63. Franckenberg, 'Theophrastia Valentiniana,' 30, 28.

64. For the meaning of this term in alchemy (remnants of which survive in current terms such as distilled 'spirits'), see e.g. Ruland, *Lexicon alchemiae*, s.v. 'Spiritus.' In medical theory, the vital spirits (construed as a subtle substance mediating between body and soul) kept the body alive; see e.g. Michael Stolberg, ' "You Have No Good Blood in Your Body": Oral Communication in Sixteenth-Century Physicians' Medical Practice,' *Medical History* 59 (2015): 63–82, on 66; Jole Shackelford, 'Paracelsianism and the Orthodox Lutheran Rejection of Vital Philosophy in Early Seventeenth-Century Denmark,' *Early Science and Medicine* 8 (2003): 210–52, on 244–46. See further the section 'Spiritual Alchemy' in the Introduction.
65. Görlitz, OLBW: LA III 409, f. 48r (emphasis added).
66. Franckenberg, 'Theophrastia Valentiniana,' 30.
67. E.g. Maul, *Zahav mi-ẓafon*, 724. On this author, see Ulrike Kummer, ' "Gold von Mitternacht"—Zu Leben und Werk des Arztpietisten Johann Philipp Maul (1662–1727),' *Pietismus und Neuzeit* 40 (2014): 134–62.
68. On the Paracelsian term *archaeus*, see e.g. Theophrastus Paracelsus, *Essential Theoretical Writings*, ed. and trans. Andrew Weeks (Leiden: Brill, 2007), 672–73; Pagel, *Paracelsus*, 104–12.
69. Franckenberg, 'Theophrastia Valentiniana,' 29–30.
70. Franckenberg, 'Theophrastia Valentiniana,' 30. See Romans 6:3–11.
71. Görlitz, OLBW: LA III 409, f. 59v.
72. Franckenberg, 'Theophrastia Valentiniana,' 32. See Franckenberg, *Trias mystica*, 8, 41.
73. Franckenberg, 'Theophrastia Valentiniana,' 34.
74. E.g. Franckenberg, 'Theophrastia Valentiniana,' 32; Franckenberg, *Raphael*, 19, 43.
75. Ruland, *Lexicon alchemiae*, s.v. 'Tinctura,' 474.
76. Ruland, *Lexicon alchemiae*, s.v. 'Tingiren und transmutiren.' See also Priesner and Figala, *Alchemie*, s.v. 'Anima solis,' 48.
77. E.g. Ruland, *Lexicon alchemiae*, s.v. 'Proiectio.' For a late-eighteenth century collection of transmutation histories, see Siegmund Heinrich Güldenfalk, *Sammlung von mehr als hundert wahrhaften Transmutationsgeschichten* (Frankfurt a.M./Leipzig: Bey Joh. Georg Fleischer, 1784). On the work and its genre, see Jürgen Strein, 'Siegmund Heinrich Güldenfalks *Sammlung von mehr als 100 Transmutationsgeschichten* (1784),' in *Iliaster: Literatur und Naturkunde in der frühen Neuzeit (Festgabe für Joachim Telle zum 60. Geburtstag)*, ed. Wilhelm Kühlmann and Wolf-Dieter Müller-Jahncke (Heidelberg: Manutius, 1999), 275–83; Principe, *Aspiring Adept*, 93–98.
78. Jacob Boehme, '*Clavis* oder Schlüssel. Das ist: Eine Erklärung der vornehmsten Puncten und Wörtern in diesen Schriften,' in *Quaestiones theosophicae, oder Betrachtung Göttlicher Offenbarung, was GOTT, Natur und Creatur, sowol Himmel, Hölle und Welt, samt allen Creaturen sind* ([Leiden?]: 1730), 75–120, on 110 (= C, 'Clavis specialis'). See Görlitz, OLBW: LA III 409, f. 29v.
79. Copenhagen, KB: Thott 49 oktav, f. 20r/v (C, para. 73–74).
80. Copenhagen, KB: Thott 49 oktav, f. 24v (C, para. 95).
81. Cf. אוּר ('*ur*, fire) and אוֹר ('*or*, light).
82. Franckenberg, *Raphael*, 4. Compare Berlin, SB–PK: Ms. germ. fol. 142, f. 135v (in Greek letters).

83. Franckenberg, 'Theophrastia Valentiniana,' 31. See Matthew 25:33.
84. Franckenberg, *Raphael*, 5, 43.
85. Durham, NC, Duke University Libraries: Harold Jantz Collection, Bound MS 148, f. 15r. See also Franckenberg, *Raphael*, 43.
86. Franckenberg, *Raphael*, 11.

Chapter 5

1. For modern accounts, see Ernestien G. E. van der Wall, 'Chiliasmus Sanctus: De toekomstverwachting van Georg Lorenz Seidenbecher (1623–1663),' *Nederlands archief voor kerkgeschiedenis* 63 (1983): 69–83; Johannes Wallmann, 'Reich Gottes und Chiliasmus in der lutherischen Orthodoxie,' in *Theologie und Frömmigkeit im Zeitalter des Barock* (Tübingen: Mohr, 1995), 105–23, on 118–20.
2. Gottfried Arnold, *Fortsetzung und Erläuterung oder Dritter und Vierdter Theil der unpartheyischen Kirchen- und Ketzer-Historie* (Frankfurt a.M.: Bey Thomas Fritschens sel. Erben, 1729), pt. 3, 136–37; pt. 4, 1091, 1151–76.
3. Most biographical accounts of Seidenbecher mention this fact, documenting the esteem in which Libavius was held; e.g. Arnold, *Fortsetzung und Erläuterung*, pt. 4, 1169; Albrecht Meno Verpoorten, *De Georgii Laurentii Seidenbecheri vita et institutis* (Danzig: Sumptibus et Typis Thomae Joannis Schreiberi, Senatus et Gymn. Typographi, 1739), 2, 22.
4. Andreas Libavius and Jacob Michael, *De millenariorum haereticorum secta.... Disputatio Casimiriana ad XXII. Junii anno Salv. MDCVI* (Coburg: Typis Casparis Bertschii, 1616); Andreas Libavius, *Wolmeinendes Bedencken, Von der Fama unnd Confession der Brüderschafft deß RosenCreutzes* (Erfurt: Bey Johann Röhbock, 1616).
5. Franckenberg, *Briefwechsel*, 357, 366.
6. Gotha, Forschungsbibliothek der Universität Erfurt (FB): Chart. A 291.
7. On this usage, see e.g. Jennifer M. Rampling, 'John Dee and the Alchemists: Practising and Promoting English Alchemy in the Holy Roman Empire,' *Studies in History and Philosophy of Science* 43 (2012): 498–508, on 502.
8. Franckenberg, *Raphael*, 27, 31, 45–46.
9. Görlitz, OLBW: LA III 409, ff. 38r–40r, on f. 39r.
10. Leiden, Universiteitsbibliotheek: BPL 157 B, ff. 1r–21v, on ff. 3v, 4v, 8r, 16v. The capitalised Latin numerals indicate the work's composition in 1616; a printed edition was published in 1618. On Bureus and his reception of Rosicrucianism, see Susanna Åkerman, *Rose Cross over the Baltic: The Spread of Rosicrucianism in Northern Europe* (Leiden: Brill, 1998), 29–67; on 65 Åkerman mistakenly attributes the Leiden manuscript's marginalia to Bureus.
11. Franckenberg, *Trias mystica*, 26, 32, 60; the questionable year is on 2.
12. Franckenberg, *Trias mystica*, 29.
13. Franckenberg, *Briefwechsel*, 163–65.

14. Munich, BSB: Nachlässe, Frankenbergiana, no. 91, vol. 7, p. 429. For a summary, see Franckenberg, *Briefwechsel*, 184–85.
15. Franckenberg, *Briefwechsel*, 231–40. Telle has little to say about König; see, however, A. Soom, *Die Politik Schwedens bezüglich des russischen Transithandels über die estnischen Städte in den Jahren 1636–1656* (Tartu: Öpetatud Eesti Selts, 1940), 230–33, 236, 241–42; Erwin Oberländer, 'Königliches Intermezzo in Kurland: Ludwig XVIII. in Mitau und Blankenfeld,' in *Ostseeprovinzen, Baltische Staaten und das Nationale: Festschrift für Gert von Pistohlkors zum 70. Geburtstag*, ed. Norbert Angermann, Michael Garleff, and Wilhelm Lenz (Münster: LIT, 2005), 165–84, on 174; Kathrin Pfister, 'Joachim Polemann: Biographische Notizen zu einem Fachschriftsteller und Alchemiker des 17. Jahrhunderts,' in *Minera discipulorum: Vorstösse in das Fachschrifttum der frühen Neuzeit. Gedenkschrift für Joachim Telle*, ed. Laura Balbiani and Kathrin Pfister (Heidelberg: Mattes, 2014), 161–70, on 165.
16. Verpoorten, *Seidenbecheri vita*, 180–82, on 181.
17. Franckenberg, *Briefwechsel*, 353–71, on 353–54. In addition, I also use the 1739 edition: Verpoorten, *Seidenbecheri vita*, 103–18.
18. Verpoorten, *Seidenbecheri vita*, 139–82. See also the manuscript copies: Gotha, FB: Chart. A 291, pp. 109–32. Telle only provides summaries of letters addressed to the Silesian mystic throughout Franckenberg, *Briefwechsel*.
19. Verpoorten, *Seidenbecheri vita*, 139–40. See Philemon 10–21.
20. Verpoorten, *Seidenbecheri vita*, 150, 153–54.
21. Franckenberg, *Briefwechsel*, 355. See also Franckenberg, *Jordans Steine*, 36.
22. Franckenberg, *Briefwechsel*, 355.
23. Abraham von Franckenberg, *Via veterum sapientum. Das ist: Weg der Alten Weisen* (Amsterdam: Gedruckt by Christoffel Cunradus, Buchdrucker. In verlegung Henrici Betkii, und Consorten, 1675), 241–50. The source for these excerpts was the edition of the *Corpus Hermeticum* and *Asclepius* appended to Francesco Patrizi, *Nova de universis philosophia* (Ferrara: Apud Benedictum Mammarellum, 1591).
24. E.g. Zurich, Zentralbibliothek (ZB): Sammlung Oskar R. Schlag, SCH R 809, f. 17v.
25. Franckenberg, *Briefwechsel*, 356; Georg Lorenz Seidenbecher, *Chiliasmus Sanctus: qui est Sabbatismus populo Dei relictus*, ed. Petrus Serrarius (Amsterdam, 1660), title page.
26. Franckenberg, *Briefwechsel*, 356.
27. The initials of the three editors appear after Franckenberg's preface: Boehme, *Theosophische Send-Schreiben*, f. A4v.
28. Verpoorten, *Seidenbecheri vita*, 143–44. For a short biography of Werdenhagen, see *Deutsche Biographie (DB)*, https://www.deutsche-biographie.de (Munich: Historische Kommission der Bayerischen Akademie der Wissenschaften, 2001 ff.), s.v.
29. Verpoorten, *Seidenbecheri vita*, 149.
30. Seidenbecher, *Chiliasmus sanctus*, 52, 278–79, esp. 442–44. Compare Erfurt, Bibliothek des Evangelischen Ministeriums: Msc 21, ff. 328r–61r, on ff. 354r–55v (CS, bk. 4, 7:5–11).
31. Franckenberg, *Briefwechsel*, 356–57.
32. Franckenberg, *Briefwechsel*, 229–31.
33. Verpoorten, *Seidenbecheri vita*, 108 and 107, resp.; Franckenberg, *Briefwechsel*, 357.

34. Verpoorten, *Seidenbecheri vita*, 145.
35. Franckenberg, *Briefwechsel*, 241.
36. Verpoorten, *Seidenbecheri vita*, 147.
37. Silesius, *Cherubinischer Wandersmann*, esp. bk. 1, nos. 87, 102–4, 147, 244, 246–50, 258, 280. The remaining five books also occasionally include alchemical motifs. For an insightful study delineating how Scheffler's mysticism, unlike spiritual alchemy, stayed true to orthodox Catholicism, see Rainer Hillenbrand, 'Cherubinische Trinitätsmystik bei Angelus Silesius,' *Daphnis* 47 (2019): 592–638.
38. Verpoorten, *Seidenbecheri vita*, 119. For Telle's modern edition, see Franckenberg, *Briefwechsel*, 231–37. Due to the way Telle dealt with symbols and Hebrew letters, his edition lacks the visual dimension of the early-modern manuscript and print versions: compare Gotha, FB: Chart. A 291, pp. 95–98; Verpoorten, *Seidenbecheri vita*, 119–24.
39. Verpoorten, *Seidenbecheri vita*, 120. The biblical allusion refers to e.g. Luke 9:54. The symbol for antimony stands for the letter *U*, even though its shape more closely resembles *O*. As discussed in Chapter 4, Franckenberg did not necessarily distinguish between these because the Hebrew letter *vav* could stand for either vowel.
40. Verpoorten, *Seidenbecheri vita*, 120–21.
41. Verpoorten, *Seidenbecheri vita*, 122. For a study on Elias Artista, see Antoine Faivre, 'Elie Artiste, ou la messie des philosophes de la nature,' 2 pts., *Aries* 2–3 (2002–3): 119–52, 25–54.
42. Verpoorten, *Seidenbecheri vita*, 125–26.
43. See Johann Valentin Andreae, *Rosenkreuzerschriften*, ed. Roland Edighoffer (Stuttgart-Bad Cannstatt: Frommann-Holzboog, 2010), 160. The first of the Rosicrucian manifestos circulated in manuscript from 1610 and appeared in print in 1614.
44. Daniel Mögling, *Speculum Sophicum Rhodo-Stauroticum Das ist: Weitläuffige Entdeckung deß Collegii unnd axiomatum von der sondern erleuchten Fraternitet Christ-RosenCreutz* (n.p., 1618), 'Ergon-Parergon' engraving. Mögling in turn had been inspired by Khunrath's oft-reproduced 'Oratorium-Laboratorium' engraving; for a discussion, see e.g. Forshaw, 'Alchemy in the Amphitheatre,' 195, 197–201.
45. Verpoorten, *Seidenbecheri vita*, 124.
46. Verpoorten, *Seidenbecheri vita*, 126.
47. Verpoorten, *Seidenbecheri vita*, 154–55.
48. E.g. Priesner and Figala, *Alchemie*, s.v. 'Hermes Trismegistos.'
49. Marsilio Ficino, ed., *Mercurii Trismegisti Pymander, de potestate et sapientia Dei* (Basel: Per Mich. Isingrinium, mense Augusto, 1532), 3–4.
50. Franckenberg, *Notae mysticae*, ch. I. The *mem* stands for 'king' (*melekh*), the *ḥet* for 'prophet' (*ḥozeh*, in contrast to the more common *navi'*). For the *shin*, the connection is less obvious, but it might have to do with the Priestly Blessing (Numbers 6:24–26): while reciting it, the priest formed the letter *shin* with his hands. On the cross, Christ would have formed a similar shape with his head and outstretched arms.
51. The idea of Hermes as a prophet can be found in Petrus Bonus and Wilhelm Christoph Kriegsmann, among others; see Mike A. Zuber, 'Between Alchemy and

Pietism: Wilhelm Christoph Kriegsmann's Philological Quest for Ancient Wisdom,' *Correspondences* 2 (2014): 67–104, on 76, 82.
52. Verpoorten, *Seidenbecheri vita*, 122–23. Regarding Dorn, Franckenberg was most likely referring to 'De spagirico artificio Jo. Trithemii sententia,' contained in Gerard Dorn, *De naturae luce physica, ex Genesi desumpta, iuxta sententiam Theophrasti Paracelsi* (Frankfurt a.M.: Apud Christophorum Corvinum, 1583), 135–58.
53. For discussions of the letter's dating and content, respectively, see Penman, 'The Broken Tradition,' 102–8; Zuber, 'Jacob Böhme and Alchemy,' 272–79.
54. On the elusive Polemann, see Pfister, 'Joachim Polemann.'
55. Verpoorten, *Seidenbecheri vita*, 157, 161–63, 166–67, 181.
56. Verpoorten, *Seidenbecheri vita*, 123. The initials stand for 'Jacobi Boehmii Teutonici.'
57. Verpoorten, *Seidenbecheri vita*, 132.
58. Didier Kahn, 'Paracelsisme, alchimie et diplomatie dans le contexte de la Paix de Westphalie,' in *République des lettres, république des arts: Mélanges offerts à Marc Fumaroli, de l'Académie Française*, ed. Christian Mouchel and Colette Nativel (Geneva: Droz, 2008), 103–21, on 116–17.
59. On this publisher, see Leigh T. I. Penman, 'A Heterodox Publishing Enterprise of the Thirty Years' War: The Amsterdam Office of Hans Fabel (1616–after 1650),' *Library* 15 (2014): 3–44; Leigh T. I. Penman, 'A Heterodox Publishing Enterprise of the Thirty Years' War: Additions to the Catalogue of Hans Fabel's Publications,' *Library* 19 (2018): 360–67.
60. Franckenberg, *Briefwechsel*, 34–37.
61. Tünde Beatrix Karnitscher, *Der vergessene Spiritualist Johann Theodor von Tschesch (1595–1649): Untersuchungen und Spurensicherung zu Leben und Werk eines religiösen Nonkonformisten* (Göttingen: Vandenhoeck & Ruprecht, 2015), 241–42. Intriguingly, Mary Anne Atwood still employed the same strategy in the early twentieth century; see Providence, RI, Brown University, John Hay Library (BU–JHL): A54785, no. 530, scans 2–3.
62. Verpoorten, *Seidenbecheri vita*, 130–32.
63. Verpoorten, *Seidenbecheri vita*, 134–35. See also Dorn, *De naturae luce physica*, 152; Forshaw, 'Ora et Labora,' 2:118–19.
64. Zurich, ZB: SCH R 809, ff. 5r, 4v, 8r.
65. Franckenberg, *Raphael*, 46. For a discussion of Dorn's involvement with the *Aurora philosophorum*, see Kahn, 'Les débuts de Gérard Dorn,' 107–16.
66. C. H. Josten, 'A Translation of John Dee's "Monas Hieroglyphica" (Antwerp, 1564), with an Introduction and Annotations,' *Ambix* 12 (1964): 84–221; Peter J. Forshaw, 'The Early Alchemical Reception of John Dee's *Monas Hieroglyphica*,' *Ambix* 52 (2005): 247–69; Federico Cavallaro, 'The Alchemical Significance of John Dee's *Monas Hieroglyphica*,' in *John Dee: Interdisciplinary Studies in English Renaissance Thought*, ed. Stephen Clucas (Dordrecht: Springer, 2006), 159–76. The literature on Dee is vast; for a recent full-length account shedding new light on Dee's biography, see Glyn Parry, *The Arch-conjuror of England: John Dee* (New Haven: Yale University Press, 2011). Franckenberg was familiar with Dee: Sibylle Rusterholz, 'Jakob Böhme und Anhänger,' in *Die Philosophie des 17. Jahrhunderts: Das Heilige Römische*

Reich Deutscher Nation, Nord- und Ostmitteleuropa, ed. Helmut Holzhey, Wilhelm Schmidt-Biggemann, and Vilem Mudroch (Basel: Schwabe, 2001), 61–102, on 93.
67. Verpoorten, *Seidenbecheri vita*, 135.
68. Rusterholz, 'Elemente christlicher Kabbala', 187–89.
69. A perceptive early reader, Franckenberg's friend Daniel Czepko highlighted this in a poem on the work, which appears under the corrupted title 'Seriphiel'; Daniel Czepko, *Sämtliche Werke*, ed. Hans-Gert Roloff and Marian Szyrocki, 6 vols. (Berlin: De Gruyter, 1980–97), I/1:307–8.
70. Matthew 28:18b.
71. E.g. Ruland, *Lexicon alchemiae*, s.v. 'Coniugium, copulatio.' See also Spike Bucklow, *The Alchemy of Paint: Art, Science and Secrets from the Middle Ages* (London: Marion Boyars, 2009), ch. 9.
72. Verpoorten, *Seidenbecheri vita*, 135. The prefixed 'quadr-' is represented by a square inscribed with a dot, in analogy to the symbol for gold and the sun. In *Raphael*, the same symbol occurs, accompanied by the words 'new creature'; Franckenberg, *Raphael*, 17. In alchemical literature, this symbol more commonly referred to urine.
73. Franckenberg, *Trias mystica*, 106.
74. Leipzig, UB: Cod. mag. 24, f. 5v. See also Franckenberg, *Conclusiones de fundamento sapientiae*, 12.
75. Franckenberg, 'Theophrastia Valentiniana', 37.
76. Franckenberg, 'Theophrastia Valentiniana', 24.
77. Verpoorten, *Seidenbecheri vita*, 135–36.
78. E.g. Karl Baier, *Meditation und Moderne: Zur Genese eines Kernbereichs moderner Spiritualität in der Wechselwirkung zwischen Westeuropa, Nordamerika und Asien*, 2 vols. (Würzburg: Königshausen & Neumann, 2009), 1:43.
79. Franckenberg, *Raphael*, e.g. 12, 17.
80. Franckenberg, *Raphael*, 27–30.
81. Verpoorten, *Seidenbecheri vita*, 136.
82. Verpoorten, *Seidenbecheri vita*, 134. The phrase *philosophia harmonica* was associated with Rosicrucianism; see Jole Shackelford, *A Philosophical Path for Paracelsian Medicine: The Ideas, Intellectual Context, and Influence of Petrus Severinus (1540/2–1602)* (Copenhagen: Museum Tusculanum Press, 2004), 338–39.

Chapter 6

1. Important publications include Friedrich Breckling, *Autobiographie: Ein frühneuzeitliches Ego-Dokument im Spannungsfeld von Spiritualismus, radikalem Pietismus und Theosophie*, ed. Johann Anselm Steiger (Tübingen: Niemeyer, 2005); Brigitte Klosterberg, Guido Naschert, and Mirjam-Juliane Pohl, eds., *Friedrich Breckling (1629–1711): Prediger, "Wahrheitszeuge" und Vermittler des Pietismus im niederländischen Exil* (Halle: Verlag der Franckeschen Stiftungen, 2011). Guido

Naschert is currently preparing the results of his research project on Breckling's networks for publication.

2. On the Zwolle years, see Paul Estié, 'Die Auseinandersetzung von Charias, Breckling, Jungius und Gichtel in der lutherischen Gemeinde zu Kampen 1661-1668,' *Pietismus und Neuzeit* 16 (1990): 31-52; Paul Estié, 'Die Entlassung Friedrich Brecklings als Pfarrer der Lutherischen Gemeinde zu Zwolle, 1667-1668,' *Pietismus und Neuzeit* 18 (1992): 9-39. On Breckling's study and semi-public library in The Hague, see Guido Naschert, 'Knorr von Rosenroth als "Wahrheitszeuge" Friedrich Brecklings,' *Morgen-Glantz* 23 (2013): 131-52, on 146-50.

3. For a summary, see Paul Hoftijzer, 'Metropolis of Print: The Amsterdam Book Trade in the Seventeenth Century,' in *Urban Achievement in Early Modern Europe: Golden Ages in Antwerp, Amsterdam and London*, ed. Patrick O'Brien et al. (Cambridge: Cambridge University Press, 2001), 249-63. For accounts of the Dutch Golden Age and its intellectual climate, see Maarten Prak, *Gouden Eeuw: het raadsel van de Republiek* (Nijmegen: SUN, 2002); Eric Jorink, *Reading the Book of Nature in the Dutch Golden Age, 1575-1715*, trans. Peter Mason (Leiden: Brill, 2010).

4. Verpoorten, *Seidenbecheri vita*, 255-56 and 202-14, resp. On Sarnov or Zarnovius, see Gotha, FB: Chart. A 306, p. 124 (no. 14). For information on Sarnov's two known works, in print and manuscript, respectively, see J. Bruckner, *A Bibliographical Catalogue of Seventeenth-Century German Books Published in Holland* (The Hague: Mouton, 1971), no. 213; Jörg Georg Becker and Nilüfer Krüger, *Die theologischen Handschriften der Staats- und Universitätsbibliothek Hamburg*, 4 vols. (Hamburg: Hauswedell, 1975-98), 2:54.

5. Gotha, FB: Chart. A 306, p. 184.

6. Breckling, *Autobiographie*, 18.

7. Gotha, FB: Chart. A 306, pp. 185-86.

8. Franckenberg, *Briefwechsel*, 363, 371.

9. Klosterberg et al., *Friedrich Breckling*, 'Zeittafel,' 155-56.

10. Verpoorten, *Seidenbecheri vita*, 251-52. Not much is known about Münster; see e.g. Gotha, FB: Chart. A 306, p. 115 (no. 2); Franckenberg, *Briefwechsel*, 330-31. On Gifftheil, see e.g. Ernst Eylenstein, 'Ludwig Friedrich Gifftheil: Zum mystischen Separatismus des 17. Jahrhunderts in Deutschland,' *Zeitschrift für Kirchengeschichte* 41 (1922): 1-62; K. Gibson, 'Apocalyptic and Millenarian Prophecy in Early Stuart Europe: Philip Ziegler, Ludwig Friedrich Gifftheil and the Fifth Monarchy,' in *Prophecy: The Power of Inspired Language in History 1300-2000*, ed. Bertrand Taithe and Tim Thornton (Stroud: Sutton, 1997), 71-84. Leigh Penman is currently preparing a monograph on Gifftheil.

11. Verpoorten, *Seidenbecheri vita*, 268-71.

12. Estié, 'Charias, Breckling, Jungius und Gichtel,' 31-32.

13. For Seidenbecher's detailed diary and additional notes, see Gotha, FB: Chart. A 291, pp. 23-52. An eighteenth-century summary in Latin is provided by Verpoorten, *Seidenbecheri vita*, 25-30.

14. Verpoorten, *Seidenbecheri vita*, 262.

15. Estié, 'Charias, Breckling, Jungius und Gichtel,' esp. 33, 46. See also Estié, 'Die Entlassung Friedrich Brecklings.' For more on the role of the Amsterdam consistory for Lutheran congregations in the Low Countries, see e.g. Frits Praamsma, *Zacharias Webber (1644–1696): Irenisch lutheraan—verlicht protestant. Kerk en theologie in het denken van een zeventiende-eeuws kunstschilder* (Delft: Eburon, 2013), ch. 3.
16. Gotha, FB: Chart. B 198, ff. 32r–34v, 390r–91v (autograph), 392r–94v. For the relevant typescript catalogue, see Gertraud Zaepernick, *Verzeichnis der Handschriftenbestände pietistischer, spiritualistischer und separatistischer Autoren des 17. und 18. Jahrhunderts in der Landesbibliothek Gotha sowie in anderen Handschriftensammlungen und Archiven in Gotha und Erfurt* (n.p., 1965/68), 75, 82.
17. Gotha, FB: Chart. B 198, f. 390v. Compare Verpoorten, *Seidenbecheri vita*, 260.
18. Verpoorten, *Seidenbecheri vita*, 250.
19. Verpoorten, *Seidenbecheri vita*, 264–66; Friedrich Breckling, *Christus iudex in et cum sanctis contra gentes, secundum iudicium et iustitiam. Das Geheimniß des Reichs von der Monarchi Christi auff Erden* ([Amsterdam], 1663), f. **6r–8v.
20. For later remarks regarding Seidenbecher, see Friedrich Breckling, *Anticalovius, sive Calovius cum asseclis suis prostratus et Jacob Bohmius cum aliis testibus veritatis defensus* (n.p.: Gedruckt vor Andream Luppium, 1688), f. F6r/v; Gotha, FB: Chart. A 306, pp. 122–23 (no. 12). Breckling's late letters to Olaus Bjorn frequently revolve around millenarianism; see e.g. Gotha, FB: Chart. B 197, esp. f. 38r/v.
21. Breckling to Francke, 15 September 1697; Gotha, FB: Chart. B 195, p. 31.
22. Estié, 'Die Entlassung Friedrich Brecklings,' 11–13. Breckling gave his wife's date of birth as 26 December 1642; Breckling, *Autobiographie*, 34.
23. Estié, 'Die Entlassung Friedrich Brecklings,' 11–16.
24. Frans A. Janssen, 'Die erste Ausgabe von Böhmes gesammelten Werken 1682,' in Harmsen, *Jacob Böhmes Weg in die Welt*, 249–54. An earlier, English version of this article is also available: Frans A. Janssen, 'Böhme's *Wercken* (1682): Its Editor, Its Publisher, Its Printer,' *Quaerendo* 16 (1986): 137–41.
25. Gichtel's long letter to Breckling from 2 February 1660 relates his experience in prison; Gotha, FB: Chart. A 413, ff. 229r–33r.
26. E.g. Friedrich Breckling, *Christus cum suis prophetis et apostolis redivivus: Gottes Wort, Welches Gott dieser gegenwärtigen Welt in allen Ständen, Secten und Oertern selbst redet* ([Amsterdam], 1661), 107.
27. Gotha, FB: Chart. A 413, f. 234r/v. Arnold had published a number of Gichtel letters in 1700 and the next year, but married during 1701, which caused the rupture of his relationship with Gichtel; Gertraud Zaepernick, 'Johann Georg Gichtels und seiner Nachfolger Briefwechsel mit den Hallischen Pietisten, besonders mit A. M. Francke,' *Pietismus und Neuzeit* 8 (1982): 74–118, on 90, 94.
28. For important remarks in this connection, see Gilly, 'Zur Geschichte und Überlieferung der Handschriften Jacob Böhmes,' 43–46, with nn. 13 and 16–17 on 403–4; see also 465 and 491 in the same volume.
29. Janssen, 'Böhme's *Wercken*.'
30. Gotha, FB: Chart. A 291, p. 35; Verpoorten, *Seidenbecheri vita*, 26; Gotha, FB: Chart. A 306, p. 117.

31. Eventually, however, Gichtel did work as a corrector and translator: Christiaan Sepp, *Geschiedkundige nasporingen*, 3 vols. (Leiden: De Breuk & Smits, 1872–75), 2:200. Sepp's source does not explicitly mention the Blaeu firm, on which see e.g. Marijke Donkersloot-de Vrij, *Drie generaties Blaeu: Amsterdamse cartografie en boekdrukkunst in de zeventiende eeuw* (Zutphen: Walburg, 1992). On proofreading as a low-income profession for the highly educated, see Anthony Thomas Grafton, *Humanists with Inky Fingers: The Culture of Correction in Renaissance Europe* (Florence: Olschki, 2011), 43–44; Ernestien G. E. van der Wall, 'De mystieke chiliast Petrus Serrarius (1600–1669) en zijn wereld' (PhD thesis, Rijksuniversiteit Leiden, 1987), 61–67.
32. Johann Georg Gichtel, *Theosophia Practica: Halten und Kämpfen ob dem H. Glauben bis ans Ende*, 3rd, augmented, and improved ed., 7 vols. (Leiden, 1722), 7:74–75; Petrus Serrarius and Benedict Bahnsen, *Catalogus variorum . . . Librorum*, ed. [Johann Georg Gichtel] (Amsterdam: Typis Jacobi van Velsen, in de Kalverstraet, op d'Ossesluys, 1670), title page.
33. On the catalogue's rediscovery, see Ernestien G. E. van der Wall, 'A Philo-Semitic Millenarian on the Reconciliation of Jews and Christians: Henry Jessey and His "The Glory and Salvation of Jehudah and Israel" (1650),' in *Sceptics, Millenarians, and Jews*, ed. David S. Katz and Jonathan I. Israel (Leiden: Brill, 1990), 161–84, on 161. On the wrong binding order, see Reinhard Breymayer, 'Auktionskataloge deutscher Pietistenbibliotheken,' in *Bücherkataloge als buchgeschichtliche Quellen in der frühen Neuzeit*, ed. Reinhard Wittmann (Wiesbaden: Harrassowitz, 1984), 113–208, on 160.
34. Serrarius and Bahnsen, *Catalogus variorum . . . Librorum*, 38–41. For more on Bahnsen's library, see Dietrich Hakelberg, 'Die fanatischen Bücher des Benedikt Bahnsen: Leben und Bibliothek eines religiösen Dissidenten,' *Bibliothek und Wissenschaft* 48 (2015): 113–46; Hartmut Beyer et al., 'Bibliotheken im Buch: Die Erschließung von privaten Büchersammlungen der Frühneuzeit über Auktionskataloge,' in *Kodikologie und Paläographie im Digitalen Zeitalter 4*, ed. Hannah Busch, Franz Fischer, and Patrick Sahle (Norderstedt: BoD, 2017), 43–70.
35. On De Raadt, see Frank van Lamoen, 'Verliefd op Sophia: Alhart de Raadt (1640–1716) en de vrienden van Jacob Boehme,' *Geschiedenis van de wijsbegeerte in Nederland* 13 (2002): 119–63.
36. On Rothé, see e.g. K. H. D. Haley, 'Sir Johannes Rothe: English Knight and Dutch Fifth Monarchist,' in *Puritans and Revolutionaries: Essays in Seventeenth Century History Presented to Christopher Hill*, ed. D. Pennington and K. Thomas (Oxford: Oxford University Press, 1978), 310–32; Frank van Lamoen, 'Chiliast contra stadhouder: Johannes Rothé (1628–1702),' *Mededelingen van de Stichting Jacob Campo Weyerman* 22 (1999): 145–59. For Breckling's portrayal of Rothé as a heretic, see Gotha, FB: Chart. A 306, p. 230 (no. 4).
37. Gichtel, *Theosophia Practica*, 7:162–63. Judging from the date, the treatise would have to be the following: Johann Georg Gichtel, *Citatie voor Godts Gericht . . . Aen het luytersche consistorie tot Amsterdam* (Kampen, 1668). See also Breckling, *Autobiographie*, 34 (n. 377).

38. Gichtel, *Theosophia Practica*, 1:105; Breckling, *Autobiographie*, 39; for Breckling's son, see 37.
39. Lamoen, 'Verliefd op Sophia,' 122–23, 136–37. On Jean de Labadie and the community he founded, see T. J. Saxby, *The Quest for the New Jerusalem: Jean de Labadie and the Labadists, 1610-1744* (Dordrecht: Nijhoff, 1987).
40. Gichtel, *Theosophia Practica*, 7:188. For a rare moment of humility, see Gichtel, *Theosophia Practica*, 3:194.
41. Gichtel, *Theosophia Practica*, 7:188.
42. Gichtel, *Theosophia Practica*, 1:115.
43. Zaepernick, 'Gichtels und seiner Nachfolger Briefwechsel,' 82–84, 86, 88–90, 92–93, 112.
44. Lucinda Martin, ' "God's Strange Providence": Jane Lead in the Correspondence of Johann Georg Gichtel,' in *Jane Lead and Her Transnational Legacy*, ed. Ariel Hessayon (London: Palgrave Macmillan, 2016), 187–212, on 195, 205. On Leade (also Lead), her life and works, see e.g. Ariel Hessayon, 'Lead's Life and Times' (pts. 1–3), in Hessayon, *Jane Lead*, 13–90; Julie Hirst, *Jane Leade: Biography of a Seventeenth-Century Mystic* (Aldershot: Ashgate, 2005); Nils Thune, *The Behmenists and the Philadelphians: A Contribution to the Study of English Mysticism in the Seventeenth and Eighteenth Centuries* (Uppsala: Almquist & Wiksells, 1948), chs. 2 and 3.2. Lucinda Martin is currently preparing an edition of Leade's extant correspondence.
45. Kaspar Bütikofer, *Der frühe Zürcher Pietismus (1689-1721): Der soziale Hintergrund und die Denk- und Lebenswelten im Spiegel der Bibliothek Johann Heinrich Lochers (1648-1718)* (Göttingen: Vandenhoeck & Ruprecht, 2009), 234–36; Harmsen, *Jacob Böhmes Weg in die Welt*, 491; Bernard Gorceix, *Johann Georg Gichtel: Théosophe d'Amsterdam* (Paris: l'Age d'Homme, 1975), 32–35.
46. Lamoen, 'Verliefd op Sophia,' 137.
47. Harmsen, *Jacob Böhmes Weg in die Welt*, 403, n. 13; see also 404, n. 16.
48. Gichtel, *Theosophia Practica*, 7:193.
49. The Hague, KB: Ritman Kerncollectie, PH266 M140, no. 5, p. 17. Exorcising the taint of these editors was part of the motivation for the third edition of Boehme's complete works; see Günther Bonheim, 'Die "große Reinigung" vom "gemeinen Geiste": Zu den Umständen der Entstehung der dritten Böhme-Gesamtausgabe 1730/31 und zu ihrem philologischen Ertrag,' in Kühlmann and Vollhardt, *Offenbarung und Episteme*, 451–62.
50. Wrocław, BU: Ms. Akc. 1977/109, p. 40. See also Gichtel, *Theosophia Practica*, 7:169–73.
51. Gichtel, *Theosophia Practica*, 7:132.
52. Gichtel, *Theosophia Practica*, 7:213; see also 424–25. Gichtel and Überfeld both characterised Andreae as a *philosophus*, which could be interpreted as a synonym for 'alchemist'; see e.g. Gichtel, *Theosophia Practica*, 7:171; The Hague, KB: Ritman Kerncollectie, PH261 M135, p. 26. For a product of Andreae's and De Raadt's increased collaboration in 1684, see Manchester, John Rylands Library: Latin MS 77.
53. London, British Library (BL): Sloane MS 2709, f. 160r/v. On Moritz and his papers, see Leigh T. I. Penman, 'Statt "Briefe Böhmes an . . ." nun eine erste "Korrespondenz

mit . . .": Nachricht von der Entdeckung zweier Briefe Paul Kayms an Jacob Böhme,' in *Morgenröte im Aufgang: Beiträge einer Tagung zum 400. Jahrestag der Entstehung von Jacob Böhmes Erstschrift*, ed. Günther Bonheim and Thomas Regehly (Berlin: Weißensee Verlag, 2017), 197–208; Mike A. Zuber and Leigh T. I. Penman, 'Robert Boyle's Anonymous "Crosey-Crucian" Identified: The German Alchemist and Religious Dissenter Peter Moritz,' *Notes and Records* 74 (2020): 95–103; Mike A. Zuber, 'Alchemical Promise, the Fraud Narrative, and the History of Science from Below: Peter Moritz's Encounter with Robert Boyle and Ambrose Godfrey,' *Ambix* 68 (2021): 28–48.

54. Gotha, FB: Chart. A 306, p. 183. The corresponding passage in the printed edition is considerably shorter: Arnold, *Fortsetzung und Erläuterung*, pt. 4, 1103.
55. Gotha, FB: Chart. A 413, f. 235r.
56. See the bibliographical descriptions and comments in Bruckner, *Bibliographical Catalogue*, nos. 432–37, 450–53, 465; Werner Buddecke, *Die Jakob Böhme-Ausgaben: Ein beschreibendes Verzeichnis*, 2 vols. (Göttingen: Dr. Ludwig Häntzschel, 1937–57), vol. 1, nos. 19, 131, 133, 136–37, 141, 144, 147, 165, 178, 183. Breckling's chronological account does not mention any of these: Breckling, *Autobiographie*, 44–48.
57. On Betke, see Willem Heijting, 'Hendrick Beets (1625?–1708), Publisher to the German Adherents of Jacob Böhme in Amsterdam,' *Quaerendo* 3 (1973): 250–80; Willem Heijting, *Profijtelijke boekskens: Boekcultuur, geloof en gewin. Historische studies* (Hilversum: Verloren, 2007), 209–42, esp. 220, 226, 230.
58. Buddecke, *Böhme-Ausgaben*, vol. 1, no. 165.
59. Friedrich Breckling, *Compendium Apocalypseos reseratae: Kurtzer Außzug Auß einem grössern Tractat, oder Außlegung über die Offenbahrung Johannis* ([Amsterdam], 1678), 11, nos. 17–18.
60. Breckling, *Autobiographie*, 53; see also 48, 54, 58, 60, 62.
61. Friedrich Breckling, *Christus mysticus, sol et sal sapientiae ex summo ac infimo coelo ac centro erumpens cum luce benedictionis et igne maledictionis, ad salvandum filios lucis, et iudicandum filios tenebrarum* ([Amsterdam], 1682), 7; Friedrich Breckling, *Pseudosophia mundi cum falsis eius doctoribus de sede sua deturbata, et vera theosophia cum datore et doctore suo summo in thronum suum regalem exaltanda* ([Amsterdam], 1682), 15. Boehme's early reception history often saw him placed in the company of new prophets; see Penman, *Hope and Heresy*, ch. 2, esp. 48–53.
62. Breckling, *Autobiographie*, 52.
63. Bruckner, *Bibliographical Catalogue*, xiii; index (s.v. 'Cunradus, Christoffel').
64. Acting as publisher himself, Breckling had Cunradus print his early *Ankündigung des Rach-tages* and *Das Ewige Evangelium* in 1660; Bruckner, *Bibliographical Catalogue*, nos. 271–72. Breckling and Cunradus' widow collaborated on the edition of Sclei's works in 1686. See also Gotha, FB: Chart. B 198, f. 112v.
65. Breckling, *Christus mysticus*, title page. See e.g. Malachi 4:2; Mark 5:13. The alchemical language does not yet appear in Breckling's announcement of related projects on mystical theology and 'spiritual agriculture' (*Agricultura Spiritualis*); see Breckling, *Compendium Apocalypseos reseratae*, 11–12, nos. 21–22.

66. Breckling, *Christus mysticus*, title page. For the alchemical meanings, e.g. Ruland, *Lexicon alchemiae*, s.v. 'Exaltatio', 'Multiplicatio'.
67. Breckling, *Christus mysticus*, 12.
68. Breckling, *Christus mysticus*, 16; Breckling, *Pseudosophia mundi*, 13.
69. Breckling, *Pseudosophia mundi*, title page.
70. Breckling, *Christus mysticus*, 12.
71. Fludd, *Clavis philosophiae et alchymiae*, 83. For recent work on Fludd, see Janacek, *Alchemical Belief*, ch. 2; Lauren Kassell, 'Magic, Alchemy and the Medical Economy in Early Modern England: The Case of Robert Fludd's Magnetical Medicine,' in *Medicine and the Market in England and Its Colonies, c. 1450–c. 1850*, ed. Mark S. R. Jenner and Patrick Wallis (Basingstoke: Palgrave Macmillan, 2007), 88–107. On Geber and the 'Geber problem,' see Principe, *The Secrets of Alchemy*, 33–45, 54–58; William R. Newman, *The* Summa Perfectionis *of Pseudo-Geber: A Critical Edition, Translation and Study* (Leiden: Brill, 1991), ch. 2.
72. Tilton, 'Alchymia Archetypica,' 194. For an earlier discussion, see Silberer, *Probleme der Mystik*, 115, 187.
73. Fludd, *Clavis philosophiae et alchymiae*, 75, 83.
74. Gotha, FB: Chart. A 310, p. 215.
75. Breckling, *Christus mysticus*, 12–13.
76. Breckling, *Pseudosophia mundi*, 13–14.
77. Breckling, *Christus mysticus*, 15.
78. 1 Corinthians 3:10–15.
79. Breckling, *Pseudosophia mundi*, 13.
80. Breckling, *Christus mysticus*, 16. See also Breckling, *Pseudosophia mundi*, 8.
81. Gotha, FB: Chart. B 195, pp. 326, 329; Chart. A 310, p. 215. See [Siebmacher], *Wasserstein*, 102–3, 114, 144. Siebmacher used Khunrath's derogatory term 'bad chymistry' (*argchimia*) and likely drew on his influential portrayal of fraudulent practices: Khunrath, *Von Hylealischen . . . Chaos*, 'Trewhertzige Warnungs-Vermanung,' 440–69. On this text, see Nummedal, *Alchemy and Authority*, 68–70.
82. Breckling, *Christus mysticus*, 15.
83. Breckling, *Pseudosophia mundi*, 14–15.
84. Breckling, *Pseudosophia mundi*, 15.
85. Breckling, *Christus mysticus*, 15. See 1 Peter 1:7; Luke 18:9–14.
86. Breckling, *Christus mysticus*, 15–16. See Psalm 118:22.
87. Breckling, *Pseudosophia mundi*, 14. One of the first among these associates was Johann Friedrich Münster; see Gotha, FB: Chart. A 306, p. 115 (no. 2). See also Breckling, *Compendium Apocalypseos reseratae*, 14.
88. Breckling, *Pseudosophia mundi*, 13.
89. Gotha, FB: Chart. A 297, p. 246; see also pp. 247–48.
90. Gotha, FB: Chart. B 195, p. 200. An influential church historian prominently took up the phrase 'Bibliothecarius Dei,' though without specifying its source; see Johannes Wallmann, *Der Pietismus* (Göttingen: Vandenhoeck & Ruprecht, 2005), 45–47, on 47.
91. From the early eighteenth century until today, catalogues and discussions of the books Breckling donated to the Halle Orphanage miss this crucial point and

usually focus on the printed ones exclusively; e.g. Halle, Archiv der Franckeschen Stiftungen (AFS): H G 1; Brigitte Klosterberg, 'Libri Brecklingici: Bücher aus dem Besitz Friedrich Brecklings in der Bibliothek des Halleschen Waisenhauses,' in *Interdisziplinäre Pietismusforschung: Beiträge zum Ersten Internationalen Kongress für Pietismusforschung*, ed. Udo Sträter (Tübingen: Niemeyer, 2005), 871–81; Brigitte Klosterberg, 'Brecklingiana in den Beständen der Franckeschen Stiftungen,' in Klosterberg et al., *Friedrich Breckling*, 35–40. Mined by generations of scholars (from Theodor Wotschke to Joachim Telle), two important manuscript volumes preserved in Halle hark back to Breckling without doubt; Halle, AFS: H B 17 a–b. The neighbouring manuscripts, H B 18 and 19, share the same provenance.

Chapter 7

1. Carlos Gilly, 'Zwischen Erfahrung und Spekulation: Theodor Zwinger und die religiöse und kulturelle Krise seiner Zeit. 1. Teil,' *Basler Zeitschrift für Geschichte und Altertumskunde* 77 (1977): 57–137, on 88, n. 73; Geyer, *Verborgene Weisheit*, 1:257–70; 2:60–65. According to one scholar, Sclei was born in 1556; Friedhelm Kemp, 'Jakob Böhme in Holland, England und Frankreich,' in *Studien zur europäischen Rezeption deutscher Barockliteratur*, ed. Leonard Forster (Wiesbaden: Harrassowitz, 1983), 211–26, on 223. As the article in question features few references, I have not been able to verify this information independently.
2. For an overview on the early history of Socinianism and its Dutch reception, see Philip Knijf, Sibbe Jan Visser, and Piet Visser, *Bibliographia Sociniana: A Bibliographical Reference Tool for the Study of Dutch Socinianism and Antitrinitarianism* (Hilversum: Verloren, 2004), 11–24.
3. A cursory comparison reveals that Franckenberg's *Pater Noster* text is considerably shorter than the one printed in 1686 as 'Orationis Dominicae Meditatio': Sclei, *Theosophische-Schrifften*, 609–815. The manuscript Franckenberg used may indeed have been inaccurate or deficient, as it did not mention the author's name and Franckenberg attributed it to Sclei himself; see Bartholomaeus Sclei, *Pater Noster: Das ist Eine geheime unnd allgemeine Außlegung Des Heiligen Vater Unsers*, ed. Abraham von Franckenberg ([Amsterdam]: [Johannes Janssonius], 1639), 3. Even as the editors of the 1686 edition did not wholly rely on Franckenberg's text of 1639, they included his preface and an appendix compiled by him: Sclei, *Theosophische-Schrifften*, 611–15, 797–815.
4. Gotha, FB: Chart. A 306, pp. 146–47 (no. 84).
5. Breckling, *Autobiographie*, 58.
6. Johann Christoph Adelung, *Geschichte der menschlichen Narrheit*, 7 vols. (Leipzig: In der Weygandschen Buchhandlung, 1785–89), 4:30.
7. Quirinus Kuhlmann, *Widerlegte Breklingsworte aus zweien Brifen an Andreas Luppius gezogen* (Amsterdam: Gedrukt vor den Autor auch zu finden bei Andrea Luppio,

Buchhändlern, 1688), f. B3r. On Kuhlmann, see Walter Dietze, *Quirinus Kuhlmann— Ketzer und Poet: Versuch einer monographischen Darstellung von Leben und Werk* (Berlin: Rütten & Loening, 1963); Eugene Kuzmin, *Alchemical Imagery in the Works of Quirinus Kuhlmann* (Wilsonville: Sirius Academic Press, 2013).

8. A famous example of this problem is the papal bull *Spondent pariter* issued by Pope John XXII in 1317, forbidding the practice of alchemy due to the danger it posed to currency; see Priesner and Figala, *Alchemie*, s.v. 'Alchemiekritik'; Principe, *The Secrets of Alchemy*, 61–62; Frieda Maria Huggenberg, 'Alchemisten und Goldmacher im 16. Jahrhundert in der Schweiz,' *Gesnerus* 13 (1956): 97–164, on 110–16.
9. Sclei, *Theosophische-Schrifften*, flyleaf at the back (The Hague, KB: Ritman Kerncollectie, PH2762).
10. Gotha, FB: Chart. A 306, pp. 230–31 (no. 5).
11. Lamoen, 'Verliefd op Sophia,' 142–43, n. 91.
12. Wrocław, BU: Ms. Akc. 1977/109, p. 162.
13. Wrocław, BU: Ms. Akc. 1977/109, p. 163.
14. Breckling, *Autobiographie*, 43.
15. Gichtel, *Theosophia Practica*, 7:198–99. See J. C. van der Does, 'Johan Georg Gichtel's verblijf in Nederland en zijn verhouding tot Jan Luyken,' *Stemmen des tijds* 18 (1929): 146–66, on 153–54. On the Sulzbach connection, see Düsseldorf, Landeskirchliches Archiv der Evangelischen Kirche im Rheinland (LKA): Nachlass Prof. J. F. Gerhard Goeters, 7 NL 015, Nr. 759, p. 55; Amsterdam, Bibliotheca Philosophica Hermetica (BPH): M 519, p. 35. The latter library is now known as the Embassy of the Free Mind.
16. Gotha, FB: Chart. B 198, f. 233r.
17. Gotha, FB: Chart. A 310, p. 58. The labyrinthine garden could be found at the corner where the Prinsengracht and the Looiersgracht meet. A faulty transcription of this letter was published by Theodor Wotschke, 'Weseler Briefe an Friedrich Breckling,' *Monatshefte für Rheinische Kirchengeschichte* 27 (1933): 178–85, on 181–82. The letter is by Johann Jacob Zimmermann, and the year can be established based on the events of his life; see Gudrun Aker, 'Johann Jakob Zimmermann 1642–1693: Ein Prophet des Tausendjährigen Reiches,' in *Vaihinger Köpfe: Biographische Porträts aus fünf Jahrhunderten*, ed. Lothar Behr et al. (Vaihingen: Selbstverlag der Stadt Vaihingen an der Enz, 1993), 71–88.
18. Halle, AFS: MF 5, pos. 153–54. For the auction catalogue of Schmidberger's library, see Gerard Block, *Bibliotheca Smidsbergiana, sive catalogus insignium et rarissimorum . . . non solum typis editi, verum etiam manuscripta exima* (The Hague: Apud Gerardum Block, Bibliopolam, 1732).
19. On Mulder and his engravings for Boehme and related literature, see Christoph Geissmar, *Das Auge Gottes: Bilder zu Jakob Böhme* (Wiesbaden: Harrassowitz, 1993), 52–55.
20. Wrocław, BU: Ms. Akc. 1977/109, p. 163.
21. Frederik Muller and Martinus Nijhoff, *Catalogue de la bibliothèque . . . formée pendant le 18e siècle par Messieurs Izaak, Johannes et le Dr Johannes Enschedé Imprimeurs-Libraires à Haarlem* (Amsterdam/The Hague: Muller/Nijhoff, 1867), no. 602.

According to an interleaved, annotated copy, Muller himself bought the Sclei manuscript for a negligible sum: Oxford, Bodleian Library (BL): 2592 d.156, interleaved page opposite 71. With his many contacts, he could have sold it on to anybody anywhere in the world. For more on Muller and his business activities, see Marja Keyser et al., eds., *Frederik Muller (1817–1881): Leven en werken* (Zutphen: Walburg, 1996); Chris Schriks, *Frederik Muller: Baanbreker in de wereld van het Nederlandse boek* (Zutphen: Walburg, 2016).

22. Martin Mulsow and Olaf Simons are preparing an edition of Stolle's manuscript diary. In the meantime, see G. E. Guhrauer, 'Beiträge zur Kenntniss des 17. u. 18. Jahrhunderts aus den handschriftlichen Aufzeichnungen Gottlieb Stolle's,' *Allgemeine Zeitschrift für Geschichte* 7 (1847): 385–436, 481–531; Martin Mulsow, 'Eine Reise durch die Gelehrtenrepublik: Soziales Wissen in Gottlieb Stolles Journal der Jahre 1703–1704,' in *Kultur der Kommunikation: Die europäische Gelehrtenrepublik im Zeitalter von Leibniz und Lessing*, ed. Johannes Ulrich Schneider (Wiesbaden: Harrassowitz, 2005), 185–201. Von der Hardt's library remained in family possession until 1786: Ferdinand Lamey, *Hermann von der Hardt in seinen Briefen und seinen Beziehungen: Neudruck mit bibliographischen Nachträgen* (Wiesbaden: Harrassowitz, 1974), 1; Paul Jacob Bruns, *Catalogus bibliothecae D. Antonii Julii von der Hardt Abbatis Michaelsteinensis* (Helmstedt: Typis Vid. Schnorrianae acad. typ., 1786), 234, no. 1988.

23. Geyer, *Verborgene Weisheit*, 1:260–61, esp. nn. 116–17. The book forms part of the Fenitzer Library, first established in 1615; for more on the library and its history, see Matthias Simon, 'Die Fenitzerbibliothek in Nürnberg,' *Zeitschrift für bayerische Kirchengeschichte* 29 (1960): 167–85; Matthias Simon, 'Zur Geschichte der Fenitzerbibliothek,' *Zeitschrift für bayerische Kirchengeschichte* 30 (1961): 101. Sclei appears in the second library catalogue of 1776: Leonhard Rinder, *Catalogus Bibliothecae Fenizerianae: Verzeichnis derjenigen Bücher welche in der Fenizerischen Bibliothek befindlich*, 2nd ed. (Nuremberg: Bey Wolfgang Schwartzkopf, 1776), 127. The book's previous owner was Johann Wilhelm Baier, professor of theology, physics, and mathematics at the University of Altdorf: Johann Wilhelm Baier, *Catalogus librorum theologicorum . . . quibus suam olim bibliothecam B. Jo. Guilielmus Baierus . . . instruxerat* (Altdorf: Prostant exemplaria catalogi in bibliopolio sub iisdem aedibus, 1731), 391, no. 23. His 'sizable collection of fanatical and mystical writings,' which had largely failed to attract buyers at an auction in June 1731, represented a significant addition to the library: Rinder, *Catalogus Bibliothecae Fenizerianae*, f. b7r.

24. Sclei, *Theosophische-Schrifften*, f. **4v (Nuremberg, Landeskirchliches Archiv [LKA]: Fen II 914 8°).

25. Sclei, *Theosophische-Schrifften*, f. *3r and 779, resp. (Nuremberg, LKA: Fen II 914 8°). In the latter case, concerning 'Die Zehende Betrachtung. Von der H. Tauffe,' the precise extent of Schmidberger's addition is not marked.

26. These often concerned the omission or translation of Latin and the replacement of dialectal terms that would not readily be understood by readers. According to the annotator, Sclei referred to the rich man (in Christ's parable of the rich man and Lazarus, Luke 16:19–31) as 'Kwesser' or 'Kwösser'; see e.g. Sclei, *Theosophische-Schrifften*, 45, 459, 482 (Nuremberg, LKA: Fen II 914 8°). Standard historical and

dialectal dictionaries do not list this word, but it is entirely plausible that it could be have been used in Sclei's German community in Lesser Poland. Similar interventions appear in another copy: Sclei, *Theosophische-Schrifften*, 459, 464, 482 (Amsterdam, Universiteitsbibliotheek [UB]: OK 65-542). The former Special Collections of the University of Amsterdam have now been rebranded as part of the Allard Pierson Collections.

27. The passage 'Und dieweil . . . einringen und kommen müssen' is highlighted as Breckling's: Sclei, *Theosophische-Schrifften*, 26 (Nuremberg, LKA: Fen II 914 8°).

28. Apart from the references to the Bible, the passage 'Wir predigen . . . Gottes Wort predigen' is highlighted: Sclei, *Theosophische-Schrifften*, 36 (Nuremberg, LKA: Fen II 914 8°). See 1 Corinthians 3:19.

29. Apart from the phrase 'Das Wort ist dir nahe' and references to the Bible, the passage 'Denn wer nicht . . . aufffahren und erhöhet werden' is highlighted: Sclei, *Theosophische-Schrifften*, 42 (Nuremberg, LKA: Fen II 914 8°).

30. Sclei, *Theosophische-Schrifften*, flyleaf at the back (The Hague, KB: PH2762).

31. The Halle database of Pietist correspondence lists two Straubes and five Mylii who were alive around 1700; see *Datenbank zu den Einzelhandschriften in den historischen Archivabteilungen*, http://fas.francke-halle.de/cgi-bin/gkdb.pl (Halle: Franckesche Stiftungen, 2008 ff.), s.v.

32. For longer manuscript additions, see e.g. Sclei, *Theosophische-Schrifften*, 63, 104, 111, 135, 718, 781, 784, 789 (Amsterdam, UB: OK 65-542). Encountered repeatedly on these pages, the spellings 'Godt' (rather than 'Gott') and 'met' (instead of 'mit') are telling examples of interference from the Dutch.

33. Sclei, *Theosophische-Schrifften*, 486-92, on 486; 604-8, on 604 (Amsterdam, UB: OK 65-542).

34. Geyer, *Verborgene Weisheit*, 3:463-71; Gilly, 'Zwischen Erfahrung und Spekulation,' 88, n. 73. Two annotated copies highlight the passage quoted by Gilly as Breckling's contribution; Sclei, *Theosophische-Schrifften*, 181 (The Hague, KB: PH2762; Amsterdam, UB: OK 65-542).

35. On Fischer, see Johann Christian Siebenkees, *Materialien zur Nürnbergischen Geschichte*, 4 vols. (Nuremberg: In Commission der A. G. Schneiderischen Kunst- und Buchhandlung, 1792-95), 1:104-9. This account is not accurate in all details; for instance, Fischer spent a much longer time studying at Leipzig, from 1655 to 1661; compare Georg Erler, *Die iüngere Matrikel der Universität Leipzig 1559-1809: Als Personen- und Ortsregister bearbeitet und durch Nachträge aus den Promotionslisten ergänzt*, 3 vols. (Nendeln: Kraus Reprint, 1976), s.v. 'Fischer, Lothus.' The burial records of Utrecht list 'Loth Visser' on 23 February 1723, and he is almost certainly identical to our Fischer; Utrecht, Utrechts Archief: 711—Burgerlijke stand gemeente Utrecht, nr. 130, p. 298.

36. Bütikofer, *Der frühe Zürcher Pietismus*, 235-39.

37. The whole book has been attributed to Überfeld; see Buddecke, *Böhme-Ausgaben*, 1:87-89 (no. 36). For an unfounded challenge to this attribution, see Geissmar, *Das Auge Gottes*, 44-45. Überfeld himself claimed that he had been the volume's publisher: Düsseldorf, LKA: Nachlass Prof. J. F. Gerhard Goeters, 7 NL 015, Nr.

720, no. 71, para. 16. Breckling identifies Fischer as the author of a specific portion of *Der rechte Weg zum Ewigen Leben;* Gotha, FB: Chart. A 297, p. 281; [Johann Wilhelm Überfeld], ed., *Der rechte Weg zum Ewigen Leben: Verfasst in Drey- und neuntzig Fragen und Antworten* ([Frankfurt a.M.], 1683), 'Einige Denckwürdige Erinnerungen,' independently paginated, 1–159. Andreae contributed the design for the frontispiece.

38. On the attribution of the German Hiël translation to Fischer, see Andreas Pietsch, 'Expanding the Boundaries of Orthodoxy? Friedrich Breckling and the 1687/90 German Edition of Hiel's Works,' *Church History and Religious Culture* 98 (2018): 91–110. On Pordage, see Thune, *The Behmenists,* chs. 1 and 3.1; Manfred Brod, 'A Radical Network in the English Revolution: John Pordage and His Circle, 1646–54,' *English Historical Review* 119 (2004): 1230–53; Arthur Versluis, *Wisdom's Children: A Christian Esoteric Tradition* (Albany: State University of New York Press, 1999), ch. 3.
39. Gotha, FB: Chart. A 297, p. 281.
40. John Pordage, 'Ein Gründlich Philosophisch Sendschreiben vom rechten und wahren Steine der Weißheit,' in *Theologia mystica: oder Geheime und verborgne göttliche Lehre von den Ewigen unsichtbahrlichkeiten: als vom Mundô et Globô Archetypô* (Amsterdam: Bey Heinrich Wettstein daselbst zu finden, 1698), 267–82. As with most of Pordage's writings, the English original is no longer extant; a flawed translation based on a later edition can be found in Arthur Versluis, ed., *Wisdom's Book: The Sophia Anthology* (St. Paul: Paragon House, 2000), 67–76.
41. See Martin Mulsow and Olaf Simons's edition of Stolle's diary (in preparation).
42. Sclei, *Theosophische-Schrifften,* index.
43. Sclei, *Theosophische-Schrifften,* 115.
44. E.g. Sclei, *Theosophische-Schrifften,* 331, 395, 396 (The Hague, KB: PH2762; Amsterdam, UB: OK 65-542).
45. E.g. [Johann Gottmann], 'Speculum Sapientiae. Das ist: Ein Buch des Geheimnisses vom Anfang der Welt,' in *Quadratum Alchymisticum: Das ist: Vier auserlesene rare Tractätgen Vom Stein der Weisen* (Hamburg: Verlegts Christian Liebezeit. Druckts Philipp Ludwig Stromer, 1705), 1–54, on 45–47. For a study of the manuscript transmission of this treatise, see Mike A. Zuber, 'The Duke, the Soldier of Fortune, and a Rosicrucian Legacy: Exploring the Roles of Manuscripts in Early-Modern Alchemy,' *Ambix* 65 (2018): 122–42.
46. Sclei, *Theosophische-Schrifften,* 115–16.
47. Breckling, *Anticalovius,* f. E3r; see also ff. B4v–B5r, E2r. For more on this work, see e.g. Johann Anselm Steiger, 'Jacob Böhmes Rettung: Friedrich Brecklings *Anticalovius* (1688) als Apologie des mystischen Spiritualismus,' in Kühlmann and Vollhardt, *Offenbarung und Episteme,* 283–94.
48. Sclei, *Theosophische-Schrifften,* 117.
49. Sclei, *Theosophische-Schrifften,* 381.
50. Sclei, *Theosophische-Schrifften,* 119–20 (The Hague, KB: PH2762).
51. See also Geyer, *Verborgene Weisheit,* 3:227–28.
52. Sclei, *Theosophische-Schrifften,* 120 (The Hague, KB: PH2762).
53. Sclei, *Theosophische-Schrifften,* 121.

54. There are a number of studies devoted to this phenomenon in the Italian context; e.g. David Gentilcore, *Medical Charlatanism in Early Modern Italy* (Oxford: Oxford University Press, 2006); David Gentilcore, '"Charlatans, Mountebanks and Other Similar People": The Regulation and Role of Itinerant Practitioners in Early Modern Italy,' *Social History* 20 (1995): 297–314; Rosa Salzberg, 'In the Mouth of Charlatans: Street Performers and the Dissemination of Pamphlets in Renaissance Italy,' *Renaissance Studies* 24 (2010): 638–53. For more on the British and central European contexts, see the articles by M. A. Katritzky, 'Marketing Medicine: The Image of the Early Modern Mountebank,' *Renaissance Studies* 15 (2001): 121–53; M. A. Katritzky, 'Quacksalber in den Schriften Christian Weises und Johann Kuhnaus: *Der Politische Quacksalber* (1693) und *Der Musicalische Quack=salber* (1700),' in *Poet und Praeceptor: Christian Weise (1642–1708) zum 300. Todestag*, ed. Peter Hesse (Dresden: Neisse-Verlag, 2009), 319–40.
55. Sclei, *Theosophische-Schrifften*, 121 (The Hague, KB: PH2762; Amsterdam, UB: OK 65-542). Breckling's references to Seth, the third son of Adam and Eve, and Malachi are obscure. For more on Seth and lore associated with him, see e.g. Flavius Josephus, *Judean Antiquities 1–4: Translation and Commentary*, ed. Louis H. Feldman (Leiden: Brill, 2000), bk. 1, para. 68–71, with copious notes. The Malachi reference would make more sense if emended to 3:3.
56. Sclei, *Theosophische-Schrifften*, index, s.v. 'Adeptus Lapidis Mystici.'
57. Sclei, *Theosophische-Schrifften*, 120–21. See Leviticus 21:23.
58. Sclei, *Theosophische-Schrifften*, 122 (The Hague, KB: PH2762).
59. Halle, AFS: MF 5, pos. 153–54; Wilhelm G. Goeters, 'Johann Overbeek in Cleve als Mitarbeiter an Gottfrieds Arnolds Kirchen- und Ketzer-Historie,' *Monatshefte für Rheinische Kirchengeschichte* 8 (1914): 3–20, on 19.
60. Breckling, *Christus Mysticus*, 13.
61. Sclei, *Theosophische-Schrifften*, 138. Compare Philippians 3:20–21.
62. Sclei, *Theosophische-Schrifften*, index, s.v. 'Processus Mysticus zur Wiedergeburt'; 541. See Hebrews 12:29.
63. Gotha, FB: Chart. A 297, p. 281. On Schardius, see Christian Schmitz, *Ratsbürgerschaft und Residenz: Untersuchungen zu Berliner Ratsfamilien, Heiratskreisen und sozialen Wandlungen im 17. Jahrhundert* (Berlin: De Gruyter, 2002), 127–30; Daniel Ernst Jablonski, *Christliche Gedächtnüß-Predigt, Als... Levin Schardius, ... Den 12. Januarii 1699. selig aus diesem Leben abgefordert, und den 19. darauf zu seiner Ruhestat gebracht worden* (Cölln a.d. Spree: Druckts Ulrich Liebpert, Churfürstl. Brandenb. Hoff-Buchdr., 1699).
64. Gotha, FB: Chart. A 297, p. 280.
65. Gotha, FB: Chart. A 297, p. 278.
66. Immediately prior to this passage, Breckling used a phrase common in late seventeenth-century alchemy and referred to Jan Baptist van Helmont as a 'philosopher by fire' (*Philosophus per ignem*); Gotha, FB: Chart. A 297, p. 278. Following in Helmont's footsteps, George Starkey (Eirenaeus Philalethes) also described himself

as a 'Philosopher by Fire'; see e.g. Newman and Principe, *Alchemy Tried in the Fire*, 99, 117.
67. E.g. Penman, *Cabala*, pl. 3, 'Mittel: Conjunctio.'
68. Gotha, FB: Chart. A 297, p. 247.
69. E.g. Shantz, *An Introduction to German Pietism*, ch. 5.
70. Gotha, FB: Chart. B 195, pp. 326–27. Breckling had been familiar with the *Wasserstein* since at least 1682; Breckling, *Christus Mysticus*, 16.
71. Christoph Friedrich Gayler, *Historische Denkwürdigkeiten der ehemaligen freien Reichsstadt, itzt Königlich Würtembergischen Kreisstadt, Reutlingen vom dritten Viertel des 16ten bis gegen die Mitte des 18ten Jahrhunderts. Nebst einem Anhang von 1789 bis 1803* (Reutlingen: Fleischhauer und Spohn, 1845), 261; Dieter Ising, 'Radikaler Pietismus in der frühen Korrespondenz Johann Albrecht Bengels,' *Pietismus und Neuzeit* 31 (2005): 152–95, on 183. Hoffstetter's letters to Breckling may be found in Gotha, FB: Chart. B 198, ff. 192r–217v; Hamburg, Staats- und Universitätsbibliothek (SUB): Cod. theol. 1894, pp. 249–50.
72. Hamburg, SUB: Cod. theol. 1894, pp. 249–50. On the woman alchemist in question, see Alexander Kraft, 'Dorothea Juliana Wallich (1657–1725) and Her Contributions to the Chymical Knowledge about the Element Cobalt,' in *Women in Their Element: Selected Women's Contributions to the Periodic System*, ed. Annette Lykknes and Brigitte van Tiggelen (Singapore: World Scientific, 2019), 57–69; Alexander Kraft, 'Dorothea Juliana Wallich, geb. Fischer (1657–1725), eine Alchemistin aus Thüringen,' *Genealogie: Deutsche Zeitschrift für Familienkunde* XXXIII/66 (2017): 539–55.
73. Halle, AFS: MF 5, pos. 151–52.
74. Halle, AFS: MF 5, pos. 159–60.
75. Halle, AFS: MF 5, pos. 151–52, 159–60; see also 137–38.
76. Significant passages of alchemical notes may be found in the following manuscripts: Hamburg, SUB: Cod. theol. 1894, pp. 299–314; Gotha, FB: Chart. B 962, ff. 158r–66v.

Chapter 8

1. For more on the Philadelphian Society, see Thune, *The Behmenists*, esp. ch. 2. For a more recent collective volume, see Hessayon, *Jane Lead*. On Leade's own Boehme-inspired spiritual alchemy, see e.g. Stefania Salvadori, 'The Restitution of "Adam's Angelical and Paradisiacal Body": Jane Lead's Metaphor of Rebirth and Mystical Marriage,' in Hessayon, *Jane Lead*, 143–65; Hirst, *Jane Leade*, ch. 3; Burkhard Dohm, *Poetische Alchimie: Öffnung zur Sinnlichkeit in der Hohelied- und Bibeldichtung von der protestantischen Barockmystik bis zum Pietismus* (Tübingen: Niemeyer, 2000), ch. 2, esp. 153–58. However, these discussions suffer from not taking into account the New Historiography of Alchemy; in this regard, only Dohm can be excused with reference to the early date of his study.

2. On the popularity of Philadelphian books in Germany, see Hans-Jürgen Schrader, *Literaturproduktion und Büchermarkt des radikalen Pietismus* (Göttingen: Vandenhoeck & Ruprecht, 1989).
3. The former two are included in what remains the standard English edition of Boehme's writings: [Dionysius Andreas Freher], 'An Illustration of the Deep Principles of Jacob Behmen, . . . in Thirteen Figures' and 'An Illustration of the Deep Principles of Jacob Behmen, . . . in Figures,' in Jacob Boehme, *The Works*, ed. William Law, 4 vols. (London: Printed for M. Richardson, in Pater-noster Row, 1764–81), towards the end of vol. 2 (ff. **Dd2r–4v) and vol. 3 (ff. 4B3r–4D2r), resp. The *Paradoxa, Emblemata* are now better known as Dionysius Andreas Freher, *The Paradoxical Emblems*, ed. Adam McLean (Edinburgh: Adam McLean, 1983).
4. Freher's autograph set also includes an additional contents volume I; London, DWL: Walton MSS I.1.5–13.
5. The exact date is known primarily due to the portraits made by Freher's disciple Jeremias Daniel Leuchter; e.g. London, BL: Add. MSS 5767–74, vol. A, f. 2r; London, Dr Williams's Library (DWL): Walton MS I.1.52a, loose frontispiece. Strangely, he was only baptised on 4 December—almost three months after his birth rather than the customary few days; see Charles A. Muses, *Illumination on Jacob Boehme: The Work of Dionysius Andreas Freher* (New York: King's Crown Press, 1951), 160, n. 10. On the family's history, see *DB*, s.v. 'Freher'; Dietrich Kornexl, 'Studien zu Marquard Freher (1565–1614): Leben, Werke und gelehrtengeschichtliche Bedeutung' (PhD thesis, Albert-Ludwigs-Universität Freiburg i.Br., 1967), ch. 1.
6. Elias von Steinmeyer, *Die Matrikel der Universität Altdorf*, 2 vols. (Würzburg: Königl. Universitätsdruckerei H. Stürtz, 1912), 1:341. On this now defunct university, see Horst Claus Recktenwald, 'Aufstieg und Niedergang der Universität Altdorf,' *Zeitschrift für Bayerische Landesgeschichte* 30 (1967): 242–63; Horst Claus Recktenwald, *Die fränkische Universität Altdorf*, 2nd ed. (Nuremberg: Spindler, 1990).
7. These exceedingly rare occasional publications are listed in the most comprehensive bibliography of German print productions during the seventeenth century: *Verzeichnis der im deutschen Sprachraum erschienenen Drucke des 17. Jahrhunderts*, http://www.vd17.de (Berlin: Gemeinsamer Bibliotheksverbund, 1966–), s.v. 'Freherus, Dionysius Andreas.' See also Leonard Forster, 'Deutsche Drucke des 17. Jahrhunderts in der Domkapitelbibliothek zu Durham/England,' *Wolfenbütteler Barock-Nachrichten* 16 (1989): 92–109, on 96.
8. Gustav Toepke and Paul Hintzelmann, *Die Matrikel der Universität Heidelberg*, 7 vols. (Heidelberg: Winter, 1884–1916), 2:358, 579.
9. Pelikan and Hotchkiss, *Creeds and Confessions*, 2:427–28.
10. Kühlmann, *Killy Literaturlexikon*, s.v. 'Freher, Dionysius Andreas.' Cecilia Muratori is currently preparing an entry on Freher for the *Verfasserlexikon*.
11. In his topographical catalogue of witnesses of the truth, Breckling listed Freher in the entry for Muscovy; Guido Naschert is currently preparing an annotated edition of this source. See also Gotha, FB: Chart. B 962, f. 29r; Amsterdam, BPH: M 519, pp. 41–42; Düsseldorf, LKA: 7 NL 015, Nr. 759, p. 66.

12. Gichtel, *Theosophia Practica*, 7:144.
13. Wrocław, BU: Ms. Akc. 1977/109, p. 161.
14. Wrocław, BU: Ms. Akc. 1977/109, p. 237.
15. Wrocław, BU: Ms. Akc. 1977/109, p. 269; Amsterdam, BPH: M 519, pp. 13–14; see also pp. 5–7.
16. Wrocław, BU: Ms. Akc. 1977/109, p. 547.
17. The Hague, KB: PH266 M140, no. 121, pp. 703–4.
18. Wrocław, BU: Ms. Akc. 1977/109, p. 566.
19. Compare Muses, *Illumination on Jacob Boehme*, 162–63, n. 33; see also 2 and 159, n. 7. By 1870, Walton had established the correct year: London, DWL: Walton MS I.1.53, verso of title page.
20. Martin, 'God's Strange Providence.' This is further confirmed in an unpublished letter to Überfeld, dated 22 August 1694; Wrocław, BU: Ms. Akc. 1977/109, p. 509.
21. Bruckner, *Bibliographical Catalogue*, no. 589.
22. Wrocław, BU: Ms. Akc. 1977/109, p. 595.
23. Muses, *Illumination on Jacob Boehme*, 16–18; Christopher Walton, *Notes and Materials for an Adequate Biography of the Celebrated Divine and Theosopher, William Law* (London: Printed for private circulation, 1854 [1848–61]), 631, 683, 687. See London, DWL: Walton MS I.1.4.
24. Donovan Dawe, *Skilbecks: Drysalters 1650–1950* (London: Skilbeck Brothers, 1950), 44–49.
25. E.g. Muses, *Illumination on Jacob Boehme*, 75–76, 151.
26. London, BL: Add. MSS 5767–74, vol. D, p. 243.
27. E.g. London, BL: Add. MSS 5767–74, vol. A, pp. 100, 168–77; vol. D, pp. 56–58, 161, 223–24; vol. F, pp. 24, 209; vol. H, p. 38.
28. London, BL: Add. MSS 5767–74, vol. F, pp. 231–33; vol. H, title page.
29. Wrocław, BU: Ms. Akc. 1977/109, p. 595.
30. London, BL: Add. MSS 5767–74, vol. D, p. 100.
31. London, BL: Add. MSS 5767–74, vol. D, p. 129.
32. London, BL: Add. MS 5784, f. 56r.
33. London, BL: Add. MSS 5767–74, vol. E, pp. 218–19; see also vol. A, pp. 190–208. Freher devoted an entire 'conference' of his *Sixteen Conferences* (no. 8) to 'the two eternal Principles, Annihilation and Transmutation'; see London, BL: Add. MSS 5775–82, vol. 3, f. 1r–93r, on f. 1r.
34. London, BL: Add. MSS 5767–74, vol. E, p. 220.
35. For Freher's short treatise 'The Growing of Vegetables (with Respect to their yearly Renewing in Spring-time),' see London, BL: Add. MSS 5767–74, vol. G, pp. 251–65.
36. London, BL: Add. MSS 5767–74, vol. A, f. 166r. The whole collection encompasses Add. MSS 5767–93.
37. Early references to the manuscripts may be found in e.g. *The Lives of Alchemystical Philosophers*, 2nd ed. (London: Printed by Macdonald and Son, Cloth Fair, for Lackington, Allen, & Co., 1815), 131; John Cochran, *A Catalogue of Manuscripts, in Different Languages, on Theology; . . . Now Selling (for Ready Money) at the Prices Affixed* (London, 1829), 28, no. 87.

38. The unfinished *Discourse of Nothing and Something* is least relevant: London, BL: Add. MSS 5767–74, vol. F.
39. London, BL: Add. MSS 5767–74, vol. H, title page.
40. London, BL: Add. MSS 5767–74, vol. H, pp. 48–49.
41. London, BL: Add. MSS 5767–74, vol. D, p. 66.
42. London, BL: Add. MSS 5767–74, vol. C, pp. 439–40.
43. London, BL: Add. MSS 5775–82, vol. 2, ff. 330v–32v, on f. 332r.
44. E.g. Jacob Boehme, *Beschreibung der drey Principien Göttliches Wesens* (Amsterdam, 1682), 226–28, 405 (TP 14:41–46, 20:9).
45. London, BL: Add. MSS 5767–74, vol. E, pp. 262–63.
46. London, BL: Add. MSS 5767–74, vol. C, pp. 439–40; vol. E, p. 262.
47. London, BL: Add. MSS 5767–74, vol. E, p. 66. For a magisterial account of medieval and early-modern cosmology, see Edward Grant, *Planets, Stars, Orbs: The Medieval Cosmos, 1200–1687*, 2 vols. (Cambridge: Cambridge University Press, 1996).
48. London, BL: Add. MSS 5767–74, vol. D, p. 32; vol. E, pp. 67–68.
49. London, BL: Add. MSS 5767–74, vol. H, p. 61; vol. E, p. 264. See 1 Corinthians 15:50.
50. London, BL: Add. MSS 5767–74, vol. C, p. 289. Compare Jacob Boehme, *Theosophische Send-Briefe, . . . Enthaltende Allerhand Gottseelige Ermahnungen zu wahrer Buß und Besserung* (Amsterdam, 1682), 131 (ET 28:12).
51. London, BL: Add. MSS 5767–74, vol. G, p. 210.
52. Boehme, *De signatura rerum*, 106 (SR 10:10); London, BL: Add. MSS 5767–74, vol. G, pp. 208–9.
53. Günther Bonheim, '"Lernet von ehe unterscheiden": Jacob Böhmes Mystik der Naturen,' in *Mystik und Natur: Zur Geschichte ihres Verhältnisses vom Altertum bis zur Gegenwart*, ed. Peter Dinzelbacher (Berlin: De Gruyter, 2009), 123–39, on 127; Pierre Deghaye, 'Die Natur als Leib Gottes in Jacob Böhmes Theosophie,' in Garewicz and Haas, *Gott, Natur und Mensch*, 71–111, on 93–94. Another English Behmenist also attached considerable weight to the term; Hanegraaff et al., *Dictionary*, s.v. 'Pordage, John,' esp. 968–69.
54. London, BL: Add. MSS 5767–74, vol. A, p. 135.
55. London, BL: Add. MSS 5767–74, vol. A, pp. 232, 271–72.
56. London, BL: Add. MS 5792, pp. 203–5.
57. London, BL: Add. MSS 5767–74, vol. A, p. 135.
58. London, BL: Add. MSS 5767–74, vol. A, pp. 135–36.
59. London, BL: Add. MSS 5767–74, vol. A, p. 141.
60. London, BL: Add. MSS 5767–74, vol. A, p. 138.
61. London, BL: Add. MSS 5767–74, vol. A, p. 143.
62. London, BL: Add. MSS 5767–74, vol. A, p. 142.
63. Boehme, *De signatura rerum*, chs. 7 and 10–12, according to London, BL: Add. MSS 5767–74, vol. G, p. 202.
64. *Lives of Alchemystical Philosophers*, 121–31. The first edition is now exceedingly rare: *The Lives of the Adepts in Alchemystical Philosophy* (London: Lackington, Allen & Co., 1814). On it see José Bouman, Theodor Harmsen, and Cis van Heertum, *'Tried and Tested': The Appreciation of Hermetic*

and *Alchemical Manuscripts from the 15th–20th Centuries*, exhibition catalogue (Amsterdam: Bibliotheca Philosophica Hermetica, 2004), 'Lives of the Adepts in Alchemystical Philosophy' entry. Like Mary Anne South, I have used the 1815 edition, which remained in her library until her dying day: *Catalogue of a Choice Selection of Books from the Valuable Library of the Late Mrs. Atwood* (Belfast: William Tait, 1912), no. 24.

65. For other versions, see Freher's autograph and a copy formerly owned by Muses; London, DWL: Walton MSS I.1.5–13, vol. G, pp. 273–332; Amsterdam, BPH: M 328, pp. 235–88. A largely reliable transcription of the British Library version is available on http://www.alchemywebsite.com/freher.html. The full text of Freher's 'Process' is also included in Walton, *Notes and Materials*, 319–28.

66. The attribution to Francis Barrett is unfounded; see Arthur Edward Waite, *Lives of Alchemystical Philosophers: Based on Materials Collected in 1815 and Supplemented by Recent Researches* (London: George Redway, 1888), 5; Francis X. King, *The Flying Sorcerer: Being the Magical and Aeronautical Adventures of Francis Barrett, Author of* The Magus (Oxford: Mandrake, 1992), 67. The latter suggests that J. P. Kellerman may have been responsible for the *Lives* volume.

67. This suggestion was first advanced in Bouman et al., *Tried and Tested*, 'Lives of the Adepts in Alchemystical Philosophy' entry.

68. *Lives of Alchemystical Philosophers*, 293–97, on 293; 60–65.

69. Walton, *Notes and Materials*, xxvii; [Mary Anne South], *A Suggestive Inquiry into the Hermetic Mystery with a Dissertation on the More Celebrated of the Alchemical Philosophers* (London: Trelawney Saunders, 1850), 54. For more on Brooke's Behmenist views, see B. J. Gibbons, *Gender in Mystical and Occult Thought: Behmenism and Its Development in England* (Cambridge: Cambridge University Press, 1996), 187–90.

70. *Lives of Alchemystical Philosophers*, 113 and 121–31, resp.

71. *Lives of Alchemystical Philosophers*, 131.

72. [South], *A Suggestive Inquiry*, 122 (n. 2), 124 (n. 1), 130–31 (n. 2), 500–2.

73. Boehme, *De signatura rerum*, 56 (SR 7:26); see also 130 (SR 11:19). Further, London, BL: Add. MSS 5767–74, vol. G, p. 205.

74. Boehme, *De signatura rerum*, 57 (SR 7:27).

75. London, BL: Add. MSS 5767–74, vol. G, pp. 226, 228–29, 231, 234–39, 241, 247.

76. London, BL: Add. MSS 5767–74, vol. G, p. 231.

77. London, BL: Add. MSS 5767–74, vol. G, p. 207.

78. London, BL: Add. MSS 5767–74, vol. D, p. 245.

79. London, BL: Add. MSS 5767–74, vol. D, p. 276; see also vol. E, pp. 99–100.

80. London, BL: Add. MSS 5767–74, vol. G, p. 202.

81. *Lives of Alchemystical Philosophers*, 121.

82. London, BL: Add. MSS 5767–74, vol. G, pp. 206–7. See *Lives of Alchemystical Philosophers*, 122; [South], *A Suggestive Inquiry*, 501–2. Compare Boehme, *De signatura rerum*, 85 (SR 8:53).

83. London, BL: Add. MSS 5767–74, vol. H, p. 48.

84. Interviewed by Mircea Eliade in 1952, Jung succinctly summarised this view; see Robert Hinshaw and Lela Fischli, eds., *C. G. Jung im Gespräch: Interviews, Reden, Begegnungen* (Zurich: Daimon, 1986), 76–86, on 79. For recent reiterations of this claim, see e.g. Christine Maillard, 'Eine Wissensform unter Heterodoxieverdacht: Die spekulative Alchemie nach 1600,' in *Heterodoxie in der frühen Neuzeit*, ed. Hartmut Laufhütte and Michael Titzmann (Tübingen: Niemeyer, 2006), 267–89, on 273. An older article on the subject is Karl Hoheisel, 'Christus und der philosophische Stein: Alchemie als über- und nichtchristlicher Heilsweg,' in *Die Alchemie in der europäischen Kultur- und Wissenschaftsgeschichte*, ed. Christoph Meinel (Wiesbaden: Harrassowitz, 1986), 61–84. See also the critical remarks on this 'soteriological' understanding of alchemy in Principe, 'Reflections on Newton's Alchemy,' 212–13.

85. E.g. Johann Hartprecht, *Der Verlangete Dritte Anfange Der Mineralischen Dinge, oder vom Philosophischen Saltz* (Amsterdam: Vor Christoffel Luycken, Buchverkauffer auff der Haarlemmer Creutzstraßen, 1656), f. A2r/v; Johann Michael von Löen, *Sod rikvon ve-serefa i.e. Das Geheimnuß der Verwesung und Verbrennung aller Dinge*, 2nd expanded ed. (Frankfurt a.M.: Bey Johann Friedrich Fleischer, 1733); *Microcosmische Vorspiele Des Neuen Himmels und der Neuen Erde*, 2nd rev. ed. (Amsterdam, 1744). The Hartprecht passage is discussed in Telle, *Alchemie und Poesie*, 2:942.

86. Forshaw, 'Ora et Labora,' 2:452–53, 458–59. Though perhaps overstating this point, it is made by Janacek, *Alchemical Belief*, 55–56. For a more judicious discussion that notes the debts of Waite and Jung to Khunrath, see Forshaw, 'Ora et Labora,' 1:262–64.

87. Boehme, *De signatura rerum*, 85 (SR 8:53).

88. For high-quality scans of Jung's personal copy of Boehme, *De Signatura Rerum*, see http://www.e-rara.ch/cgj/content/titleinfo/1500794.

89. London, BL: Add. MSS 5767–74, vol. B, pp. 196–97.

90. London, BL: Add. MSS 5767–74, vol. H, p. 46.

91. London, BL: Add. MSS 5767–74, vol. G, pp. 202, 206–7; *Lives of Alchemystical Philosophers*, 121–22; [South], *A Suggestive Inquiry*, 500–502; Mary Anne Atwood, *A Suggestive Inquiry into the Hermetic Mystery with a Dissertation on the More Celebrated of the Alchemical Philosophers*, 3rd ed. (Belfast: William Tait, 1920), 528–29.

92. Boehme, *De signatura rerum*, 118 (SR 10:48).

93. Boehme, *De signatura rerum*, 128 (SR 11:11).

94. London, BL: Add. MSS 5767–74, vol. E, p. 81.

95. London, BL: Add. MS 5792, pp. 69–70, 276. Gottfried Arnold was another author mentioned by name; e.g. London, BL: Add. MS 5783, f. 2r–15v.

96. London, BL: Add. MSS 5767–74, vol. G, p. 206.

97. London, BL: Add. MSS 5767–74, vol. G, p. 207.

98. London, BL: Add. MSS 5767–74, vol. G, p. 214.

99. London, BL: Add. MSS 5767–74, vol. G, pp. 207–8. See John 1:12.

100. Boehme, *De signatura rerum*, 56 (SR 7:25).

101. London, BL: Add. MSS 5767–74, vol. G, p. 205. See Genesis 3:15.

258 NOTES

102. London, BL: Add. MSS 5767–74, vol. G, p. 222; *Lives of Alchemystical Philosophers*, 124–25. See Boehme, *De signatura rerum*, 58–59, 128–29 (SR 7:34, 11:11).
103. *Lives of Alchemystical Philosophers*, 121.
104. [South], *A Suggestive Inquiry*, 500–2 and 130–31, resp.; see also 124, 493.

Chapter 9

1. *Lives of Alchemystical Philosophers*, 202–3. On Welling, see Telle, 'Zum *Opus magocabbalisticum*'; Petra Jungmayr, *Georg von Welling (1655–1727): Studien zu Leben und Werk* (Stuttgart: Franz Steiner, 1990).
2. Principe, 'A Revolution Nobody Noticed?'; Principe, 'The End of Alchemy?'; Principe, 'Transmuting Chymistry into Chemistry'. Principe mainly discusses London and Paris; for Leiden and Halle, see e.g. John C. Powers, *Inventing Chemistry: Herman Boerhaave and the Reform of the Chemical Arts* (Chicago: University of Chicago Press, 2012); Kevin Chang, 'Georg Ernst Stahl's Alchemical Publications: Anachronism, Reading Market, and a Scientific Lineage Redefined,' in Principe, *New Narratives*, 23–43.
3. Principe, *The Secrets of Alchemy*, ch. 5.
4. Though South only married in 1859, almost ten years after writing her *Suggestive Inquiry*, all later editions—the first appeared anonymously—give her name as Mary Anne Atwood, under which she became known to the great majority of her readers. Since she wrote the work before changing her name, as well as to emphasise potential differences between her youthful and mature views, I refer to her by both names as appropriate.
5. [South], *A Suggestive Inquiry*, 138.
6. Versluis, *Wisdom's Children*, chs. 5 and 7; Joscelyn Godwin, 'A Behemist Circle in Victorian England,' *Hermetic Journal* 15 (1992): 48–71.
7. Law owned Freher manuscripts, whose authorship his literary executors mistakenly attributed to their possessor. Walton rediscovered Freher as he researched Law's life; he then amassed what remains the most complete collection of Freher manuscripts, now held in London at Dr Williams's Library. Its availability there was announced in 'Literary Gossip,' *Athenaeum*, no. 2577 (17 March 1877): 353–54, on 353. Mostly ignored by scholarship, Penny was one of the leading Boehme interpreters of the Victorian era: A. J. Penny, *An Introduction to the Study of Jacob Boehme's Writings* (New York: Grace Shaw Duff, 1901). Muses noted her profound knowledge of Freher's works when he republished selections from her works in his short-lived *Jacob Boehme Society Quarterly*; see Charles A. Muses, 'Ann Judith Penny (née Brown) 1825–1893,' *Jacob Boehme Society Quarterly* 1 (1954): 4–5.
8. Providence, BU–JHL: A54785, no. 580, scan 8. The collection can be accessed online: https://repository.library.brown.edu/studio/collections/id_685. I provide the number of the manuscript (given in square brackets online) and the count of the digital scans.

9. London, DWL: Walton MS 189.3, nos. 153–83, no. 169, f. 2v. The foliation counts are my own; if a letter consists of more than one sheet, I indicate this by using Roman numerals.
10. Godwin, 'A Behemist Circle,' 52–53. On Greaves, see J. E. M. Latham, *Search for a New Eden. James Pierrepont Greaves (1777–1842): The Sacred Socialist and His Followers* (Madison, NJ: Fairleigh Dickinson University Press, 1999).
11. Providence, BU–JHL: A54785, no. 70, scan 12.
12. James Pierrepont Greaves, *New Theosophic Revelations: From the Ms. Journal* (London: John Chapman, 1847), e.g. 92, 97, 108, 123, 132, 135–37, 151, 155, 179, 254.
13. [Christopher Walton], ed., *On the Present, Past, and Future, with Regard to the Creation* (London: T. Ward & Co., 1847). The treatise contained therein is sometimes attributed to Greaves; Godwin, 'A Behemist Circle,' 58; Versluis, *Wisdom's Children*, 359. The only specialist on Greaves has called this into doubt: Latham, *Search for a New Eden*, 254, n. 24. The style makes it obvious that Walton could not have penned this treatise, yet he edited and published it.
14. London, DWL: Walton MS 189.3, no. 154, f. 1r.
15. [Walton], *On the Present*, 24–25.
16. London, DWL: Walton MS 189.3, no. 154, f. 1r/v.
17. [Walton], *On the Present*, 28.
18. London, DWL: Walton MS 189.3, no. 154, f. 2r/v. Pierre Poiret was a close associate of Antoinette Bourignon and eventually a prominent mystical author in his own right; on them, see Max Wieser, *Peter Poiret: Der Vater der romanischen Mystik in Deutschland. Zum Ursprung der Romantik in Deutschland* (Munich: Müller, 1932); Marjolaine Chevallier, *Pierre Poiret 1646–1719: Du protestantisme à la mystique* (Geneva: Labor et Fides, 1994); Mirjam de Baar, *'Ik moet spreken': Het spiritueel leiderschap van Antoinette Bourignon (1616–1680)* (Zutphen: Walburg, 2004).
19. London, DWL: Walton MS 189.3, no. 155, ff. 1v–2v.
20. London, DWL: Walton MS 189.3, no. 156, f. 2r/v.
21. Godwin, 'A Behemist Circle,' 58.
22. Louisa was still alive in 1907, despite some health issues, and may even have survived her sister; Providence, BU–JHL: A54785, no. 590, scan 8. In the years 1853 and 1854, Thomas and Mary Anne South corresponded with Christopher Walton regarding Louisa's husband, who apparently defrauded the family of significant sums of money (partly in stock-exchange speculations concerning 'South Australian Land Shares'), upon which her father 'cut him off from any possibility of sharing in right of his wife or children in what I may leave behind'; London, DWL: Walton MS 189.3, nos. 166–70, 178, on no. 167, f. 1r; no. 169, f. 2v.
23. London, DWL: Walton MS 189.3, no. 157, f. 1v; no. 160, f. 2v. Today, the street is simply known as Coram Street.
24. London, DWL: Walton MS 189.3, no. 153, f. 1r. This letter is undated; I have dated it based on its contents and links to other letters. It is possible that South's stay extended into the spring or even summer of 1849, though the letter must have been written before 18 July 1849.

25. Zoe Stansell, Manuscripts Reference Services, British Library, email message to author, 19 July 2016.
26. Walton, *Notes and Materials*, 258–459. In addition, on 461–91, Walton printed parts of vol. I (London, DWL: Walton MS I.1.13), the contents of Freher's *Fundamenta mystica*, omitting the page references.
27. Walton, *Notes and Materials*, 385. Sheet AAA corresponds to 361–68.
28. Walton, *Notes and Materials*, 319–28. The relevant sheets, SS and TT, must have been printed prior to AAA.
29. Walton, *Notes and Materials*, 489 (sheet RRR).
30. London, DWL: Walton MS 189.3, no. 161, f. 2r/v.
31. London, DWL: Walton MS 189.3, no. 171, ff. I1v–III1r. See Godwin, 'A Behemist Circle,' 57.
32. London, DWL: Walton MS 189.3, no. 154, f. 1r.
33. London, DWL: Walton MS 189.3, no. 158, f. 1r/v. For another instance of South comparing 'rail and steam' to 'the electric wire,' see [Thomas South and Mary Anne South], *Early Magnetism in Its Higher Relations to Humanity, as Veiled in the Poets and the Prophets* (London: H. Baillière, 1846), 104.
34. London, DWL: Walton MS 189.3, no. 159, ff. 1r, 2v. See also no. 154, f. 2v; no. 155, ff. 1r/v and 2v.
35. London, DWL: Walton MS 189.3, no. 156, f. 2r.
36. Alchemy is only mentioned as having been superseded by chemistry: [South and South], *Early Magnetism*, 36. In addition, on 65 they reproduced Heinrich Khunrath's owl, though they may also have encountered it in contexts other than Khunrath's alchemical writings. In a 1907 letter, however, Mary Anne Atwood did mention 'Kuhnrath's Owl'; Providence, BU–JHL: A54785, no. 593, scan 4. For more on the subject, see Joseph L. Rabinowitz, 'The Owl of Heinrich Khunrath: Its Origins and Significance,' *Chymia* 3 (1950): 243–50.
37. Atwood, *A Suggestive Inquiry*, (4), (37), (41). The pagination begins anew at the actual start of the treatise, hence the brackets.
38. Providence, BU–JHL: A54785, no. 698, scan 2. This remark would most likely refer to [South and South], *Early Magnetism*, 1–61.
39. [South and South], *Early Magnetism*, 21.
40. [South and South], *Early Magnetism*, 120.
41. Godwin, 'A Behemist Circle,' 55.
42. [Walton], *On the Present*, 24.
43. Christopher Walton, *An Introduction to Theosophy, or the Science of the 'Mystery of Christ,' That is, of Deity, Nature, and Creature* (London: John Kendrick, 1854), 498. See Versluis, *Wisdom's Children*, 115. On Walton's engagement with Spiritualism (in the nineteenth-century sense of the term), see Godwin, 'A Behemist Circle,' 60.
44. [South and South], *Early Magnetism*, 118.
45. [South and South], *Early Magnetism*, 107.
46. [South and South], *Early Magnetism*, 55–56.
47. [South and South], *Early Magnetism*, 8, 29.
48. [South and South], *Early Magnetism*, 16.

49. [South and South], *Early Magnetism*, 49.
50. J. Jeffrey Franklin, 'The Evolution of Occult Spirituality in Victorian England and the Representative Case of Edward Bulwer-Lytton,' in *The Ashgate Research Companion to Nineteenth-Century Spiritualism and the Occult*, ed. Tatiana Kontou and Sarah A. Wilburn (Farnham: Ashgate, 2012), 123–41, on 126. The literature on Mesmerism in Britain is vast; for a classic study, see e.g. Alison Winter, *Mesmerized: Powers of Mind in Victorian Britain* (Chicago: University of Chicago Press, 1998).
51. E.g. Providence, BU–JHL: A54785, no. 528, scan 7.
52. London, DWL: Walton MS 189.3, no. 157, ff. 1v–2v.
53. London, DWL: Walton MS 189.3, no. 160, f. 1r.
54. Providence, BU–JHL: A54785, no. 528, scan 6.
55. London, DWL: Walton MS 189.3, no. 160, f. 1v.
56. London, DWL: Walton MS 189.3, no. 163, f. 1r.
57. London, DWL: Walton MS 189.3, no. 172, f. 1v.
58. London, DWL: Walton MS 189.3, no. 174, f. 2v. The reference is likely to Walton, *Notes and Materials*, 658–63.
59. London, DWL: Walton MS 189.3, no. 179, f. 2r/v.
60. Jayne Elisabeth Archer, 'The Philosopher's Stone and the Key to All Mythologies: Mary Anne South, George Eliot and the Object of Knowledge,' in *Literary Bric-à-Brac and the Victorians: From Commodities to Oddities*, ed. Jonathon Shears and Jen Harrison (Farnham: Ashgate, 2013), 163–78, on 163.
61. Atwood, *A Suggestive Inquiry*, 'Introduction,' (1)–(64), on (5)–(8).
62. An announcement of Thomas's poem ('The Enigma of Alchemy and Œdipus Resolved. A Poem in Five Parts') was included at the back of [South], *A Suggestive Inquiry*, 533. For the surviving fragments, see Thomas South, 'The Enigma of Alchemy,' ed. Walter Leslie Wilmshurst, *The Quest* 10 (1919): 213–25. On 2 December, adverts for the *Suggestive Inquiry* appeared: 'New Works Published from the 14th to the 30th of November,' *Publisher's Circular* 13, no. 317 (2 December 1850): 386–96, on 389, s.v. 'Suggestive Inquiry'; 395, no. 1059. Staff at Oxford's Bodleian Library noted that the legal deposit examplar had arrived by late December 1850; Oxford, BL: Library Records c. 864, 'List of Books sent to Bodleian Library Dec. 28. 1850' (no pagination).
63. '[Classified Advertisements],' *Morning Post*, no. 24,005 (16 November 1850): 8.
64. Elizabeth Severn, 'Some Mystical Aspects of Alchemy,' *Journal of the Alchemical Society* 2 (May 1914): 110–19, on 118. For a copy bought at the exceptional price mentioned by Waite, see Invictus, 'Suggestive Inquiry into the Hermetic Mystery,' *Historic Magazine* 25 (1907): 224e. More than ten copies survive at public institutions to this day, most of them in England and Scotland.
65. Beyond occasional mentions, see Archer, 'The Philosopher's Stone'; Kerry E. Koitzsch, 'Mrs Atwood and the Utopian Tradition: A Nineteenth-Century Alchemist as Utopian Theorist,' in *The Individual and Utopia: A Multidisciplinary Study of Humanity and Perfection*, ed. Clint Jones and Cameron Ellis (Farnham: Ashgate, 2015), 99–114.
66. Franckenberg, *Via veterum sapientum*, 239–58.
67. [South], *A Suggestive Inquiry*, 262. For more on ancient theurgy and subtle bodies, see e.g. Addey, 'In the Light of the Sphere.'

68. [South], *A Suggestive Inquiry*, 462–63 (Los Angeles, Getty Research Institute [GRI]: Manly P. Hall Collection, QD25 .A89 1850). Manuscript corrections and later editions change 'initiation' to 'consummation' and emend 'exemplary' to read 'exemplar'.
69. [South], *A Suggestive Inquiry*, 20.
70. [South], *A Suggestive Inquiry*, 219.
71. [South], *A Suggestive Inquiry*, 205.
72. [South], *A Suggestive Inquiry*, 191.
73. [South], *A Suggestive Inquiry*, 188.
74. [South], *A Suggestive Inquiry*, 176.
75. [South], *A Suggestive Inquiry*, 238.
76. [South], *A Suggestive Inquiry*, 92.
77. South preferred to avoid the phrase 'mystical union,' though she employed near-synonyms, such as 'Divine union,' 'Divine Union,' 'Theurgic union,' and 'spiritual union'; e.g. [South], *A Suggestive Inquiry*, 169–70, 347, 237, 411.
78. [South], *A Suggestive Inquiry*, 416; [South and South], *Early Magnetism*, 118. In the appendix compiled for later editions, Atwood spoke of the 'individual Logos' or 'the λογος in man' (based on the prologue of John's Gospel, which established the identity of Christ and *logos*) as yet another variation on *Christus in nobis*; Atwood, *A Suggestive Inquiry*, 579, no. 101; 594, no. 171.
79. [South], *A Suggestive Inquiry*, 138. See 1 Corinthians 3:16–17 and 6:19, the former quoted in [South], *A Suggestive Inquiry*, 453. See further the appendix of later editions, which on various occasions explicitly refers to the latter verse as well as the *lapis-Christus* analogy: Atwood, *A Suggestive Inquiry*, 563, no. 11; 568, no. 35; 590, no. 147.
80. [South], *A Suggestive Inquiry*, 300.
81. [South], *A Suggestive Inquiry*, 54, 279–80, 290, 297.
82. Gotha, FB: Chart. A 297, p. 280.
83. [South], *A Suggestive Inquiry*, 493 (Los Angeles, GRI: QD25 .A89 1850). A manuscript correction emends 'Kuhnrath' to the correct spelling.
84. [South], *A Suggestive Inquiry*, 55; see also 47, 109, 116, 185, 289, 397, 459.
85. Atwood, *A Suggestive Inquiry*, 571, no. 58.
86. [South], *A Suggestive Inquiry*, 90 (emphasis added).
87. [South], *A Suggestive Inquiry*, 523.
88. See Galatians 3:27.
89. [South], *A Suggestive Inquiry*, 507. The 'dim beholding' alludes to 1 Corinthians 13:12.
90. South used cognates of deification, such as 'Divinization,' or paraphrases, including 'divine assimilation,' several times throughout her work; e.g. [South], *A Suggestive Inquiry*, 158–59, 246, 257, 335, 496.

Chapter 10

1. 'A Suggestive Inquiry into the Hermetic Mystery; with a Dissertation on the more Celebrated of the Alchemical Philosophers. Saunders' (review), Athenaeum, no. 1228 (10 May 1851): 497; Archer, 'The Philosopher's Stone,' 170, n. 32.
2. Ellic Howe, ed., *The Alchemist of the Golden Dawn: The Letters of the Revd W. A. Ayton to F. L. Gardner and Others 1886-1905* (Wellingborough: Aquarian Press, 1985), 50.
3. Both of these are preserved in London, Wellcome Collection Library (WCL): EPB/B/49072; DWL: Walton Collection, (W) C.6.9.
4. London, WCL: EPB/B/49072, flyleaf at the back.
5. For mention of 'a dirty old copy of "the Enquiry" which I secured from Watkins the bookseller' around 1900, see Providence, BU–JHL: A54785, no. 625, scan 4. It is with a great degree of understatement that Waite described Atwood as chasing these books 'for some years subsequently'; Arthur Edward Waite, 'The Hermetic Tradition,' *Occult Review* (1918): 44–46, on 44.
6. London, DWL: Walton MS 189.3, no. 162, f. 2r/v.
7. An announcement appeared in 'Literary Gossip,' 353.
8. 'Deaths,' *Hampshire Telegraph and Sussex Chronicle*, no. 3062 (12 June 1858): 5.
9. Rev. Atwood's first wife, Georgiana Moore, died on 13 May 1858; 'Deaths,' *Yorkshire Gazette* 40, no. 2039 (22 May 1858): 3.
10. Providence, BU–JHL: A54785, no. 675, scan 2.
11. [South], *A Suggestive Inquiry*, front flyleaf (Los Angeles, GRI: QD25.A89 1850). See *Catalogue of a Choice Selection*, no. 42. On Massey, see Jeffrey D. Lavoie, *A Search for Meaning in Victorian Religion: The Spiritual Journey and Esoteric Teachings of Charles Carleton Massey* (Bethlehem, PA: Lehigh University Press, 2014).
12. Atwood, *A Suggestive Inquiry*, (11), (13); Edward Maitland, *Anna Kingsford: Her Life, Letters, Diary and Work*, 2 vols. (Cambridge: Cambridge University Press, 2011), 2:242; see also 212–13 and esp. 222.
13. Mark S. Morrisson, *Modern Alchemy: Occultism and the Emergence of Atomic Theory* (Oxford: Oxford University Press, 2007), ch. 1; Alex Owen, *The Place of Enchantment: British Occultism and the Culture of the Modern* (Chicago: University of Chicago Press, 2004), 123–25.
14. Alfred Percy Sinnett, *Autobiography* (London: Theosophical History Centre, 1986), 38. For a complementary account, see Isabelle de Steiger, *Memorabilia: Reminiscences of a Woman Artist and Writer* (London: Rider, 1927), 237–38.
15. Providence, BU–JHL: A54785, no. 625, scan 2.
16. Waite's reminiscences regarding Sinnett after his death may be found in Ralph Shirley, 'Notes of the Month,' *Occult Review* 34 (1921): 65–73, on 69.
17. On Waite's early engagement with alchemy, see Gilbert, *A. E. Waite*, 92–96. On the unlikely path that led him from popular fiction to interest in all things occult, see Christine Ferguson, 'Reading with the Occultists: Arthur Machen, A. E. Waite, and the Ecstasies of Popular Fiction,' *Journal of Victorian Culture* 21 (2016): 40–55, on 44–48.

18. Arthur Edward Waite, 'A New Light of Mysticism: To the Editor of "Light,"' *Light* 8, no. 402 (1888): 461–62, on 461–62, nos. I and V, resp.
19. Waite, *Lives of Alchemystical Philosophers*, 6, 9, and 17, resp.; see also 14–17, 30, 34–37.
20. Arthur Edward Waite, 'What Is Alchemy? [First Paper.],' *The Unknown World* 1 (1894): 7–11, on 11. For a study on anonymity in Victorian publishing, see Ian Hesketh, *Victorian Jesus: J. R. Seeley, Religion, and the Cultural Significance of Anonymity* (Toronto: University of Toronto Press, 2017).
21. Waite, *Azoth*, 60.
22. Patience Sinnett, 'Alchemy as a Spiritual Science,' *Lucifer* 14 (1894): 211–18.
23. Lover of Philalethes, *A Short Enquiry concerning the Hermetic Art*, ed. William Wynn Westcott (London: Theosophical Publishing Society, 1894), 5, 12. Signed 'N. O. M.' (*Non Omnis Moriar*), Westcott's preface mentioned the 'survivor of the two authors' responsible for the *Suggestive Inquiry*, yet the 'Introduction to Alchemy' by 'S. S. D. D.' (*Sapientia Sapienti Dono Data*), that is, Florence Farr, simply referred to the author using the male pronoun.
24. Waite, *Lives of Alchemystical Philosophers*, 10–14; see also 24–25. It should be noted that Waite appears to have been unaware of Hitchcock's rare 1855 publication: Hitchcock, *Remarks upon Alchymists*.
25. Waite, *Azoth*, 72.
26. Sinnett, 'Alchemy as a Spiritual Science,' 211.
27. Sinnett, 'Alchemy as a Spiritual Science,' 211–12; see also 215.
28. [Alban Thomas Atwood and Mary Anne Atwood], 'A Review: "Arcana of Christianity," etc.,' *The Recipient* 2 (April 1868): 336–48, on 344.
29. Arthur Edward Waite, 'What is Alchemy? [Second Paper.],' *The Unknown World* 1 (1894): 80–84, on 82.
30. Isabelle de Steiger, 'The Hermetic Mystery,' *Journal of the Alchemical Society* 2 (November 1913): 17–32, on 32.
31. Evelyn Underhill, *Mysticism: A Study in the Nature and Development of Man's Spiritual Consciousness* (London: Methuen, 1911), 167–77; also 122, 272, 480, 500, 517. See further Evelyn Underhill, 'A Defence of Magic,' *Fortnightly Review* 82 (1907): 754–65; Evelyn Stuart Moore [Underhill], 'Magic and Mysticism To-day,' *Hibbert Journal* 6 (1908): 373–86. For a scholarly account, see Michael Stoeber, 'Evelyn Underhill on Magic, Sacrament, and Spiritual Transformation,' *Worship* 77 (2003): 132–51.
32. Waite and most critics of Darwin motivated by religious sentiment favoured theories inspired by Jean-Baptiste Lamarck with their emphasis on 'the autonomous striving of the individual'; see Egil Asprem, *The Problem of Disenchantment: Scientific Naturalism and Esoteric Discourse, 1900–1939* (Leiden: Brill, 2014), 185–98, on 191; see also 450–52. For more on this context, see James R. Moore, *The Post-Darwinian Controversies: A Study of the Protestant Struggle to Come to Terms with Darwin in Great Britain and America 1870–1900* (Cambridge: Cambridge University Press, 1979). Contemporary Spiritualists also formulated 'models of progressive spiritual evolution'; see e.g. Franklin, 'The Evolution of Occult Spirituality,' 129. Conversely, some leading proponents of evolution, including Darwin's co-discoverer Alfred Russell Wallace, closely engaged with Spiritualism; e.g. Peter Pels, 'Spiritual Facts and

Super-Visions: The "Conversion" of Alfred Russel Wallace,' *Etnofoor* 8 (1995): 69–91; Christine Ferguson, 'Other Worlds: Alfred Russel Wallace and Cross-cultural Spiritualism,' *Victorian Review* 41 (2015): 177–91.
33. Waite, *Azoth*, 88.
34. Waite, *Azoth*, 10 and 'Perfection Consists' (prior to Contents); see also 10–11, 50–51, 79–80, 178–79.
35. Waite, *Azoth*, 51.
36. Waite, *Azoth*, 60.
37. Waite, *Azoth*, 113–14.
38. Waite, *Azoth*, 88.
39. Providence, BU–JHL: A54785, no. 522, scan 16.
40. Providence, BU–JHL: A54785, nos. 111, scans 4–5; 120, scan 3.
41. Waite, *Azoth*, 142.
42. Waite, *Azoth*, 191.
43. Waite, *Azoth*, 141.
44. Waite, *Azoth*, 136, 205; see also 50, 117.
45. Steiger, *Memorabilia*, 236. The year is mentioned on 234; see also 188–89.
46. Godwin, 'A Behemist Circle,' 48–53.
47. Steiger, *Memorabilia*, 189.
48. Providence, BU–JHL: A54785, no. 609, scan 1. Pencilled notes question whether this missive dated from 1911, 1904, or 1903, yet the most likely date for this letter is 14 January 1910, a Friday, as noted in the letter: Atwood did not live to see 1911, and the date rendered doubtful by a correction can be identified using calendars and a process of elimination.
49. Steiger, *Memorabilia*, 281; the month is mentioned on 282. For the year, see Gilbert's entry in the *Oxford Dictionary of National Biography* (*ODNB*), http://www.oxforddnb.com (Oxford: Oxford University Press, 2004 ff.), s.v. 'Steiger, Isabelle de.'
50. Morrisson, *Modern Alchemy*, 136–38.
51. Providence, BU–JHL: A54785, no. 588, scans 3–4. See Isabelle de Steiger, *On a Gold Basis: A Treatise on Mysticism*, 2nd ed. (London: Rider, 1909), 94, 126–36, 267.
52. Steiger, *Gold Basis*, xiii–xv.
53. Steiger, *Gold Basis*, 342.
54. Steiger, *Gold Basis*, 140.
55. Steiger, *Gold Basis*, 138.
56. Steiger, *Gold Basis*, 112 (with the alternative spelling 'arch history'), 133, 199, 210.
57. Steiger, *Gold Basis*, 137; see also 173, 190.
58. Providence, BU–JHL: A54785, no. 128, scans 3, 5; see also nos. 375, 'On Alchemy,' scan 1; 520, scan 4–5; 598 (26 May 1908), scan 6. Compare e.g. Steiger, *Gold Basis*, 347.
59. Steiger, *Gold Basis*, 23; see also 99, 110–11.
60. Steiger, *Gold Basis*, 68.
61. Steiger, *Gold Basis*, 142–43.
62. Steiger, *Gold Basis*, 130.
63. Steiger, *Gold Basis*, 104–5.

64. Steiger, *Gold Basis*, 26 (emphasis in the original).
65. Steiger, *Gold Basis*, 297.
66. Steiger, *Gold Basis*, 320.
67. Steiger, *Gold Basis*, 224. Compare 1 Corinthians 15:22 (KJV): 'For as in Adam all die, even so in Christ shall all be made alive.'
68. Steiger, *Gold Basis*, 221 (emphasis in the original).
69. Steiger, *Gold Basis*, 260; see also 102.
70. Steiger, *Gold Basis*, 49 (emphases in the original).
71. Steiger, *Gold Basis*, 12.
72. Steiger, *Gold Basis*, 18; see also 134.
73. Steiger, *Gold Basis*, 122–23; see also 67.
74. Steiger, *Gold Basis*, 201.
75. Steiger, *Gold Basis*, 187; see also 220–21.
76. Steiger, *Gold Basis*, 13 (emphasis in the original).
77. Gilbert, *A. E. Waite*, 151–52. For summaries of Waite's developing understanding of alchemy, see Principe and Newman, 'Some Problems,' 395; Morrisson, *Modern Alchemy*, 57–58.
78. Isabelle de Steiger, 'To the Editor of the *Occult Review*,' *Occult Review* 14 (1911): 346–49.
79. A. E. Waite, 'To the Editor of the *Occult Review*,' *Occult Review* 15 (1912): 50.
80. H. Stanley Redgrove, 'The Quest for Truth in Alchemy,' *Occult Review* 42 (1928): 42–45, on 44; Gilbert, *A. E. Waite*, 151–52. For more on this society, see e.g. Morrisson, *Modern Alchemy*, 49–64, 205–8; Asprem, *The Problem of Disenchantment*, 248–59.
81. Steiger, 'The Hermetic Mystery.' A note on the Society's meeting of 8 October 1915 and the announcement of the publication of Atwood's essay under Isabelle de Steiger's editorship may be found in 'The Alchemical Society,' *Light* 35 (1915): 509. See also H. Stanley Redgrove, 'The Alchemical Society,' *Occult Review* (1918): 49–50. No fewer than five rivalling understandings of alchemy within the Alchemical Society are discussed in Morrisson, *Modern Alchemy*, 57–59. For an edition, see R. A. Gilbert, ed., *Journal of the Alchemical Society 1913-1915* (Swindon: Imagier, 2017).
82. Steiger, 'The Hermetic Mystery,' 21–25. Compare e.g. Providence, BU–JHL: A54785, no. 528, scans 6–7.
83. Steiger, *Gold Basis*, 158; see also 145.
84. A. W. H. Bates, *Anti-vivisection and the Profession of Medicine in Britain: A Social History* (London: Palgrave Macmillan, 2017).
85. See Waite's observation that 'Mrs. Atwood' had 'recognised something beyond mesmerism' in alchemy; Severn, 'Some Mystical Aspects,' 118.
86. Steiger, 'The Hermetic Mystery,' 23.
87. Providence, BU–JHL: A54785, no. 531, scan 20 (note that the same number is also used for a different letter dated March 1903); see further nos. 663, scans 2–3; 443, scan 16.
88. Providence, BU–JHL: A54785, no. 116 (20 August 1908), scan 4; see also no. 610 (9 November 1908), scan 8.
89. Atwood, *A Suggestive Inquiry*, (13); *ODNB*, s.v. 'Steiger, Isabelle de.'

90. Atwood, *A Suggestive Inquiry*, (28)–(30), (38)–(49), on (38)–(39). See [Atwood and Atwood], 'Arcana of Christianity.'
91. Walter Leslie Wilmshurst, 'The Later Mysticism of Mrs. Atwood,' 2 pts., *The Quest* 10–11 (1919): pt. 1, 487–507; pt. 2, 31–53, on 494–97; 33–36, 40–42, 51–53. In Wilmshurst's introduction, a vague statement on reincarnation, which Atwood supposedly 'entirely accepted as a fact, but not as a hope,' may betray an effort to portray her in ways better suited to her occultist readership; see Atwood, *A Suggestive Inquiry*, (18). Most Victorians viewed the Buddhist doctrine of metempsychosis 'with something little short of horror'; Philip C. Almond, *The British Discovery of Buddhism* (Cambridge: Cambridge University Press, 1988), 84. Further research is needed to better understand Atwood's stance on Christianity both in the context of her time and as it changed through the course of her long life. For Atwood, there clearly was a tension between continued insistence on the veracity of the Gospels and an unwillingness to take them literally; see e.g. Providence, BU–JHL: A54785, no. 108, scans 2–3. Despite this, she repeatedly criticised the liberal theology of the Broad Church movement; e.g. nos. 450, scan 4; 521, scans 3–4; 621, scans 1–3; 625, scans 11–12; 631, scans 7–9. In view of her biography and status as a clergyman's widow who remained involved in the local church community, it would be no injustice to characterise Atwood as a devout, if idiosyncratic, Christian.
92. In a footnote, Wilmshurst mentioned that her 'private . . . papers' were 'now in my care'; Atwood, *A Suggestive Inquiry*, (46).
93. I am grateful to the collector S. Brown for sharing photographs of these manuscripts with me.
94. Providence, BU–JHL: A54785, no. 119, scans 4–5.
95. Atwood, *A Suggestive Inquiry*, 580, no. 103. In what is probably a joint publication under her husband's initials, the couple discuss Swedenborg and alchemy: [Atwood and Atwood], 'Arcana of Christianity.'
96. Mark S. Morrisson, 'The Periodical Culture of the Occult Revival: Esoteric Wisdom, Modernity and Counter-public Spheres,' *Journal of Modern Literature* 31, no. 2 (2008): 1–22.
97. Atwood, *A Suggestive Inquiry*, 586, no. 126.
98. Providence, BU–JHL: A54785, no. 117, scan 3. Such a view had already been articulated by William Law; see Alan Gregory, ' "No New Truths of Religion": William Law's Appropriation of Jacob Boehme,' in Hessayon and Apetrei, *An Introduction to Jacob Boehme*, 142–61, on 144. It was further disseminated by Walton, *Notes and Materials*, e.g. 80 and esp. 558. In the twentieth century, this claim was debated by scholars but ultimately dismissed for want of evidence; for a summary still coloured by national pride, see Wollgast, *Philosophie in Deutschland*, 727–40.
99. See Cecilia Muratori, *The First German Philosopher: The Mysticism of Jakob Böhme as Interpreted by Hegel*, trans. Richard Dixon and Raphaëlle Burns (Dordrecht: Springer, 2016).
100. Atwood, *A Suggestive Inquiry*, 577, no. 90 (emphases in the original).

101. Atwood, *A Suggestive Inquiry*, 584, no. 117 (emphasis in the original).
102. Providence, BU–JHL: A54785, no. 160: 'Theurgy,' scan 9.
103. Providence, BU–JHL: A54785, no. 625, scans 8–9.
104. Providence, BU–JHL: A54785, no. 594, scans 3–4.
105. Providence, BU–JHL: A54785, no. 531 (8 February 1903), scans 18–19; see also e.g. nos. 67, scan 8; 121, scan 2; 588, scan 2; 591, scan 3. Compare John 3:5a.7b.
106. Providence, BU–JHL: A54785, no. 705: 'The Stone,' f. 3.
107. Providence, BU–JHL: A54785, no. 531, scan 13. See also Wilmshurst, 'The Later Mysticism of Mrs. Atwood,' pt. 1, 496–98.
108. Providence, BU–JHL: A54785, no. 506, scan 7; see also scan 10.
109. Providence, BU–JHL: A54785, no. 529, scan 2.
110. Providence, BU–JHL: A54785, no. 705: 'The Stone,' ff. 2, 4.
111. Providence, BU–JHL: A54785, no. 613, scan 2. An earlier draft with more corrections is preserved as no. 129, scans 2–3. For yet another version, see no. 614, scan 3. Compare Romans 8:17.
112. Providence, BU–JHL: A54785, no. 591, scan 3.
113. Providence, BU–JHL: A54785, no. 705: 'The Stone,' f. 2. See Genesis 3:21.
114. Steiger, *Gold Basis*, 51–52. Compare John 1:29 (KJV): 'Behold the Lamb of God, which taketh away the sin of the world.'
115. Providence, BU–JHL: A54785, no. 705: 'The Stone,' f. 3.
116. Hans Lassen Martensen, *Jacob Boehme: His Life and Teaching. Or Studies in Theosophy*, trans. T. Rhys Evans (London: Hodder and Stoughton, 1885), 31 (emphases in the original). Compare Providence, BU–JHL: A54785, no. 185, scans 2–4. On Martensen's Boehme monograph, see George Pattison, 'H. L. Martensen on Jacob Boehme,' in Hessayon and Apetrei, *An Introduction to Jacob Boehme*, 244–62.
117. Atwood, *A Suggestive Inquiry*, (59). Compare Martensen, *Jacob Boehme*, 32; Providence, BU–JHL: A54785, no. 185, scan 4.
118. Atwood, *A Suggestive Inquiry*, 573, no. 69.
119. Atwood, *A Suggestive Inquiry*, 562, no. 5.
120. Atwood, *A Suggestive Inquiry*, 571, no. 56.
121. Providence, BU–JHL: A54785, no. 598 (26 May 1908), scans 6–7.
122. Atwood, *A Suggestive Inquiry*, 365. See 1 Corinthians 15:50.
123. Atwood, *A Suggestive Inquiry*, 564, no. 20.
124. London, BL: Add. MSS 5767–74, vol. D, p. 264.
125. Atwood, *A Suggestive Inquiry*, 568, no. 34.
126. Providence, BU–JHL: A54785, nos. 590, scan 10; 578, scan 6.
127. Providence, BU–JHL: A54785, no. 595, scan 4 (emphases are underlined in the original). The parenthetical remark unfortunately skips over some words that likely would have addressed the reversal of the Fall.
128. Providence, BU–JHL: A54785, no. 594, scan 6.
129. Providence, BU–JHL: A54785, no. 609, scan 4.

Epilogue

1. E.g. Lawrence M. Principe, *Alchemy and Chemistry: Breaking Up and Making Up (Again and Again). Dibner Library Lecture, December 11, 2014* (Washington, D.C.: Smithsonian Libraries, 2017).
2. Zuber, 'Jacob Böhme and Alchemy,' esp. 279–84.
3. Hitchcock, *Remarks upon Alchymists*, 11; see also 30.
4. Waite, *Azoth*, 60.
5. E.g. Newman, *Newton the Alchemist*, 216. The phrase is also used in other fields of learning; sometimes it appears with qualifiers such as 'almost' (*paene*) or 'nearly' (*fere*).
6. Principe and Newman, 'Some Problems,' 401–4, 408–12.
7. The development outlined here can already be observed to have taken place in the work of Hereward Tilton, who has a background in Jungian psychoanalysis. In 2003 he still endorsed a very broad concept of spiritual alchemy with the aim of defending Jung; by 2012 he drew attention to the existence of several different kinds of alchemies that might be subsumed under the umbrella term ' "spiritual" alchemical traditions': Tilton, *The Quest for the Phoenix;* Tilton, 'Alchymia Archetypica,' 180.
8. On religionism and the study of esotericism, see Hanegraaff, *Esotericism and the Academy*, esp. 295–314.
9. Waite, *Azoth*, 60; Taylor, *The Alchemists*, 227–28; Principe and Newman, 'Some Problems,' 399–400.
10. Neugebauer, 'The Study of Wretched Subjects.'

Works Cited

Manuscript and Archival Sources

Amsterdam
Bibliotheca Philosophica Hermetica (now Embassy of the Free Mind): M 328, M 519.

Berlin
Staatsbibliothek Berlin—Preußischer Kulturbesitz: Ms. germ. fol. 142; Ms. germ. fol. 1070; Ms. germ. quart. 1525.

Copenhagen
Kongelige Bibliotek: Thott 49 oktav.

Durham, NC
Duke University Libraries: Harold Jantz Collection, Bound MS 148.

Düsseldorf
Landeskirchliches Archiv der Evangelischen Kirche im Rheinland: Nachlass Prof. J. F. Goeters, 7 NL 015, Nr. 720; Nr. 759.

Erfurt
Augustinerkloster, Bibliothek des Evangelischen Ministeriums: Msc 21.

Görlitz
Oberlausitzische Bibliothek der Wissenschaften: LA III 409.

Gotha
Forschungsbibliothek der Universität Erfurt: Chart. A 291; Chart. A 297; Chart. A 306; Chart. A 310; Chart. A 413; Chart. B 195; Chart. B 197–98; Chart. B 962.

The Hague
Koninklijke Bibliotheek: 72 E 14; Ritman Kerncollectie, PH261 M135; PH266 M140; PH317 M197; PH404 M315.

Halle
Archiv der Franckeschen Stiftungen: H B 17 a–b; H G 1; MF 5.
Universitäts- und Landesbibliothek: 14 B 22; 23 B 11.

Hamburg
Staats- und Universitätsbibliothek: Cod. theol. 1894.

Heidelberg
Universitätsbibliothek: Cod. Pal. Germ. 782.

Karlsruhe
Badische Landesbibliothek: Cod. Allerheiligen 3.

Leiden
Universiteitsbibliotheek: BPL 157 B.

Leipzig
Universitätsbibliothek: Cod. mag. 24; Ms 0356.

London
British Library: Add. MSS 5767–84; Add. MS 5792; Sloane MS 2709.
Dr Williams's Library: Walton MSS I.1.4–13, Walton MS I.1.52a, Walton MSS I.1.52–55; Walton MS 189.3.

Manchester
John Rylands Library: Latin MS 77.

Munich
Bayerische Staatsbibliothek: Cgm 4416. 9; Nachlässe, Frankenbergiana, no. 91, vol. 7.

Oxford
Bodleian Library: Library Records c. 864.

Providence, RI
Brown University, John Hay Library: A54785.

Schleswig
Landesarchiv Schleswig-Holstein: Abt. 7, Nr. 2059:3.

Utrecht
Utrechts Archief: 711—Burgerlijke stand gemeente Utrecht, nr. 130.

Wolfenbüttel
Herzog August Bibliothek: Cod. Guelf. 65 Noviss. 4°.

Wrocław
Biblioteka Uniwersytecka: Ms. Akc. 1975/252; Ms. Akc. 1975/255; Ms. Akc. 1975/271; Ms. Akc. 1977/109.

Zurich
Zentralbibliothek: Sammlung Oskar R. Schlag, SCH R 809.

Printed and Electronic Sources

Abbri, Ferdinando. 'Alchemy and Chemistry: Chemical Discourses in the Seventeenth Century.' *Early Science and Medicine* 5 (2000): 214–26.

Addey, Crystal. 'In the Light of the Sphere: The "Vehicle of the Soul" and Subtle-Body Practices in Neoplatonism.' In Samuel and Johnston, *Religion and the Subtle Body*, 149–67.
Adelung, Johann Christoph. *Geschichte der menschlichen Narrheit*. 7 vols. Leipzig: In der Weygandschen Buchhandlung, 1785–89.
Aker, Gudrun. 'Johann Jakob Zimmermann 1642–1693: Ein Prophet des Tausendjährigen Reiches.' In *Vaihinger Köpfe: Biographische Porträts aus fünf Jahrhunderten*. Edited by Lothar Behr, Otto-Heinrich Elias, Manfred Scheck, and Ernst Eberhard Schmidt, 71–88. Vaihingen: Selbstverlag der Stadt Vaihingen an der Enz, 1993.
Åkerman, Susanna. *Rose Cross over the Baltic: The Spread of Rosicrucianism in Northern Europe*. Leiden: Brill, 1998.
'The Alchemical Society.' *Light* 35 (1915): 509.
Almond, Philip C. *The British Discovery of Buddhism*. Cambridge: Cambridge University Press, 1988.
Andersson, Bo, Leigh T. I. Penman, Lucinda Martin, and Andrew Weeks, eds. *Jacob Böhme and His World*. Leiden: Brill, 2019.
Andreae, Johann Valentin. *Rosenkreuzerschriften*. Edited by Roland Edighoffer. Stuttgart-Bad Cannstatt: Frommann-Holzboog, 2010.
Archer, Jayne Elisabeth. 'The Philosopher's Stone and the Key to All Mythologies: Mary Anne South, George Eliot and the Object of Knowledge.' In *Literary Bric-à-Brac and the Victorians: From Commodities to Oddities*. Edited by Jonathon Shears and Jen Harrison, 163–78. Farnham: Ashgate, 2013.
Arndt, Johann. *Vier Bücher Von wahrem Christenthumb*. 4 vols. Magdeburg: Durch Joachim Böel, In verlegung Johan Francken, 1610.
Arndt, Johann. *Das große Geheimniß der Menschwerdung des ewigen Worts. In einem Sendschreiben an seinen guten Freund Erasmum Wolfartum, Notar. Publ. Caes. etc.* N.p., 1676.
Arnold, Gottfried. *Fortsetzung und Erläuterung oder Dritter und Vierdter Theil der unpartheyischen Kirchen- und Ketzer-Historie*. Frankfurt a.M.: Bey Thomas Fritschens sel. Erben, 1729. First published 1700.
Artis auriferae, quam chemiam vocant, volumen primum: quod continet Turbam Philosophorum. Basel: Excudebat Conr. Waldkirch, Expensis Claudii de Marne, et Joan. Aubry, 1593.
Asprem, Egil. *The Problem of Disenchantment: Scientific Naturalism and Esoteric Discourse, 1900–1939*. Leiden: Brill, 2014.
[Atwood, Alban Thomas, and Mary Anne Atwood]. 'A Review: "Arcana of Christianity," etc.' *The Recipient* 2 (April 1868): 336–48.
Atwood, Mary Anne. *A Suggestive Inquiry into the Hermetic Mystery with a Dissertation on the More Celebrated of the Alchemical Philosophers*. 3rd ed. Belfast: William Tait, 1920. First published 1850.
Baar, Mirjam de. *'Ik moet spreken': het spiritueel leiderschap van Antoinette Bourignon (1616–1680)*. Zutphen: Walburg, 2004.
Bach, Jeff. *Voices of the Turtledoves: The Sacred World of Ephrata*. University Park: Pennsylvania State University Press, 2002.
Baier, Johann Wilhelm. *Catalogus librorum theologicorum . . . quibus suam olim bibliothecam B. Jo. Guilielmus Baierus . . . instruxerat*. Altdorf: Prostant exemplaria catalogi in bibliopolio sub iisdem aedibus, 1731.

Baier, Karl. *Meditation und Moderne: Zur Genese eines Kernbereichs moderner Spiritualität in der Wechselwirkung zwischen Westeuropa, Nordamerika und Asien*. 2 vols. Würzburg: Königshausen & Neumann, 2009.

Barnes, Robin Bruce. *Prophecy and Gnosis: Apocalypticism in the Wake of the Lutheran Reformation*. Stanford: Stanford University Press, 1988.

Bates, A. W. H. *Anti-Vivisection and the Profession of Medicine in Britain: A Social History*. London: Palgrave Macmillan, 2017.

Baur, Jörg. 'Ubiquität.' In *Creator est Creatura: Luthers Christologie als Lehre von der Idiomenkommunikation*. Edited by Oswald Bayer and Benjamin Gleede, 186–301. Berlin: De Gruyter, 2007.

Becker, Jörg Georg, and Nilüfer Krüger. *Die theologischen Handschriften der Staats- und Universitätsbibliothek Hamburg*. 4 vols. Hamburg: Hauswedell, 1975–98.

Berns, Jörg Jochen. 'Peregrinatio academica und Kavalierstour: Bildungsreisen junger Deutscher in der Frühen Neuzeit.' In *Rom—Paris—London: Erfahrung und Selbsterfahrung deutscher Schriftsteller und Künstler in den fremden Metropolen*. Edited by Conrad Wiedemann, 155–81. Stuttgart: Metzler, 1988.

Beyer, Hartmut, Jörn Münkner, Katrin Schmidt, and Timo Steyer. 'Bibliotheken im Buch: Die Erschließung von privaten Büchersammlungen der Frühneuzeit über Auktionskataloge.' In *Kodikologie und Paläographie im Digitalen Zeitalter 4*. Edited by Hannah Busch, Franz Fischer, and Patrick Sahle, 43–70. Norderstedt: BoD, 2017.

[Biedermann, Benedict]. *Theologia Weigelii. Das ist: Offentliche Glaubens Bekändtnüß*. Newstatt [Magdeburg]: Bey Johann Knuber [Johann Francke], 1618.

Block, Gerard. *Bibliotheca Smidsbergiana, sive catalogus insignium et rarissimorum... non solum typis editi, verum etiam manuscripta exima*. The Hague: Apud Gerardum Block, Bibliopolam, 1732.

Boehme, Jacob. *Bedencken Uber Esaiae Stiefels Büchlein: Von Dreyerley Zustandt des Menschen, unnd dessen Newen Geburt. Geschrieben Anno Christi 1621*. [Amsterdam]: [Johannes Janssonius], 1639.

Boehme, Jacob. *Beschreibung der drey Principien Göttliches Wesens*. Amsterdam, 1682.

Boehme, Jacob. '*Clavis* oder Schlüssel. Das ist: Eine Erklärung der vornehmsten Puncten und Wörtern in diesen Schriften.' In *Quaestiones theosophicae, oder Betrachtung Göttlicher Offenbarung, was GOTT, Natur und Creatur, sowol Himmel, Hölle und Welt, samt allen Creaturen sind*, 75–120. [Leiden?], 1730.

Boehme, Jacob. *De signatura rerum, Das ist: Von der Gebuhrt und Bezeichnung aller Wesen*. Amsterdam, 1682.

Boehme, Jacob. *De tribus principiis, oder Beschreibung der Drey Principien Göttliches Wesens (Of the Three Principles of Divine Being, 1619)*. Translated by Andrew Weeks. Leiden: Brill, 2019.

Boehme, Jacob. *Epistolae theosophicae, oder Theosophische Send-Briefe*. [Leiden?], 1730.

Boehme, Jacob. *Erste Apologia wider Balthasar Tilken: Eine Verantwortung des Authoris*. Amsterdam: Gedruckt bey Christoffel Cunradus, Vor Henricus Betkius, 1677.

Boehme, Jacob. *Josephus redivivus: Das ist Die Uberaus Lehr und Trostreiche Historia von dem Ertzvatter Joseph*. Amsterdam: [Johann and Siegfried Saccus] zu finden bey Veit Heinrichs Boeckverkoper, 1631.

Boehme, Jacob. 'Metapsychica de terrestri et coelesti mysterio, ex cognitione mysterii magni concepta, contemplatio.' In Franckenberg, *Trias mystica*, 65–98.

Boehme, Jacob. *Mysterium magnum, Oder Erklärung über das Erste Buch Mosis*. 2nd, corrected ed. Amsterdam: Auff Kosten Henrici Betkii, und Consorten, 1678.
Boehme, Jacob. *Theosophia . . . Oder: Alle Werke*. Edited by [Johann Otto Glüsing]. 2 vols. [Hamburg/Altona], 1715.
Boehme, Jacob. *Theosophische Send-Briefe, . . . Enthaltende Allerhand Gottseelige Ermahnungen zu wahrer Buß und Besserung*. Amsterdam, 1682.
Boehme, Jacob. *Theosophische Send-Schreiben*. Amsterdam: Verlegt durch Henrico Betkio, 1658.
Boehme, Jacob. *Von der Gnaden-Wahl, oder dem Willen Gottes über die Menschen*. Amsterdam: Auff kosten Henrici Betkii verlegt, und bey Christoff Cunraden gedruckt, 1665.
Boehme, Jacob. *Von der Menschwerdung Jesu Christi*. Amsterdam: Bey Henrico Betkio, 1660.
Boehme, Jacob. *The Works*. Edited by William Law. 4 vols. London: Printed for M. Richardson, in Pater-noster Row, 1764–81.
Böhme, Jacob. *Aurora (Morgen Röte im auffgang, 1612) and Fundamental Report (Gründlicher Bericht, Mysterium Pansophicum, 1620)*. Edited and translated by Andrew Weeks and Günther Bonheim. Leiden: Brill, 2013.
Böhme, Jacob. *Werke: Morgenröte. De signatura rerum*. Edited by Ferdinand van Ingen. Frankfurt a.M.: Deutscher Klassiker Verlag, 1997.
Bonheim, Günther. 'Die "große Reinigung" vom "gemeinen Geiste": Zu den Umständen der Entstehung der dritten Böhme-Gesamtausgabe 1730/31 und zu ihrem philologischen Ertrag.' In Kühlmann and Vollhardt, *Offenbarung und Episteme*, 451–62.
Bonheim, Günther. '"Lernet von ehe unterscheiden": Jacob Böhmes Mystik der Naturen.' In *Mystik und Natur: Zur Geschichte ihres Verhältnisses vom Altertum bis zur Gegenwart*. Edited by Peter Dinzelbacher, 123–39. Berlin: De Gruyter, 2009.
Bonheim, Günther. 'Zur Entstehung und Verbreitung der *Aurora*.' *Böhme-Studien* 4 (2017): 17–49.
Bonus, Petrus. *Pretiosa margarita novella de thesauro, ac pretiosissimo philosophorum lapide: Artis huius divinae typus, et methodus*. Edited by Janus Lacinius. Venice: Apud Aldi filios, 1546.
Bonus, Petrus. *Introductio in artem chemiae integra, ab ipso authore inscripta margarita preciosa novella*. Montbéliard: Apud Jacobum Foillet, 1602.
Bouman, José, Theodor Harmsen, and Cis van Heertum. *'Tried and Tested': The Appreciation of Hermetic and Alchemical Manuscripts from the 15th– 20th Centuries* (exhibition catalogue). Amsterdam: Bibliotheca Philosophica Hermetica, 2004.
Brecht, Martin, Johannes van den Berg, Friedhelm Ackva, Martin Sallmann, and Hartmut Lehmann, eds. *Geschichte des Pietismus*. 4 vols. Göttingen: Vandenhoeck & Ruprecht, 1993–2004.
Breckling, Friedrich. *Anticalovius, sive Calovius cum asseclis suis prostratus et Jacob Bôhmius cum aliis testibus veritatis defensus*. N.p.: Gedruckt vor Andream Luppium, 1688.
Breckling, Friedrich. *Autobiographie: Ein frühneuzeitliches Ego-Dokument im Spannungsfeld von Spiritualismus, radikalem Pietismus und Theosophie*. Edited by Johann Anselm Steiger. Tübingen: Niemeyer, 2005.

Breckling, Friedrich. *Christus cum suis prophetis et apostolis redivivus: Gottes Wort, Welches Gott dieser gegenwärtigen Welt in allen Ständen, Secten und Oertern selbst redet.* [Amsterdam], 1661.

Breckling, Friedrich. *Christus iudex in et cum sanctis contra gentes, secundum iudicium et iustitiam: Das Geheimniß des Reichs von der Monarchi Christi auff Erden.* [Amsterdam], 1663.

Breckling, Friedrich. *Christus mysticus, sol et sal sapientiae ex summo ac infimo coelo ac centro erumpens cum luce benedictionis et igne maledictionis, ad salvandum filios lucis, et iudicandum filios tenebrarum.* [Amsterdam], 1682.

Breckling, Friedrich. *Compendium Apocalypseos reseratae: Kurtzer Außzug Auß einem grössern Tractat, oder Außlegung über die Offenbahrung Johannis.* [Amsterdam], 1678.

Breckling, Friedrich. *Pseudosophia mundi cum falsis eius doctoribus de sede sua deturbata, et vera theosophia cum datore et doctore suo summo in thronum suum regalem exaltanda.* [Amsterdam], 1682.

Breymayer, Reinhard. 'Auktionskataloge deutscher Pietistenbibliotheken.' In *Bücherkataloge als buchgeschichtliche Quellen in der frühen Neuzeit.* Edited by Reinhard Wittmann, 113–208. Wiesbaden: Harrassowitz, 1984.

Breymayer, Reinhard, ed. *Johann Valentin Andreae: Ein geistliches Gemälde. Entworfen und aufgezeichnet von Huldrich StarkMann Diener des Evangeliums.* Tübingen: Noûs-Verlag Thomas Heck, 1991.

Brod, Manfred. 'A Radical Network in the English Revolution: John Pordage and His Circle, 1646–54.' *English Historical Review* 119 (2004): 1230–53.

Bröer, Ralf. 'Friedenspolitik durch Verketzerung: Johannes Crato (1519–1585) und die Denunziation der Paracelsisten als Arianer.' *Medizinhistorisches Journal* 37 (2002): 139–82.

Broszinski, Hartmut. *Manuscripta chemica in quarto.* Wiesbaden: Harrassowitz, 2011.

Bruckner, J. *A Bibliographical Catalogue of Seventeenth-Century German Books Published in Holland.* The Hague: Mouton, 1971.

Bruckner, János. *Abraham von Franckenberg: A Bibliographical Catalogue with a Short-List of His Library.* Wiesbaden: Otto Harrassowitz, 1988.

Bruckner, John. 'Abraham von Franckenberg, Johann Scheffler und Johann Theodor von Tschesch in einem "Quaker-Buche" (1680).' In *Literatur und Volk im 17. Jahrhundert: Probleme populärer Kultur in Deutschland.* Edited by Wolfgang Brückner, 579–88. Wiesbaden: Harrassowitz, 1985.

Bruckner, John. 'A Bibliography of Abraham von Franckenberg: Problems and Propositions.' *German Life and Letters* 36 (1983): 213–18.

Bruns, Paul Jacob. *Catalogus bibliothecae D. Antonii Julii von der Hardt Abbatis Michaelsteinensis.* Helmstedt: Typis Vid. Schnorrianae acad. typ., 1786.

Bucklow, Spike. *The Alchemy of Paint: Art, Science and Secrets from the Middle Ages.* London: Marion Boyars, 2009.

Buddecke, Werner, ed. *Jacob Böhme: Die Urschriften.* 2 vols. Stuttgart-Bad Cannstatt: Frommann, 1963–66.

Buddecke, Werner. *Die Jakob Böhme-Ausgaben: Ein beschreibendes Verzeichnis.* 2 vols. Göttingen: Dr. Ludwig Häntzschel, 1937–57.

Buddecke, Werner. *Verzeichnis von Jakob Böhme-Handschriften.* Göttingen: Dr. Ludwig Häntzschel, 1934.

Buddecke, Werner, and Matthias Wenzel. *Jacob Böhme: Verzeichnis der Handschriften und frühen Abschriften.* Görlitz: Oberlausitzische Bibliothek der Wissenschaften, 2000.

Buddecke, Wolfram. 'Die Jakob-Böhme-Autographen: Ein historischer Bericht.' *Wolfenbütteler Beiträge* 1 (1972): 61–87.

Bütikofer, Kaspar. *Der frühe Zürcher Pietismus (1689–1721): Der soziale Hintergrund und die Denk- und Lebenswelten im Spiegel der Bibliothek Johann Heinrich Lochers (1648–1718)*. Göttingen: Vandenhoeck & Ruprecht, 2009.

Butterfield, Herbert. *The Origins of Modern Science 1300–1800*. London: G. Bell, 1949.

Călian, George-Florin. '*Alkimia Operativa* and *Alkimia Speculativa*: Some Modern Controversies on the Historiography of Alchemy.' *Annual of Medieval Studies* 16 (2010): 166–90.

[Capito, Johann]. *Libellus theosophiae de veris reliquiis seu semine Dei in nobis post lapsum relicto*. Newstadt [Frankfurt a.M.]: Zu finden bey Lucas Jennis, 1618.

Catalogue of a Choice Selection of Books from the Valuable Library of the Late Mrs. Atwood. Belfast: William Tait, 1912.

Cavallaro, Federico. 'The Alchemical Significance of John Dee's *Monas Hieroglyphica*.' In *John Dee: Interdisciplinary Studies in English Renaissance Thought*. Edited by Stephen Clucas, 159–76. Dordrecht: Springer, 2006.

Chang, Kevin. 'Georg Ernst Stahl's Alchemical Publications: Anachronism, Reading Market, and a Scientific Lineage Redefined.' In Principe, *New Narratives*, 23–43.

Chevallier, Marjolaine. *Pierre Poiret 1646–1719: du protestantisme à la mystique*. Geneva: Labor et Fides, 1994.

'[Classified Advertisements].' *Morning Post*, no. 24,005 (16 November 1850): 8.

Clericuzio, Antonio. 'William R. Newman and Lawrence M. Principe, *Alchemy Tried in the Fire: Starkey, Boyle, and the Fate of Helmontian Chymistry*' (review). *Annals of Science* 62 (2005): 406–8.

Cochran, John. *A Catalogue of Manuscripts, in Different Languages, on Theology;... Now Selling (for Ready Money) at the Prices Affixed*. London, 1829.

Cohen, I. Bernard. 'Ethan Allen Hitchcock: Soldier—Humanitarian—Scholar. Discoverer of the "True Subject" of the Hermetic Art.' *Proceedings of the American Antiquarian Society* 61 (1951): 29–136.

Colberg, Ehregott Daniel. *Das Platonisch-Hermetisches Christenthum, Begreiffend Die Historische Erzehlung vom Ursprung und vielerley Secten der heutigen Fanatischen Theologie*. 2 vols. Frankfurt a.M./Leipzig: Bey Moritz Georg Weidmann, Druckts Joh. Köler, 1690–91.

Crisciani, Chiara. 'The Conception of Alchemy as Expressed in the *Pretiosa Margarita Novella* of Petrus Bonus of Ferrara.' *Ambix* 20 (1973): 165–81.

Crollius, Oswald. *Alchemomedizinische Briefe 1585 bis 1597*. Edited by Wilhelm Kühlmann and Joachim Telle. Stuttgart: Steiner, 1998.

Crowley, Aleister. *777 and Other Qabalistic Writings*. Edited by Israel Regardie. Boston: Weiser Books, 1973.

Curry, Patrick. *Prophecy and Power: Astrology in Early Modern England*. Princeton: Princeton University Press, 1989.

Czepko, Daniel. *Sämtliche Werke*. Edited by Hans-Gert Roloff and Marian Szyrocki. 6 vols. Berlin: De Gruyter, 1980–97.

Dan, Joseph. 'The Kabbalah of Johannes Reuchlin and Its Historical Significance.' In *The Christian Kabbalah: Jewish Mystical Books and Their Christian Interpreters*. Edited by Joseph Dan, 55–84. Cambridge: Harvard University Press, 1997.

Daniel, Dane T. 'Paracelsus' *Astronomia magna* (1537/38): Bible-Based Science and the Religious Roots of the Scientific Revolution.' PhD thesis, Indiana University, 2003.

Daniel, Dane T. 'Paracelsus on Baptism and the Acquiring of the Eternal Body.' In *Paracelsian Moments: Science, Medicine, and Astrology in Early Modern Europe*. Edited by Gerhild Scholz Williams and Charles D. Gunnoe, 117–34. Kirksville: Truman State University Press, 2002.

Datenbank zu den Einzelhandschriften in den historischen Archivabteilungen. http://fas.francke-halle.de/cgi-bin/gkdb.pl. Halle: Franckesche Stiftungen, 2008 ff.

Dawe, Donovan. *Skilbecks: Drysalters 1650–1950*. London: Skilbeck, 1950.

'Deaths.' *Hampshire Telegraph and Sussex Chronicle*, no. 3062 (12 June 1858): 5.

'Deaths.' *Yorkshire Gazette* 40, no. 2039 (22 May 1858): 3.

Deghaye, Pierre. *La naissance de Dieu ou la doctrine de Jacob Boehme*. Paris: Albin Michel, 1985.

Deghaye, Pierre. 'Die Natur als Leib Gottes in Jacob Böhmes Theosophie.' In Garewicz and Haas, *Gott, Natur und Mensch*, 71–111.

Deutsche Biographie (DB). https://www.deutsche-biographie.de. Munich: Historische Kommission der Bayerischen Akademie der Wissenschaften, 2001 ff.

Deutsches Wörterbuch von Jacob Grimm und Wilhelm Grimm. http://woerterbuchnetz.de/DWB. Trier: Universität Trier, 1998 ff.

DeVun, Leah. 'The Jesus Hermaphrodite: Science and Sex Difference in Premodern Europe.' *Journal of the History of Ideas* 69 (2008): 193–218.

Dietze, Walter. *Quirinus Kuhlmann—Ketzer und Poet: Versuch einer monographischen Darstellung von Leben und Werk*. Berlin: Rütten & Loening, 1963.

Dobbs, B. J. T. *The Foundations of Newton's Alchemy: Or, 'The Hunting of the Greene Lyon.'* Cambridge: Cambridge University Press, 1975.

Dobbs, B. J. T. *The Janus Faces of Genius: The Role of Alchemy in Newton's Thought*. Cambridge: Cambridge University Press, 1991.

Does, J. C. van der. 'Johan Georg Gichtel's verblijf in Nederland en zijn verhouding tot Jan Luyken.' *Stemmen des tijds* 18 (1929): 146–66.

Dohm, Burkhard. *Poetische Alchimie: Öffnung zur Sinnlichkeit in der Hohelied- und Bibeldichtung von der protestantischen Barockmystik bis zum Pietismus*. Tübingen: Niemeyer, 2000.

Donkersloot-de Vrij, Marijke. *Drie generaties Blaeu: Amsterdamse cartografie en boekdrukkunst in de zeventiende eeuw*. Zutphen: Walburg, 1992.

Döring, Detlef. *Katalog der Handschriften der Universitätsbibliothek Leipzig: Die neuzeitlichen Handschriften der Nullgruppe*. 4 vols. Wiesbaden: Harrassowitz, 2000–5.

Dorn, Gerard. *De naturae luce physica, ex Genesi desumpta, iuxta sententiam Theophrasti Paracelsi*. Frankfurt a.M.: Apud Christophorum Corvinum, 1583.

Dünnhaupt, Gerhard. *Personalbibliographien zu den Drucken des Barock*. 2nd, improved, and expanded ed. 6 vols. Stuttgart: Hiersemann, 1990–93.

Eberlein, Paul Gerhard. *Ketzer oder Heiliger? Caspar von Schwenckfeld, der schlesische Reformator und seine Botschaft*. Metzingen: Franz, 1998.

Egerding, Michael. *Die Metaphorik der spätmittelalterlichen Mystik*. 2 vols. Paderborn: Schöningh, 1997.

Ehrentreich, Alfred. 'Valentin Weigels religiöser "Dialogus" als literarische Schöpfung.' *Zeitschrift für Religions- und Geistesgeschichte* 21 (1969): 42–54.

Eliade, Mircea, ed. *The Encyclopedia of Religion*. 16 vols. New York: Macmillan, 1987.

Eliade, Mircea. *The Forge and the Crucible*. Translated by Stephen Corrin. London: Rider, 1962. First published 1956.

Erler, Georg. *Die iüngere Matrikel der Universität Leipzig 1559–1809: Als Personen- und Ortsregister bearbeitet und durch Nachträge aus den Promotionslisten ergänzt.* 3 vols. Nendeln: Kraus Reprint, 1976. First published 1909.

Estié, Paul. 'Die Auseinandersetzung von Charias, Breckling, Jungius und Gichtel in der lutherischen Gemeinde zu Kampen 1661–1668.' *Pietismus und Neuzeit* 16 (1990): 31–52.

Estié, Paul. 'Die Entlassung Friedrich Brecklings als Pfarrer der Lutherischen Gemeinde zu Zwolle, 1667–1668.' *Pietismus und Neuzeit* 18 (1992): 9–39.

Eylenstein, Ernst. 'Ludwig Friedrich Gifftheil: Zum mystischen Separatismus des 17. Jahrhunderts in Deutschland.' *Zeitschrift für Kirchengeschichte* 41 (1922): 1–62.

Faivre, Antoine. 'Elie Artiste, ou la messie des philosophes de la nature.' 2 pts. *Aries* 2–3 (2002–3): 119–52, 25–54.

Fallend, Karl. '"Über den Wolken": Herbert Silberer—"Führer erster Classe" und Mitglied der Wiener Psychoanalytischen Vereinigung.' *Zeitschrift für Psychoanalyse und Gesellschaftskritik* 5 (1988): 67–86.

Ferguson, Christine. 'Other Worlds: Alfred Russel Wallace and Cross-Cultural Spiritualism.' *Victorian Review* 41 (2015): 177–91.

Ferguson, Christine. 'Reading with the Occultists: Arthur Machen, A. E. Waite, and the Ecstasies of Popular Fiction.' *Journal of Victorian Culture* 21 (2016): 40–55.

Ferguson, John. *Bibliotheca Chemica: A Bibliography of Books on Alchemy, Chemistry and Pharmaceutics.* 2 vols. London: Derek Verschoyle, 1954. First published 1906.

Feuerstein-Herz, Petra, and Stefan Laube, eds. *Goldenes Wissen: Die Alchemie—Substanzen, Synthesen, Symbolik.* Wiesbaden: Harrassowitz, 2014.

Ficino, Marsilio, ed. *Mercurii Trismegisti Pymander, de potestate et sapientia Dei.* Basel: Per Mich. Isingrinium, mense Augusto, 1532.

Ficino, Marsilio. *Three Books on Life: A Critical Edition and Translation with Introduction and Notes.* Edited and translated by Carol V. Kaske and John R. Clark. 3rd ed. Tempe, AZ: Renaissance Society of America, 2002. First published 1989.

Fictuld, Hermann. *Der längst gewünschte und versprochene Chymisch-Philosophische Probier-Stein.* Frankfurt a.M./Leipzig: Bey Michael Blochberger, 1740.

Fictuld, Hermann. *Des Längst gewünschten und versprochenen Chymisch-Philosophischen Probier-Steins Erste Claß.* 2nd, expanded ed. Frankfurt a.M./Leipzig: Bey Veraci Orientali Wahrheit und Ernst Lugenfeind, 1753.

Fictuld, Hermann. *Des Längst gewünschten und versprochenen Chymisch-Philosophischen Probier-Steins Erste Classe.* 3rd ed. Dresden: In der Hilscherschen Buchhandlung, 1784.

Fink, David C. 'Was There a "Reformation Doctrine of Justification"?' *Harvard Theological Review* 103 (2010): 205–35.

Fludd, Robert. *Clavis philosophiae et alchymiae Fluddanae.* Frankfurt a.M.: Prostat apud Guilhelmum Fitzerum, 1633.

Forshaw, Peter. '"Alchemy in the Amphitheatre": Some Considerations of the Alchemical Content of the Engravings in Heinrich Khunrath's *Amphitheatre of Eternal Wisdom* (1609).' In *Art & Alchemy.* Edited by Jacob Wamberg, 195–220. Copenhagen: Museum Tusculanum Press, 2006.

Forshaw, Peter J. 'Ora et Labora: Alchemy, Magic, and Cabala in Heinrich Khunrath's *Amphitheatrum sapientiae aeternae* (1609).' 2 vols. PhD thesis, Birkbeck, University of London, 2003.

Forshaw, Peter J. 'The Early Alchemical Reception of John Dee's *Monas Hieroglyphica*.' *Ambix* 52 (2005): 247–69.

Forshaw, Peter J. 'Subliming Spirits: Physical-Chemistry and Theo-Alchemy in the Works of Heinrich Khunrath (1560–1605).' In Linden, *Mystical Metal*, 255–75.

Forshaw, Peter J. '"Chemistry, that Starry Science": Early Modern Conjunctions of Astrology and Alchemy.' In *Sky and Symbol: Proceedings of the Ninth Annual Sophia Centre Conference, 2011.* Edited by Nicholas Campion and Liz Greene, 143–84. Lampeter: Sophia Centre Press, 2013.

Forster, Leonard. 'Deutsche Drucke des 17. Jahrhunderts in der Domkapitelbibliothek zu Durham/England.' *Wolfenbütteler Barock-Nachrichten* 16 (1989): 92–109.

Franckenberg, Abraham von. *Briefwechsel.* Edited by Joachim Telle. Stuttgart-Bad Cannstatt: Frommann-Holzboog, 1995.

Franckenberg, Abraham von. *Conclusiones de fundamento sapientiae theorico-practicae. Das ist, Endlicher Beschluß Vom Grunde der Weißheit, Von etlichen Liebhabern der Wahrheit zusammen getragen.* Königstein [Amsterdam]: [Hans Fabel], 1646.

Franckenberg, Abraham von. *Jordans Steine, welche Einem nach dem Lande der Lebendigen reisenden Mit-Pilgrim, Auß dem Wege zu räumen.* Frankfurt a.M./Leipzig: Bey Andräe Lupplo [*recte*: Luppio], Buchhändlern in Nimmägen, 1684.

Franckenberg, Abraham von. 'Kurtz- jedoch gründtlich- und warhaffter Bericht, von dem Leben und Abscheid des in Gott seelig ruhenden JACOB BOEMENS.' In *Von Erschaffung des Menschen zu Gottes Ebenbilde... Alles aus J. B. T. Schrifften gezogen: Der IV. Theil.* Edited by [Gottfried Richter], ff. A2v–C2r. [Toruń]: [Michael Karnall], 1652/53.

Franckenberg, Abraham von. 'Kurtze Beschreibung Des Lebens und wandels Jacobi Böhmens.' In Boehme, *Josephus Redivivus*, ff. (0)3r–(0)5v.

Franckenberg, Abraham von. *Notae mysticae et mnemonicae ad Bechinas Olam sive examen mundi R. Jedaja Happenini.* Edited by Hilarius Prache. N.p., 1673.

Franckenberg, Abraham von. *Raphael oder Artzt-Engel.* Amsterdam: Gedruckt bey Jacob von Felsen, wohnhaft in der Utrechtschen Gasse am Reguliers Marckt, 1676.

Franckenberg, Abraham von. 'Theophrastia Valentiniana. Das ist: Ein unpartheyischer Schrifft- und Natur-mäßiger Bericht Uber ein *Fragmentum* Von der Lehre *Valentini*.' In Gottfried Arnold, *Supplementa, Illustrationes und Emendationes Zur Verbesserung Der Kirchen-Historie,* 11–49. Frankfurt a.M.: Bey Thomas Fritschen, 1703.

Franckenberg, Abraham von. *Trias mystica: In quâ 1. Speculum apocalypticum: 2. Mysterium metapsychicum: 3. Epistolium chronometricum: Ad ecclesiam quae est in Philadelphia et Laodiceia.* Amsterdam: Typis Georgii Trigg, 1651.

Franckenberg, Abraham von. *Via veterum sapientum. Das ist: Weg der Alten Weisen.* Amsterdam: Gedruckt by Christoffel Cunradus, Buchdrucker. In verlegung Henrici Betkii, und Consorten, 1675.

Franklin, J. Jeffrey. 'The Evolution of Occult Spirituality in Victorian England and the Representative Case of Edward Bulwer-Lytton.' In *The Ashgate Research Companion to Nineteenth-Century Spiritualism and the Occult.* Edited by Tatiana Kontou and Sarah A. Wilburn, 123–41. Farnham: Ashgate, 2012.

Fraser, Kyle A. 'Zosimos of Panopolis and the Book of Enoch: Alchemy as Forbidden Knowledge.' *Aries* 4 (2004): 125–47.

Freher, Dionysius Andreas. *The Paradoxical Emblems.* Edited by Adam McLean. Edinburgh: McLean, 1983.

Furcha, E. J. 'Key Concepts in Caspar von Schwenckfeld's Thought: Regeneration and the New Life.' *Church History* 37 (1968): 160–73.

Gajek, Konrad. 'Georg Philipp Harsdörffers Brief vom 30. Mai 1652 an Abraham von Franckenberg.' In *Studien zur Literatur des 17. Jahrhunderts: Gedenkschrift für Gerhard Spellerberg (1937–1996).* Edited by Hans Feger, 403–12. Amsterdam: Rodopi, 1997.

Gantenbein, Urs Leo. 'Cross and Crucible: Alchemy in the Theology of Paracelsus.' *Ambix* 67 (2020): 88–99.

Gantenbein, Urs Leo. '"Himmlische Philosophia" bei Paracelsus und Caspar Schwenckfeld.' *Daphnis* 48 (2020): 296–318.

Gantenbein, Urs Leo. 'The New Adam: Jacob Böhme and the Theology of Paracelsus (1493/94–1541).' In Andersson et al., *Jacob Böhme and His World*, 166–96.

Ganzenmüller, W. 'Das Buch der heiligen Dreifaltigkeit: Eine Deutsche Alchemie aus dem Anfang des 15. Jahrhunderts.' In *Beiträge zur Geschichte der Technologie und der Alchemie*, 231–72. Weinheim: Verlag Chemie, 1956.

Garewicz, Jan, and Alois Maria Haas, eds. *Gott, Natur und Mensch in der Sicht Jacob Böhmes und seiner Rezeption*. Wiesbaden: Harrassowitz, 1994.

Gayler, Christoph Friedrich. *Historische Denkwürdigkeiten der ehemaligen freien Reichsstadt, itzt Königlich Württembergischen Kreisstadt, Reutlingen vom dritten Viertel des 16ten bis gegen die Mitte des 18ten Jahrhunderts. Nebst einem Anhang von 1789 bis 1803*. Reutlingen: Fleischhauer und Spohn, 1845.

Geissmar, Christoph. *Das Auge Gottes: Bilder zu Jakob Böhme*. Wiesbaden: Harrassowitz, 1993.

Gennrich, P. *Die Lehre von der Wiedergeburt, die christliche Zentrallehre in dogmengeschichtlicher und religionsgeschichtlicher Beleuchtung*. Leipzig: Deichert, 1907.

Gentilcore, David. '"Charlatans, Mountebanks and Other Similar People": The Regulation and Role of Itinerant Practitioners in Early Modern Italy.' *Social History* 20 (1995): 297–314.

Gentilcore, David. *Medical Charlatanism in Early Modern Italy*. Oxford: Oxford University Press, 2006.

Geyer, Hermann. *Verborgene Weisheit: Johann Arndts 'Vier Bücher vom Wahren Christentum' als Programm einer spiritualistisch-hermetischen Theologie*. 3 vols. Berlin: De Gruyter, 2001.

Gibbons, B. J. *Gender in Mystical and Occult Thought: Behmenism and Its Development in England*. Cambridge: Cambridge University Press, 1996.

Gibson, K. 'Apocalyptic and Millenarian Prophecy in Early Stuart Europe: Philip Ziegler, Ludwig Friedrich Gifftheil and the Fifth Monarchy.' In *Prophecy: The Power of Inspired Language in History 1300–2000*. Edited by Bertrand Taithe and Tim Thornton, 71–84. Stroud: Sutton, 1997.

Gichtel, Johann Georg. *Citatie voor Godts Gericht. . . Aen het luytersche consistorie tot Amsterdam*. Kampen, 1668.

Gichtel, Johann Georg. *Theosophia Practica: Halten und Kämpfen ob dem H. Glauben bis ans Ende*. 3rd, augmented, and improved ed. 7 vols. Leiden, 1722.

Gilbert, R. A. *A. E. Waite: Magician of Many Parts*. Wellingborough: Thorsons, 1987.

Gilbert, R. A., ed. *Journal of the Alchemical Society 1913–1915*. Swindon: Imagier, 2017.

Gilly, Carlos. 'Abraham von Franckenberg und die Rosenkreuzer: Zur Datierung der Tabula Universalis Theosophica Mystica et Cabalistica von 1623.' In *Rosenkreuz als europäisches Phänomen im 17. Jahrhundert*. Edited by Bibliotheca Philosophica Hermetica, 212–32. Amsterdam: In de Pelikaan, 2002.

Gilly, Carlos. 'Das Bekenntnis zur Gnosis von Paracelsus bis auf die Schüler Jacob Böhmes.' In *From Poemandres to Jacob Böhme: Gnosis Hermetism and the Christian Tradition*. Edited by Roelof van den Broek and Cis van Heertum, 385–425. Amsterdam: In de Pelikaan, 2000.

Gilly, Carlos. 'Das Sprichwort "Die Gelehrten die Verkehrten" oder der Verrat der Intellektuellen im Zeitalter der Glaubensspaltung.' In *Forme e destinazione del messagio religioso: aspetti della propaganda religiosa nel Cinquecento*. Edited by Antonio Rotondò, 229–375. Florence: Olschki, 1991.

Gilly, Carlos. 'Khunrath und das Entstehen der frühneuzeitlichen Theosophie.' In *Amphitheatrum Sapientiae Aeternae—Schauplatz der ewigen allein wahren Weisheit: Vollständiger Reprint des Erstdrucks von [Hamburg] 1595 und des zweiten und letzten Drucks Hanau 1609*. Edited by Carlos Gilly, Anja Hallacker, Hanns-Peter Neumann, and Wilhelm Schmidt-Biggemann, 9–22. Stuttgart-Bad Cannstatt: Frommann-Holzboog, 2014.

Gilly, Carlos. 'On the Genesis of L. Zetzner's *Theatrum Chemicum* in Strasbourg.' In Gilly and Van Heertum, *Magic, Alchemy and Science*, 1:417–67.

Gilly, Carlos. '"Theophrastia sancta": Paracelsianism as a Religion, in Conflict with the Established Churches.' In Grell, *Paracelsus*, 151–85.

Gilly, Carlos. 'Wege der Verbreitung von Jacob Böhmes Schriften in Deutschland und den Niederlanden.' In Harmsen, *Jacob Böhmes Weg in die Welt*, 71–98.

Gilly, Carlos. 'Zur Entstehung und Wirkung der Handschriftensammlung Abraham Willemsz van Beyerlands.' In Harmsen, *Jacob Böhmes Weg in die Welt*, 99–132.

Gilly, Carlos. 'Zur Geschichte der Böhme-Biographie des Abraham von Franckenberg.' In Harmsen, *Jacob Böhmes Weg in die Welt*, 365–81.

Gilly, Carlos. 'Zur Geschichte und Überlieferung der Handschriften Jacob Böhmes.' In Harmsen, *Jacob Böhmes Weg in die Welt*, 39–54.

Gilly, Carlos. 'Zwischen Erfahrung und Spekulation: Theodor Zwinger und die religiöse und kulturelle Krise seiner Zeit. 1. Teil.' *Basler Zeitschrift für Geschichte und Altertumskunde* 77 (1977): 57–137.

Gilly, Carlos, and Cis van Heertum, eds. *Magic, Alchemy and Science, 15th–18th Centuries: The Influence of Hermes Trismegistus*. 2 vols. Florence: Centro Di, 2002.

Glorez, Andreas. *Des Mährischen Albertus Magnus . . . Eröffnetes Wunderbuch von Waffensalben*. Regensburg/Stadtamhof, 1700 [1850?].

Godwin, Joscelyn. 'A Behemist Circle in Victorian England.' *Hermetic Journal* 15 (1992): 48–71.

Goeters, Wilhelm G. 'Johann Overbeek in Cleve als Mitarbeiter an Gottfrieds Arnolds Kirchen- und Ketzer-Historie.' *Monatshefte für Rheinische Kirchengeschichte* 8 (1914): 3–20.

Goldammer, Kurt. 'Paracelsus, Osiander and Theological Paracelsism in the Middle of the 16th Century: Some Remarks Concerning a Paracelsian Pseudepigraphon on the Ten Commandments.' Translated by Victor J. Gustitus. In *Science, Medicine and Society in the Renaissance: Essays to Honor Walter Pagel*. Edited by Allen G. Debus, 2 vols., 1:105–20. London: Heinemann, 1972.

Gorceix, Bernard. *Johann Georg Gichtel: théosophe d'Amsterdam*. Paris: l'Age d'Homme, 1975.

Göttler, Christine, and Wolfgang Neuber, eds. *Spirits Unseen: The Representation of Subtle Bodies in Early Modern European Culture*. Leiden: Brill, 2008.

[Gottmann, Johann]. '*Speculum Sapientiae*. Das ist: Ein Buch des Geheimnisses vom Anfang der Welt.' In *Quadratum Alchymisticum: Das ist: Vier auserlesene rare Tractätgen Vom Stein der Weisen*, 1–54. Hamburg: Verlegts Christian Liebezeit. Druckts Philipp Ludwig Stromer, 1705.

Grafton, Anthony Thomas. *Humanists with Inky Fingers: The Culture of Correction in Renaissance Europe*. Florence: Olschki, 2011.

Grant, Edward. *Planets, Stars, Orbs: The Medieval Cosmos, 1200–1687.* 2 vols. Cambridge: Cambridge University Press, 1996.
Greaves, James Pierrepont. *New Theosophic Revelations: From the Ms. Journal.* London: John Chapman, 1847.
Gregory, Alan. '"No New Truths of Religion": William Law's Appropriation of Jacob Boehme.' In Hessayon and Apetrei, *An Introduction to Jacob Boehme*, 142–61.
Grell, Ole Peter, ed. *Paracelsus: The Man and His Reputation, His Ideas and Their Transformation.* Leiden: Brill, 1998.
Grunsky, Hans. *Jacob Böhme.* 2nd ed. Stuttgart-Bad Cannstatt: Frommann-Holzboog, 1984. First published 1956.
Guhrauer, G. E. 'Beiträge zur Kenntniss des 17. u. 18. Jahrhunderts aus den handschriftlichen Aufzeichnungen Gottlieb Stolle's.' *Allgemeine Zeitschrift für Geschichte* 7 (1847): 385–436, 481–531.
Güldenfalk, Siegmund Heinrich. *Sammlung von mehr als hundert wahrhaften Transmutationsgeschichten.* Frankfurt a.M./Leipzig: Bey Joh. Georg Fleischer, 1784.
Haberling, W. 'Alexander von Suchten, ein Danziger Arzt und Dichter des 16. Jahrhunderts.' *Zeitschrift des Westpreussischen Geschichtsvereins* 69 (1929): 177–230.
Haferland, Harald. 'Eine kurze Theoriegeschichte der alchemistischen *multiplicatio* und der *Vorbothe der am philosophischen Himmel hervorbrechenden Morgenröthe* des Johannes de Monte Raphaim (Amsterdam 1703).' In *Magia daemoniaca, magia naturalis, zouber: Schreibweisen von Magie und Alchemie in Mittelalter und Früher Neuzeit.* Edited by Peter-André Alt, Jutta Eming, Tilo Renz, and Volkhard Wels, 393–417. Wiesbaden: Harrassowitz, 2015.
Hakelberg, Dietrich. 'Die fanatischen Bücher des Benedikt Bahnsen: Leben und Bibliothek eines religiösen Dissidenten.' *Bibliothek und Wissenschaft* 48 (2015): 113–46.
Haley, K. H. D. 'Sir Johannes Rothe: English Knight and Dutch Fifth Monarchist.' In *Puritans and Revolutionaries: Essays in Seventeenth Century History Presented to Christopher Hill.* Edited by D. Pennington and K. Thomas, 310–32. Oxford: Oxford University Press, 1978.
Hanegraaff, Wouter J. 'The Birth of Esotericism from the Spirit of Protestantism.' *Aries* 10 (2010): 197–216.
Hanegraaff, Wouter J. *Esotericism and the Academy: Rejected Knowledge in Western Culture.* Cambridge: Cambridge University Press, 2012.
Hanegraaff, Wouter J. 'Forbidden Knowledge: Anti-Esoteric Polemics and Academic Research.' *Aries* 5 (2005): 225–54.
Hanegraaff, Wouter J., and Ruud M. Bouthoorn. *Lodovico Lazzarelli (1447–1500): The Hermetic Writings and Related Documents.* Tempe, AZ: Arizona Center for Medieval and Renaissance Studies, 2005.
Hanegraaff, Wouter J., Antoine Faivre, Roelof van den Broek, and Jean-Pierre Brach, eds. *Dictionary of Gnosis and Western Esotericism.* Leiden: Brill, 2007.
Hannak, Kristine. *Geist=reiche Critik: Hermetik, Mystik und das Werden der Aufklärung in spiritualistischer Literatur der Frühen Neuzeit.* Berlin: De Gruyter, 2013.
Hannaway, Owen. *The Chemists and the Word: The Didactic Origins of Chemistry.* Baltimore: Johns Hopkins University Press, 1975.
Ha-Penini, Yedayah. *Beḥinot ha-ʿolam . . . Examen mundi, R. J. Badreshitae: Latina interpretatione, atque animadversionibus illustratum.* Edited and translated by Allard Uchtman. Leiden: Ex Officina Joannis Maire, 1650.

Harmsen, Theodor, ed. *Jacob Böhmes Weg in die Welt: Zur Geschichte der Handschriftensammlung, Übersetzungen und Editionen von Abram Willemsz van Beyerland*. Amsterdam: In de Pelikaan, 2007.

Harrison, Peter. *The Territories of Science and Religion*. Chicago: University of Chicago Press, 2015.

Hartprecht, Johann. *Der Verlangete Dritte Anfange Der Mineralischen Dinge, oder vom Philosophischen Saltz*. Amsterdam: Vor Christoffel Luycken, Buchverkauffer auff der Haarlemmer Creutzstraßen, 1656.

Haug, Johann Heinrich, ed. *Die Heilige Schrift Altes und Neues Testaments, Nach dem Grund-Text aufs neue übersehen und übersetzet*. 8 vols. Berleburg, 1726–42.

Heijting, Willem. 'Hendrick Beets (1625?–1708), Publisher to the German Adherents of Jacob Böhme in Amsterdam.' *Quaerendo* 3 (1973): 250–80.

Heijting, Willem. *Profijtelijke boekskens: boekcultuur, geloof en gewin. Historische studies*. Hilversum: Verloren, 2007.

Hesketh, Ian. *Victorian Jesus: J. R. Seeley, Religion, and the Cultural Significance of Anonymity*. Toronto: University of Toronto Press, 2017.

Hessayon, Ariel, and Sarah Apetrei, eds. *An Introduction to Jacob Boehme: Four Centuries of Thought and Reception*. London: Routledge, 2014.

Hessayon, Ariel. 'Boehme's Life and Times.' In Hessayon and Apetrei, *An Introduction to Jacob Boehme*, 13–37.

Hessayon, Ariel, ed. *Jane Lead and Her Transnational Legacy*. London: Palgrave Macmillan, 2016.

Hessayon, Ariel. 'Lead's Life and Times,' 3 pts. In Hessayon, *Jane Lead*, 13–90.

Hillenbrand, Rainer. 'Cherubinische Trinitätsmystik bei Angelus Silesius.' *Daphnis* 47 (2019): 592–638.

Hinshaw, Robert, and Lela Fischli, eds. *C. G. Jung im Gespräch: Interviews, Reden, Begegnungen*. Zurich: Daimon, 1986.

Hirai, Hiro. 'The World-Spirit and Quintessence in the Chymical Philosophy of Joseph Du Chesne.' In López Pérez et al., *Chymia*, 247–61.

Hirst, Julie. *Jane Leade: Biography of a Seventeenth-Century Mystic*. Aldershot: Ashgate, 2005.

Hitchcock, Ethan Allen. *Remarks upon Alchemy and the Alchemists, Indicating a Method of Discovering the True Nature of Hermetic Philosophy*. Boston: Crosby, Nichols, and Company, 1857.

Hitchcock, Ethan Allen. *Remarks upon Alchymists, and the Supposed Object of Their Pursuit; Showing that the Philosopher's Stone is a Mere Symbol*. Carlisle: Herald Office, 1855.

Hoftijzer, Paul. 'Metropolis of Print: The Amsterdam Book Trade in the Seventeenth Century.' In *Urban Achievement in Early Modern Europe: Golden Ages in Antwerp, Amsterdam and London*. Edited by Patrick O'Brien, Derek Keene, Marjolein 't Hart, and Herman van der Wee, 249–63. Cambridge: Cambridge University Press, 2001.

Hoheisel, Karl. 'Christus und der philosophische Stein: Alchemie als über- und nichtchristlicher Heilsweg.' In *Die Alchemie in der europäischen Kultur- und Wissenschaftsgeschichte*. Edited by Christoph Meinel, 61–84. Wiesbaden: Harrassowitz, 1986.

Hooker, Thomas. *The Application of Redemption, By the effectual Work of the Word, and Spirit of Christ*. 2 vols. London: Printed by Peter Cole at the sign of the Pringting-press [sic] in Cornhil, neer the Royal Exchange, 1656–57.

Hooykaas, Reyer. 'Chemical Trichotomy before Paracelsus?' In *Selected Studies in History of Science*, 105–19. Coimbra: Por ordem da Universidade, 1983.

Hoppe, Günther. 'Zwischen Augsburg und Anhalt: Der rosenkreuzerische Briefwechsel des Augsburger Stadtarztes Carl Widemann mit dem Plötzkauer Fürsten August von Anhalt.' *Zeitschrift des historischen Vereins für Schwaben* 90 (1997): 125–87.

Howe, Ellic, ed. *The Alchemist of the Golden Dawn: The Letters of the Revd W. A. Ayton to F. L. Gardner and Others 1886–1905*. Wellingborough: Aquarian Press, 1985.

Hubicki, Włodzimierz. 'Alexander von Suchten.' *Sudhoffs Archiv* 44 (1960): 54–63.

Huggenberg, Frieda Maria. 'Alchemisten und Goldmacher im 16. Jahrhundert in der Schweiz.' *Gesnerus* 13 (1956): 97–164.

Humberg, Oliver. 'Die Verlassenschaft des oberösterreichischen Landschaftsarztes Alexander von Suchten.' *Wolfenbütteler Renaissance-Mitteilungen* 31 (2007): 31–50.

Hunnius, Nicolaus. *Christliche Betrachtung Der Newen Paracelsischen und Weigelianischen Theology*. Wittenberg: Gedruckt bey Johan Gorman, In verlegung Caspar Heiden Buchh., 1622.

Huss, Boaz. 'The Sacred Is the Profane, Spirituality Is Not Religion: The Decline of the Religion/Secular Divide and the Emergence of the Critical Discourse on Religion.' *Method and Theory in the Study of Religion* 27 (2015): 97–103.

Ihde, Aaron J. 'Alchemy in Reverse: Robert Boyle on the Degradation of Gold.' *Chymia* 9 (1964): 47–57.

Illg, Thomas. *Ein anderer Mensch werden: Johann Arndts Verständnis der imitatio Christi als Anleitung zu einem wahren Christentum*. Göttingen: V&R unipress, 2011.

Ingen, Ferdinand van. 'Die Edition von Jacob Böhmes "Aurora" und die Bedeutung eines Variantenapparats.' In *Probleme der Edition von Texten der Frühen Neuzeit: Beiträge zur Arbeitstagung der Kommission für die Edition von Texten der Frühen Neuzeit*. Edited by Lothar Mundt, Hans-Gert Roloff, and Ulrich Seelbach, 15–25. Tübingen: Niemeyer, 1992.

Ingen, Ferdinand van. 'Die Jungfrau Sophia und die Jungfrau Maria bei Jakob Böhme.' In Garewicz and Haas, *Gott, Natur und Mensch*, 147–63.

Ingen, Ferdinand van. *Jacob Böhme in seiner Zeit*. Stuttgart-Bad Cannstatt: Frommann-Holzboog, 2015.

Invictus. 'Suggestive Inquiry into the Hermetic Mystery.' *Historic Magazine* 25 (1907): 224e.

Ising, Dieter. 'Radikaler Pietismus in der frühen Korrespondenz Johann Albrecht Bengels.' *Pietismus und Neuzeit* 31 (2005): 152–95.

Jablonski, Daniel Ernst. *Christliche Gedächtnüß-Predigt, Als . . . Levin Schardius, . . . Den 12. Januarii 1699. selig aus diesem Leben abgefordert, und den 19. darauf zu seiner Ruhestat gebracht worden*. Cölln a.d. Spree: Druckts Ulrich Liebpert, Churfürstl. Brandenb. Hoff-Buchdr., 1699.

Janacek, Bruce. *Alchemical Belief: Occultism in the Religious Culture of Early Modern England*. University Park: Pennsylvania State University Press, 2011.

Janssen, Frans A. 'Böhme's *Wercken* (1682): Its Editor, Its Publisher, Its Printer.' *Quaerendo* 16 (1986): 137–41.

Janssen, Frans A. 'Die erste Ausgabe von Böhmes gesammelten Werken 1682.' In Harmsen, *Jacob Böhmes Weg in die Welt*, 249–54.

Jöcher, Christian Gottlieb. *Allgemeines Gelehrten-Lexicon*. 4 vols. Leipzig: In Johann Friedrich Gleditschens Buchhandlung, 1750–51.

Jorink, Eric. *Reading the Book of Nature in the Dutch Golden Age, 1575-1715*. Translated by Peter Mason. Leiden: Brill, 2010.

Josephus, Flavius. *Judean Antiquities 1-4: Translation and Commentary*. Edited by Louis H. Feldman. Leiden: Brill, 2000.

Josten, C. H. 'A Translation of John Dee's "Monas Hieroglyphica" (Antwerp, 1564), with an Introduction and Annotations.' *Ambix* 12 (1964): 84-221.

Jung, C. G. 'The Bologna Enigma.' *Ambix* 2 (1946): 182-91.

Jung, C. G. *Psychologie und Alchemie*. 2nd ed. Olten: Walter-Verlag, 1972. First published 1943/51.

Jungmayr, Petra. *Georg von Welling (1655-1727): Studien zu Leben und Werk*. Stuttgart: Steiner, 1990.

Junker, Uwe. *Das 'Buch der Heiligen Dreifaltigkeit' in seiner zweiten alchemistischen Fassung (Kadolzburg 1433)*. Cologne: Forschungsstelle des Instituts für Geschichte der Medizin der Universität zu Köln, 1986.

Kahn, Didier. 'Les débuts de Gérard Dorn d'après le manuscrit autographe de sa *Clavis totius Philosophiæ Chymisticæ* (1565).' In Telle, *Analecta Paracelsica*, 59-126.

Kahn, Didier. 'Paracelsisme, alchimie et diplomatie dans le contexte de la Paix de Westphalie.' In *République des lettres, république des arts: mélanges offerts à Marc Fumaroli, de l'Académie Française*. Edited by Christian Mouchel and Colette Nativel, 103-21. Geneva: Droz, 2008.

Kahn, Didier. 'Recherches sur le *Livre* attribué au prétendu Bernard le Trévisan (fin du XVe siècle).' In *Alchimia e medicina nel Medioevo*. Edited by Chiara Crisciani and Agostino Paravicini Bagliani, 265-336. Florence: Sismel—Edizioni del Galluzzo, 2003.

Kämmerer, Ernst Wilhelm. *Das Leib-Seele-Geist-Problem bei Paracelsus und einigen Autoren des 17. Jahrhunderts*. Wiesbaden: Steiner, 1971.

Karnitscher, Tünde Beatrix. *Der vergessene Spiritualist Johann Theodor von Tschesch (1595-1649): Untersuchungen und Spurensicherung zu Leben und Werk eines religiösen Nonkonformisten*. Göttingen: Vandenhoeck & Ruprecht, 2015.

Karpenko, Vladimír. 'Martin Rulands *Lexicon Alchemiae* im Kontext der chemischen Sprache und Systematik.' *Studia Rudolphina* 11 (2011): 102-26.

Kassell, Lauren. 'Magic, Alchemy and the Medical Economy in Early Modern England: The Case of Robert Fludd's Magnetical Medicine.' In *Medicine and the Market in England and Its Colonies, c. 1450-c. 1850*. Edited by Mark S. R. Jenner and Patrick Wallis, 88-107. Basingstoke: Palgrave Macmillan, 2007.

Katritzky, M. A. 'Marketing Medicine: The Image of the Early Modern Mountebank.' *Renaissance Studies* 15 (2001): 121-53.

Katritzky, M. A. 'Quacksalber in den Schriften Christian Weises und Johann Kuhnaus: *Der Politische Quacksalber* (1693) und *Der Musicalische Quack=salber* (1700).' In *Poet und Praeceptor: Christian Weise (1642-1708) zum 300. Todestag*. Edited by Peter Hesse, 319-40. Dresden: Neisse-Verlag, 2009.

Kemp, Friedhelm. 'Jakob Böhme in Holland, England und Frankreich.' In *Studien zur europäischen Rezeption deutscher Barockliteratur*. Edited by Leonard Forster, 211-26. Wiesbaden: Harrassowitz, 1983.

Keyser, Marja, J. F. Heijbroek, and Ingeborg Verheul, eds. *Frederik Muller (1817-1881): leven en werken*. Zutphen: Walburg, 1996.

Khunrath, Heinrich. *Von Hylealischen, Das ist Pri-Materialischen Catholischen, oder Algemeinen Natürlichen Chaos, Der Naturgemessen Alchymiae und Alchymisten*. Magdeburg: Durch Andreas Genen Erben, 1597.

King, Francis X. *The Flying Sorcerer: Being the Magical and Aeronautical Adventures of Francis Barrett, Author of* The Magus. Oxford: Mandrake, 1992.

Klosterberg, Brigitte. 'Brecklingiana in den Beständen der Franckeschen Stiftungen.' In Klosterberg et al., *Friedrich Breckling*, 35–40.

Klosterberg, Brigitte. 'Libri Brecklingici: Bücher aus dem Besitz Friedrich Brecklings in der Bibliothek des Halleschen Waisenhauses.' In *Interdisziplinäre Pietismusforschung: Beiträge zum Ersten Internationalen Kongress für Pietismusforschung*. Edited by Udo Sträter, 871–81. Tübingen: Niemeyer, 2005.

Klosterberg, Brigitte, Guido Naschert, and Mirjam-Juliane Pohl, eds. *Friedrich Breckling (1629–1711): Prediger, 'Wahrheitszeuge' und Vermittler des Pietismus im niederländischen Exil*. Halle: Verlag der Frankeschen Stiftungen, 2011.

Knijf, Philip, Sibbe Jan Visser, and Piet Visser. *Bibliographia Sociniana: A Bibliographical Reference Tool for the Study of Dutch Socinianism and Antitrinitarianism*. Hilversum: Verloren, 2004.

Kober, Tobias. 'Umständlicher Bericht . . . von der Kranckheit, Absterben und Begräbniß des sel. *Autoris Theosophi*, an die Edlen Herren von Schweinichen.' In Jacob Boehme, *De vita et scriptis*, 40–52. [Leiden?], 1730.

Koitzsch, Kerry E. 'Mrs Atwood and the Utopian Tradition: A Nineteenth-Century Alchemist as Utopian Theorist.' In *The Individual and Utopia: A Multidisciplinary Study of Humanity and Perfection*. Edited by Clint Jones and Cameron Ellis, 99–114. Farnham: Ashgate, 2015.

Kornexl, Dietrich. 'Studien zu Marquard Freher (1565–1614): Leben, Werke und gelehrtengeschichtliche Bedeutung.' PhD thesis, Albert-Ludwigs-Universität Freiburg i.Br., 1967.

Koyré, Alexandre. *La philosophie de Jacob Boehme*. Paris: Librarie philosophique J. Vrin, 1929.

Kraft, Alexander. 'Dorothea Juliana Wallich, geb. Fischer (1657–1725), eine Alchemistin aus Thüringen.' *Genealogie: Deutsche Zeitschrift für Familienkunde* XXXIII/66 (2017): 539–55.

Kraft, Alexander. 'Dorothea Juliana Wallich (1657–1725) and Her Contributions to the Chymical Knowledge about the Element Cobalt.' In *Women in Their Element: Selected Women's Contributions to the Periodic System*. Edited by Annette Lykknes and Brigitte van Tiggelen, 57–69. Singapore: World Scientific, 2019.

Kress, Berthold. *Divine Diagrams: The Manuscripts and Drawings of Paul Lautensack (1477/78–1558)*. Leiden: Brill, 2014.

Kuhlmann, Quirinus. *Widerlegte Brecklingsworte aus zweien Brifen an Andreas Luppius gezogen*. Amsterdam: Gedrukt vor den Autor auch zu finden bei Andrea Luppio, Buchhändlern, 1688.

Kühlmann, Wilhelm, ed. *Killy Literaturlexikon: Autoren und Werke des deutschsprachigen Kulturraumes*. 2nd, completely reworked ed. 13 vols. Berlin: De Gruyter, 2008–11.

Kühlmann, Wilhelm, and Joachim Telle. *Der Frühparacelsismus (Corpus Paracelsisticum)*. 3 vols. Berlin: De Gruyter, 2001–13.

Kühlmann, Wilhelm, and Friedrich Vollhardt, eds. *Offenbarung und Episteme: Zur europäischen Wirkung Jakob Böhmes im 17. und 18. Jahrhundert*. Berlin: De Gruyter, 2012.

Kummer, Ulrike. '"Gold von Mitternacht"—Zu Leben und Werk des Arztpietisten Johann Philipp Maul (1662–1727).' *Pietismus und Neuzeit* 40 (2014): 134–62.

Kuzmin, Eugene. *Alchemical Imagery in the Works of Quirinus Kuhlmann*. Wilsonville: Sirius Academic Press, 2013.

Lamey, Ferdinand. *Hermann von der Hardt in seinen Briefen und seinen Beziehungen: Neudruck mit bibliographischen Nachträgen*. Wiesbaden: Harrassowitz, 1974.

Lamoen, Frank van. 'Chiliast contra stadhouder: Johannes Rothé (1628–1702).' *Mededelingen van de Stichting Jacob Campo Weyerman* 22 (1999): 145–59.

Lamoen, Frank van. 'Verliefd op Sophia: Alhart de Raadt (1640–1716) en de vrienden van Jacob Boehme.' *Geschiedenis van de wijsbegeerte in Nederland* 13 (2002): 119–63.

Latham, J. E. M. *Search for a New Eden. James Pierrepont Greaves (1777–1842): The Sacred Socialist and His Followers*. Madison, NJ: Farleigh Dickinson University Press, 1999.

Lavoie, Jeffrey D. *A Search for Meaning in Victorian Religion: The Spiritual Journey and Esoteric Teachings of Charles Carleton Massey*. Bethlehem, PA: Lehigh University Press, 2014.

Lehmann-Brauns, Sicco. *Weisheit in der Weltgeschichte: Philosophiegeschichte zwischen Barock und Aufklärung*. Tübingen: Niemeyer, 2004.

Lemper, Ernst-Heinz. *Jakob Böhme: Leben und Werk*. Berlin: Union, 1976.

Lévi, Eliphas. *Dogme et rituel de la haute magie*. 2nd, expanded ed. 2 vols. Paris: Germer Baillière, 1861.

Libavius, Andreas. *Wolmeinendes Bedencken, Von der Fama unnd Confession der Brüderschafft deß RosenCreutzes*. Erfurt: Bey Johann Röhbock, 1616.

Libavius, Andreas, and Jacob Michael. *De millenariorum haereticorum secta.... Disputatio Casimiriana ad XXII. Junii anno Salv. MDCVI*. Coburg: Typis Casparis Bertschii, 1616.

Linden, Stanton J., ed. *Mystical Metal of Gold: Essays on Alchemy and Renaissance Culture*. New York: AMS Press, 2007.

'Literary Gossip.' *Athenaeum*, no. 2577 (17 March 1877): 353–54.

The Lives of Alchemystical Philosophers. 2nd ed. London: Printed by Macdonald and Son, Cloth Fair, for Lackington, Allen, & Co., 1815. First published 1814.

The Lives of the Adepts in Alchemystical Philosophy. London: Lackington, Allen & Co., 1814.

Löen, Johann Michael von. *Sod rikvon ve-serefa i.e. Das Geheimnuß der Verwesung und Verbrennung aller Dinge*. 2nd, expanded ed. Frankfurt a.M.: Bey Johann Friedrich Fleischer, 1733.

López Pérez, Miguel, Didier Kahn, and Mar Rey Bueno, eds. *Chymia: Science and Nature in Medieval and Early Modern Europe*. Newcastle: Cambridge Scholars, 2010.

Love, Harold. *The Culture and Commerce of Texts: Scribal Publication in Seventeenth-Century England*. 2nd ed. Amherst: University of Massachusetts Press, 1998. First published 1993.

Luther, Martin. *Das dise wort Christi (Das ist meyn leyb etc.) noch fest stehen: widder die Schwermgeyster*. Zwickau: Gedruckt durch Gabriel Kantz, 1527.

Luther, Martin. *Werke: Kritische Gesamtausgabe* (Abt. Tischreden). 6 vols. Weimar: Böhlau, 1912–21.

Maillard, Christine. 'Eine Wissensform unter Heterodoxieverdacht: Die spekulative Alchemie nach 1600.' In *Heterodoxie in der frühen Neuzeit*. Edited by Hartmut Laufhütte and Michael Titzmann, 267–89. Tübingen: Niemeyer, 2006.

Maitland, Edward. *Anna Kingsford: Her Life, Letters, Diary and Work*. 2 vols. Cambridge: Cambridge University Press, 2011. First published 1896.

Margolin, Jean-Claude, and Sylvain Matton, eds. *Alchimie et philosophie à la Renaissance: actes du colloque international de Tours (4–7 Décembre 1991)*. Paris: Librairie philosophique J. Vrin, 1993.
Marquet, Jean-François. 'Philosophie et alchimie chez Gerhard Dorn.' In Margolin and Matton, *Alchimie et philosophie*, 215–21.
Martensen, Hans Lassen. *Jacob Boehme: His Life and Teaching. Or Studies in Theosophy*. Translated by T. Rhys Evans. London: Hodder and Stoughton, 1885.
Martin, Lucinda. '"God's Strange Providence": Jane Lead in the Correspondence of Johann Georg Gichtel.' In Hessayon, *Jane Lead*, 187–212.
Martin, Lucinda. 'Jakob Böhmes "göttliche Sophia" und Emanzipationsansätze bei pietistischen Autorinnen.' In Kühlmann and Vollhardt, *Offenbarung und Episteme*, 241–57.
Martinón-Torres, Marcos. 'Some Recent Developments in the Historiography of Alchemy.' *Ambix* 58 (2011): 215–37.
Marx, Jacques. 'Alchimie et palingénésie.' *Isis* 62 (1971): 274–89.
Matton, Sylvain. 'Marsile Ficin et l'alchimie: sa position, son influence.' In Margolin and Matton, *Alchimie et philosophie*, 123–92.
Matus, Zachary A. 'Alchemy and Christianity in the Middle Ages.' *History Compass* 10 (2012): 934–45.
Maul, Johann Philipp. *Zahav mi-ẓafon sive medicina theologica, chymico irenica, et christiano-cabbalistica, Vorgestellet in der Ersten Continuation curioser und erbaulicher Gespräche Vom Gold von Mitternacht*. 2nd ed. Wesel: Bey Jacobus von Wesel, Buchh., 1713. First published 1709.
Mayer, Paola. *Jena Romanticism and Its Appropriation of Jakob Böhme: Theosophy, Hagiography, Literature*. Montreal: McGill-Queen's University Press, 1999.
McDowell, Nicholas. 'Dead Souls and Modern Minds? Mortalism and the Early Modern Imagination, from Marlowe to Milton.' *Journal of Medieval and Early Modern Studies* 40 (2010): 559–92.
McGinn, Bernard. *The Mystical Thought of Meister Eckhart: The Man from Whom God Hid Nothing*. New York: Crossroad, 2001.
McLaughlin, R. Emmet. 'Spiritualism: Schwenckfeld and Franck and Their Early Modern Resonances.' In *A Companion to Anabaptism and Spiritualism, 1521–1700*. Edited by John D. Roth and James M. Stayer, 119–61. Leiden: Brill, 2007.
Mertens, Michèle, ed. *Zosime de Panopolis: Mémoires authentiques*. Paris: Les Belles Lettres, 1995.
Microcosmische Vorspiele Des Neuen Himmels und der Neuen Erde. 2nd, revised ed. Amsterdam, 1744.
Mögling, Daniel. *Speculum Sophicum Rhodo-Stauroticum Das ist: Weitläuffige Entdeckung deß Collegii unnd axiomatum von der sondern erleuchten Fraternitet Christ-RosenCreutz*. N.p., 1618.
Mohr, Jan. 'Konvergenzen in der "poetischen" Böhme-Rezeption Abraham von Franckenbergs und Daniel Czepkos.' In Kühlmann and Vollhardt, *Offenbarung und Episteme*, 93–123.
Moore, James R. *The Post-Darwinian Controversies: A Study of the Protestant Struggle to Come to Terms with Darwin in Great Britain and America 1870–1900*. Cambridge: Cambridge University Press, 1979.
Moran, Bruce T. 'The Alchemist's Reality.' *Halcyon* 9 (1987): 133–48.

Moran, Bruce T. 'Alchemy, Prophecy, and the Rosicrucians: Raphael Eglinus and Mystical Currents of the Early Seventeenth Century.' In *Alchemy and Chemistry in the 16th and 17th Centuries*. Edited by Piyo Rattansi and Antonio Clericuzio, 103–19. Dordrecht: Kluwer, 1994.

Moran, Bruce T. *Andreas Libavius and the Transformation of Alchemy: Separating Chemical Cultures with Polemical Fire*. Sagamore Beach: Science History, 2007.

Moran, Bruce T. 'Introduction.' *Isis* 102 (2011): 300–4.

Morrisson, Mark S. *Modern Alchemy: Occultism and the Emergence of Atomic Theory*. Oxford: Oxford University Press, 2007.

Morrisson, Mark S. 'The Periodical Culture of the Occult Revival: Esoteric Wisdom, Modernity and Counter-Public Spheres.' *Journal of Modern Literature* 31, no. 2 (2008): 1–22.

Muller, Frederik, and Martinus Nijhoff. *Catalogue de la bibliothèque ... formée pendant le 18e siècle par Messieurs Izaak, Johannes et le Dr Johannes Enschedé Imprimeurs-Libraires à Haarlem*. Amsterdam/The Hague: Muller/Nijhoff, 1867.

Mulsow, Martin. 'Eine Reise durch die Gelehrtenrepublik: Soziales Wissen in Gottlieb Stolles Journal der Jahre 1703–1704.' In *Kultur der Kommunikation: Die europäische Gelehrtenrepublik im Zeitalter von Leibniz und Lessing*. Edited by Johannes Ulrich Schneider, 185–201. Wiesbaden: Harrassowitz, 2005.

Muratori, Cecilia. *The First German Philosopher: The Mysticism of Jakob Böhme as Interpreted by Hegel*. Translated by Richard Dixon and Raphaëlle Burns. Dordrecht: Springer, 2016.

Muses, Charles A. 'Ann Judith Penny (née Brown) 1825–1893.' *Jacob Boehme Society Quarterly* 1 (1954): 4–5.

Muses, Charles A. *Illumination on Jacob Boehme: The Work of Dionysius Andreas Freher*. New York: King's Crown Press, 1951.

Naschert, Guido. 'Knorr von Rosenroth als "Wahrheitszeuge" Friedrich Brecklings.' *Morgen-Glantz* 23 (2013): 131–52.

Neugebauer, O. 'The Study of Wretched Subjects.' *Isis* 42 (1951): 111.

Neumann, Hanns-Peter. *Natura sagax—Die geistige Natur: Zum Zusammenhang von Naturphilosophie und Mystik in der frühen Neuzeit am Beispiel Johann Arndts*. Tübingen: Niemeyer, 2004.

'New Works Published from the 14th to the 30th of November.' *Publisher's Circular* 13, no. 317 (2 December 1850): 386–96.

Newman, William R. 'Brian Vickers on Alchemy and the Occult: A Response.' *Perspectives on Science* 17 (2009): 482–506.

Newman, William R. '"*Decknamen* or Pseudochemical Language"? Eirenaeus Philalethes and Carl Jung.' *Revue d'histoire des sciences* 49 (1996): 159–88.

Newman, William R. *Newton the Alchemist: Science, Enigma, and the Quest for Nature's 'Secret Fire.'* Princeton: Princeton University Press, 2019.

Newman, William R. *Promethean Ambitions: Alchemy and the Quest to Perfect Nature*. Chicago: University of Chicago Press, 2004.

Newman, William R. *The Summa Perfectionis of Pseudo-Geber: A Critical Edition, Translation and Study*. Leiden: Brill, 1991.

Newman, William R., and Lawrence M. Principe. *Alchemy Tried in the Fire: Starkey, Boyle, and the Fate of Helmontian Chemistry*. Chicago: University of Chicago Press, 2002.

Newman, William R., and Lawrence M. Principe. 'Alchemy vs. Chemistry: The Etymological Origins of a Historiographic Mistake.' *Early Science and Medicine* 3 (1998): 32–65.

Nitzschke, Bernd. 'Herbert Silberer—Luftschiffer und Halluzinationsforscher—Stichworte zu seinem Leben und Werk.' In *Aus dem Kreis um Sigmund Freud: Zu den Protokollen der Wiener Psychoanalytischen Vereinigung*. Edited by Ernst Federn and Gerhard Wittenberger, 170-75. Frankfurt a.M.: Fischer-Taschenbuch-Verlag, 1992.

Nowotny, Otto. 'Paracelsus und die Transmutation.' In *Rosarium litterarum: Beiträge zur Pharmazie- und Wissenschaftsgeschichte*. Edited by Christoph Friedrich, Sabine Bernschneider-Reif, and Daniela Schierhorn, 251-58. Eschborn: Govi-Verlag, 2003.

Nummedal, Tara. 'The Alchemist.' In *A Companion to the History of Science*. Edited by Bernard Lightman, 58-70. Chichester: Wiley Blackwell, 2016.

Nummedal, Tara. *Alchemy and Authority in the Holy Roman Empire*. Chicago: University of Chicago Press, 2007.

Nummedal, Tara. 'Alchemy and Religion in Christian Europe.' *Ambix* 60 (2013): 311-22.

Nummedal, Tara. *Anna Zieglerin and the Lion's Blood: Alchemy and End Times in Reformation Germany*. Philadelphia: University of Pennsylvania Press, 2019.

Nummedal, Tara, and Donna Bilak, eds. *Furnace and Fugue: A Digital Edition of Michael Maier's* Atalanta fugiens *(1618) with Scholarly Commentary*. https://doi.org/10.26300/bdp.ff. Charlottesville: University of Virginia Press, 2019.

Oberländer, Erwin. 'Königliches Intermezzo in Kurland: Ludwig XVIII. in Mitau und Blankenfeld.' In *Ostseeprovinzen, Baltische Staaten und das Nationale: Festschrift für Gert von Pistohlkors zum 70. Geburtstag*. Edited by Norbert Angermann, Michael Garleff, and Wilhelm Lenz, 165-84. Münster: LIT, 2005.

Obrist, Barbara. *Les débuts de l'imagerie alchimique (XIVe-XVe siècles)*. Paris: Editions le Sycomore, 1982.

Osiander, Andreas. *Disputationes duae: Una, de lege et evangelio, habita nonis Aprilis. 1549. Altera, de iustificatione, habita 9. cal. Novembris. 1550*. Königsberg: Ex officina haeredum Joannis Lufftii, 1550.

Owen, Alex. *The Place of Enchantment: British Occultism and the Culture of the Modern*. Chicago: University of Chicago Press, 2004.

Oxford Dictionary of National Biography (*ODNB*). http://www.oxforddnb.com. Oxford: Oxford University Press, 2004 ff.

Oxford English Dictionary: The Definitive Record of the English Language. http://www.oed.com. Oxford: Oxford University Press, 1992 ff.

Pagel, Walter. 'Jung's Views on Alchemy.' *Isis* 39 (1948): 44-48.

Pagel, Walter. *Paracelsus: An Introduction to Philosophical Medicine in the Era of the Renaissance*. 2nd, revised ed. Basel: Karger, 1982. First published 1958.

Pagel, Walter. 'The Vindication of "Rubbish."' In *Religion and Neoplatonism in Renaissance Medicine*. Edited by Marianne Winder, 1-14. London: Variorum Reprints, 1985.

Paracelsus, Theophrastus. *Essential Theoretical Writings*. Edited and translated by Andrew Weeks. Leiden: Brill, 2007.

Paracelsus, Theophrastus. *Sämtliche Werke. 1. Abteilung: Medizinische, naturwissenschaftliche und philosophische Schriften*. Edited by Karl Sudhoff. 14 vols. Berlin: Oldenbourg, 1922-33.

Park, Katharine. 'The Organic Soul.' In *The Cambridge History of Renaissance Philosophy*. Edited by Quentin Skinner, Eckhard Kessler, and Jill Kraye, 464-84. Cambridge: Cambridge University Press, 1988.

Parry, Glyn. *The Arch-Conjuror of England: John Dee*. New Haven: Yale University Press, 2011.

Pasi, Marco. *Aleister Crowley and the Temptation of Politics*. Durham: Acumen, 2014.

Patrizi, Francesco. *Nova de universis philosophia*. Ferrara: Apud Benedictum Mammarellum, 1591.

Pattison, George. 'H. L. Martensen on Jacob Boehme.' In Hessayon and Apetrei, *An Introduction to Jacob Boehme*, 244–62.

Paulus, Julian. 'Alchemie und Paracelsismus um 1600: Siebzig Porträts.' In Telle, *Analecta Paracelsica*, 335–406.

Pelikan, Jaroslav, and Valerie Hotchkiss, eds. *Creeds and Confessions of Faith in the Christian Tradition*. 4 vols. New Haven: Yale University Press, 2003.

Pels, Peter. 'Spiritual Facts and Super-Visions: The "Conversion" of Alfred Russel Wallace.' *Etnofoor* 8 (1995): 69–91.

Penman, Leigh. 'The Broken Tradition: Uncovering Errors in the Correspondence of Jacob Böhme.' *Aries* 18 (2018): 96–125.

Penman, Leigh T. I. 'Boehme's Intellectual Networks and the Heterodox Milieu of His Theosophy, 1600–1624.' In Hessayon and Apetrei, *An Introduction to Jacob Boehme*, 57–76.

Penman, Leigh T. I., ed. *Cabala: Mirror of Art and Nature. Editio trilingua: A Critical Edition of the German and Latin Editions 1615-1616, Published by Stephan Michelspacher in Augsburg, together with an Annotated English Translation*. Seattle: Ouroboros Press, 2015.

Penman, Leigh T. I. 'Climbing Jacob's Ladder: Crisis, Chiliasm, and Transcendence in the Thought of Paul Nagel (†1624), a Lutheran Dissident during the Time of the Thirty Years' War.' *Intellectual History Review* 20 (2010): 201–26.

Penman, Leigh T. I. 'The First Appearance of Jacob Böhme's Work in Print.' *Notes and Queries* 57 (2010): 419–21.

Penman, Leigh T. I. 'A Heterodox Publishing Enterprise of the Thirty Years' War: Additions to the Catalogue of Hans Fabel's Publications.' *Library* 19 (2018): 360–67.

Penman, Leigh T. I. 'A Heterodox Publishing Enterprise of the Thirty Years' War: The Amsterdam Office of Hans Fabel (1616–after 1650).' *Library* 15 (2014): 3–44.

Penman, Leigh T. I. *Hope and Heresy: The Problem of Chiliasm in Lutheran Confessional Culture, 1570–1630*. Dordrecht: Springer, 2019.

Penman, Leigh T. I. 'Jacob Böhme and His Networks.' In Andersson et al., *Jacob Böhme and His World*, 98–120.

Penman, Leigh T. I. '*Paraluther*: Explaining an Unexpected Portrait of Paracelsus in Andreas Hartmann's *Curriculum Vitae Lutheri* (1601).' In *Religion, the Supernatural and Visual Culture in Early Modern Europe: An Album Amicorum for Charles Zika*. Edited by Jennifer Spinks and Dagmar Eichberger, 161–84. Leiden: Brill, 2015.

Penman, Leigh T. I. ' "Repulsive Blasphemies": Paul Nagel's Appropriation of Unprinted Works of Jakob Böhme and Valentin Weigel in His *Prodromus astronomiae apocalypticae* (1620).' *Daphnis* 38 (2009): 597–620.

Penman, Leigh T. I. 'Statt "Briefe Böhmes an . . ." nun eine erste "Korrespondenz mit . . .": Nachricht von der Entdeckung zweier Briefe Paul Kayms an Jacob Böhme.' In *Morgenröte im Aufgang: Beiträge einer Tagung zum 400. Jahrestag der Entstehung von Jacob Böhmes Erstschrift*. Edited by Günther Bonheim and Thomas Regehly, 197–208. Berlin: Weißensee Verlag, 2017.

Penny, A. J. *An Introduction to the Study of Jacob Boehme's Writings*. New York: Grace Shaw Duff, 1901.

Peuckert, Will-Erich. *Das Leben Jakob Böhmes*. Jena: Diederichs, 1924.

Peuckert, Will-Erich. *Pansophie: Ein Versuch zur Geschichte der weissen und schwarzen Magie*. Edited by Rolf Christian Zimmermann. 2nd, revised ed. Berlin: Schmidt, 1973. First published 1928.

Pfefferl, Horst. 'Christoph Weickhart als Paracelsist: Zu Leben und Persönlichkeit eines Kantors Valentin Weigels.' In Telle, *Analecta Paracelsica*, 407–23.

Pfefferl, Horst. 'Die Überlieferung der Schriften Valentin Weigels (Teildruck).' PhD thesis, Philipps-Universität Marburg, 1991.

Pfefferl, Horst. 'Valentin Weigel und Paracelsus.' In *Paracelsus und sein dämonengläubiges Jahrhundert*. Edited by Sepp Domandl, 77–95. Vienna: Verband der Wissenschaftlichen Gesellschaften Österreichs, 1988.

Pfister, Kathrin. 'Joachim Polemann: Biographische Notizen zu einem Fachschriftsteller und Alchemiker des 17. Jahrhunderts.' In *Minera discipulorum: Vorstösse in das Fachschrifttum der frühen Neuzeit. Gedenkschrift für Joachim Telle*. Edited by Laura Balbiani and Kathrin Pfister, 161–70. Heidelberg: Mattes, 2014.

Philalethes, Lover of. *A Short Enquiry concerning the Hermetic Art*. Edited by Non Omnis Moriar [William Wynn Westcott]. London: Theosophical Publishing Society, 1894.

Pietsch, Andreas. 'Expanding the Boundaries of Orthodoxy? Friedrich Breckling and the 1687/90 German Edition of Hiel's Works.' *Church History and Religious Culture* 98 (2018): 91–110.

Poortman, J. J. *Vehicles of Consciousness: The Concept of Hylic Pluralism (Ochēma)*. Translated by N. D. Smith. 4 vols. Utrecht: Theosophical Society, 1978.

Pordage, John. 'Ein Gründlich Philosophisch Sendschreiben vom rechten und wahren Steine der Weißheit.' In *Theologia mystica: oder Geheime und verborgne göttliche Lehre von den Ewigen unsichtbahrlichkeiten: als vom Mundô et Globô Archetypô*, 267–82. Amsterdam: Bey Heinrich Wettstein daselbst zu finden, 1698.

Powers, John C. *Inventing Chemistry: Herman Boerhaave and the Reform of the Chemical Arts*. Chicago: University of Chicago Press, 2012.

Praamsma, Frits. *Zacharias Webber (1644–1696): irenisch lutheraan—verlicht protestant. Kerk en theologie in het denken van een zeventiende-eeuws kunstschilder*. Delft: Eburon, 2013.

Prak, Maarten. *Gouden Eeuw: het raadsel van de Republiek*. Nijmegen: SUN, 2002.

Priesner, Claus, and Karin Figala, eds. *Alchemie: Lexikon einer hermetischen Wissenschaft*. Munich: Beck, 1998.

Principe, Lawrence M. *Alchemy and Chemistry: Breaking Up and Making Up (Again and Again). Dibner Library Lecture, December 11, 2014*. Washington: Smithsonian Libraries, 2017.

Principe, Lawrence M. 'Alchemy Restored.' *Isis* 102 (2011): 305–12.

Principe, Lawrence M. *The Aspiring Adept: Robert Boyle and His Alchemical Quest*. Princeton: Princeton University Press, 1998.

Principe, Lawrence. '"Chemical Translation" and the Role of Impurities in Alchemy: Examples from Basil Valentine's *Triumph-Wagen*.' *Ambix* 34 (1987): 21–30.

Principe, Lawrence M. 'The Development of the Basil Valentine Corpus and Biography: Pseudepigraphic Corpora and Paracelsian Ideas.' *Early Science and Medicine* 24 (2019): 549–72.

Principe, Lawrence M. 'The End of Alchemy? The Repudiation and Persistence of Chrysopoeia at the Académie Royale des Sciences in the Eighteenth Century.' In *Chemical Knowledge in the Early Modern World*. Edited by Matthew D. Eddy, Seymour

H. Mauskopf, and William R. Newman, 96–116. Chicago: University of Chicago Press, 2014.

Principe, Lawrence M., ed. *New Narratives in Eighteenth-Century Chemistry: Contributions from the First Francis Bacon Workshop, 21–23 April 2005, California Institute of Technology, Pasadena, California.* Dordrecht: Springer, 2007.

Principe, Lawrence M. 'Reflections on Newton's Alchemy in Light of the New Historiography of Alchemy.' In *Newton and Newtonianism: New Studies.* Edited by James E. Force and Sarah Hutton, 205–19. Dordrecht: Kluwer, 2004.

Principe, Lawrence M. 'Revealing Analogies: The Descriptive and Deceptive Roles of Sexuality and Gender in Latin Alchemy.' In *Hidden Intercourse: Eros and Sexuality in the History of Western Esotericism.* Edited by Wouter J. Hanegraaff and Jeffrey J. Kripal, 209–29. New York: Fordham University Press, 2011.

Principe, Lawrence M. 'A Revolution Nobody Noticed? Changes in Early Eighteenth-Century Chymistry.' In Principe, *New Narratives*, 1–22.

Principe, Lawrence M. *The Secrets of Alchemy.* Chicago: University of Chicago Press, 2013.

Principe, Lawrence M. 'Transmuting Chymistry into Chemistry: Eighteenth-Century Chrysopoeia and Its Repudiation.' In *Neighbours and Territories: The Evolving Identity of Chemistry.* Edited by José Ramón Bertomeu-Sánchez, Duncan Thorburn Burns, and Brigitte van Tiggelen, 21–34. Leuven: Mémosciences, 2008.

Principe, Lawrence M., and William R. Newman. 'Some Problems with the Historiography of Alchemy.' In *Secrets of Nature: Astrology and Alchemy in Early Modern Europe.* Edited by William R. Newman and Anthony Grafton, 385–431. Cambridge: MIT Press, 2001.

Principe, Lawrence M., and Andrew Weeks. 'Jacob Boehme's Divine Substance *Salitter*: Its Nature, Origin, and Relationship to Seventeenth Century Scientific Theories.' *British Journal for the History of Science* 22 (1989): 53–61.

Prinke, Rafał T. 'Beyond Patronage: Michael Sendivogius and the Meanings of Success in Alchemy.' In López Pérez et al., *Chymia*, 175–231.

Prinke, Rafał T. 'New Light on the Alchemical Writings of Michael Sendivogius (1566–1636).' *Ambix* 63 (2016): 217–43.

Prinke, Rafał T. 'The Twelfth Adept: Michael Sendivogius in Rudolfine Prague.' In *The Rosicrucian Enlightenment Revisited.* Edited by Ralph White, 143–92. Hudson: Lindisfarne Books, 1999.

Prinke, Rafał T., and Mike A. Zuber. '"Learn to Restrain Your Mouth": Alchemical Rumours and Their Historiographical Afterlives.' *Early Science and Medicine* 25 (2020): 413–52.

Pseudo-Weigel. *Dritter Theil Deß Gnothi Seauton Oder Cognosce Teipsum genannt.* Newstadt [Magdeburg]: Bey Johan Knuber [Johann Francke], 1618.

Pseudo-Weigel. *Himmlisch Manna, Azoth et Ignis, das ist: güldenes Kleinod, handelnde von dem köstlichen Eckstein der Natur und desselben wunderbaren unaussprechlichen Kräften und Tugenden.* Amsterdam, 1787.

Pseudo-Weigel. *Zwey schöne Büchlein, Das Erste, Von dem leben Christi, . . . Das Ander, Eine kurtze außführliche Erweisung.* Edited by [Johann Siebmacher]. Newstatt [Frankfurt a.M.]: [Lucas Jennis], 1618/21?

Pumfrey, Stephen. 'The Spagyric Art; or, the Impossible Work of Separating Pure from Impure Paracelsianism: A Historiographical Analysis.' In Grell, *Paracelsus*, 21–51.

Putscher, Marielene. *Pneuma, Spiritus, Geist: Vorstellungen vom Lebensantrieb in ihren geschichtlichen Wandlungen.* Wiesbaden: Steiner, 1973.

Quispel, Gilles. 'The Original Doctrine of Valentinus the Gnostic.' *Vigiliae Christianae* 50 (1996): 327–52.
Quispel, Gilles. *Valentinus de gnosticus en zijn Evangelie der Waarheid*. Amsterdam: In de Pelikaan, 2003.
Rabinowitz, Joseph L. 'The Owl of Heinrich Khunrath: Its Origins and Significance.' *Chymia* 3 (1950): 243–50.
Rampling, Jennifer M. 'John Dee and the Alchemists: Practising and Promoting English Alchemy in the Holy Roman Empire.' *Studies in History and Philosophy of Science* 43 (2012): 498–508.
Recktenwald, Horst Claus. 'Aufstieg und Niedergang der Universität Altdorf.' *Zeitschrift für Bayerische Landesgeschichte* 30 (1967): 242–63.
Recktenwald, Horst Claus. *Die fränkische Universität Altdorf*. 2nd ed. Nuremberg: Spindler, 1990.
Redgrove, H. Stanley. 'The Alchemical Society.' *Occult Review* 28 (1918): 49–50.
Redgrove, H. Stanley. 'The Quest for Truth in Alchemy.' *Occult Review* 42 (1928): 42–45.
Rhenanus, Johannes, ed. *Dyas chymica tripartita, Das ist: Sechs Herrliche Teutsche Philosophische Tractätlein*. Frankfurt a.M.: Bey Luca Jennis zu finden, 1625.
Rinder, Leonhard. *Catalogus Bibliothecae Fenizerianae: Verzeichnis derjenigen Bücher welche in der Fenizerischen Bibliothek befindlich*. 2nd ed. Nuremberg: Bey Wolfgang Schwartzkopf, 1776. First published 1736.
Rittgers, Ronald K., and Vincent Evener, eds. *Protestants and Mysticism in Reformation Europe*. Leiden: Brill, 2019.
Rocke, A. J. 'Agricola, Paracelsus, and "Chymia."' *Ambix* 32 (1985): 38–45.
Roellenbleck, Georg. 'Lodovico Lazzarelli, Opusculum de bombyce.' In *Literatur und Spiritualität: Hans Sckommodau zum siebzigsten Geburtstag*. Edited by Hans Rheinfelder, Pierre Christophorov, and Eberhard Müller-Bochat, 213–31. Munich: Fink, 1978.
Ronca, Italo. 'Religious Symbolism in Medieval Islamic and Christian Alchemy.' In *Western Esotericism and the Science of Religion*. Edited by Antoine Faivre and Wouter J. Hanegraaff, 95–116. Leuven: Peeters, 1998.
Roos, Anna Marie. 'The Experimental Approach towards a Historiography of Alchemy (Reviewing L. M. Principe, *The Secrets of Alchemy*).' *Studies in History and Philosophy of Biological and Biomedical Sciences* 44 (2013): 787–89.
Rosarium philosophorum. Frankfurt a.M.: Ex officina Cyriaci Jacobi, mense Junio, 1550.
Ross, Tricia M. 'Anthropologia: An (Almost) Forgotten Early Modern History.' *Journal of the History of Ideas* 79 (2018): 1–22.
Ruh, Kurt, Gundolf Keil, Werner Schröder, Burghart Wachinger, and Franz Josef Worstbrock, eds. *Verfasserlexikon: Die deutsche Literatur des Mittelalters*. Berlin: De Gruyter, 1978–2008.
Ruland, Martin. *Lexicon alchemiae sive dictionarium alchemisticum*. Frankfurt a.M.: Cura ac sumtibus Zachariae Palthenii, Librarii ac D., 1612.
Rusterholz, Sibylle. 'Abraham von Franckenbergs Verhältnis zu Jacob Böhme: Versuch einer Neubestimmung aufgrund kritischer Sichtung der Textgrundlagen.' In *Kulturgeschichte Schlesiens in der Frühen Neuzeit*. Edited by Klaus Garber, 205–41. Tübingen: Niemeyer, 2005.
Rusterholz, Sibylle. 'Elemente christlicher Kabbala bei Abraham von Franckenberg.' In *Christliche Kabbala*. Edited by Wilhelm Schmidt-Biggemann, 183–97. Ostfildern: Thorbecke, 2003.

Rusterholz, Sibylle. 'Jacob Böhme im Lichte seiner Gegner und Anhänger: Die zentralen Argumente der Streitschriften von ihren Anfängen zu Lebzeiten Böhmes bis zum Ende des 17. Jahrhunderts.' In Kühlmann and Vollhardt, *Offenbarung und Episteme*, 7–32.

Rusterholz, Sibylle. 'Jacob Böhme im Spiegel totalitären Denkens: Hans Alfred Grunskys nationalsozialistische Sicht des *Philosophus teutonicus*.' *Böhme-Studien* 3 (2013): 91–116.

Rusterholz, Sibylle. 'Jakob Böhme und Anhänger.' In *Die Philosophie des 17. Jahrhunderts: Das Heilige Römische Reich Deutscher Nation, Nord- und Ostmitteleuropa*. Edited by Helmut Holzhey, Wilhelm Schmidt-Biggemann, and Vilem Mudroch, 61–102. Basel: Schwabe, 2001.

Rusterholz, Sibylle. 'Zum Verhältnis von *Liber Naturae* und *Liber Scripturae* bei Jacob Böhme.' In Garewicz and Haas, *Gott, Natur und Mensch*, 129–46.

Salvadori, Stefania. 'The Restitution of "Adam's Angelical and Paradisiacal Body": Jane Lead's Metaphor of Rebirth and Mystical Marriage.' In Hessayon, *Jane Lead*, 143–65.

Salzberg, Rosa. 'In the Mouth of Charlatans: Street Performers and the Dissemination of Pamphlets in Renaissance Italy.' *Renaissance Studies* 24 (2010): 638–53.

Samuel, Geoffrey, and Jay Johnston, eds. *Religion and the Subtle Body in Asia and the West: Between Mind and Body*. London: Routledge, 2013.

Saxby, T. J. *The Quest for the New Jerusalem: Jean de Labadie and the Labadists, 1610–1744*. Dordrecht: Nijhoff, 1987.

Schlechter, Armin, and Gerhard Stamm. *Die kleinen Provenienzen*. Wiesbaden: Harrassowitz, 2000.

Schmauch, Hans. 'Neue Funde zum Lebenslauf des Coppernicus.' *Zeitschrift für die Geschichte und Altertumskunde Ermlands* 28 (1943): 54–99.

Schmidt, Martin. 'Christian Hoburg and Seventeenth-Century Mysticism.' *Journal of Ecclesiastical History* 18 (1967): 51–58.

Schmidt-Biggemann, Wilhelm. 'Abraham von Franckenberg.' In *Geschichte der christlichen Kabbala*. 4 vols., 2:235–57. Stuttgart-Bad Cannstatt: Frommann-Holzboog, 2013.

Schmidt-Biggemann, Wilhelm. 'Abraham von Franckenberg als christlicher Kabbalist.' In *Realität als Herausforderung: Literatur in ihren konkreten historischen Kontexten*. Edited by Ralf Bogner, Ralf Georg Czapla, Robert Seidel, and Christian von Zimmermann, 233–48. Berlin: De Gruyter, 2011.

Schmidt-Biggemann, Wilhelm. *Philosophia Perennis: Historical Outlines of Western Spirituality in Ancient, Medieval and Early Modern Thought*. Dordrecht: Springer, 2004.

Schmitz, Christian. *Ratsbürgerschaft und Residenz: Untersuchungen zu Berliner Ratsfamilien, Heiratskreisen und sozialen Wandlungen im 17. Jahrhundert*. Berlin: De Gruyter, 2002.

Schneider, Daniel. *Gläubiger Christen Hertzens-Freude. . . . Bey ansehnlicher Leichbestattung Des . . . Benedicti Hinckelmanns, . . . Welcher im Jahr 1659. den 17. Aprilis . . . eingeschlaffen*. Dresden: Gedruckt durch Melchior Bergen, Churfürstl. Sächs. Hoff-Buchdr., 1662.

Schneider, Hans. *Der fremde Arndt: Studien zu Leben, Werk und Wirkung Johann Arndts (1555–1621)*. Göttingen: Vandenhoeck & Ruprecht, 2006.

Schneider, Hans. 'Das *Platonisch-hermetische Christenthum*: Ehre Gott Daniel Colbergs Bild des frühneuzeitlichen Spiritualismus.' In *Hermetik: Literarische Figurationen zwischen Babylon und Cyberspace*. Edited by Nicola Kaminski, Heinz J. Drügh, Michael Herrmann, and Andreas Beck, 21–42. Tübingen: Niemeyer, 2002.

Schneider, Heinrich, ed. *Abraham von Franckenbergs Raphael oder Artzt-Engel (Cod. Guelferbytan. Blancob. No. 160)*. 2 vols. Wolfenbüttel: Verlag der Freude (Georg Koch und Paul Zieger), 1924.

Schoeps, Hans-Joachim. *Vom himmlischen Fleisch Christi: Eine dogmengeschichtliche Untersuchung*. Tübingen: Mohr, 1951.

Schrader, Hans-Jürgen. *Literaturproduktion und Büchermarkt des radikalen Pietismus*. Göttingen: Vandenhoeck & Ruprecht, 1989.

Schriks, Chris. *Frederik Muller: baanbreker in de wereld van het Nederlandse boek*. Zutphen: Walburg, 2016.

Scialdone, Maria Paola. '"Aller heilsamste MUM IAH": *Lebensbalsam* (pseudo-) Paracelsiano e *Selbsterlösung* nel *Raphael* di Abraham von Franckenberg.' *Studi Germanici* 39 (2001): 7–35.

Sclei, Bartholomaeus. *Pater Noster: Das ist Eine geheime unnd allgemeine Außlegung Des Heiligen Vater Unsers*. Edited by Abraham von Franckenberg. [Amsterdam]: [Johannes Janssonius], 1639.

Sclei, Bartholomaeus. *Theosophische-Schrifften: Oder Eine Allgemeine und Geheime, jedoch Einfältige und Teutsche THEOLOGIA*. Edited by [Friedrich Breckling]. Amsterdam: [Christoffel Cunradus' widow], 1686.

Secret, François. 'Palingenesis, Alchemy and Metempsychosis in Renaissance Medicine.' *Ambix* 26 (1979): 81–92.

Secret, François. 'Alchimie, palingénésie et métempsychose chez Guillaume Postel.' *Chrysopœia* 3 (1989): 3–60.

[Seidenbecher, Georg Lorenz]. *Chiliasmus sanctus: qui est sabbatismus populo Dei relictus*. Edited by [Petrus Serrarius]. Amsterdam, 1660.

Sepp, Christiaan. *Geschiedkundige nasporingen*. 3 vols. Leiden: De Breuk & Smits, 1872–75.

Serrarius, Petrus, and Benedict Bahnsen. *Catalogus variorum . . . librorum*. Edited by [Johann Georg Gichtel]. Amsterdam: Typis Jacobi van Velsen, in de Kalverstraet, op d'Osse-sluys, 1670.

Severn, Elizabeth. 'Some Mystical Aspects of Alchemy.' *Journal of the Alchemical Society* 2 (May 1914): 110–19.

Shackelford, Jole. 'Paracelsianism and the Orthodox Lutheran Rejection of Vital Philosophy in Early Seventeenth-Century Denmark.' *Early Science and Medicine* 8 (2003): 210–52.

Shackelford, Jole. *A Philosophical Path for Paracelsian Medicine: The Ideas, Intellectual Context, and Influence of Petrus Severinus (1540/2-1602)*. Copenhagen: Museum Tusculanum Press, 2004.

Shantz, Douglas H. 'The Origin of Pietist Notions of New Birth and the New Man: Alchemy and Alchemists in Gottfried Arnold and Johann Heinrich Reitz.' In *The Pietist Impulse in Christianity*. Edited by Christian T. Collins Winn, Christopher Gehrz, G. William Carlson, and Eric Holst, 29–41. Eugene: Pickwick, 2011.

Shantz, Douglas H. *An Introduction to German Pietism: Protestant Renewal at the Dawn of Modern Europe*. Baltimore: Johns Hopkins University Press, 2013.

Shantz, Douglas H. 'Valentin Weigel.' In Rittgers and Evener, *Protestants and Mysticism*, 243–64.

Shirley, Ralph. 'Notes of the Month.' *Occult Review* 34 (1921): 65–73.

Siebenkees, Johann Christian. *Materialien zur Nürnbergischen Geschichte*. 4 vols. Nuremberg: In Commission der A. G. Schneiderischen Kunst- und Buchhandlung, 1792–95.

[Siebmacher, Johann]. '*Introductio Hominis, Oder Kurtze Anleitung zu einem Christlichen Gottseligen Leben.*' In *Philosophia Mystica, Darinn begriffen Eilff unterschidene Theologico-Philosophische, doch teutsche Tractätlein, zum theil auß Theophrasti Paracelsi, zum theil auch M. Valentini Weigelii*. Edited by [Benedictus Figulus], 228–72. Newstadt [Frankfurt a.M.]: Zu finden bey Lucas Jennis, Buchhändler, 1618.

[Siebmacher, Johann]. *Wasserstein der Weysen, Das ist, Ein Chymisch Tractätlein, darin der weg gezeiget, die Materia genennet, und der Proceß beschrieben wird, zu dem hohen geheymnuß der Universal Tinctur zukommen*. Frankfurt a.M.: Bey Lucas Jennis zufinden, 1619.

[Siebmacher, Johann]. *Das Güldne Vließ, Oder Das Allerhöchste, Edelste, Kunstreichste Kleinod, und der urälteste verborgene Schatz der Weisen*. Leipzig: Bey Samuel Benjamin Walthern, 1736.

Silberer, Herbert. *Probleme der Mystik und ihrer Symbolik*. Vienna: Heller, 1914.

Silesius, Angelus. *Cherubinischer Wandersmann: Kritische Ausgabe*. Edited by Louise Gnädinger. Stuttgart: Reclam, 2000. First published 1984.

Simon, Matthias. 'Die Fenitzerbibliothek in Nürnberg.' *Zeitschrift für bayerische Kirchengeschichte* 29 (1960): 167–85.

Simon, Matthias. 'Zur Geschichte der Fenitzerbibliothek.' *Zeitschrift für bayerische Kirchengeschichte* 30 (1961): 101.

Simpson, Anne, and J. K. Rowling. 'Casting a Spell over Young Minds.' *Herald* (Edinburgh, 7 December 1998).

Sinnett, Alfred Percy. *Autobiography*. London: Theosophical History Centre, 1986.

Sinnett, Patience. 'Alchemy as a Spiritual Science.' *Lucifer* 14 (1894): 211–18.

Smith, Pamela H. 'Preface to the New Paperback Edition.' In *The Business of Alchemy: Science and Culture in the Holy Roman Empire*, xi–xxv. Princeton: Princeton University Press, 2016.

[Söldner, Johann Anton]. *Fegfeuer der Chymisten, Worinnen Für Augen gestellt die wahren Besitzer der Kunst; Wie auch Die Ketzer, Betrieger, Sophisten und Herren gern-Grosse*. Amsterdam, 1701.

[Söldner, Johann Anton]. *Keren Happuch, Posaunen Eliae des Künstlers, oder Teutsches Fegfeuer der Scheide-Kunst*. Hamburg: Bey Gottfried Libernickel, im Dohm, 1702.

Soom, A. *Die Politik Schwedens bezüglich des russischen Transithandels über die estnischen Städte in den Jahren 1636–1656*. Tartu: Öpetatud Eesti Selts, 1940.

[South, Mary Anne]. *A Suggestive Inquiry into the Hermetic Mystery with a Dissertation on the More Celebrated of the Alchemical Philosophers*. London: Trelawney Saunders, 1850.

South, Thomas. 'The Enigma of Alchemy.' Edited by Walter Leslie Wilmshurst. *The Quest* 10 (1919): 213–25.

[South, Thomas, and Mary Anne South]. *Early Magnetism in Its Higher Relations to Humanity, as Veiled in the Poets and the Prophets*. London: H. Baillière, 1846.

Sparling, Andrew. 'Paracelsus, a Transmutational Alchemist.' *Ambix* 67 (2020): 62–87.

Stavenhagen, Lee, ed. *A Testament of Alchemy: Being the Revelations of Morienus, Ancient Adept and Hermit of Jerusalem to Khalid ibn Yazid Muʿawiyya, King of the Arabs of the Divine Secrets of the Magisterium and Accomplishment of the Alchemical Art*. Hanover: Brandeis University Press, 1974.

Steiger, Isabelle de. 'The Hermetic Mystery.' *Journal of the Alchemical Society* 2 (November 1913): 17–32.

Steiger, Isabelle de. *Memorabilia: Reminiscences of a Woman Artist and Writer*. London: Rider, 1927.

Steiger, Isabelle de. *On a Gold Basis: A Treatise on Mysticism*. 2nd ed. London: Rider, 1909. First published 1907.

Steiger, Isabelle de. 'To the Editor of the *Occult Review*.' *Occult Review* 14 (1911): 346–49.

Steiger, Johann Anselm. 'Jacob Böhmes Rettung: Friedrich Brecklings *Anticalovius* (1688) als Apologie des mystischen Spiritualismus.' In Kühlmann and Vollhardt, *Offenbarung und Episteme*, 283–94.

Steinmeyer, Elias von. *Die Matrikel der Universität Altdorf*. 2 vols. Würzburg: Königl. Universitätsdruckerei H. Stürtz, 1912.

Stockum, Th. C. van. *Zwischen Jakob Böhme und Johann Scheffler: Abraham von Franckenberg (1593–1652) und Daniel Czepko von Reigersfeld (1605–1660)*. Amsterdam: N.V. Noord-Hollandsche Uitgevers Maatschappij, 1967.

Stoeber, Michael. 'Evelyn Underhill on Magic, Sacrament, and Spiritual Transformation.' *Worship* 77 (2003): 132–51.

Stolberg, Michael. '"You Have No Good Blood in Your Body": Oral Communication in Sixteenth-Century Physicians' Medical Practice.' *Medical History* 59 (2015): 63–82.

Strein, Jürgen. 'Siegmund Heinrich Güldenfalks *Sammlung von mehr als 100 Transmutationsgeschichten* (1784).' In *Iliaster: Literatur und Naturkunde in der frühen Neuzeit (Festgabe für Joachim Telle zum 60. Geburtstag)*. Edited by Wilhelm Kühlmann and Wolf-Dieter Müller-Jahncke, 275–83. Heidelberg: Manutius, 1999.

Strube, Julian. *Sozialismus, Katholizismus und Okkultismus im Frankreich des 19. Jahrhunderts: Die Genealogie der Schriften von Eliphas Lévi*. Berlin: De Gruyter, 2016.

Stuart Moore [Underhill], Evelyn. 'Magic and Mysticism To-day.' *Hibbert Journal* 6 (1908): 373–86.

'*A Suggestive Inquiry into the Hermetic Mystery; with a Dissertation on the more Celebrated of the Alchemical Philosophers*. Saunders' (review). *Athenaeum*, no. 1228 (10 May 1851): 497.

Szulakowska, Urszula. 'The Alchemical Medicine and Christology of Robert Fludd and Abraham von Franckenberg.' In Linden, *Mystical Metal*, 277–98.

Taylor, F. Sherwood. *The Alchemists: Founders of Modern Chemistry*. New York: Arno Press, 1974. First published 1949.

Telle, Joachim. 'Alchemie II. Historisch.' In *Theologische Realenzyklopädie*. Edited by Horst Balz, Gerhard Krause, and Gerhard Müller. 36 vols., 2:199–227. Berlin: De Gruyter, 1978.

Telle, Joachim. *Alchemie und Poesie: Deutsche Alchemikerdichtungen des 15. bis 17. Jahrhunderts*. 2 vols. Berlin: De Gruyter, 2013.

Telle, Joachim, ed. *Analecta Paracelsica: Studien zum Nachleben Theophrast von Hohenheims im deutschen Kulturgebiet der frühen Neuzeit*. Stuttgart: Steiner, 1994.

Telle, Joachim. 'Jakob Böhme unter den deutschen Alchemikern der frühen Neuzeit.' In Kühlmann and Vollhardt, *Offenbarung und Episteme*, 165–82.

Telle, Joachim. *Sol und Luna: Literar- und alchemiegeschichtliche Studien zu einem altdeutschen Bildgedicht*. Hürtgenwald: Pressler, 1980.

Telle, Joachim. 'Zum *Opus mago-cabbalisticum et theosophicum* von Georg von Welling.' *Euphorion* 77 (1983): 359–79.

Thumm, Theodor, Georg Hehl, and Marcus Hailand. *Brevis consideratio trium quaestionum, nostro seculo maximè controversiarium*. Tübingen: Typis Theodorici Werlini, 1624.

Thune, Nils. *The Behmenists and the Philadelphians: A Contribution to the Study of English Mysticism in the Seventeenth and Eighteenth Centuries*. Uppsala: Almquist & Wiksells, 1948.

Tilton, Hereward. 'Alchymia Archetypica: Theurgy, Inner Transformation and the Historiography of Alchemy.' *Quaderni di studi indo-mediterranei* 5 (2012): 179–215.

Tilton, Hereward. *The Quest for the Phoenix: Spiritual Alchemy and Rosicrucianism in the Work of Count Michael Maier (1569–1622)*. Berlin: De Gruyter, 2003.

Toepke, Gustav, and Paul Hintzelmann. *Die Matrikel der Universität Heidelberg*. 7 vols. Heidelberg: Winter, 1884–1916.

Trepp, Anne-Charlott. *Von der Glückseligkeit alles zu wissen: Die Erforschung der Natur als religiöse Praxis in der Frühen Neuzeit*. Frankfurt a.M.: Campus Verlag, 2009.

Trevisanus, Bernardus. *Von der Hermetischen Philosophia, das ist, von dem Gebenedeiten Stain der Weisen*. Strasbourg: Bey Christian Müller, 1574.

[Überfeld, Johann Wilhelm], ed. *Der rechte Weg zum Ewigen Leben: Verfasst in Drey- und neuntzig Fragen und Antworten*. [Frankfurt a.M.], 1683.

Underhill, Evelyn. 'A Defence of Magic.' *Fortnightly Review* 82 (1907): 754–65.

Underhill, Evelyn. *Mysticism: A Study in the Nature and Development of Man's Spiritual Consciousness*. London: Methuen, 1911.

Vainio, Olli-Pekka. *Justification and Participation in Christ: The Development of the Lutheran Doctrine of Justification from Luther to the Formula of Concord (1580)*. Leiden: Brill, 2008.

Vergil. *Aeneidos liber sextus*. Edited by R. G. Austin. Oxford: Clarendon Press, 1977.

Verpoorten, Albrecht Meno. *De Georgii Laurentii Seidenbecheri vita et institutis*. Danzig: Sumptibus et typis Thomae Joannis Schreiberi, Senatus et Gymn. Typographi, 1739.

Versluis, Arthur, ed. *Wisdom's Book: The Sophia Anthology*. St. Paul: Paragon House, 2000.

Versluis, Arthur. *Wisdom's Children: A Christian Esoteric Tradition*. Albany: State University of New York Press, 1999.

Verzeichnis der im deutschen Sprachraum erschienenen Drucke des 17. Jahrhunderts. http://www.vd17.de. Berlin: Gemeinsamer Bibliotheksverbund, 1966 ff.

Vickers, Brian. 'The "New Historiography" and the Limits of Alchemy.' *Annals of Science* 65 (2008): 127–56.

Voss, Karen-Claire. 'Spiritual Alchemy: Interpreting Representative Texts and Images.' In *Gnosis and Hermeticism from Antiquity to Modern Times*. Edited by Roelof van den Broek and Wouter J. Hanegraaff, 147–82. New York: State University of New York Press, 1995.

Waite, A. E. 'To the Editor of the *Occult Review*.' *Occult Review* 15 (1912): 50.

Waite, Arthur Edward. 'The Hermetic Tradition.' *Occult Review* 28 (1918): 44–46.

Waite, Arthur Edward. *Lives of Alchemystical Philosophers: Based on Materials Collected in 1815 and Supplemented by Recent Researches*. London: George Redway, 1888.

Waite, Arthur Edward. *A New Light of Mysticism: Azoth; or, The Star in the East. Embracing the First Matter of the Magnum Opus*. London: Theosophical Publishing Society, 1893.

Waite, Arthur Edward. 'A New Light of Mysticism: To the Editor of "Light."' *Light* 8, no. 402 (1888): 461–62.

Waite, Arthur Edward. 'What is Alchemy? [First Paper.]' *The Unknown World* 1 (1894): 7–11.

Waite, Arthur Edward. 'What is Alchemy? [Second Paper.]' *The Unknown World* 1 (1894): 80–84.

Walker, D. P. 'The Astral Body in Renaissance Medicine.' *Journal of the Warburg and Courtauld Institutes* 21 (1958): 119–33.
Walker, D. P. *Spiritual and Demonic Magic: From Ficino to Campanella.* Notre Dame: University of Notre Dame Press, 1975. First published 1958.
Wall, Ernestien G. E. van der. 'Chiliasmus Sanctus: de toekomstverwachting van Georg Lorenz Seidenbecher (1623–1663).' *Nederlands archief voor kerkgeschiedenis* 63 (1983): 69–83.
Wall, Ernestien G. E. van der. 'De mystieke chiliast Petrus Serrarius (1600–1669) en zijn wereld.' PhD thesis, Rijksuniversiteit Leiden, 1987.
Wall, Ernestien G. E. van der. 'A Philo-Semitic Millenarian on the Reconciliation of Jews and Christians: Henry Jessey and His "The Glory and Salvation of Jehudah and Israel" (1650).' In *Sceptics, Millenarians, and Jews.* Edited by David S. Katz and Jonathan I. Israel, 161–84. Leiden: Brill, 1990.
Wälli, J. 'Raphael Egli (1559–1622).' *Zürcher Taschenbuch* 28 (1905): 154–92.
Wallmann, Johannes. 'Reich Gottes und Chiliasmus in der lutherischen Orthodoxie.' In *Theologie und Frömmigkeit im Zeitalter des Barock,* 105–23. Tübingen: Mohr, 1995.
Wallmann, Johannes. *Der Pietismus.* Göttingen: Vandenhoeck & Ruprecht, 2005.
Walton, Christopher. *An Introduction to Theosophy, or the Science of the 'Mystery of Christ,' That is, of Deity, Nature, and Creature.* London: John Kendrick, 1854.
Walton, Christopher. *Notes and Materials for an Adequate Biography of the Celebrated Divine and Theosopher, William Law.* London: Printed for private circulation, 1854 [1848–61].
[Walton, Christopher], ed. *On the Present, Past, and Future, with Regard to the Creation.* London: T. Ward & Co., 1847.
Ward, W. R. *Early Evangelicalism: A Global Intellectual History.* Cambridge: Cambridge University Press, 2006.
Webster, Charles. *Paracelsus: Medicine, Magic and Mission at the End of Time.* New Haven: Yale University Press, 2008.
Weeks, Andrew. *Boehme: An Intellectual Biography of the Seventeenth-Century Philosopher and Mystic.* Albany: State University of New York Press, 1991.
Weeks, Andrew. *Paracelsus: Speculative Theory and the Crisis of the Early Reformation.* Albany: State University of New York Press, 1997.
Weeks, Andrew. *Valentin Weigel (1533–1588): German Religious Dissenter, Speculative Theorist, and Advocate of Tolerance.* Albany: State University of New York Press, 2000.
Weeks, Andrew. 'Valentin Weigel and Anticlerical Tradition.' *Daphnis* 48 (2020): 140–59.
Weigel, Valentin. *Dialogus de Christianismo: Das ist, Ein Christliches, hochwichtiges, nothwendiges Colloquium oder Gespräche, dreyer fürnembsten Personen in der Welt.* Halle: In verlegung Joachim Krusicken, 1614.
Weigel, Valentin. *Schriften: Neue Edition.* Edited by Horst Pfefferl. 14 vols. Stuttgart-Bad Cannstatt: Frommann-Holzboog, 1996–2015.
Weigelt, Horst. *Spiritualistische Tradition im Protestantismus: Die Geschichte des Schwenckfeldertums in Schlesien.* Berlin: De Gruyter, 1973.
Weigelt, Horst. *Von Schlesien nach Amerika: Die Geschichte des Schwenckfeldertums.* Cologne: Böhlau, 2007.
Weiß, Ulman. *Die Lebenswelten des Esajas Stiefel oder Vom Umgang mit Dissidenten.* Stuttgart: Steiner, 2007.
Wengert, Timothy John. *Defending Faith: Lutheran Responses to Andreas Osiander's Doctrine of Justification, 1551–1559.* Tübingen: Mohr Siebeck, 2012.

Wiedeburg, Heinrich, and Christoph Tobias Wiedeburg. *Disputatio theologica inauguralis qua theologiae fanaticae fundamentum de tribus partibus hominis corpore anima et spiritu.* Helmstedt: Typis Georgii Wolfgangi Hammii, Acad. Typogr., 1695.

Wieser, Max. *Peter Poiret: Der Vater der romanischen Mystik in Deutschland. Zum Ursprung der Romantik in Deutschland.* Munich: Müller, 1932.

Willard, Thomas. 'Two Early References to "Spiritual Chemists."' *Cauda Pavonis* 3 (1984): 3–4.

Wilmshurst, Walter Leslie. 'The Later Mysticism of Mrs. Atwood.' 2 pts. *The Quest* 10–11 (1919): pt. 1, 487–507; pt. 2, 31–53.

Winckelmann, Johann, and Balthasar Werner. *Disputatio theologica de partibus hominis, contra novam opinionem quorundam tres partes substantialiter differentes constituentium.* Gießen: Ex officina typographica Casparis Chemlini, 1623.

Winter, Alison. *Mesmerized: Powers of Mind in Victorian Britain.* Chicago: University of Chicago Press, 1998.

Wollgast, Siegfried. *Philosophie in Deutschland zwischen Reformation und Aufklärung 1550–1650.* 2nd ed. Berlin: Akademie-Verlag, 1993. First published 1988.

Wollgast, Siegfried. 'Zur Wirkungsgeschichte des Paracelsus im 16. und 17. Jahrhundert.' In *Resultate und Desiderate der Paracelsus-Forschung.* Edited by Peter Dilg and Hartmut Rudolph, 113–44. Stuttgart: Steiner, 1993.

Wotschke, Theodor. 'Weseler Briefe an Friedrich Breckling.' *Monatshefte für Rheinische Kirchengeschichte* 27 (1933): 178–85.

Zaepernick, Gertraud. 'Johann Georg Gichtels und seiner Nachfolger Briefwechsel mit den Hallischen Pietisten, besonders mit A. M. Francke.' *Pietismus und Neuzeit* 8 (1982): 74–118.

Zaepernick, Gertraud. *Verzeichnis der Handschriftenbestände pietistischer, spiritualistischer und separatistischer Autoren des 17. und 18. Jahrhunderts in der Landesbibliothek Gotha sowie in anderen Handschriftensammlungen und Archiven in Gotha und Erfurt.* N.p., 1965/68.

Zalta, Edward N., ed. *The Stanford Encyclopedia of Philosophy.* Summer 2015 ed. https://plato.stanford.edu. Stanford: Stanford University, 2015.

Zeilfelder, Wilhelm. *Ungetauffter kinderlein Predigt.* Gera: Durch Martinum Spiessen, 1611.

Zeller, Winfried. *Die Schriften Valentin Weigels: Eine literarkritische Untersuchung.* Berlin: Ebering, 1940.

Žemla, Martin. 'From Paracelsus to Universal Reform: The (Pseudo-)Paracelsian-Weigelian *Philosophia Mystica* (1618).' *Daphnis* 48 (2020): 184–213.

Žemla, Martin. 'Valentin Weigel and Alchemy.' In *Latin Alchemical Literature of Czech Provenance: Proceedings from the Centre for Renaissance Texts Conference (16–17 October 2014).* Edited by Tomáš Nejeschleba and Jiří Michalík, 21–49. Olomouc: Univerzita Palackého, 2015.

Zika, Charles. 'Reuchlin's *De verbo mirifico* and the Magic Debate of the Late Fifteenth Century.' *Journal of the Warburg and Courtauld Institutes* 39 (1976): 104–38.

Zuber, Mike A. 'Alchemical Promise, the Fraud Narrative, and the History of Science from Below: Peter Moritz's Encounter with Robert Boyle and Ambrose Godfrey.' *Ambix* 68 (2021): 28–48.

Zuber, Mike A. 'Between Alchemy and Pietism: Wilhelm Christoph Kriegsmann's Philological Quest for Ancient Wisdom.' *Correspondences* 2 (2014): 67–104.

Zuber, Mike A. 'The Duke, the Soldier of Fortune, and a Rosicrucian Legacy: Exploring the Roles of Manuscripts in Early-Modern Alchemy.' *Ambix* 65 (2018): 122–42.

Zuber, Mike A. 'Franckenberg, Abraham von.' In *Literaturwissenschaftliches Verfasserlexikon: Frühe Neuzeit in Deutschland 1620–1720*. Edited by Stefanie Arend et al., vol. 3: F–H, s.v. Berlin: De Gruyter, forthcoming.

Zuber, Mike A. 'Jacob Böhme and Alchemy: A Transmutation in Three Stages.' In Andersson et al., *Jacob Böhme and His World*, 262–85.

Zuber, Mike A. 'Surely Born-Again Christianity Has Nothing to Do with Occult Stuff Like Alchemy?' In *Hermes Explains: Thirty Questions on Western Esotericism*. Edited by Wouter J. Hanegraaff, Peter Forshaw, and Marco Pasi, 252–60. Amsterdam: Amsterdam University Press, 2019.

Zuber, Mike A. 'Theosophische Spekulation und erbauliche Frömmigkeit: Jacob Böhme, die neue Wiedergeburt und ihre Alchemisierung.' In *Grund und Ungrund: Der Kosmos des mystischen Philosophen Jacob Böhme*. Edited by Claudia Brink and Lucinda Martin, 114–29. Dresden: Sandstein, 2017.

Zuber, Mike A., and Leigh T. I. Penman. 'Robert Boyle's Anonymous "Crosey-Crucian" Identified: The German Alchemist and Religious Dissenter Peter Moritz.' *Notes and Records* 74 (2020): 95–103.

Index

Page ranges (e.g. 40–41) refer to the paragraph(s) in which indexed terms appear.

Figures are indicated by *f* following the page number

Acts of the Apostles, 59–60
Adam 52–53
   as name, meaning of, 77
   prelapsarian or crystalline body of, 75–76, 149–50
   See also Curse; Fall; Eve
Ad dialogum de morte (A Conversation on Death), 25–27
   on antimony in alchemy, 27–29
   Boehme and, 28–29
   circulation of, 30
   connection of spiritual rebirth and alchemy in, 19
   copies and editions of, 25–26
   influences on, 25–26
   on justification, 26
   and Nagel, 43
   as pseudepigraphical addition to Weigel's *Dialogus de Christianismo*, 25–26
   on spiritual alchemy, 26–27
albedo (whiteness), 37, 104
Alchemical Society, 187–88
alchemy
   as concept spanning science and religion, 5–6
   definition of, 1–2, 197
   marginalisation after early eighteenth century, 2, 160, 199–200
   and mining, 14–15
   spiritual interpretation of, 2–3, 5, 160
   spread in British occultist circles, 178
   three common views of, 1, 2–6
   combining with German mysticism, 14, 16–17

alchemy, as religion and psychology, 1, 2–4
   criticisms of, 5
alchemy, as science and natural philosophy, 1, 2, 4–5
   and New Historiography, 4–6
alchemy, as superstition and fraud, 1
Ambix (periodical), 3–4, 12
Anabaptism, 15–16
ancient wisdom (*prisca sapientia*), 12–13, 69–70, 73–74, 101–3, 167, 170, 192
Andreae, Michael, 113–15, 128, 129*f*, 131–32
Angelic Brethren, 114–15, 158–59
Anhalt-Plötzkau, Duke August of, 40–41
annihilation, 147
anthropology, 9, 185
   See also dichotomous anthropology; trichotomous anthropology
Antichrist, 23, 34
antimony, 27–29, 35–36
   star regulus of (*stella antimonii*), 58
antinomianism, 62, 63
archaeus, 82
Arndt, Johann, 17–18, 71, 91
   Vier Bücher Vom wahren Christenthumb (Four Books on True Christianity), 17
Arnold, Gottfried, 73–74, 110
   Unparteyische Kirchen- und Ketzer-Historie (Impartial History), 73–74, 87–88, 140
Arnoldi, Marcus, 126
Artista, Elias, 95
Ascension of Christ, 58, 60, 75, 152
astrology, 47, 178

Athanasian Creed, 56
Atwood, Mary Anne (*née* South)
   and alchemy, 160, 195
   and Boehme, 160–61, 189–92, 193–94
   and Christian lineage, 192–93
   and Christian socialism, 161–62
   contribution to *Early Magnetism*, 166, 167
   correspondence with Walton, 161–62, 167–68, 169
   donation of library to Sinnett, 178–79, 183
   and English Behmenists, 161
   and Freher, 148, 152–54, 156, 158–59, 161, 169, 189, 196
   Freher manuscript owned by, 189, 190*f*
   on her works, as misunderstood by most, 192
   influences on, 194
   and spiritual alchemy, 12, 161–62, 164
   later views on spiritual alchemy, 191–96
   and *Lives of Alchemystical Philosophers*, 160
   in London, 163
   and magnetism (Mesmerism), 166–68, 171, 174, 192
   marriage, 177, 258n.4
   on occultism, 192
   on Spiritualists, 192
   'The Stone,' 192
   and Theosophical Society of London, 183, 192, 200
   views on Gospels, 184–85, 267n.91
   on Waite, 182
   See also Suggestive Inquiry into the Hermetic Mystery (Atwood)
Atwood, Thomas Alban, 177
Augsburg Confession, 91
Aurora philosophorum, 101
azoth, 40, 43–46, 47, 95–96
   Christ as, 45–46
   healing power of, 44
   and *imitatio Christi*, 44–45
   as philosophers' stone, 43, 46
   and spiritual alchemy, 43–46
   as union of two things, 46–47
Azoth et Ignis (Azoth and Fire), 19–25
   on antimony, 28
   on *Christus in nobis*, 23–25
   circulation of, 30
   connection of spiritual rebirth and alchemy in, 19, 24–25
   first page of Nagel copy, 22*f*
   influence on *Ad dialogum de morte*, 25–26
   on justification, 24
   on knowledge of Christ as secret to alchemical success, 23
   on 'Know thyself' imperative, 24
   on mystical identification with Christ, 24
   number of the beast (666) in, 20, 21–23
   on parallels between alchemy and theology, 23–24
   on philosophers' stone, 24–25
   as pseudo-Weigelian text, 19–20
   related texts and copies, 20–21, 111–12

Bahnsen, Benedict, 111
baptism, 9, 15–16, 37, 167, 170–71
   and spiritual alchemy, 14–18, 39, 50, 58, 59–60, 64, 166–67, 170–71, 192
Barnes, Robin B., 65
beautitude, 194–95
Beets, Hendrick. *See* Betke, Heinrich
Bethabor, Floretus à, 89–90
Betke, Heinrich (Hendrick Beets), 92–93, 107, 115–16
Betke, Joachim, 107
Beyerland, Abraham Willemsz van, 72–73, 112–13, 115–16
Bible, books of the. *See specific books*
Biedermann, Benedict, 20, 41–42
   Theologia Weigelii, 20, 41–42, 46
Boehme, Jacob
   on Adam, 52–53
   and *Ad dialogum de morte*, 28–29
   on alchemy, 48, 49–50, 155
   Apologia, Betreffend Die Vollkommenheit des Menschen, 48–49, 63, 66
   Atwood on, 172–73
   availability of works, 160–61
   on baptism, 59–60
   Bedencken über Esaiä Stiefels, von Langensaltza, Büchlein, 49

Beschreibung der Drey Principien Göttliches Wesens, 39–40, 51–55
on born-again believers as both human and divine, 62
on Christ's life and passion as alchemical process, 67–68
on Christ's humanity and divinity, 56
on *Christus in nobis*, 55
Clavis specialis, 71–72, 84
death of, 72
differences compared to Paracelsus, 14–16
early life and education, 48
Ein Gründlicher Bericht, Latin translation of, 72–73
on eternal nature, 150–51
on Fall, 51–53, 54, 55–57, 60, 65–67, 84, 156
familiarity with pseudo-Weigelian alchemy, 30, 40, 48–49, 51
on godhead as dynamic, 49–50
on Incarnation of Christ, 56–60, 63
influence on Franckenberg, 71, 98–99
influence on Freher, 142
influences on, 16, 17–18, 29, 49, 52, 54
on three principles (theosophy), 150–51
Morgen Röte im auffgang (*Aurora*), 39–40, 48, 49–51, 71–72, 73
Mysterium magnum, 52–53, 71, 72–73, 115–16
opera omnia, 106–7, 110–16, 125–26, 131–32
on Pentecost, 58, 59–60, 67–68
on philosophers' stone, 51–52, 55, 57
on prelapsarian pure matter (one element), 52–53, 54, 154–55
on *proto-evangelium* 47
on restoration of nature through alchemy, 156–57
and revelation of alchemy's secrets, 160–61
on salvation history, 56
and separation of baptism and rebirth, 16
on seven source spirits, 148–49
Siebmacher's influence on, 30
on Sophia (wisdom), 53–54
and Stiefel, 48–49, 60–63
Tabula principiorum, 71–72
Theosophische Send-Schreiben, 92–93
On the Threefold Life of Man, 55, 63–64, 98–99
on tincture, 59, 62–64, 67–68, 84
Tröstliche Erclärung Uber etliche . . . spruche der H. Göttlichen Schrifft, 61–63
Ungrund, 101–3
on union of God and man, 157
Viertzig Fragen von der Seelen, 92–93
Von der Menschwerdung Jesu Christi, 56
Weg zu Christo, 71, 98–99
Weigel and, 17–18
works, editions by Betke and Cunradus, 115–16
works, in Bahnsen's library, 111–12
See also Signatura rerum (Boehme)
Boehme, and spiritual alchemy, 12, 197
as bridge between speculative and devotional work, 52, 225n.22
and Christ as philosophers' stone, 57–60
Christus in nobis as goal of, 55, 57, 60
close connection of spiritual and bodily renewal in, 63–64
as completed only at resurrection, 62, 63–65
departures from traditional alchemy, 65
development of theory, 48–49
explicit comparisons to alchemical processes, 58–60
first account of, 52
identification with Christ as means to, 56
as literal and physical, 51–52, 55
as necessary for understanding alchemy, 34
new body in, as made from holy element of Christ's body, 54–55, 198
new body in, 62–63
physical effects of, 171
regaining of heavenly bodiliness through, 53–54
renewal of soul through, 62
reversal of Fall through, 51–52, 53, 54
spanning all of salvation history, 67–68
transformation sought by, as inward and real, 11

308 INDEX

Boehme's network, 21, 39–40, 51
Bonheim, Günther, 71–72
Bonus, Petrus, *Pretiosa margarita novella* (Precious New Pearl), 6–7, 34, 39, 40
Bosch, Hieronymus, 4
Brecht, Martin, 17–18
Breckling, Friedrich
  Anticalovius, 115–16, 132
  and Arnold's *Impartial History*, 140
  and Boehme, 115, 116, 123–24, 138, 139–41
  and Boehme experts, struggle for dominance among, 114–15
  and Boehme's *opera omnia*, publication of, 106–7, 110–11, 116
  career of, 106–7
  Christus iudex, 108–9
  Christus mysticus, sol et sal sapientiae, 106–7, 116, 118–19, 123–24, 136–37
  on church as Christ's spiritual body, 120–21
  collaboration with Cunradus, 115–17
  correspondence, 138–39
  De studio universalissimo et pansophico, 139
  expulsions from ministry posts, 107–8, 109–10
  on false alchemists (ministers), 121–24, 134–35
  and Gifftheil, 107, 109–10
  and laboratory alchemy, 140, 198–99
  on multiplication, 118, 133, 170–71
  and network of religious dissenters, 107–8, 110–11
  on persecuted believers, 122–24
  Pseudosophia mundi, 106–7, 116, 118, 121–22, 123–24
  publications of 1681–82, 116–17
  scandal at Zwolle, 109–10
  and Seidenbecher, 106, 107–10
  sparing use of paper by, 116–17, 117*f*
  on spiritual alchemy, 119–21, 131, 138–41
  Veritatis triumphus (Truth's Triumph), 107–8
  See also *Theosophische-Schrifften* (Sclei)
Brooke, Henry, 153–54

Bureus, Johannes, *FaMa è sCanzIa reDVX*, 88–89
Butterfield, Herbert, 2

calcination, 42, 45–46, 82, 138–39, 184
cauda pavonis (peacock's tail), 37
chemistry (chymistry), 4–5
Chesne, Joseph du (Quercetanus), 49
Christ
  and antimony, 27–29
  as *azoth*, 45–46
  death of, *mumIAH* created by, 76–77
  De Steiger on, 184–85
  doctrine of ubiquity of, and spiritual alchemy, 197–98
  as God-man, 103–4
  identification with philosophers' stone, 6–7, 19–20, 21–23, 28–29, 55, 57–60, 65, 67–68, 97–98, 101–3, 139, 154, 155
  as 'stone that the builders rejected,' 23, 28–29, 122–23, 172
  as tincture, 152
  transformation through death, 152
Christ's body
  as spiritual essence of prelapsarian world, 76–77
  ubiquity of, in Luther, 54
Christus in nobis, 23–25, 36, 39, 55, 57, 60, 79–80, 121–22, 135, 166–67, 170–72, 182–83
  as *archaeus*, 82
  as gold, 42–43, 44–46
  history of phrase, 209–10n.51
  and introspection as contemplation, 23–24
  and trichotomous anthropology, 9–10
  See also lapis-Christus in nobis three-way analogy
citrinitas (yellow), 37, 104
Clarke, Lindsay, *The Chymical Wedding*, 169–70
coagulation (*coagulatio*), 59, 138–39, 184
cohobation, 138–39
Colberg, Ehregott Daniel, 9
colours, 104
  See also specific colours

Concerning the Dialogue on Death. See
  Ad dialogum de morte
Copernicus, Nicolaus, *De revolutionibus
  orbium coelestium*, 16–17
Corinthians, First Epistle to, 54–55,
  120, 172
Croll, Oswald, 18, 21
  Basilica chymica, 88–89
Crouse, Elisabeth, 109–10
crystalline body after rebirth, 75, 76–77,
  80–82, 137, 193–94
crystalline body of Adam, 149–50
Cunradus, Christoffel, 112, 115–17
Curry, Patrick, 12
Curse (of creation), 44, 47, 79, 84, 148–49,
  155, 156, 157–58
  See also Fall

damnation, 46–47, 84–85
Daniel (biblical book), 97
Darwin, Charles, *On the Origin of
  Species*, 181
Das Güldne Vließ (Siebmacher), 31–32
  See also *Wasserstein der Weysen*
Dee, John, *Monas hieroglyphica*, 101
Deichmann, Heinrich, 145
deification, 8–9, 11, 95–96, 120, 134–35,
  157–58, 161–62, 168, 191, 195
De Raadt, Alhardt. *See* Raadt, Alhardt de.
Der Weeg zum Ewigen Leben, 131–32
De Steiger, Isabelle. *See* Steiger, Isabelle de.
dichotomous anthropology (soul and
  body), 9
digestion, 37, 45–46, 194
distillation, 103–4, 184
Dobbs, Betty Jo Teeter, 3–4
Dorn, Gerard, 18, 21, 98
  *De spagirico artificio Jo. Trithemii
  sententia*, 101

Eckhart, Meister, 14
Egli, Raphael, 21–23
Ein Gesprech vom Tode. See *Ad dialogum
  de morte*
Eliade, Mircea, 3, 200–1
elixir, 155
Elliot, Scott, 178–79
Ender von Sercha, Carl, 50–51

English Behmenists, 161
Enlightenment, views on alchemy, 2, 160,
  199–200
Enoch (apocryphal book), 6–7
ergon/parergon, 96, 119–21, 237n.44
Estié, Paul, 106–7
eternal nature, 150–52
ether, 171, 185, 197–98
  See also quintessence
Eucharist, 9, 14–15, 16, 53–54, 170–
  71, 193–94
Eve, 52–53
  prelapsarian or crystalline body
  of, 75–76
  See also Adam; Curse; Fall
evolution, 155–56, 181–82, 264n.32
exaltation, 118

Fabel, Johann, 99–100
Fall, 52–53, 65–67, 77–78, 80, 84, 156,
  182, 185
  reversal of, 9–10, 38, 43–45, 51–53, 54,
  55, 60, 78, 104, 148–49, 151–52, 155–
  56, 161–62, 166–67, 186–87, 196
Fama Fraternitatis, 96
  See also Rosicrucianism
fermentation, 26–27, 194, 195, 196
Ficino, Marsilio, 8–9, 97–98
fire, 21–23, 45, 95–96, 135–36, 137
  See also *Azoth et Ignis*
fire and wrath, eternal principle of, 52,
  84–85, 150–51
  See also light and love; temporal
  principle; three principles
Formula of Concord, 56
Fischer, Loth, 113, 131–33, 144–45
fixation (*fixatio*), 59, 75
Fludd, Robert, 119
Fontenelle, Bernard le Bovier de, 2
four elements, 53, 149–50, 185, 196
Francke, August Hermann, 117f, 139, 140
Francke, Johann, 25–26
Franckenberg, Abraham von, 48
  and alchemy, 87, 88–90, 198–99
  authors influencing, 71, 98–99, 170
  and Boehme, 69–70, 71–73, 77, 85–86,
  89, 92–93, 115–16
  on Christ's Incarnation, 75

Franckenberg, Abraham von (*cont.*)
  on *Christus in nobis*, 79–80
  Conclusiones de fundamento sapientiae, 69–71, 73, 81, 88–89, 98–99
  as consumer of heterodox literature, 70–71
  correspondence, 88–90, 94–97, 103
  on dust of primordial chaos, 79
  elevated state of being experienced by, 167–68
  on Fall, 77, 79
  and Gifftheil, 107–8
  on heavenly Jerusalem, 80
  on individuals' experience as mirrored in history, 95
  instruction in spiritual alchemy for disciples, 94–100
  Josephus redivivus, 72–73
  Klage-Schreiben uber und wider den Greuwel der Verwüstung, 77
  and 'Know thyself' formula, 95
  on Mary, 79–80
  millenarianism of, 91–92
  on Nagel, 95–96
  Notae mysticae et mnemonicae, 78–79
  on the One, return to, 101–3
  on persecution of believers, 82
  Raphael, 69–70, 76, 79, 85–86, 88–89, 95, 98–99, 101, 104, 230n.7
  Reg[imen] Cabal[isticum], 99, 100–5
  religious awakening of, 70
  and sabbathism (millenarianism), 91–92
  Sephiriel, 85, 91–92, 100–3, 102*f*
  Speculum Apocalypticum, references to alchemy in, 89
  on substance of Christ's body, 76–77, 80
  on terms used for humanity, as inspiration to seek prelapsarian virtue, 77–78
  Theophrastia Valentiniana, 69–70, 73–75, 76, 81–82, 85–86, 88–89, 98–99, 103–4, 136–37
  Trias mystica, 72–73, 89
  on union of opposites in alchemy, 101–4
  Verpoorten's condemnation of, 87–88
  Via veterum sapientum, 72, 95, 170
  works by, in Bahnsen's library, 111–12
  See also Seidenbecher, and Franckenberg
Franckenberg, and spiritual alchemy, 69–70, 73–86, 87, 95–96
  and believer's daily death and rebirth, 82–83
  and blurring of body/spirit distinction, 81–82
  Boehme's influence on, 73–74
  and Christ as *mumIAH*, 76–77
  crystalline body attained through, 75, 76–77, 80–82, 193–94
  death necessary for, 81–82
  differences from Boehme, 78
  linking to ancient wisdom, 69–70, 170
  and new birth hidden in old body, 79–80
  and seed of light (spiritual essence) of prelapsarian humanity, 75–77, 78, 79–80
  as spiritual resurrection prefiguring bodily resurrection, 83
  in Valentinus, 74–75
Franklin, J. Jeffrey, 167
Freher, Dionysius Andreas
  on alchemy, 150
  and Amsterdam group editing Sclei's works, 142
  Atwood on, 172–73
  background of, 143
  and Boehme, 142–43
  career of, 146–47
  Hieroglyphica sacra, 142–43
  in Holland, 143–46
  images by, popularity of, 142–43
  influence of works, 160–61
  as interpreter of spiritual alchemy for English audiencs, 158–59
  on three principles (theosophy), 150–51
  Leade and, 144–46
  and London, 142–43, 144–46
  in *Lives of Alchemystical Philosophers*, 152–53, 160
  mentors of, 147–48
  Paradoxa, emblemata, aenigmata, hieroglyphica de uno, toto, puncto, centro, 142–43
  and Philadelphian Society, 145–46

and Quaker congregation of Bow Lane, 145–46
on rebirth, as requirement for successful practice of alchemy, 150
on restoration of nature through alchemy, 156–57
and separation of spiritual and laboratory alchemy, 199
on spiritual alchemy, bodily effects of, 171
The Substance of a Conference betwixt a German Theosophist, and an English Divine, 146–47
Three Tables, 142–43
and Überfeld, 142, 143–45
See also *Fundamenta mystica Jacobi Behmen, explicata* (Freher); 'The Process in the Philosophical Work' (Freher)
Freud, Sigmund, 2–3
Fuchs, Georg Christian, 113–14
Fundamenta mystica Jacobi Behmen, explicata (Freher), 142–43, 146–59
alchemical concepts used in, 147–48
Atwood's copy of, 189, 190*f*
on Boehme's lack of practical alchemical knowledge, 150–51
and explanation of Boehme to English audiences, 158–59
and Freher's limited grasp of alchemy, 147–48, 150–51, 155–56
manuscripts of, 147–48
on prelapsarian pure matter (one element), 149–50, 171, 196
responses to questions in, 146–47
on restoration of nature through alchemy, 157
on seven planets and metals, 148–49
on spiritual and laboratory alchemy, 148–49
on tincture and transformation, 148–52
on union of heaven and earth, 157–58

Galatians (biblical epistle), 262n.88
Gallus, Friedrich, 99
See also *Reise Frieder[ich] Galli*
Gantenbein, Urs Leo, 15–16

gems
Christ's body as like, 80
New Jerusalem as made of, 80
Genesis, 66, 73, 77–78, 79, 158, 223n.79, 233n.49, 233n.51
German mysticism, combining with alchemy, 14, 16–17
Geyer, Hermann, 128
Gichtel, Johann Georg
as Boehme expert, 111
and Boehme, early lack of interest in, 111–13
and Boehme's *opera omnia*, publication of, 110–11, 112–16
and Breckling, 110–11, 112
on Breckling's *Anticalovius*, 115–16
correspondence, 127, 143–44
and Raadt, friendship with, 112–13
and Freher, 143–44, 145, 147–48
influences on, 114–15
inheritance of Bahnsen's library, 111–12
and Leade, 144–45
and Sclei's *Theosophische-Schrifften*, 125–26, 127, 128–30
Gifftheil, Ludwig Friedrich, 107–8, 109–10
Gilly, Carlos, 73–74
Glüsing, Otto, 113–14
gnosticism, 69–70, 73–74, 75–76
Godwin, Joscelyn, 161–62, 163
Goethals, Johannes, 112–14
gold, 21–24, 38–39, 42, 49–50, 55, 65–67, 70, 78, 79, 80, 103, 104, 118, 119–20, 122–23, 133–37, 147, 155
Christus in nobis as, 42–43, 45
purification of, 35–36, 42, 48
transmutation of, 84, 197
Grasse, Johann, 172–73
Greaves, James Pierrepont, 161–62, 183

Hakelberg, Dietrich, 111–12
Hanegraaff, Wouter J., 5–6, 73–74
heaven, 80
new, after destruction of world, 23–24
preparation for, through spiritual alchemy, 10, 43, 64, 80, 85, 137, 148–49, 171–72, 193–94, 195–96
transmutation of earth into, 63–65
uniting with earth, 103, 157–58

heavenly stone (*lapis coelestis*), 21–23
Hebrews (biblical epistle), 137
Hegenicht, Ehrenfried, 69–70, 85–86
Heidelberg Catechism, 143
hell, 61–62, 154–55
heresy, 9, 87–88, 91–92
hermaphrodite, 36, 103–4
Hermes Trimegistus, 97–98, 170
   Emerald Tablet, 98–99
Hirsch, Christoph, 106
   Gemma magica (Magical Jewel), 93
Hitchcock, Ethan Allen, 2–3, 11, 199–200
   Alchemy and the Alchemists, 180
Hoburg, Christian, 107
Hoffstetter, Gottlieb, 140
Holy Spirit, 34, 38, 53, 59–60, 63, 67–68,
   76, 79–80, 81–82, 83, 96
Huss, Boaz, 8
Huygens, Willem Gozewijn, 112–14

illumination (*illuminatio*), 10–11, 119–20
Incarnation of Christ, 17, 18, 36–37, 48–49,
   56–60, 63, 67–68, 75, 79–80, 103–4,
   139, 152–53, 154–55, 158–59, 172–73
   within the believer, mystical, 17–18, 38–
      39, 57, 182–83, 184–85, 195
incineration, 42, 44–45
Introductio hominis (Siebmacher), 30,
   31–35, 119, 138
   on alchemy and philosophers' stone,
      32, 34–35
   authorship of, 31–32
   as companion piece to
      Wasserstein, 32–34
   date of composition, 32
   influence on Franckenberg, 71
   influences on, 32–34
   on 'Know thyself' imperative, 32–34
   on number of the beast (666), 34–35
   title page of, 33f
iron, 55
Isaiah, 97
Isis (periodical), 2

Johann Capito, *Libellus theosophiae*, 81
John (gospel), 14, 233n.56
Jung, C. G., 3–4, 156, 169–70,
   182–83, 200–1

justification, forensic, 16–17, 19, 24, 26,
   38–39, 56

kabbalah, 69–70, 95, 104
Kahn, Didier, 99
Kerzenmacher, Petrus, *Alchimi und
   Bergwerck*, 14–15
Khunrath, Heinrich, 119, 172–73
   Amphitheatrum sapientiae aeternae,
      18, 101
   on antimonialists, 27
   influence on Franckenberg, 88–89
   and origin of spiritual alchemy, 18
   on philosophers' stone, 21
   and 'Pray and work!' motto, 95
   on restoration of nature through
      alchemy, 156
Kings, First Book of, 222n.49
Kingsford, Anna, 178
Know thyself (*gnothi se auton, nosce te
   ipsum*), 23–24, 32–34, 95, 119
Knuber, Johann, 25–26
Kober, Tobias, 72
König (von Königfels), Tobias, 89–90,
   94–96, 98–99
Koschwitz, Jonas Daniel, 98
Kress, Berthold, 20
Kuhlmann, Quirinus, 126

Lamoen, Frank van, 127
lapis angularis, 172
lapis-Christus in nobis three-way analogy
   (philosophers' stone, Christ
   incarnate, and believer), 9–10, 36,
   48–49, 57, 154–55, 172–73, 174
lapis-Christus two-way analogy
   (philosophers' stone and Christ
   incarnate), 9–10, 36–37, 97–98,
   101–3, 104, 139, 154–55, 174
lapis philosophorum. See
   philosophers' stone
Last Judgement
   as rebirth (palingenesis), 26–27
   and soul sleep, 65
   and spiritual alchemy, 9–10, 11
Lautensack, Paul, 20–21, 35, 41–42
Law, William, 161–62, 163, 164,
   169, 258n.7

lead, 65–67, 79, 147, 173–74
Leade, Jane, 113, 132, 142, 144–46, 162–63
  The Heavenly Cloud Now Breaking, 144–45
Le Blon, Michel, 92–93
Leppington, Allen, 145–46
Leuchter, Jeremias Daniel, 145–46
Lévi, Eliphas, 180
Libavius, Andreas
  Alchemia, 4–5, 87–88
  maternal grandfather of Seidenbecher, 87–88
Liber Azoth sive de ligno et linea vitae, 20–21
Liber Trinitatis (1410s), 6–7, 36–37, 221n.26
Light (periodical), 183
light and love, as eternal principle, 52, 54–55, 57, 67–68, 69–86, 150–52, 195
  See also fire and wrath; temporal principle; three principles
Lion of Judah, 47, 66
The Lives of Alchemystical Philosophers (1814/15; 1888), 152–54, 155–56, 158–59, 160, 179–80
Lucifer (periodical), 180
Luke (gospel), 233n.56
Luther, Martin, 10, 16–17, 26–27, 76–77
Lutheranism
  on baptism, 15–16
  and dichotomous anthropology, 9
  and spiritual alchemy, 2, 9–11, 16–17
  and various authors, 24, 26, 38–39, 56, 65, 70, 79–80, 87–88, 91, 106, 108, 120–21, 198

magi, 28, 55, 118
magic
  alchemy and, 1–2, 134–35
  in ancient Egypt, 46–47
  Franckenberg on, 95
  and narratives of human progress, 1
magic squares, 20–21
magnesia, 135
magnetism. *See* Mesmerism
Maitland, Edward, 178
Malachi (biblical book), 135–37
manuscript annotations/annotated
    exemplars (Sclei edition), 125–26, 128–33, 140–41

manuscript collection(s)
  of alchemical works, 20–21, 94, 98, 107, 111–12, 127–28, 147–48, 175, 177, 178–79, 183
  of Boehme's writings, 72–73, 112–13, 115–16
  of Freher's writings, 147–48, 163, 164, 169
  Franckenberg's use in teaching, 99–100, 104–5
manuscript collector(s), 72–73, 88, 92–93, 98–99, 111–13, 114–15, 116–17, 123, 128, 137, 140, 163, 164, 169, 189, 190f
manuscripts
  circulation of, 19–20, 25–26, 30, 32–34, 50–51, 72–73, 110–11
  publication of, 110–11, 112–16
  scribal transmission of, 19–20, 50–51, 88, 99–100, 105, 128, 161
Mark (gospel), 233n.56
Martensen, Hans Lassen, 194
Martin, Lucinda, 144–45
Massey, Charles Carleton, 178
Matthew (gospel), 26–27, 50, 233n.56
Melanchthon, Philipp, 16–17
Menius, Justus, 16–17
mercurius philosophorum, 21–23
mercury, 9, 19, 21–24, 36, 45, 47, 58, 59, 65–66, 103, 193–94
Mesmerism, 166–68, 171, 174, 197–98
Methodism, 17–18
millenarianism, 87–88, 91–92, 108–9, 125
  See also sabbathism
mind/matter distinction, 9–10
mining, 14–15
Mögling, Daniel, *Speculum sophicum rhodo-stauroticum*, 96
Moran, Bruce T., 21–23
Morgan, John Minter, 161–62
Morienus, *Testament*, 19
Moritz, Peter, 115
Moseley, Walter, 178
Mulder, Joseph, 128, 129f
multiplication (*multiplicatio*), 38, 59, 118, 133, 170–71
mumia, 76–77, 135–36
Münster, Johann Friedrich, 107–8
Muses, Charles A., 146

mysticism, 2–3, 101–3, 123–24, 158, 160–61, 165–66, 167, 173–74, 175–76, 177, 179, 181, 182–83, 184, 188–89, 195
   definition of, 210n.54
   and equanimity (*Gelassenheit*), 45–46
   German, combining with alchemy, 14, 16–17
   and Mesmerism (magnetism), 2–3, 167, 173–74
   and Sophia (wisdom), 53–54
   and spiritual alchemy, 10–11
   three paths of, 45, 119–20, 135–36
   See also deification; illumination; purification; union

Nagel, Paul
   Aurum divinum 666. centenariorum, 40–43
   on *azoth*, 43–46
   and *Azoth et Ignis*, 21–23, 24–25, 30, 39–40, 42–43
   and Boehme, 21, 39–40
   on born-again believers as both human and divine, 62
   on *Christus in nobis*, 42–43, 44–46
   conflation of theology and alchemy, 42–46
   and Franckenberg, 95–96
   on God as first and last, 46
   and laboratory alchemy, 198–99
   Leo rugiens, 23, 40, 42–46
   millenarianism of, 47, 91–92
   on number of the beast, 40–42
   and pseudo-Weigelian alchemy, 39–40, 43
   on spiritual alchemy, 96–97
Naschert, Guido, 106–7
nature, restoration of prelapsarian state through alchemy, 156
   See also Curse
Neo-Platonism, 8–9, 189–91
new body through spiritual alchemy, 54–55, 61, 62–63, 64, 75, 76–77, 79–82, 137, 173–74, 193–94, 198
New Historiography of Alchemy, 4–6, 201–2, 204–5n.16
Newman, William R.
   'Alchemy vs. Chemistry,' 4–5
   on continuity of spiritual alchemy, 12
   and New Historiography of Alchemy, 4–6
   'Some Problems with the Historiography of Alchemy,' 5, 200–1
New Theosophic Revelations (Greaves), 161–62
Nicodemus, 14
nigredo (blackness) 81–82, 104, 105
   association with Christ's temptation and death, 37, 58
number of the beast (666), 34–35, 40–42
   appearances in Bible, 40–41
   association with Christ, 23
   in *Azoth et Ignis*, 20, 21–23
Nummedal, Tara, 12

Obrist, Barbara, 4
occultism, 5, 180, 189–91, 192
Occult Review, 156
Oculus sidereus (Franckenberg), 89
Old, Walter Gorn, 156
opus magnum (Great Work), 37, 154, 160
Osiander, Andreas, 16–17, 24
Overbeek, Johann, 136–37
Owen, Robert, 161–62

palingenesis, 26–27, 42
panacea, 118, 132–33, 135, 139
Paracelsianism, 9, 14, 118, 133
Paracelsus (Hohenheim, Theophrastus Bombastus von), 14–15
   influence on Boehme, 29, 52
   separation of theology and alchemy in, 15–16
   theories compared to Boehme, 14–16
   and trichotomous anthropology, 9, 208n.45
parergon, 119–21
   See also *ergon*
Park, Katharine, 8–9
Paul, Epistles of, 174
Penman, Leigh, 39–40
Penny, Anne Judith, 161, 183–84
Pentecost, 58, 59–60, 67–68
Peuckert, Will-Erich, 25–26

Pfefferl, Horst, 20
Philadelphian Society, 142, 145–46
Philemon (biblical epistle), 90–91
Philippians (biblical epistle), 137–38
philosophers' stone (*lapis philosophorum*),
    2, 3–4, 18, 21–23, 24–25, 32, 34–37,
    38, 39, 51–52, 55, 57–58, 97–98, 100,
    104, 114–15, 118, 120–21, 122–23,
    136–37, 139, 154, 158, 173–74,
    192, 193–94
  and *azoth*, 43, 46
  Christ's identification with, 6–7, 19–20,
    21–23, 28–29, 55, 57–60, 65, 67–68,
    97–98, 101–3, 139, 154, 155
  healing power of, 44
  See also lapis-Christus in nobis three-way
    analogy; *lapis-Christus* two-way analogy
Philosophia mystica (Paracelsus and
    Weigel), 31–32, 138
Pietism, 17–18
Pietsch, Roland, 143
Poiret, Pierre, 162–63, 259n.18
Polemann, Joachim, 98–99
Polish Brethren, 125
Pordage, John, 132, 162–63
  'A Thorough Philosophical Epistle,' 132
postlapsarian humanity, 77
  See also Adam; Curse; Eve; Fall
prayer and spiritual alchemy, 95–97
prelapsarian state
  of Adam and Eve, 75–76
  of nature, restoration through
    alchemy, 156
  See also Curse; Fall: reversal of
Preston, John, 176f, 176–77
prima materia, 21–23, 36
Principe, Lawrence M., 4–6, 7, 12, 58, 160
  'Alchemy vs. Chemistry,' 4–5
  'Some Problems with the
    Historiography of Alchemy,' 5, 200–1
prisca sapientia. *See* ancient wisdom
'The Process in the Philosophical Work'
    (Freher), 152–59
  as chapter in *Fundamenta
    mystica*, 152–53
  and explanation of alchemy in terms of
    salvation, 155–56
  and *lapis-Christus in nobis* analogy,
    154–55, 158–59

linking early-modern to modern
    spiritual alchemy, 152–54,
    155–56, 158–59
  publication of, 152–53, 158–59, 164
  on restoration of prelapsarian world as
    goal of alchemy, 155–56
  on spiritual alchemy, 154–59
projection (*proiectio*), 59, 75
proto-evangelium, 47, 57, 66, 154, 158
Prunius, Heinrich, 72–73
Psalms, 23, 97
pseudo-Weigelian texts, 19–25
  See also Ad dialogum de morte; *Azoth
    et Ignis*
purification (*purificatio*), 10–11, 35–36,
    49, 62, 80, 81, 82–83, 118, 119–20,
    138–39, 166–67, 195
putrefaction, 26–27, 42, 45–46, 58–59, 64,
    97, 138–39, 194
Putscher, Marielene, 8–9

quintessence, 8–9, 54–55, 67–68, 79,
    149–50, 171, 173–74, 185, 197–98

Raadt, Alhardt de, 112–15
rebirth (palingenesis), 26–27, 50
rebirth (*Wiedergeburt*), 54, 166–67
  and baptism, dissociation of, 14–18
  and born-again Christians, 209–10n.51
  and justification doctrine, 16–17
  in late medieval German writings, 14
  and modern evangelicalism, 17–18
  and mystical incarnation of Christ
    within believer, 17
  and spiritual alchemy, 9–10
  in spiritual alchemy compared to
    Lutheranism, 9–11, 16–17
  and *spiritus*, 11–12
  terms for, 14
rebis. *See* hermaphrodite
Redgrove, H. Stanley, 156
Reformation, 12–13, 20, 24–25, 70,
    170–71
  radical, 14–15
regeneration, 1–13, 14–29, 30–47,
    87–105, 125–41, 142–59,
    161–62, 184, 191, 194–95, 196
  See also rebirth (*Wiedergeburt*)
Reise Frieder[ich] Galli, 99–100, 105

religion, compared to spirituality, as terms, 8
religious/spiritual dimensions of alchemy, 6–7
resurrection
　baptism and, 16, 39
　of Christ, 63
　and Christ's transformation into tincture, 152
　at Last Judgement, 50
　and lifting of the Curse, 148–49
　new body received following, 76, 80, 137, 174, 192–93, 196
　of plants (palingenesis), 42
　spiritual alchemy as preparation for, 9–10, 11, 62, 83, 85, 198
　spiritual alchemy as type of, 18, 23–24, 26–27, 36–37, 45, 50, 58, 59, 63–65, 67–68, 76–77, 80–81, 120–21, 123–24, 139, 152–53, 171, 172
Revelation (biblical book), 23, 26–27, 47, 50, 83, 222n.48, 223n.76, 223n.78
reverberation, 45–46
Richter, Gregor, 50–51, 71–72
rites/rituals, 167, 170–72
　in spiritual alchemy, 9, 10–11, 135, 171–72
　spiritualists' dismissal of, 16, 122, 171
Rosarium philosophorum, 6–7, 36–37, 57–58
Rosicrucianism, 40–41, 61, 69, 87–88, 93, 96, 98–99, 119
Rothe, Johann, 72–73
Rothé, Johannes, 112
rubedo (redness), 37, 104
Ruland, Martin, *Lexicon alchemiae*, 42, 83–84
Rusterholz, Sibylle, 17–18, 73–74

sabbathism, 91–92
　See also millenarianism
sal niter, 49
salt, 9, 118, 194
Sarnov, Johann, 107
Schardius, Levin, 138
Scheffler, Johann. *See* Silesius, Angelus
Schmidberger, Isaac, 127–30
Schweinichen, Johann Siegmund von, the younger, 71–72

Schwenckfeld (von Ossig), Caspar, 14–16, 19, 29, 54
Sclei, Bartholomaeus, 125–26
　Pater Noster, 125, 246n.3
　See also Theosophische-Schrifften (Sclei)
scribal publications, 21, 23, 30, 40, 50–51, 91
Seidenbecher, Georg Lorenz
　and alchemy, 98
　biological father, strained relationship with, 90–91
　Boehme's influence on, 92–93
　and Breckling, 106, 107–10
　Chiliasmus sanctus, 91–93
　'Conversation with Ancient Virtue and Faith' *(Conversatio cum Antiqua Virtute Fideque)*, 90–91
　correspondence, 107–9
　and Gifftheil, 107–8
　investigation for heresy, 87–88
　and millenarianism, 91–92, 108–9
　and network of religious dissenters, 106, 107–8, 111
　on spiritual alchemy, 96–97
Seidenbecher, and Franckenberg
　assistance as amanuensis, 93–95, 99
　authors discussed by, 92–93
　connections to religious dissenters, 106
　correspondence, preservation of, 89–90, 93–95
　first meeting of, 87, 90–91
　friendship between, 90–94
　millenarianism discussed by, 91–92
　spiritual alchemy discussed by, 88, 91, 94, 96–97, 98, 99–100, 104–5
　as spiritual father, 87, 90–91
Sendivogius, Michael, 21
　Novum lumen chymicum, 49
Serrarius, Petrus, 108–9, 111–12
seven degrees of regenerative process, 138–39, 184
seven planets/metals, 50, 148–49
seven source spirits/properties, 50, 148–49
seven stages in alchemical processes, 49, 138–39
Shantz, Douglas H., 17–18
Siebmacher, Johann
　on alchemical king, 39, 40
　and *Azoth et Ignis*, 30, 32–34, 35

influence on Franckenberg, 71
pseudonym of, 31–32
Zwey schöne Büchlein, 31–32
See also *Introductio hominis*
(Siebmacher); *Wasserstein der
Weysen* (Siebmacher)
Signatura rerum (Boehme), 65–66, 152–54
on antimony, 28–29
Breckling and, 120, 138
on Christ as philosophers' stone, 57–58
events of salvation history and
alchemical processes, 58–60
on Fall, 67
Franckenberg and, 71, 98–99
and *lapis-Christus in nobis* analogies,
39–40, 48–49, 154–55
on prelapsarian human's ability to
tinge, 77
on *proto-evangelium*, 158
spiritual alchemy in, 139–40
Silberer, Herbert, *Probleme der Mystik und
ihrer Symbolik*, 2–3
Silesius, Angelus (Johann
Scheffler), 157
Cherubinischer Wandersmann, 94
silver, 21–23, 38–39, 49–50, 82, 103
Sinnett, Alfred Percy, 178–79
Sinnett, Patience, 179–80
Smith, Pamela H., 6–7
snakes, 46–47
Socinianism, 125
Solomon, 40–41
solution, 184
Sophia (wisdom), 53–54
soteriology, 23–24, 155–56
soul sleep (doctrine), 65
South, Louisa, 163, 259n.22
South, Mary Anne. *See* Atwood, Mary
Anne (*née* South)
South, Thomas
on alchemy and rebirth, 174
correspondence with Walton, 161–66,
167–69, 174
death of, 177
Early Magnetism, 162–63, 166,
167, 169
and Freher, 161, 162–65, 167
interest in Mesmerism, 2–3, 166–68
in London, 163

on mystical union with divine, 166–67,
168–69
and spiritual alchemy, 161–63, 164, 165
and *Suggestive Inquiry*, 160–61
turn from Mesmerism to alchemy, 166,
168–69, 171
Sozzini, Lelio and Fausto, 125
Sperber, Julius, 93
spirit (*spiritus*), 8–9, 11–12, 197–98
spiritual alchemy, 24–25, 26–27, 42–43,
44–45, 80–82, 151
basic principles of, 12
continuity into nineteenth century, 201
definition of, 9–10, 197
as hybrid of science and
religion, 198–99
as literal and real for believers, 9–10,
11, 197–98
as neither science nor religion, 1
origin(s) of, 11, 12, 14, 19–29, 197–99
particulars of individual interpretations
of, need for study of, 200–2
practice of, 12
relation to laboratory alchemy, 199–
200, 201–2
similar terms, 8
and *spiritus*, early modern meanings
of, 8–9
as term, 7–8
three stages/paths of mystical quest,
10–11, 119–20, 135–36
transformation sought in, 9–12,
197–98
as type of Protestant mysticism, 10–11
unravelling of, 197, 199–200
See also Boehme, and spiritual alchemy;
Franckenberg, and spiritual alchemy;
other specific authors
spiritual body, 14–15, 16, 38, 62, 63–65,
67–68, 120–21, 122–23, 133, 174,
186, 193–94, 195–96
spiritualism (theology), 15–16, 19, 20–21,
28, 132, 154–55, 184–85
and separation of baptism and
rebirth, 15–16
Spiritualism (Victorian), 192, 212n.13
spirituality, compared to religion, as
term, 8
spiritus mundi, 8–9

Steiger, Isabelle de, 183–89
   as Atwood's friend and disciple, 175–76, 183–84
   and Atwood's papers, 188, 189
   and Atwood's *Suggestive Inquiry*, republication of, 188–89, 267n.91
   Boehme's influence on, 184
   defence of Atwood's view of spiritual alchemy, 156–88
   on ether, 185
   on evolution, 155–56
   On a Gold Basis (1907), 184–86, 187–88, 191–92, 193
   on Mesmerism, 187–88
   and spiritual alchemy, 178, 184–87
   views on Gospels, 184–85
   and Waite, debate with, 156
Steiner, Rudolf, 182–83
stella antimonii (star regulus of antimony), 58
Stiefel, Esaias
   Boehme's interaction with, 48–49, 60–63
   response to Boehme's criticisms, 61
   Tractätlein von zweyen Sprüchen, 60–61
Stolle, Gottlieb, 128, 132
Stumm, Nicolaus, 108
sublimation, 45, 103–4, 118, 184, 194
Suchten, Alexander von, 27
Suggestive Inquiry into the Hermetic Mystery (Atwood), 169–74
   on actual efficacy of early Christian rites, 170–71
   on alchemical adepts as inheritors of ancient wisdom on rebirth, 172–73
   on alchemy and Mesmerism, 2–3
   on ancient wisdom on rebirth, 170–72, 174
   availability of copies, 175
   Atwood's copy of, gifted to Steiger, 183–84
   Atwood's greater openness about, in later life, 178–79
   and Boehme, 170, 174
   on *Christus in nobis*, 170–72
   contents of, 160–61
   copies lent to friends, 175, 176f, 176–77
   Steiger's republication of, 188–89, 194–95, 267n.91
   on divine germ of humanity, 171–72
   early reception of, 175, 177–83
   on ether, 171–72, 173–74
   on ethereal body, 173–74
   on experiences of elevated states of being, 168
   on Freher, 169
   influence of, 169–70
   influences on, 160
   lapis-Christus in nobis three-way analogy in, 172–73
   on Mesmerism, 171, 172–73
   notable early readers of, 175–79
   on philosophers' stone, 173–74
   as rare collectors' item, 169–70
   reviews of, 179, 180–81
   rival works, 180
   and separation of spiritual and laboratory alchemy, 199–200
   Souths' destruction of copies of, 160–61, 169–70, 177, 188, 191–92
   on spiritual alchemy, 170–74, 175–76
   Taylor on, 12
   on transformation necessary to enter heaven, 195–96
   and unravelling of spiritual alchemy, 200
   writing of, 169–70
sulphur, 9, 36, 79, 103, 194

Tackius, Johann, 115
Tauler, Johann, 71, 91, 107
Taylor, Sherwood, *The Alchemists*, 12
Telle, Joachim, 7, 69, 90–91, 99–100
temporal principle, as visible world, 52
   See also fire and wrath; light and love; three principles
Theologia Germanica, 70, 72, 91
theology, 14–17, 23, 121, 128–30, 133–34, 143, 195
   Lutheran, and spiritual alchemy, 9, 24, 26, 32–34
   Socinian, 125
   and spiritual alchemy, 23–24, 26, 128–30, 197–98
   and *spiritus* as term, 8, 9

Theosophical Society of London, 178, 180, 183, 192, 200
Theosophische-Schrifften (Sclei), 125, 129f
  annotated printed copies of, 128–32
  Breckling's contributions to, 125–26, 127, 128–30, 133–38, 248n.26
  Breckling's work on publication of, 125–26, 127–28
  on Christ as tincture, 134–36
  group working on publication of, 125–26, 127–31
  index in, 131–33
  manuscripts of, 128
  motives for writing, 125
  preface to second part, Breckling's contribution to, 132–33
  spiritual alchemy in, as Breckling's addition, 131, 133–38, 140–41
theosophy (Boehme), 73–74, 81, 115, 116, 118, 129f, 146, 148, 150, 158–59, 160–61, 170, 183, 189–91, 195, 200
  and ancient wisdom, 73–74
  on body of Christ, 67–68
  godhead in, 49–50
  on Incarnation of Christ, 75
  influence of, 9–10
  influences on, 16, 19
theurgy, 171–72, 174, 181
Thomas à Kempis, 91
Thompson, E. P., 12
three paths of mysticism, 45, 119–20, 135–36
three principles
  according to Paracelsus, 9, 118
  according to theosophy (Boehme), 39–40, 52–53, 54–55, 84–85, 100–1, 116, 150–51
  See also fire and wrath; light and love; temporal principle
Tilton, Hereward, 119, 269n.7
tincture, 23–24, 36, 38–39, 59, 62–64, 67–68, 75, 76, 77–78, 79, 81–82, 83–85, 95, 100, 118, 120, 122–23, 132–33, 135–37, 138–39, 147, 148–49, 151–52, 155–56, 158, 184
  definitions of, 83–84

Titus (biblical epistle), 50
trance (magnetic), 166, 167, 168
Transfiguration of Christ, 80, 85, 95
transmutation, 35–36, 38–39, 43, 44–45, 49, 51, 57, 58, 59–60, 61–65, 75, 134–35, 138–39, 147, 148, 150–52, 161–62, 184, 193–94
  alchemy and, 4–5, 11–12, 15–16, 27, 28
  definition of, 84
  of earth into heaven, 63–65
  philosophers' stone and, 2
  spiritual alchemy and, 2–3, 9–10, 18, 19–20, 24, 28–29
Trautmannsdorf (fictional adept), 100
Trevisanus, Bernardus, *Practica*, 28–29
trichotomous anthropology (body, soul, and spirit)
  compared to dichotomous anthropology, 9
  and *lapis-Christus in nobis* analogy, 9–10
  as context for spiritual alchemy, 9
Trismegistus, Hermes, 34, 164
  Tabula smaragdina, 157
Tschesch, Johann Theodor von, 99–100

Überfeld, Johann Wilhelm, 113–15, 127–30
  Der Weeg zum Ewigen Leben, 131–32
  and Freher, 142, 143–45, 147–48, 158–59
Underhill, Evelyn, 181
union (*unio*), 10–11, 14–29, 30–47, 87–105, 119–20, 157, 166–67
University of Heidelberg, 143

Valentinus, Basilius, 27, 69–70, 73–74, 79–80
Verpoorten, Albrecht Meno
  De Georgii Laurentii Seidenbecheri vita, 87–88
  on Franckenberg's influence on Seidenbecher, 99
vitriol, 89
Von dem Ohrte der Seelen (1644), 89
Von der Hardt, Hermann, 128

Waite, Arthur Edward
  and Alchemical Society, founding of, 156
  and Atwood's library, 179
  and Atwood's *Suggestive Inquiry*, 156, 175–76, 179–80
  Azoth; or, The Star in the East, 179–80, 181, 182
  Darwin's influence on, 181–82, 264n.32
  on Fall, 182
  on spiritual interpretations of alchemy, 180
  'A New Light of Mysticism,' 179
  on physical beauty as goal, 181–82, 193
  The Secret Tradition in Freemasonry, 156
  on spiritual alchemy, 182–83, 199–200
  and Steiger, debate with, 156
Walker, D. P., 8
Wallich, Dorothea Juliana, 140
Walther, Balthasar, 39–40, 60–61
Walton, Christopher
  Atwood's correspondence with, 161–66, 167–69, 174
  and Atwood's *Suggestive Inquiry*, 177
  Freher excerpts, publication of, 164
  Freher's influence on, 161
  interest in magnetism, 166, 167–68
  Notes and Materials, 164
  On the Present, Past and Future, 162–63, 165–66
  publications, 162–63
Waple, Edward, 146–47, 148
Ward W. R., 17–18
Wasserstein der Weysen (Siebmacher), 30, 35–39, 98, 121, 139, 172–73
  on *Christus in nobis*, 36, 39
  editions of, 31
  establishing authorship of, 30–32
  on human agency in salvation, 39
  on incarnation of Christ within believer, 38–39
  influence of pseudo-Weigelian alchemy on, 30, 39
  and *Introductio hominis*, 32
  on justification, 38–39
  on philosophers' stone, 37
  on rebirth, restoration of prelapsarian state by, 38
  and related texts, 31–32
  on spiritual alchemy, 35, 37–39
  on suffering leading to salvation, alchemical parallels to, 37–38, 39
  theology and alchemy in, 35–38
Webster, Charles, 14–15
Weeks, Andrew, 19
Weickhart, Christoph, 20
Weigel, Valentin
  Dialogus de Christianismo, 19, 25–26, 43
  Gnothi seauton, 23, 32–34
  influence on later authors, 16, 17–18, 29, 41–42, 52, 71
  lack of alchemical approach to rebirth, 19
  Paracelsus' influence on, 17
  and separation of baptism and rebirth, 14–15, 16, 17
  and spiritualism, 16
  spiritualised notion of baptism and rebirth, 15–16
  on spiritual rebirth, 19
Welling, Georg von, 160
Werdenhagen, Johann Angelius von, 92–93, 103
white stone, 47
Widemann, Carl, 30–31
Wiedergeburt (rebirth). *See* rebirth (*Wiedergeburt*)
Wilberforce, Basil, 189
Wilmshurst, Walter Leslie, 166, 169–70, 175–76, 178
  and Atwood's papers, 189
  'The Later Mysticism of Mrs. Atwood,' 188–89
  and republishing of Atwood's *Suggestive Inquiry*, 188–89, 194–95, 267n.91
Wisdom of Solomon, 18

Zoroaster, 170
Zosimos of Panopolis, 6–7